PICTURING CUBA

Picturing Cuba

Art, Culture, and Identity on the Island and in the Diaspora

EDITED BY

JORGE DUANY

University of Florida Press
Gainesville

Funding provided by the Darlene M. and Jorge M. Pérez Cuban Art Collection at Florida International University.

Published in the United States of America

First cloth printing, 2019
First paperback printing, 2021

29 28 27 26 25 6 5 4 3 2

Library of Congress Cataloging-in-Publication Data
Names: Duany, Jorge, editor.
Title: Picturing Cuba : art, culture, and identity on the island and in the diaspora / edited by Jorge Duany.
Description: Gainesville : University of Florida Press, 2019. | Includes bibliographical references and index.
Identifiers: LCCN 2018055515 | ISBN 9781683400905 (cloth)
ISBN 9781683402091 (pbk.)
Subjects: LCSH: Arts and society—Cuba—History. | Arts, Cuban—History. | Nationalism and art—Cuba.
Classification: LCC NX525.A1 P53 2019 | DDC 700.97291—dc23 LC record available at https://lccn.loc.gov/2018055515

UF PRESS
UNIVERSITY OF FLORIDA

University of Florida Press
2046 NE Waldo Road
Suite 2100
Gainesville, FL 32609
http://upress.ufl.edu

This volume is dedicated to Professor Juan A. Martínez,
in recognition of his multiple contributions to the understanding,
preservation, and exhibition of Cuban and Cuban-American art.

CONTENTS

ILLUSTRATIONS

Figures

Plates

Plates follow page 84

Introduction

Cuba, a Moveable Nation

Jorge Duany

Since the late eighteenth century, prominent Cuban intellectuals have portrayed their country as a fatherland (*patria*) or nation with a distinctive character. Indeed, patriotism—as a sense of emotional attachment and devotion to the island, its people and its culture—emerged well before the establishment of an independent Cuban nation in 1902. One of the recurring themes in Cuban thought has been interpreting the island's cultural identity out of a troubled colonial and slave past, characterized by mass immigration of Spanish, African, and other peoples, as well as the more recent exodus to the United States and other countries. As the Cuban-American literary and art critic Andrea O'Reilly Herrera writes, "Just as Cuba and its people have absorbed and been transformed by diverse presences and cultural elements, it has also become a moveable nation, a traveling, prismatic site of rupture and continuity resulting from continuous out-migrations and scatterings."[1]

Several generations of Cuban writers and artists on the island and abroad have drawn the contours of their "moveable nation," according to different historical junctures, geographic locations, and ideological perspectives. Expressions of Cuban patriotism became stronger during the early 1800s, both in Cuba and in its incipient diaspora in the United States. An iconic moment was the publication of José María Heredia's romantic ode, "Niagara" (1825), in which the exiled poet contemplates the beauty of the falls while reminiscing about "the delicious palms" on the plains of his "ardent fatherland."

Throughout the nineteenth century, the island's native elite articulated a growing sense of "Cubanness" (*cubanía*), as opposed to an identification with peninsular Spain. Initially, most authors limited their purview of the nation to the descendants of Spanish immigrants in Cuba (especially the white Creole elite). The concept of the nation eventually embraced blacks and *mulatos*,[2] as well as the working classes. During the first half of the twentieth century, essayists often pondered the failure of the Cuban republic to achieve national sovereignty, social justice, and racial equality. Cuba's dependence on the United States was also a constant concern for the island's intellectuals. Asserting a separate cultural identity became an even more pressing demand for Cuban and Cuban-American writers and artists after the 1959 Revolution.[3]

The search for and affirmation of Cuba's national identity molded the visual arts, as well as literature, music, and other cultural expressions. According to several historians, the sense of belonging to the island evolved gradually between the sixteenth and eighteenth centuries, first recorded in literature and later in painting and music.[4] The epic poem "Espejo de paciencia" ("Mirror of Patience," 1608), written in Cuba by an immigrant from the Canary Islands, Silvestre de Balboa (1563–ca. 1644), is usually considered the first literary work to exalt the island's exuberant nature.[5] One of the earliest Cuban composers was Esteban Salas (1725–1803), who taught and wrote baroque music for the Catholic Church, while one of the first prominent Cuban painters, Vicente Escobar (1757–1834), excelled in portraits of the island's elite in a classical European style.

Whereas vernacular expressions of literature, music, and art appeared to be isolated in the seventeenth century, the eighteenth century witnessed a notable intellectual awakening in Cuba and other Spanish colonies of the Americas. Influenced by the European Enlightenment, numerous Cuban intellectuals, most of them born on the island, set out to foster progress and renovation through culture and education. Thus, in the early 1800s, the institutionalization of art teaching in Cuba was part of the deliberate attempt by a budding local intelligentsia to promote art as the embodiment of a *criollo* identity, while disseminating European standards of culture.[6] Modeled after the French and Spanish royal academies, the San Alejandro Academy of Fine Arts, established in Havana in 1818, continues to this day.

Since the Spanish Conquest, itinerant European artists had been producing widespread representations of the environment and inhabitants of the "New World." In Cuba, such artists included the French-born lithographers Frédéric Mialhe (1810–81) and Édouard Laplante (1818–60). The visual chronicler of nineteenth-century Cuban society, the Basque painter Víctor Patricio de Landaluze (1829–89), arrived in Havana in the 1850s and stayed in Cuba for the rest of his life.[7] Many of these artists' images remain popular representations of Cuban landscapes, characters, and history, and they formed part of the emerging discourse on national identity on the island.

The nineteenth century witnessed a growing Romantic interest among visual artists in local themes and landscapes. The depiction of things Cuban comprised a wide range of subjects, from public buildings, street and country scenes, and Afro-Cuban processions to portraits, historical events, and still lifes. One of the recurring themes of this period was the bucolic portrayal of the island as a fertile paradise, full of lush vegetation and bathed in a brilliant tropical light.[8] The end of the century set the stage for the *vanguardia* (avant-garde) movement in the first decades of the twentieth century. This transition accompanied shifting political, social, and cultural circumstances as the island's status changed from Spanish colony to independent republic (1902).

During the first half of the twentieth century, many artists and intellectuals from different generations sought to delineate the cultural tropes of the young republic. Cuban art underwent an intense process of identity exploration, emphasizing the depiction of autochthonous scenes and customs, including rural landscapes (usually dotted with palm trees) and folk types (especially the *guajiro* or peasant). In the 2013 retrospective exhibition at the Vero Beach Art Museum, *Cuban Art & Identity: 1900–1950*, art critic and curator Juan A. Martínez explored four leitmotifs that helped modern and traditional painters visualize collective identity: the Cuban countryside, Havana interiors, Afro-Cuban religion, and popular music.[9] Both groups of artists depicted a similar subject matter, though they differed in their perspectives: whereas traditional painters favored naturalistic representations, modern painters tended toward expressionist or abstract images.

Art historian Abigail McEwen has discussed how a new generation of Cuban artists took up abstraction during the 1950s. These artists, too, framed their work within the nationalist discourse of cubanía, even while abandoning the mimetic pretensions of art.[10] Abstract artists affiliated with the third-generation vanguardia, grouped around Los Diez and Los Once, were increasingly drawn to universalist and cosmopolitan trends in modern art. Yet they found ideological legitimacy in earlier *cubanista* codes that had survived the political turmoil of Fulgencio Batista's dictatorship (1952–58). After the triumph of the Cuban Revolution on January 1, 1959, the new regime increasingly identified abstract art with bourgeois, capitalist, and elitist values.

The revolution inaugurated a new era for Cuban art. Under the emerging political order—officially proclaimed socialist by Fidel Castro in April 1961—artists experienced moments of extreme tension. The early 1960s represented the radicalization of revolutionary ideology, as the country's political leaders imposed conceptual boundaries on artistic creation. The revolution also exacerbated state censorship, which politicized the appraisal of art and placed new pressures on those artists who tried to evade government restrictions on creative expression. The so-called Gray Years (*Quinquenio Gris*, 1971–76) were probably the worst period of bureaucratic control over the visual arts in Cuba.[11]

Nevertheless, the postrevolutionary history of Cuban art reveals a wide spectrum of styles and coexisting trends; several generations who introduced substantial renovation within the artistic scenario; the rise of the diaspora and the formation of Cuban artistic communities throughout the world; the active presence of Cuban and Cuban-American artists in the international scenarios of contemporary art; the emergence of a more fluid dialogue between artists on and off the island; and the effects of all these elements on the constant redefinition of Cuban collective imaginaries.

As the capital of the Cuban diaspora since 1959, and one of the leading artistic hubs of Latin America and the Caribbean since the 1990s, Miami has become a crossroads for Cuban art and culture. Furthermore, the introduction of Art Basel Miami Beach in 2002 expanded the international dimensions of the local art scene, together with Art Miami, established in 1990, and Miami Art Week, started in 2001. Similarly, Art Wynwood has become a leading exhibition center for modern and contemporary art since its inception in 2012. It is in Miami that a Cuban diasporic identity has flourished most powerfully in the visual arts as well as in other cultural expressions, such as creative literature and popular music.

The Present Work

Through its comprehensive coverage, this book will expand readers' knowledge and appreciation of Cuban history and culture, as well as Cubans' contributions to various U.S. communities, especially in South Florida. *Picturing Cuba: Art, Culture, and Identity on the Island and in the Diaspora* delves into several defining moments of Cuba's artistic evolution from a multidisciplinary perspective, including art history, architecture, photography, history, literary criticism, and cultural studies. Situating Cuban art within a wider context of complex references, internal and external influences, and sociohistorical connections, fifteen prominent scholars and collectors scrutinize the enduring links between Cuban art and cultural identity. Covering the main periods in Cuban art (the colonial, republican, and postrevolutionary phases, as well as the contemporary diaspora), the contributors identify both the constant and changing elements and symbols in the visual representation of cubanía or *cubanidad* (Cubanhood).[12]

The present volume is chronologically divided into four main parts:

1. The origins of Cuban art in the nineteenth century
2. The consolidation of Cuban art during the first half of the twentieth century
3. The development of Cuban art after 1959
4. Cuban art in the diaspora

Contributors were asked to explore the following topics:

1. The construction of Cuban national identity or cubanía
2. Spanish and other European influences on Cuban art and architecture
3. The contribution of the African legacy to Cuban art
4. Gender and the visual representation of women
5. The links among academic, avant-garde, and popular arts
6. The impact of the Cuban Revolution on the island's artistic landscape and new proposals in the visual arts
7. The emergence of a Cuban diasporic identity through the visual arts and architecture
8. The history and status of Cuban artistic communities

throughout the world (Havana, Miami, New York, Madrid, Paris, and San Juan)
9. Cultural encounters and cross-fertilization between artistic communities in Cuba and its diaspora
10. The relationship between Cuban-American and other Latino artists in the United States

The Colonial Period

The collector and independent scholar Emilio Cueto opens the edited volume with a historical inventory of seventeen graphic images of Cuba, printed during the late Spanish colonial period (1762–1898). These images became the most widely circulated visual representations of the island, particularly the capital of Havana, largely authored by non-Spanish and non-Cuban artists, primarily Dutch, English, French, and German. Despite their fanciful and often inaccurate character, these prints depicted the landscape, architecture, people, and customs of the island. They became part of a well-known visual repertoire that fixed Cuba as an exotic tropical location in the global imagination. As Cueto underlines, "It was through engravings and lithographs that Cuba first became known both on the island and abroad. Colonial Cuba was defined by its prints."

In her contribution to this volume, art historian and curator E. Carmen Ramos focuses on the pioneering but problematic work of the nineteenth-century Spanish painter and caricaturist Víctor Patricio de Landaluze, who spent much of his adult life in colonial Cuba. Despite his opposition to Cuba's independence from Spain, Landaluze was one of the leading practitioners of *costumbrismo* (the literary and artistic representation of local customs) on the island, portraying human "types" such as Creole landowners, slaves, former slaves, *mulatas*, and *guajiros*. According to Ramos's analysis, Landaluze documented many aspects of Afro-Cuban daily life, including religion, music, and dance, while perpetuating racial stereotypes of African savagery, common in other former slave societies such as Brazil, the United States, and Puerto Rico at the end of the nineteenth century. A close look at one of Landaluze's most famous paintings, *Corte de caña* (*Cutting Sugar Cane*, 1874), reveals the racial anxieties among the peninsular Spanish, as well as some members of the Creole elite, provoked by the slaves' emancipation and the war of national liberation in Cuba.

In the final essay on the Spanish colonial era in Cuba, art historian Alison Fraunhar examines how graphic and fine arts helped trace the contours of national identity well before the island's independence. Fraunhar dwells on maps and other visual representations of rural and urban landscapes, people, and historical events that were critical to imagining Cuba as a separate nation with its own culture. The author demonstrates that late nineteenth-century views of the island's geography, history, and culture continue to be significant visual markers for contemporary Cuban artists.

The Republican Period

Art historian Anelys Alvarez reviews the tumultuous first three decades of the Cuban Republic (1902–30) and their impact on painting and other visual arts such as sculpture. First, she questions the conventional dichotomy between traditional (or academic) and avant-garde (or modernist) art in Cuba during this period. She then recovers several forgotten artists, such as Antonio Rodríguez Morey (1874–1967), María Capdevila (1881–1991), and Manuel Mesa (1895–1971), who were active on the island before the rise of modernism in the 1930s. Alvarez reappraises a whole generation of painters who served as an artistic bridge between the late nineteenth century and the first generation of avant-garde (*vanguardista*) painters who burst into the scene in 1927.

Art collector Ramón Cernuda discusses how Cuban art was consolidated during the first half of the twentieth century, especially after the emergence of two generations of modern artists, now considered the core of the vanguardia (also known as the Havana School). Cernuda notes that the international art market increasingly valued the work of Cuban artists such as Amelia Peláez (1896–1968), Víctor Manuel García (1897–1969), and René Portocarrero (1912–85)—not to mention Wifredo Lam (1902–82). These artists appeared in numerous individual and collective exhibitions in major museums and private galleries, as well as in specialized art magazines and books. As Cernuda underlines, Cuban vanguardia painters first reached a broad audience with Alfred H. Barr Jr.'s 1944 exhibition, *Modern Cuban Painters*, at the Museum of Modern Art (MoMA) in New York City. Ironically, the wide success of Cuban artists abroad was what led Cuban collectors to pay attention to them.

Art historian Carol Damian laments the scarcity of Cuban women artists from the early nineteenth century to the mid-twentieth century. Damian explains this trend based on women's traditional exclusion from art academies and exhibition circuits, as well as on their difficulties in traveling abroad and establishing their own studios. Yet she documents the work of eight major women artists in Cuba during the first half of the twentieth century, including Mirta Cerra (1904–86) and Gina Pellón (1926–2014). Most of these artists were associated with the San Alejandro Academy in Havana, participated in numerous exhibitions, and received critical acclaim during their lifetimes. However, most critics now neglect them in favor of the canonized male leaders of the Cuban vanguardia, except for the work of Amelia Peláez. Damian concludes with a call for further research and reflection on the careers of lesser-known female figures and their contributions to Cuban art before and after the country's independence in 1902.

For their part, architectural historians Victor Deupi and Jean-François Lejeune assess the legacy of the "modernist generation" of Cuban architects, active on the island between the late 1930s and 1959. Deupi and Lejeune focus on how this generation struggled "to be modern and Cuban at the same time," and how this tension informed their residential designs. Many Cuban architects sought to adapt modern aesthetics and building techniques to a tropical climate in their blueprints for private houses, public buildings, and urban planning. Architect Eugenio Batista (1900–92) codified the main elements of vernacular Cuban houses as "the three ps"—*persianas* (louvers), *patios* (courtyards), and *portales* (arcades)—which other architects adopted. Deupi and Lejeune have followed the careers of numerous Cuban architects who moved abroad after the Revolution and left a "transnational and transcultural" imprint in the built environments of their host countries, particularly the United States, Puerto Rico, and Venezuela.

In her chapter, art historian Abigail McEwen focuses on the so-called *concretos*, a generation of abstract Cuban painters that emerged during the 1950s and included the Romanian-born Sandú Darié (1908–91), Luis Martínez Pedro (1910–2010), Mario Carreño (1913–99), and José M. Mijares (1921–2005). According to McEwen, the concretos saw themselves as the last generation of the island's artistic avant-garde, which contradicted their predecessors' quest for a vernacular expression of national identity in the visual arts, while striving for modernization and cosmopolitanism. She shows that the abstract turn in Cuba was both an aesthetic revolt against figurative art and a political protest against the Batista regime. The abstract art movement gradually waned after the triumph of the Cuban Revolution, with its preference for narrative and representational art.

The Postrevolutionary Period

Art historian and curator Iliana Cepero analyzes how some photographers deviated from the official discourse of the 1959 Revolution as an epic and messianic process of liberation from imperialism and class oppression. Instead, as Cepero highlights, several artists (such as María Eugenia Haya—aka Marucha [1944–91]—and José Alberto Figueroa [b. 1946] in the 1960s) used photography as a medium of self-expression and to explore alternative narratives of daily life in Cuba. More recently, a new generation of photographers—among them, Eduardo García (b. 1978)—has documented the scarcity, poverty, marginalization, racial discrimination, and other intractable problems of contemporary Cuban society. Cepero concludes, "Cuban photography today, both in its documentary and conceptual approaches, aspires to dismantle the epic paradigm with which the Revolution came to be known as a visual phenomenon."

In her analysis of the olive-green leitmotif in Cuban visual arts since 1959, sociologist María A. Cabrera Arús dissects the iconography of the Cuban Revolution and its ironic appropriation by contemporary Cuban artists. Cabrera Arús demonstrates that the celebration of the sartorial guerrilla identity of the 1960s has largely given way to a critical perspective on the epic narrative in the post-Soviet era, exemplified by painters like Carlos Rodríguez Cárdenas (b. 1962) and photographers like José Ángel Toirac (b. 1966). In recent artworks produced in Cuba, the olive-green uniform of the revolutionary army appears more often as a symbol of oppression than as a metaphor for a utopian vision.

The Diaspora

Art critic and collector Ricardo Pau-Llosa proposes that certain "tropes of identity"—common metaphors inherited from previous generations of modern Cuban artists—continue to shape the work of contemporary Cuban-American artists. Pau-Llosa underlines the trope of theatricality as a form of representing "the poetics of shelter (from time, history, persecution, and other forces)." The early work in exile of Carreño and Cundo

Bermúdez (1914–2008) launched a diasporic sensibility in Cuban art that resonates in the more recent work of Emilio Sánchez (1921–99), María Brito (b. 1947), and José Bedia (b. 1959). From this perspective, theatricality ties together several generations of Cuban modern artists and those who left the island after 1959.

Art historian Lynette M. F. Bosch concentrates on the first generation of postrevolutionary exile artists, which she calls the "Cuban-American Exile Vanguardia," who arrived in the United States between 1959 and 1980. Bosch emphasizes that many members of this diasporic generation explore "identity, hybridity, transnationalism, and the emotional and experiential territory of exile." She also argues that these artists recast traditional notions of *lo cubano* (Cubanness) as *lo cubanoamericano* (Cuban-Americanness) through visual representations of "life on the hyphen,"[13] that is, the blending of Cuban and American cultural practices. Examples of these hybrid exile artists include Humberto Calzada (b. 1944), Jake Fernandez (b. 1951), and Arturo Rodríguez (b. 1956).

The next essay in this collection, authored by Andrea O'Reilly Herrera, analyzes an itinerant art exhibition known as *CAFÉ* (Cuban American Foremost Exhibitions), curated by Leandro Soto (b. 1956) since 2001. Herrera argues that the artists participating in this exhibition raise many of the same issues as earlier vanguardia artists in Cuba, including the significance of the island's African and Indigenous roots, landscape, and architecture, although they do not claim to represent the entire Cuban diaspora. Still, Herrera's analysis of the artwork of several *cafeteros*, such as Soto, Bedia, and Raúl Villarreal (b. 1964), identifies recurrent themes, especially displacement and transculturation—which in the end "allude to the all-embracing nature of Cuban culture itself."

In my final contribution to this volume, I examine the shifting cultural ties between Cuba and the United States since 1959, and how they have reframed relations between Cubans on and off the island. I argue that the cultural politics of Miami's Cuban community have changed substantially because of demographic and generational transitions over the last three decades. Until the 1980s, most Cuban artists and other intellectuals in the United States remained isolated from their island counterparts. However, it is now customary for U.S. museums and galleries to collect and exhibit artworks produced in post-1959 Cuba without much protest from Cuban Americans. Although some exile artists and critics still believe that U.S. cultural institutions should not display such artworks, the fault lines between Cubans residing on the island and abroad seem more porous than in the past. I conclude that the visual arts may serve as cultural bridges across the Florida Straits.

In sum, the essays collected in this volume provide insightful information on and interpretation of the historical trajectory of Cuban and Cuban-American art. From colonial engravers to contemporary photographers, several generations of Cuban artists have been fascinated—perhaps even obsessed—with picturing Cuba's landscapes, architecture, people, and customs. Each generation of artists has focused on various tropes of Cuban identity, whether it be the tropical environment, the lights and colors of the island, certain human types, the fusion of European and African traditions, or the uprootedness produced by exile and resettlement in another country. Even when artists shed the attempt to represent their subject matter realistically, they sought to contribute to a long-standing *cubanista* tradition in dialogue with a broader international scenario. The cumulative result of more than two centuries of Cuban art is a kaleidoscopic view of the island's nature, population, culture, and history that resonates with the metaphor of a "moveable nation," across both space and time.

Acknowledgments

When I first arrived at Florida International University (FIU) in Miami in August 2012, John Stack proudly told me that he was giving me a welcoming gift: the great news that Darlene and Jorge Pérez were donating their collection of Cuban art to the university. And what a generous gift it was! My first words of gratitude go to the Darlene M. and Jorge M. Pérez Collection of Cuban Art at FIU, for providing financial assistance and infrastructural support for public events. I am equally pleased to acknowledge the steadfast support of John Stack, Founding Dean of the Steven J. Green School of International and Public Affairs at FIU. I am also happy to recognize Carol Damian, former Director of the Frost Art Museum, for her indefatigable efforts to promote Cuban and Cuban-American art. The current Director of the Frost Art Museum, Jordana Pomeroy, also collaborated with this project.

Art historian Anelys Alvarez was one of the first scholars who worked with me on a proposal to hold a summer institute for teachers on Cuban art at FIU in 2015. Art collector Ramón Cernuda, education professor

Bárbara Cruz, and artist Humberto Calzada also gave generously of their time during the first edition of our institute. I am grateful to several colleagues who kindly served as moderators at the 2017 conference on Cuban art and cultural identity: historian Michael Bustamante, architect Marilys Nepomechie, literary and cultural critic Raúl Rubio, and Liesl Picard, Associate Director of the Kimberly Green Latin American and Caribbean Center (LACC). I appreciate the intellectual and pedagogical support of my daughter Patricia Duany.

The staff of the Cuban Research Institute—Public Affairs Manager Aymee Correa, Associate Director Sebastián Arcos, Program Assistant Paola Salavarria, Student Assistant Lennie Gómez, and College Work Study students Alfredo González and Daylen Fiallo—provided indispensable administrative assistance. We also counted on LACC's logistical and financial support through its U.S. Department of Education Title VI Grant. The Frost Art Museum—and especially Klaudio Rodríguez, then Chief Art Curator, and Miriam Machado, Curator of Education—was instrumental in the success of our activities. Staff members at the Pérez Art Museum Miami, especially Mari Robles, from the Division of Education and Public Programs, coordinated field visits to the museum. I thank the Miami-Dade County Public Schools, Division of Academic Support, Visual and Performing Arts, especially Alina Rodríguez, Mabel Morales, and Ray Azcuy, for helping us reach out to K-12 teachers.

At the University of Florida Press, Stephanye Hunter provided efficient and enthusiastic support in the process of reviewing and approving the book manuscript. I also want to acknowledge the collaboration of Eleanor O. Deumens, who later served as project editor. Isabel Alvarez-Borland and another, anonymous reviewer made useful comments and suggestions to the contributors of this edited volume. Kel Pero expertly copyedited the manuscript and improved its readability. The Darlene M. and Jorge M. Pérez Cuban Art Collection at FIU helped to cover the cost of reproducing the book's illustrations. Finally, I am grateful to the Cernuda Arte gallery in Miami for facilitating copies of numerous images illustrating the book as well as the permissions to reproduce them.

Notes

1. Andrea O'Reilly Herrera, *Cuban Artists across the Diaspora*, 2.

2. The popular term *mulato/a*, as used in Cuba from colonial times to this day, refers to people of mixed race, mainly the descendants of people of African and European background.

3. The first two paragraphs of this introduction draw on my earlier essay on "Cuban Thought and Cultural Identity." I want to recognize the collaboration of Anelys Alvarez, who helped me draft the intellectual rationale for a conference on "Picturing Cuba: Art, Culture, and Identity" at FIU during the summer of 2015.

4. See, for instance, Consuelo Naranjo Orovio, ed., *Historia de Cuba*, especially the chapters by Rafael Rojas, Françoise Moulin-Civil, and Zoila Lapique Becali.

5. See Graciella Cruz-Taura, *Espejo de paciencia y Silvestre de Balboa*.

6. See Narciso G. Menocal, "An Overriding Passion."

7. Emilio Cueto, *Mialhe's Colonial Cuba*; Justo G. Cantero, *Los ingenios*. For a discussion of Landaluze and other colonial artists in Cuba, see Evelyn Carmen Ramos-Alfred, *A Painter of Cuban Life*; Gary R. Libby, *Cuba: A History in Art*.

8. Paul Niell, "The Cuban Academy of San Alejandro and the Atlantic World"; Liliana Gómez, "El discurso colonial en la iconografía cubana."

9. Juan A. Martínez, "Representing *Lo Cubano*," 3.

10. Abigail McEwen, *Revolutionary Horizons*.

11. Fidel Castro's famous speech, known as *Palabras a los intelectuales* (*Words to the Intellectuals*), delivered in 1961 at Havana's National Library, signaled the radicalization of cultural policy in revolutionary Cuba. The speech may be found in Lee Baxandall, ed., *Radical Perspectives in the Arts*, 267–98. On the *Quinquenio Gris*, see Doreen Weppler-Grogan, "Cultural Policy, the Visual Arts, and the Advance of the Cuban Revolution."

12. A classic formulation of the definition of Cuban national identity is Fernando Ortiz, "Los factores humanos de la cubanidad." See also Duany, "Reconstructing Cubanness."

13. Gustavo Pérez Firmat, *Life on the Hyphen*.

Bibliography

Baxandall, Lee, ed. *Radical Perspectives in the Arts*. Baltimore: Penguin Books, 1972.

Cantero, Justo G. *Los ingenios: Colección de vistas de los principales ingenios de azúcar de la isla de Cuba*. Madrid: Doce Calles, 2005.

Cruz-Taura, Graciella. *Espejo de paciencia y Silvestre de Balboa en la historia de Cuba*. Frankfurt: Iberoamericana/Vervuert, 2009.

Cueto, Emilio. *Mialhe's Colonial Cuba: The Prints That Shaped the World's View of Cuba*. Miami: Historical Association of Southern Florida, 1994.

Duany, Jorge. "Cuban Thought and Cultural Identity: Populism, Nationalism, and *Cubanía*." In *Cuba: People, Culture, History*, edited by Alan West-Durán, 109–16. New York: Charles Scribner's Sons, 2011.

———. "Reconstructing Cubanness: Changing Discourses of National Identity on the Island and in the Diaspora during the Twentieth Century." In *Cuba, the Elusive Nation: Interpretations of National Identity*, edited by Damián J. Fernández and Madeline Cámara Betancourt, 17–42. Gainesville: University Press of Florida, 2000.

Gómez, Liliana. "El discurso colonial en la iconografía cubana: Paisaje, urbanización y narrativas de lo rural del siglo XIX." In *Caleidoscopios coloniales: Transferencias culturales en el Caribe del siglo XIX*, edited by Ottmar Ette and Gesine Müller, 121–38. Madrid: Iberoamericana, 2010.

Herrera, Andrea O'Reilly. *Cuban Artists across the Diaspora: Setting the Tent against the House*. Austin: University of Texas Press, 2011.

Libby, Gary R. *Cuba: A History in Art*. 2nd ed. Gainesville: University Press of Florida, 2015.

Martínez, Juan A. "Representing *Lo Cubano*: Cuban Painting, 1900–1950." In *Cuban Art & Identity: 1900–1950*, 3–18. Vero Beach, FL: Vero Beach Museum of Art, 2013.

McEwen, Abigail. *Revolutionary Horizons: Art and Polemics in 1950s Cuba*. New Haven: Yale University Press, 2016.

Menocal, Narciso G. "An Overriding Passion—The Quest for a National Identity in Painting." *Journal of Decorative and Propaganda Arts* 22 (1996): 186–219.

Naranjo Orovio, Consuelo, ed. *Historia de Cuba*. Madrid: Doce Calles, 2009.

Niell, Paul. "The Academy of San Alejandro and the Atlantic World." In *Cuban Art in the Twentieth Century: Cultural Identity and the International Avant Garde*, 17–32. Tallahassee: Florida State University Museum of Fine Arts, 2016.

Ortiz, Fernando. "Los factores humanos de la cubanidad." *Revista Bimestre Cubana* 45, no. 2 (1940): 161–86.

Pérez Firmat, Gustavo. *Life on the Hyphen: The Cuban-American Way*. Rev. ed. Austin: University of Texas Press, 2012.

Ramos-Alfred, Evelyn Carmen. *A Painter of Cuban Life: Víctor Patricio de Landaluze and 19th-Century Cuban Politics (1850–1889)*. PhD diss., University of Chicago, 2011.

Weppler-Grogan, Doreen. "Cultural Policy, the Visual Arts, and the Advance of the Cuban Revolution." *Cuban Studies* 41 (2010): 143–65.

I

Cuban Colonial Prints

Constructing Our National Identity through Seventeen Projects

Emilio Cueto

Over the 120 years that elapsed between the 1760s and 1880s, various artists produced works designed to describe and divulge Cuba's cultural identity and, eventually, its identity as a nation.[1] At the same time, the artists also needed to sell their works; the images thus tended to be pleasant views of their subject matter. By the 1880s, these Cuban-themed prints formed a large and valuable corpus of images, allowing people all over the world to get to know the island. This chapter briefly describes seventeen projects involving these prints.[2] Together, the images discussed in this essay generally reflect what may be called a "colonial gaze," that is, the visual representation of Cuba and other non-European societies to European audiences (as well as to Cuban and U.S. audiences) by foreign artists. This gaze tended to portray the island as an exotic tropical paradise, with picturesque landscapes and characters that attracted the attention of various imperial nations, such as France, England, and Holland.[3]

Spain "discovered" Cuba in 1492 and began its colonization process in 1511. Only eight different images of the island were preserved over the following 270 years. Moreover, except for one, those images were not made in Spain or by Spaniards, as one would have expected, and none of them was accurate.

The first two Cuba-related views rendered of the country appeared in Theodor de Bry's compilation about the New World in 1595; they depicted the sacking and burning of Havana by French pirates in 1536 and then again in 1556 (see Plate 1).[4] De Bry's engravings were among the first visual representations of the Americas, which helped Europeans to familiarize themselves with the far-away places and peoples now under European control. The engravings also contributed to the propagation of the Black Legend of Spanish colonialism in the Americas, which promoted a negative view of Spaniards, accusing them of being cruel, intolerant, and backward. Plate 1 depicts Havana as a small colonial outpost, with a poorly defended harbor and full of fabulous treasures to be plundered by the rivals of Spain's empire in the New World.

At the beginning of the seventeenth century, the "classic" view of Havana was first produced, with El Morro Castle topped by an onion-like dome more reminiscent of the Kremlin than of a Spanish-Italian fortress. At first, this image showed up in the ornate vignettes of Dutch maps of the Western Hemisphere, and by 1671, it had been enlarged to fit a larger page.[5]

Also around that time, Belgian artist Jan van Kessel the Elder (1626–79) painted a small view of Havana to accompany a larger composition of the American continent (1666). That painting hangs today in Munich's *Alte Pinakothek*.[6] Nevertheless, it was an original oil, not a print, and thus had little impact on how people got to see Havana, as it was not widely distributed, as a print would have been.

Next, we turn to two views depicting the capture of the Spanish Silver Fleet by Dutch admiral and privateer Piet Heyn (1577–1629) off the coast of Matanzas in 1628. The first view, originally published in Amsterdam in the same year, was often reproduced, sometimes with variations, as the victorious Dutch exploit was a popular subject at the time. A second, different rendition of the events was printed in 1630.[7]

Finally, two whimsical views of Santiago de Cuba's harbor depicted the departure of Hernán Cortés (1485–1547), then mayor of the city, for the conquest of Mexico in 1519. The first view was printed for the 1691 French edition of Solís's account of the Mexican adventure (other editions followed)[8] and was designed by a Dutch marine painter then residing in France, Jan Karel Donatus van Beecq (1638–1722). The second view appeared as a vignette on the title page of the 1726 edition of Antonio de Herrera's *History of the West Indies, Second Decade*.[9]

Then the British arrived. The military conquerors of Havana landed in 1762 with artists to record views and make maps "on the spot." And thus the *first* serious project of revealing our identity was born—the six views sketched onsite by English military engineer Elias Durnford (1739–94), engraved in London a few years later with the help of five artists: Pierre-Charles Canot (ca. 1710–77), William Elliot (1727–66), Thomas Morris (1750–?), Edward Rooker (ca. 1712–74), and Paul Sandby (1731–1809). These were views in and about Havana (the entrance, the harbor, Jesús del Monte, the marketplace, and the Franciscan Church, which was used for Anglican services during the occupation).[10]

We must wait sixty more years for the *second* project: six views of Havana sketched in the capital by Frenchman Hippolyte Garneray (1787–1858) around 1824 and printed in aquatint some years later by François Bulla in Paris (see Plate 2). This project featured views of the harbor, a general view of the city, the Arms Square, the Old Square (the market), Paula Avenue, and the Prado Promenade.[11] The bird's-eye view of the Arms Square shows a tranquil and well-ordered urban scene against the backdrop of El Morro Castle, including two large buildings and smaller dwellings in the foreground. Garneray highlights local colorful characters of different social classes: several gentlemen conversing next to their carriage, workers transporting cargo in their carts, and a black woman carrying merchandise atop her head. This French artist has been justly credited with initiating a tradition of genre painting (*costumbrismo*) in Cuba.

Since the sixteenth century, other European powers had coveted and occupied parts of Spain's territories in the New World. Consequently, Spain distrusted foreign travelers to its colonies.[12] It made a significant exception, however, for Alexander von Humboldt, the Prussian naturalist and explorer. Humboldt and his team of natural scientists arrived in Caracas, Venezuela, in 1799 and visited Cuba twice, in 1801 and 1804. Upon completing his American voyages, Humboldt published his impressions, which were quickly translated into several languages.[13] Humboldt's narratives had an enormous impact on European learned circles. Put another way, Humboldt placed Cuba and Spanish America on the world map. Excited and seduced by his descriptions, many European artists traveled to the Americas to portray the exotic continent.[14]

Until the early nineteenth century, only Havana had been painted (if we exclude the earlier, unrealistic Matanzas and Santiago harbor views), but that would change quickly. Around 1837 or 1838, Cuba's preeminent think-tank, the Sociedad Económica de Amigos del País (Economic Society of the Friends of the Country), had a brilliant idea: invite a French lithographer to come to Cuba to live in, and travel around, the country—not just the capital—and, for the first time, show us who we really were and how we looked. The man was Frédéric Mialhe and his first major work—which is our *third* project—was the *Isla de Cuba Pintoresca* collection (1839–41).

Mialhe's compilation included approximately fifty-three different views, covering much of the island: Pinar del Río (8), Havana (39), Matanzas (3), Oriente (2), and one undetermined view of a sugar mill. Most important, it was the first set of prints of this kind to be printed in Cuba, not abroad.[15] Moreover, unlike the earlier views, which were engraved, these were printed with a new technique, lithography, which used stone rather than metal. The printing was done at the establishment of the Royal Society, dubbed "the lithographic studio of the Frenchmen."

Shortly after Mialhe began his pioneering series, he found he had competition. A trio of Spanish artists, Fernando (1804–70) and Francisco de la Costa y Prades and Laureano Cuevas, began their own project—the *fourth* by my count—to lithograph the island. It was called *Paseo pintoresco por la isla de Cuba* (1841–42). The Litografía del Gobierno published the eighty-five different images (there were some minor variations in otherwise-duplicate prints). In doing so, the Litografía got the nickname "the lithographic studio of the Spaniards."

After composing seventy-six views of Havana, the artists moved on to Matanzas. However, they went bankrupt and could only finish nine of the projected Matanzas views and none of other localities farther east.[16] It was, nonetheless, a remarkable venture, not only because of the large number of images produced, but also because the artists portrayed many Havana buildings whose images have survived only because of their efforts.

Project number *five* was, once again, the work of Mialhe, who had remained in Cuba and, by 1848, had a new set of views to share with the public. This time he produced not only city and countryside pictures, but also genre views, capturing the soul of Cubans with images such as the *zapateo* dance, the poultry seller, the baker, the cockfight, and slaves dancing in public on Three Kings Day. This 1848 album—*Viaje pintoresco al rededor de la isla de Cuba*—also included views of Matanzas, Remedios, Sagua la Grande, Trinidad, Nuevitas, Santiago, the Turquino Peak, and Baracoa. All told, the album had thirty prints: sixteen from Havana, two from Matanzas, three from Villa Clara, one from Camagüey, five from Oriente, and three genre views without a specific geographic reference.

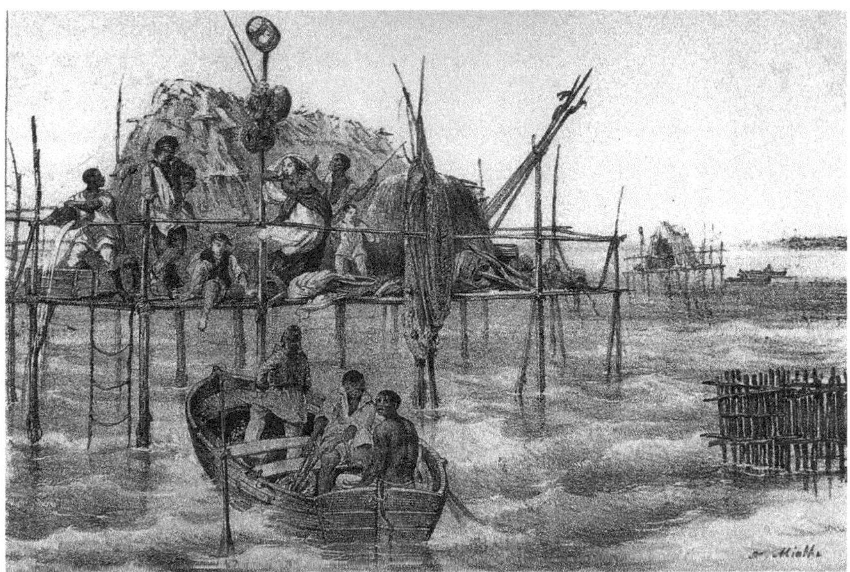

Figure 1.1. Frédéric Mialhe, *Vivienda de los pescadores de esponjas, Bahía de Nuevitas* (*Houses of Sponge Fishermen, Nuevitas Bay*), 1848. In *Viaje pintoresco al-rededor de la Isla de Cuba.* Havana, Luis Marquier.

Mialhe's panoramic view of colonial Cuba was one of the most ambitious enterprises of its kind ever attempted on the island. Among other prints, his detailed lithograph of the sponge fishers' dwellings in Nuevitas Bay has been reproduced many times since the mid-nineteenth century (see Figure 1.1). In this and other images produced by Mialhe, Cubans were no longer in the background. Instead, they took center stage, becoming the focus of attention of the artist and, hence, the viewer. In this regard, Mialhe was one the first major exponents of costumbrismo in Cuba.

Mialhe had produced a true masterpiece—so much so that a German company based in Havana decided to plagiarize his images. Therefore, around 1853 and under the name of Bernardo May, the first *Album pintoresco de la isla de Cuba*, probably printed in Hamburg with twenty-seven copies of the thirty Mialhe prints—the *sixth* project—hit the streets of Havana, to the dismay of the true author. The Frenchman sued, but was unable to produce evidence that he had secured the copyright for his work. He settled out of court, departed for France shortly thereafter, and left behind what would eventually become a very confusing bibliography.

This German project was soon followed by its twin brother—the *seventh* such project—another *Album pintoresco de la isla de Cuba* (1855), this time with twenty-six views chromolithographed in Berlin. Unlike the black-and-white version, the images in this collection were not quite exact copies of Mialhe's work, as had appeared in the earlier album. And, as it happened, the color version would contain what is probably the most reproduced view of Cuban colonial life. Pity that the Germans got it all wrong: the wheels of the *quitrín* (carriage) would have been larger than depicted, the three ladies in the picture would not have fit in the carriage where they all sit toward the back, and elegant women did not then commonly walk in the streets of Havana. Nobody seemed to care about these inaccuracies, however. In addition, the color version has been circulated far more widely than the original, accurate one. As well, the original was done in black and white, and adding color makes the image far more attractive—another case of "if it's pretty, it must be right."

During the 1850s, five new projects were unveiled. Two of them attempted to cover the entire island, one concentrated on Havana, another one on Matanzas, and the last one had no geographical focus, but instead depicted Cubans in their occupations.

Basque artist Víctor Patricio de Landaluce/Landaluze, recently arrived on the island, conceived a manual of Cuban types—the *eighth* project—after earlier French and Spanish models. This resulted in a small 1852 book about Cubans as seen by themselves, with eighteen wood engravings by Cuban artist José Robles. Parading before our eyes, we see the milkman, the cigar maker, the cock fighter, the old healer, the bureaucrat, the lovers, the teacher, the amateur musician, and many others.[17] Landaluce would return to this project three decades later.

German artist Adolf Hoeffler (1825–98) was responsible for project number *nine*. He visited Cuba in 1851 and published some of his views of the island in illustrated periodicals. He also sketched six larger views, to be lithographed in Paris by Eugène Ciceri (1813–90) and Félix Benoist (1818–96) and printed by Goupil & Cie around 1854. Three were images of Havana (a panoramic view, the cathedral, and Arms Square), and the others depicted Matanzas, Trinidad, and Santiago.[18]

Basque artist Leonardo Barañano (1822–?) teamed up with Frenchman Eduardo Laplante (1818–60) to produce a set of panoramas (our *tenth* project) depicting eight of the most important Cuban cities: Havana, Matanzas, Cárdenas, Villa Clara, Cienfuegos, Trinidad, Puerto Príncipe (Camagüey), and Santiago. The set also included a view of the Yumurí Valley in Matanzas. The images were lithographed at various Havana printing establishments (Fanjul, Gobierno, Martín, and Mercantil) around 1856. I have no explanation as to why the same image was printed at various places. This multiple print-run is a first in the history of Cuban colonial prints.[19]

The *eleventh* project was the brainchild of Englishman James Gay Sawkins (1806–78), who lived in Cuba from 1835 until he was expelled in 1847. He took his six Havana sketches, painted around 1838, to the workshop of Thierry Frères in Paris and, with the help of Frenchmen Louis-Julien Jacottet (1806–80) and Félix Achille Saint-Aulaire (1801–89?), had the views lithographed—Havana Port; a general view of Havana; Arms and St. Francis Squares; Military Road; and Havana's Indian fountain sculpture.[20]

Working for the Litografía Matancera, artist José López Martínez, born in Cárdenas, issued a set of pictures of Matanzas (our *twelfth* project). Apparently, the set consisted of twenty-five images, but only twelve have been located in Havana's National Library. They include bridges, squares (Arms, Vigía, market), streets, homes, and a fortress.[21] It remains a mystery why so few have been found.

The *thirteenth* project will take us to Santiago de Cuba, where two Frenchmen, Charles Collet and Emile Lamy, embarked on a monumental undertaking: to depict the most important sites in the eastern half of the island. One of the views realistically depicts the harbor of Santiago de Cuba during the mid-nineteenth century as a placid area with a mountainous landscape in the background (see Plate 3). The engraving is much more accurate than earlier portraits of the city, as it was based on firsthand observation.

Thirty-two images of the Departamento Oriental (eastern province) were originally scheduled for depiction, although to date only nineteen have been located. They include views of Camagüey, Nuevitas, Holguín, Gibara, Santiago, El Cobre, and Guantánamo. Presumably, Las Tunas, Bayamo, Manzanillo, and Baracoa were part of the plan, but they were either never published, or they are hidden somewhere.[22] (My hypothesis is that the venture was dissolved and the set was left incomplete.) This was the most important Cuban lithographic undertaking outside of Havana during the nineteenth century.

To give a different twist to the role played by colonial prints, we would include a *fourteenth* project. I am referring to the set of views of twenty-five sugar mills (and one of the Regla warehouse) commissioned by the wealthy sugar baron from Trinidad, Justo Germán Cantero (1815–71). They were done in lithography by Laplante, then colored by hand at the Marquier printing establishment in Havana, and distributed in eight installments between 1855 and 1857.[23]

Unlike the other albums mentioned before, this collection of views concentrated on only one aspect of our island: sugar production. However, its geographical scope was wide, as it included mills in Mariel (Asunción), Guanajay (San José de la Angosta), Güines (La Amistad), Matanzas (Acana, Armonía, Santa Rosa, Trinidad), Cárdenas (Alava, Concepción/Purísima Concepción, Flor de Cuba, Intrépido, Monserrate, El Narciso, La Ponina, El Progreso, San Martín, San Rafael, Santa Teresa/Agüica, Tinguaro, Unión, Victoria), Cienfuegos (Santa Susana), and Trinidad (Buena-Vista, Güinia, Manaca). Because it focused on Cuba's largest economic sector, and one that employed both black slaves and Chinese indentured servants, this set of views opened a new window into Cuba's economic activity as well as its demographic makeup and identity.

Tobacco provided the *fifteenth* project. No matter how good a product is, marketing specialists hold that it needs to be presented in an attractive fashion to gain, and sustain, the public's attention. This was the concept behind the colorful and instructive cigar labels that would be printed in Cuba and Germany to wrap Cuba's second-best-known industrial product. La Honradez, La Charanga de Villergas, La Real Fábrica de Eduardo Guilló, and La Africana were some of the factories involved.

Although most of the images were unrelated to Cuba (birds, romantic scenes, letters of the alphabet, uniforms, history), some of these *marquillas cigarreras* were quite representative of the island's physical and human landscape. In addition to reproducing some of Laplante's city views and sugar mills, the original series depicting the rise and fall of a woman of mixed race (*Vida y muerte de la mulata*) was significant, as it touched upon a taboo subject—the eroticism associated with free women of color—and must have made quite an impact. Printed by the thousands, these labels reached many homes throughout the island as well as abroad.[24]

We now turn to France for our *sixteenth* project and direct our attention to nine wood engravings that appeared in the Parisian periodical *Le Tour du Monde* in December 1860, accompanying an article on Cuba by Richard Dana.[25] One of the engravings highlighted the lush tropical vegetation that dominated the landscape in the southern part of Havana Harbor (see Figure 1.2). The semirural character of the small huts (*bohíos*)

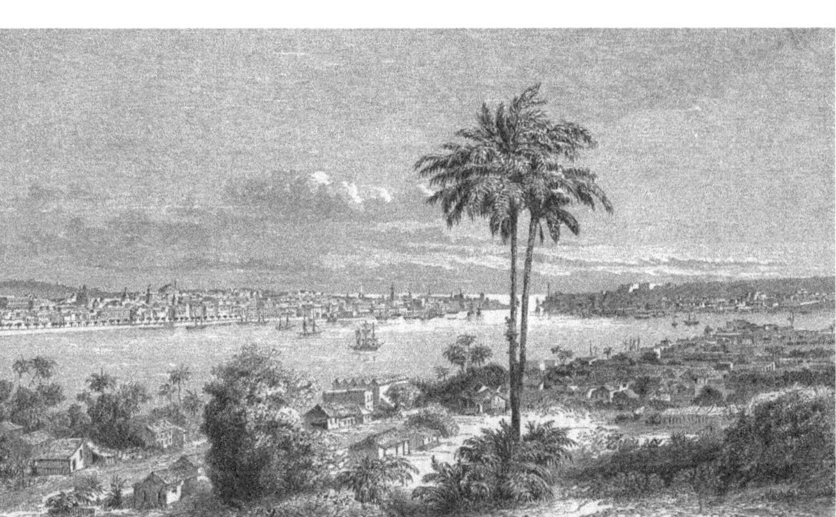

Figure 1.2. Dieudonné Lancelot (delineator) and Edward Therington (engraver), *Ansicht von La Habana* (*View of Havana*), 1895. *Die Katholischen Missionen* (Freiburg), Vol. 23, December, p. 281.

contrasted sharply with the compact settlement along the north coast of the city.

The views represented in Dana's article included the following scenes and places:

1. The Havana Harbor with two palm trees in the foreground (Lancelot and Therington)
2. An alley of palms (de Bérard and Manini)
3. Havana Cathedral (Navlet and Thienon)
4. A market scene (Pottin and Hildibrand)
5. The *volante* carriage (Adam and Huyot)
6. The Güines valley (Huet and Gusmand, after Mialhe)
7. The Gibara hills in Pinar del Río (Huet and Morand, after Moreau and Mialhe)
8. Matanzas (Lancelot and Gauchard, taken from Hoeffler, not Mialhe)
9. Three Chinese indentured workers in a cane field (Pelcoq, from a photograph)

The publication was a great success, and soon the Cuban images were being published in many countries and languages: English (Ainsworth,

All Round the World), Spanish (Charton, *La vuelta al mundo*), Italian (*Il Giro del Mondo*), Dutch (*Aarde en haar volken*), German (*Die Katolischen Millionen*), and even Japanese (Masao Uchida's geography book *Yochishiryaku*). Cuba was indeed traveling, through prints, all around the world.

Finally, we reach the *seventeenth* important print project of the nineteenth century: *Tipos y costumbres de la isla de Cuba* (1881), with texts by the most prominent writers of the day and illustrations by Landaluce/Landaluze. The artist had approached the subject thirty years earlier, but this time the images would be larger, far more detailed, and quite attractive. The twenty pictures show us the whole spectrum of Cuban society: the midwife, the lottery ticket seller, the country doctor, the firefighter, the peasant, the fruit stand operator, the carriage driver, the parasite. . . .

The editors used a novel printing procedure that required the aid of photography and, to that effect, engaged the services of the Portuguese-born Alfredo Pereira Taveira (1844–1913). The lithographed frontispiece—the often-reproduced *negros curros* (free urban blacks)—bears the signature of a certain A. Gallice, apparently Mexican, whose identity and biography have eluded me and, apparently, everybody else.[26]

Many other Cuban prints were issued during this period. However, they were mostly scattered in books and periodicals, not conceived as a purposeful, self-contained set.[27]

All told, between the 1760s and the 1880s, at least 358 different views of Cuba (plus countless cigar wrappers) were published, forming part of the seventeen projects discussed in this chapter. Moreover, these images circulated throughout the world, as many of them were copied time and again and published in the illustrated periodicals of the time: in the United States (*Ballou's Pictorial*, *Harper's Weekly*, *Lesliés Weekly*); in France (*El Correo de Ultramar*, *L'Illustration*, *Le Monde Illustré*, *Le Tour du Monde*, *L'Univers Illustré*); in England (*The Illustrated London News*, *Illustrated News*, *The Graphic*); in Spain (*El Bazar*, *La Ilustración Española y Americana*, *El Mundo Pintoresco*); in Germany (*Illustrirte Zeitung*, *Über Land und Meer*); and in Italy (*L'Illustrazione Italiana*, *L'Illustrazione Popolare*, *Il Mondo Illustrato*). Furthermore, many of these images also made it onto dinnerware sets produced in England, Spain, and Holland.[28] Imagine a Liverpool merchant, a Galician teacher, and a Dutch cabinetmaker having dinner from a plate bearing the image of a Cuban city, a cockfight, or a country dance.

Except for the small Matanzas views by López, and the engravings by Robles after Landaluze, all the artists were foreigners (English, French, Spanish, German, Belgian, Dutch), which speaks volumes. Bear in mind, also, that all the original images were printed in Havana, Matanzas, Santiago de Cuba, London, Paris, Hamburg, and Berlin—none in Madrid or Barcelona—food for thought. The so-called colonial gaze reflected in most of the graphic arts in Cuba until well into the nineteenth century was doubly colonial—it represented primarily non-Spanish and non-Cuban views of the island, largely from the perspectives of leading rivals of the Spanish empire.

Watercolors and oil paintings are, needless to say, very important in our understanding of Cuban reality. However, such works mostly remained in the homes of their owners, and, unless and until they were shown in an exhibition, a museum, or a publication (much rarer in colonial times), they would have had little impact on others; limited access means limited influence. Prints, on the other hand, were and are meant to circulate widely. It was through engravings and lithographs that Cuba first became known both on the island and abroad. Colonial Cuba was defined by its prints. Eventually, photographs took over the descriptive role of prints. However, for 120 years—and beyond—the seventeen projects here described were our most accurate and comprehensive mirror and our first true ambassadors to the world.

Notes

1. For an overview of Cuban colonial prints, see Jorge R. Bermúdez, *De Gutenberg a Landaluze*; Emilio Cueto, "A Short Guide to Old Cuban Prints"; *Grabados coloniales cubanos*; Adelaida de Juan, *Pintura y grabado coloniales cubanos*; Zoila Lapique Becali, *La memoria en las piedras*; Jorge Rigol, *Apuntes sobre la pintura y el grabado en Cuba*; Juan Sánchez, *El grabado en Cuba*; and Mario Sánchez Roig, *Notas inéditas sobre el grabado en Cuba*.

2. In addition to the prints discussed here, other colonial projects sought to describe our flora and fauna, such as Antonio Parra's *Descripción de diferentes piezas de historia natural*, with seventy-five prints, and the monumental *Histoire physique, politique et naturelle de l'île de Cuba* by Ramón de La Sagra, with 276 copperplate engravings published in Paris over the course of twenty years (1838–57). Because of their nature, they fall outside the scope of this chapter. For a panoramic overview on this subject, see Cueto, *Illustrating Cuba's Flora and Fauna*.

3. Apart from these mostly beautiful, picturesque images, during times of war in Cuba (the 1850s, 1868–78, and 1895–98), the foreign periodical press regularly depicted

many bloody scenes of combat and warfare. I have prepared an inventory of such prints for the period of the Ten Years' War (1868–78), scheduled for publication in a forthcoming issue of the *Revista de la Biblioteca Nacional de Cuba José Martí.*

4. De Bry, *America*, engravings number V 5 and 6, respectively.

5. See, for example, Johannes Hondius, *America*; Arnoldus Montanus, *De Nieuwe en Onbekende Weereld.*

6. The Havana image was reproduced in Cueto, *Illustrating Cuba's Flora and Fauna*, 85.

7. Claes Janszoon Visscher, Amsterdam, 1628; De Bry, *America*, engraving number 13.

8. Antonio de Solís, *Histoire de la conquête du Mexique*. The same image appeared in several Spanish versions of the Solís book, engraved by Spanish artists, but they were merely copying a foreign original, not offering a new version. A third, different, image of the same event appeared in the 1783 Spanish version of Solís (*Historia de la conquista de México*), but this one falls outside the scope of this pre-1762 section.

9. Antonio de Herrera, *Historia general*, frontispiece.

10. A contemporary set of twelve views of the seizure of Havana by Phillip Orsbridge (?–1766) and Dominic Serres (1722–93) is not included in this chapter because its purpose was not so much to paint Havana as to glorify the English military victory over the Spaniards. See *Grabados de Dominique Serres sobre la toma de La Habana en 1762* and *La toma de La Habana por los ingleses.*

11. See *Grabados coloniales cubanos*, 7, 79, 81, 83, and 85.

12. Spain was very laconic in divulging information about its American colonies. For example, in the field of cartography, it kept secret the geographic information and maps it accumulated in the Casa de Contratación (Chamber of Commerce) in Seville, and foreigners had to resign themselves to publishing more or less acceptable approximations of Spain's territories in the Americas. See Emilio Cueto, *Cuba in Old Maps*. Similarly, Spain rarely allowed foreign explorers to visit its colonies. A notable exception, during the Bourbon period, was the 1735 French expedition to measure the length of the Equator, to which Spain agreed on the condition that it include the Spanish naval officers Jorge Juan y Antonio de Ulloa.

13. See Alexander von Humboldt, *Voyage aux régions équinoxiales du Nouveau Continent*. On Humboldt's reflections about Cuba, see his *Ensayo Político sobre la Isla de Cuba*. See also Oficina del Historiador de la Ciudad de La Habana, *Alejandro de Humboldt en Cuba.*

14. By the 1820s, most Spanish colonies had become independent from the metropole and the new American republics placed few obstacles in the way of foreign visitors to their countries. Among the best-known nineteenth-century artists who traveled to Latin America and the Caribbean were Claudio Linati, Daniel Thomas Egerton, Frederick Catherwood, Carl Nebel, and Pierre-Frédéric Lehnert in Mexico; Johann Moritz Rugendas and Jean-Baptiste Debret in Brazil; L. Stobwasser in Antigua; John Augustine Waller in Barbados; Gaspard-Théodore Mollien in Colombia; César H. Bacle and Emeric Essex Vidal in Argentina and Uruguay; and Léonce Angrand and Alcide d'Orbigny in Peru and Bolivia.

15. See Cueto, *Mialhe's Colonial Cuba* and *La Cuba pintoresca de Frédéric Mialhe.*

16. See Cueto, "Los grabados del paseo pintoresco por la isla de Cuba." See also Lapique Becali, 99–129.

17. *Los Cubanos pintados por sí mismos*; *Les Français peints par eux-mêmes*; *Los Españoles pintados por sí mismos*.

18. See *Harper's New Monthly Magazine* (New York), January 1853, and *Illustrirte Zeitung* (Leipzig), 1869. See also *Grabados coloniales cubanos*, 89, 91, 93, 95, and 97.

19. *Grabados coloniales cubanos*, 109, 111, 113, 115, and 117.

20. Unable to date with certainty the printing of these images, I have tentatively placed them in the early 1850s, but further research may lead to a different conclusion. Some of the original watercolors of this series were housed in Havana's National Library, where I consulted them in the 1980s. Unfortunately, they were improperly removed (probably during the "Special Period" of the 1990s) and their whereabouts are unknown today.

21. See Lapique Becali, 134–38.

22. See Cueto, *Las litografías santiagueras del Departamento Oriental de la isla de Cuba*.

23. See *Grabados coloniales cubanos*, 119–77; Justo G. Cantero and Eduardo Laplante, *Los ingenios de la isla de Cuba*.

24. See Antonio Núñez Jiménez, *Marquillas cigarreras cubanas*.

25. Richard Dana, "Voyage à l'île de Cuba."

26. *Colección de artículos*. In November 1985, I examined the original glass pictures for seventeen of these images at the Museum of Art in Havana.

27. Samuel Hazard, *Cuba with Pen & Pencil*, contains mostly recycled, not original, images and is not separately discussed in this essay.

28. See Cueto, "Cuba en el grabado italiano (1792–1899)," 109–24; Cueto, *La Cuba pintoresca*; and María Josefa Fernández-España, *Dibujos de colecciones, Real Fábrica Sargadelos*.

Bibliography

Bermúdez, Jorge R. *De Gutenberg a Landaluze*. Havana: Editorial Letras Cubanas, 1990.

Cantero, Justo G., and Eduardo Laplante. *Los ingenios de la isla de Cuba: Colección de vistas de los principales ingenios de azúcar*. Madrid: Consejo Superior de Investigaciones Científicas/Doce Calles, 2005.

———. *Los ingenios de la isla de Cuba: Colección de vistas de los principales ingenios de azúcar*. Havana: Biblioteca Nacional de Cuba José Martí, Imagen Contemporánea, 2011.

Colección de artículos: Tipos y costumbres de la isla de Cuba, por los mejores autores de este género. Fototipia Taveira. Havana: Miguel de Villa, 1881.

Los Cubanos pintados por sí mismos: Colección de tipos cubanos. Havana: Barcina, 1852.

Cueto, Emilio. "Cuba en el grabado italiano (1792–1899)." In *II Seminario sobre emigración y presencia italiana en Cuba*. Havana: Embajada de Italia en Cuba, Sociedad Dante Alighieri de Cuba, 2015.

———. *Cuba in Old Maps*. Miami: Historical Museum of Southern Florida, 1999.

———. *La Cuba pintoresca de Frédéric Mialhe*. Havana: Biblioteca Nacional de Cuba José Martí, 2010.

———. "Los grabados del paseo pintoresco por la isla de Cuba." In *Paseo pintoresco por la isla de Cuba*. Miami: Herencia Cultural Cubana, Ediciones Universal, 1999.

———. *Illustrating Cuba's Flora and Fauna*. Miami: Historical Museum of Southern Florida, 2002.

———. *Las litografías santiagueras del Departamento Oriental de la isla de Cuba*. Havana: Biblioteca Nacional de Cuba José Martí, 2014.

———. *Mialhe's Colonial Cuba: The Prints That Shaped the World's View of Cuba*. Miami: Historical Association of Southern Florida, 1994.

———. "A Short Guide to Old Cuban Prints." *Cuban Studies* 14, no. 1 (1984): 27–42.

Dana, Richard. "Voyage à l'île de Cuba." In *Le Tour du Monde*, edited by Édouard Charton, Vols. 1–2, 353–68. Paris: Librairie de L. Hachette et Cie., 1860.

De Bry, Theodor. *America*. Fifth Book. Frankfurt, 1595.

Los Españoles pintados por sí mismos. Madrid: Boix, 1844.

Fernández-España, María Josefa. *Dibujos de colecciones, Real Fábrica Sargadelos*. La Coruña, Spain: La Voz de Galicia, 1978.

Les Français peints para eux-mêmes. Paris: L. Curmer, 1840–42.

Fraunhar, Alison. "*Marquillas cigarreras cubanas*: Nation and Desire in the Nineteenth Century." *Hispanic Research Journal* 9, no. 5 (2008): 458–78.

Grabados coloniales cubanos. Havana and Málaga: Museo Nacional de Cuba and Diputación de Málaga, 1999.

Grabados de Dominique Serres sobre la toma de La Habana en 1762. Havana: Biblioteca Nacional José Martí, 1962.

Hazard, Samuel. *Cuba with Pen & Pencil*. Hartford, CT: Hartford Publishing Co., 1871.

Herrera, Antonio de. *Historia general de los hechos de los castellanos en las islas i tierra firme del mar océano*. Madrid: Imprenta de Real de Nicolás Rodíquez Franco, 1726.

Hondius, Johannes. *America*. Amsterdam, 1634.

Humboldt, Alejandro von. *Ensayo Político sobre la Isla de Cuba*. Havana: Lex, 1960.

———. *Voyage aux régions équinoxiales du Nouveau Continent, fait en 1799, 1800, 1801, 1802, 1803 et 1804 par Alexandre de Humboldt et Aimé Bonpland, rédigé par A. de Humboldt*. Paris: Librairie Grecque-Latine-Allemande, 1815–26.

Juan, Adelaida de. *Pintura y grabado coloniales cubanos*. 2nd ed. Havana: Editorial Pueblo y Educación, 1985.

Lapique Becali, Zoila. *La memoria en las piedras: Historia de la litografía en Cuba*. Havana: Boloña, 2002.

Montanus, Arnoldus. *De Nieuwe en Onbekende Weereld*. Amsterdam: Jacob van Meurs, 1671.

Núñez Jiménez, Antonio. *Marquillas cigarreras cubanas*. Madrid: Tabapress, 1989.

Oficina del Historiador de la Ciudad de La Habana. *Alejandro de Humboldt en Cuba: Catálogo para la exposición en la Casa Humboldt, Habana Vieja, octubre 1997–enero 1998*. Augsburg, Germany: Wissner, 1997.

Parra, Antonio. *Descripción de diferentes piezas de historia natural, las más del ramo marino*. Havana: Imprenta de la Capitanía General, 1787.

Rigol, Jorge. *Apuntes sobre la pintura y el grabado en Cuba: De los orígenes a 1927*. Havana: Letras Cubanas, 1983.

Sagra, Ramón de la. *Histoire physique, politique et naturelle de l'île de Cuba*. Paris: Arthus Bertrand, 1840.

Sánchez, Juan. *El grabado en Cuba*. Havana: Talleres Tipográficos de Impresora Mundial, 1955.

Sánchez Roig, Mario. *Notas inéditas sobre el grabado en Cuba*. Havana: Biblioteca Nacional José Martí, 1966.

Solís, Antonio de. *Histoire de la Conquête du Mexique*. Paris: Compagnie des Libraires, 1691.

———. *Historia de la conquista de México*. Madrid: Sancha, 1783.

Tipos y costumbres de la isla de Cuba. Havana: Editorial Biblioteca Nacional de Cuba José Martí, 2010.

La toma de La Habana por los ingleses. Havana: Biblioteca Nacional de Cuba José Martí, 2012.

2

Between Civilization and Barbarism

Víctor Patricio de Landaluze's Paintings during the Ten Years' War in Cuba (1868–1878)

E. Carmen Ramos

In the early 1870s, after a thriving career as a caricaturist and publisher in Havana, Cuba, Víctor Patricio de Landaluze moved to the nearby town of Guanabacoa in an effort to slow down his hectic lifestyle in light of his failing health.[1] While continuing to publish political caricatures in Spanish satirical journals against the armed struggle for Cuban independence that had begun in 1868, he also decisively turned to painting and created some of the most ambitious canvases he had produced since his arrival in Cuba from Spain in the 1850s. One of those paintings, *Día de Reyes en La Habana* (*Three Kings Day in Havana*, ca. early 1870s), is undoubtedly one of the best-known (and most widely reproduced) depictions of the festival of the Epiphany celebrated in nineteenth-century Cuba (Plate 4). It portrays a local variant of the annual Christian celebration held every January 6 in remembrance of the day when the three kings, or three wise men, brought gifts to the infant Jesus. As the central scene of the painting readily conveys, in colonial Cuba the Epiphany was commonly associated with slaves and free persons of color who came together for a day of carnival-like celebration. On this occasion, Afro-Cubans would parade and perform in urban centers and ask spectators for an *aguinaldo* or Christmas tip.[2] Indeed, this richly detailed painting, which captures Afro-Cuban costuming, musical, and performative traditions, provides a glimpse of sorts into nineteenth-century Cuban society. Drawn to the realistic portrayal of Afro-Cuban cultural expressions in this and other works, many scholars, starting with the foundational Cuban ethnologist Fernando Ortiz, have turned to Landaluze's work for its anthropological value. For Ortiz, Landaluze's works represent a veritable "ethnographic museum" of Afro-Cuban types, which he and later scholars routinely mined in their considerations of African diasporic culture in Cuba and beyond.[3]

As valuable as these studies are in plumbing the depths of African tradition in the New World, they do not necessarily engage the politics of Landaluze's imagery, which he created during a period of profound racial transformation in one of the last bastions of the Spanish empire and slavery in the Americas. From this perspective, Cuba and Landaluze are not unique; many nineteenth-century artists working in places like Brazil, the United States, and Puerto Rico wrestled with representations of black subjects as their respective regions moved toward ending slavery and integrating former slaves and free people of color into society. In seeking to understand the black image in nineteenth-century Latin American art, it is imperative to move beyond the lure of pictorial realism to explore the politics of racial representation during these remarkably transitional times.[4]

In Cuba's and Landaluze's case, these politics directly relate to Cuba's long struggle for national sovereignty and the quest for emancipation and racial equality, both of which played a critical role in Cuba's independence wars. Between 1868 and 1878, Cuban insurgents unleashed a guerilla war—later known as the Ten Years' War—against Spanish colonialism, which threw the interrelated issues of slavery and independence into high relief. Landaluze was not a disinterested outside observer of these times but a politically active *peninsular* (a person born in Spain) and image-maker who actively defended the Spanish presence in Cuba. From his earliest days on the island, Landaluze published caricatures for some of the most staunchly conservative journals, which supported Spanish colonialism, a perspective abetted by his long military service on the island as part of *Los Voluntarios*.[5] Over the course of his almost forty-year residence in Cuba, he also became the colony's foremost visual *costumbrista* (genre artist), producing paintings and lithographs, as well as illustrating anthologies that represented unique Cuban types and scenes, right when this genre was widely associated with burgeoning Creole nationalist sentiment across Latin America and the cartographic ambitions of the new nations. Even though many questions remain about the circulation of Landaluze's paintings during his lifetime, much can still be learned by hinging his works to their momentous historical context.[6]

A careful analysis of two key paintings and related visual culture from the late 1860s and early 1870s will position Landaluze's representations of Afro-Cuban subjects as charged stage sets performing the tensions of his time. Far from transparent picture windows into the past, Landaluze's works, which he produced during the Ten Years' War, represent two sides of the same coin. On the one hand, his wartime caricature represented the racialized barbarism of the insurgency, which Spanish authorities argued would take over the whole island if the insurrection were successful. These images circulated within a larger field of visual propaganda that touted the civilizing authority of Spain. On the other hand, Landaluze's paintings, while ostensibly about Cuban customs, depict the Cuban colony as a place where slaves continue to labor peacefully on plantations, and Afro-Cubans and their culture are still held widely in contempt. My intent is to show that Landaluze's paintings both evince and deny a racial and colonial world in transition.[7]

From Africanization to Savage Insurrection

The prominence of black imagery in Landaluze's oeuvre mirrors the centrality of race in late colonial Cuban society. The enduring political ties between Cuba and Spain during the nineteenth century are directly tied to the aftermath of the Haitian Revolution (1791–1804). Following the Haitian Revolution, Creole elites in Cuba decided to take advantage of the decline of Haiti's sugar economy to expand their sugar enterprises by modernizing their plantations and importing vast numbers of enslaved African laborers. This economically motivated turn of events had profound social implications, as many residents in Cuba lived in fear of a potential race war, which Spaniards argued could only be avoided by Spain's strong, protective colonial presence. The fear of "Africanization" and the subsequent financial ruin that it came to represent kept elite Creoles tied to the Spanish empire, even as many colonies in South and North America fought for and achieved independence.

The fear of a slave uprising in Cuba similar to that of Haiti, however, did not entirely stave off efforts to reform colonial relations, or to free Cuba from Spain's hold. By 1868, Cuba's first major battle for independence was brewing, yet its historical unfolding did not adhere to the image Spain had touted since the late eighteenth century. Rather than a revolution instigated by rebelling slaves, the 1868 insurrection was orchestrated by white Creole patrician leaders based in Santiago de Cuba in the eastern, less industrialized part of the island. Led by Carlos Manuel de Céspedes, the insurrection had its origins in the failure of colonial reforms in the mid-1860s to bring about political and economic change. Knowing that the existence of slavery kept many Creole slave and property owners tied to the Spanish empire, Céspedes and his supporters strategically addressed the nagging racial dilemma in Cuban politics: they publicly supported abolition, and some insurgent leaders freed their slaves if they joined the insurgency. Over the course of the long war, the insurgent leadership and rank and file became increasingly multiracial, with slaves and free persons of color joining the battle. Ratifying their own constitution, the insurgents established a Republic in Arms, complete with a president, and set about to capture towns and regions throughout the east using guerrilla tactics, such as torching sugar plantations and using the tools of sugar cultivation, machetes, as makeshift weapons. By 1871, the insurgent leadership publicly supported complete emancipation and increasingly projected a rhetoric of racial equality as a goal of an independent Cuba. This radical challenge to the racial status quo of a slave society was organic rather than planned and fraught with significant, at times crippling, tensions within the insurgency itself. Nonetheless, in theory and sometimes in practice, the insurrection and its aftermath brought forth new possibilities for Afro-Cubans in society, who accounted for a substantial portion of the island's population.[8]

From the onset of the insurrection, Landaluze's imagery undermined these social changes by visualizing old Africanization arguments and prejudiced views of Afro-Cubans. His caricatures, which either portrayed insurrectionists or allegorized the war itself, directly and repeatedly invoked race. In one caricature, published in October 1869 around the first anniversary of the start of the war in the town of Yara, Landaluze portrayed the president of the Republic in Arms and his supporters celebrating in the manner of Afro-Cuban *cabildos*[9] (Figure 2.1). Shirtless, wearing a feather headdress and raffia hoopskirt, and shaking a pair of rattles, Céspedes presides over a barbaric topsy-turvy Epiphany celebration where drunkenness, bestiality, and miscegenation prevail. Numerous caricatures would follow, including some that portray masked and

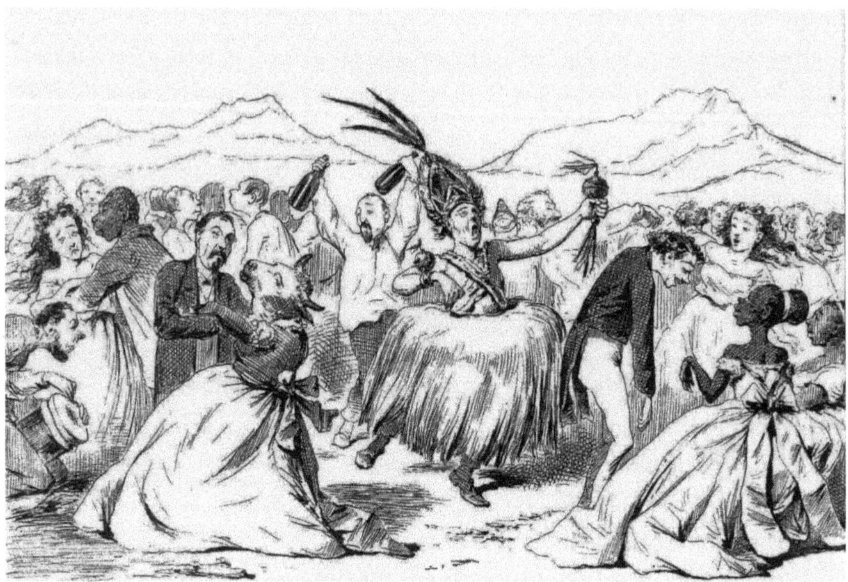

Figure 2.1. Víctor Patricio de Landaluze, "El presidente Céspedes celebrando en medio de su corte el aniversario de lo de Yara" ("President Céspedes Celebrating amidst His Court on the Anniversary of Yara"), 1869, *Don Junípero* 6, no. 53, 17 October. Collection of the National Library of Spain, Madrid.

drunken insurgents deferentially referring to President Céspedes as a slave would his master, and many that envision the threat of the insurgency by way of allegory. In a piercing caricature from 1871 titled "Isla de Cuba" ("Island of Cuba," Figure 2.2), Landaluze personifies Cuba as a young, perhaps Native American maiden, who pleads with the Spanish Overseas Minister to intervene to stop the spread of blackness overcoming her body.[10] The darkness that consumes her not only transforms her skin color from light to dark, but also her hair and behavioral disposition. On her left side, her long hair no longer hangs over her shoulder, but is short, coarse, and tightly curled. On the darker side, her earrings, armlet, and bare shoulder call attention to her physicality and receptive sexuality, further implied by the open palm of her hand. The text beneath her also undergoes transformation; the phrase "Isla de Cuba," rendered in narrow, bubble letters, is gradually being filled in with the color black. These visual cues suggest that unless Spanish authorities intervene, political and racial disorder are likely results.

As an image-maker allied with the Spanish cause, Landaluze was uniquely poised to depict what historian Ada Ferrer has called the rhetoric

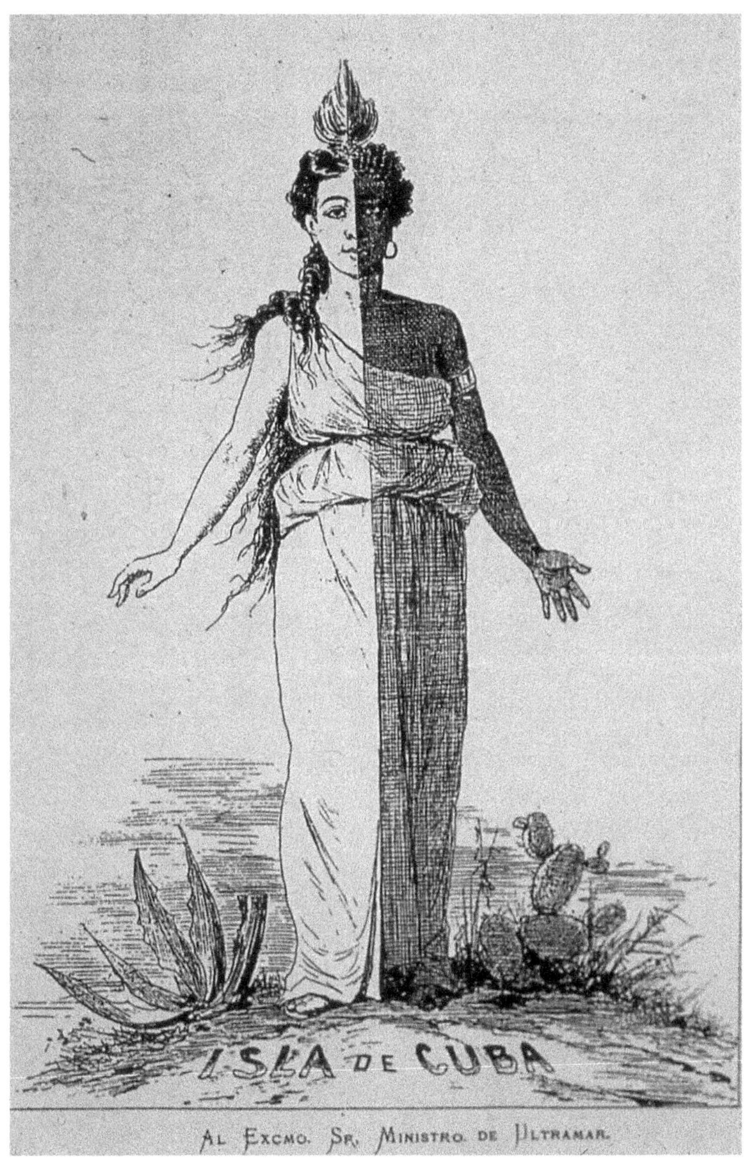

Figure 2.2. Víctor Patricio de Landaluze, "Isla de Cuba" ("Island of Cuba"), 1873, *Juan Palomo*, 30 November. Courtesy of the Cuban Heritage Collection, University of Miami Libraries, Coral Gables, FL.

of Spanish counterinsurgency. Ferrer argues that since the inception of the war, Spanish authorities had sought to construct an image of the rebellion as leading to a race war. This outlook found expression in military pronouncements and assessments of the war, as well as in the Spanish political war strategy itself. For example, at the onset of the insurrection, Captain General Francisco Lersundi—the highest Spanish official on the island between 1866 and 1869—argued that the rebellion was preparing Cuba for the kind of

> civilization and happiness . . . [present in Haiti and Santo Domingo where] . . . polygamy is permitted and practiced by all their inhabitants who settle their affairs with machetes and who live deprived of all that is indispensable to civilization, although they are entirely free to run naked if they so desire.[11]

To argue that the Ten Years' War was preparing Cuba to become a black republic, however, entailed making this threat palpable in ways that residents of Cuba could understand. As is ironically implied in the captain general's statement above, this strategy involved invoking notions of civilization and its inverse, barbarism, in a particularly Cuban way.

Like Lersundi's verbal lampoon, Landaluze's caricatures predominantly attack the insurrection on racial and, by extension, cultural and moral terms. Instead of valiant and principled white leaders (and eventually Afro-Cuban ones as well) marshaling a multiracial coalition of insurrectionists, Landaluze's images suggest that the communion of white and black soldiers on the field is leading down a path of social disorder. Landaluze achieved this feat by staging a kind of scene of miscegenation, or mixing references to the insurrection with those that signified Afro-Cuban culture. In this way, Landaluze's wartime caricatures correspond to what Jan Nederveen Pieterse has called "niggering," the presentation of images that malign ethnic or political groups by rendering them black.[12] However, Landaluze does not resort to racialized physical caricature; the white figures in this caricature are not depicted with Negroid features. Rather, a cultural and performative association—their nakedness, their deviant and interracial sexuality, in some cases their racially marked speech—renders them "black." By presenting white insurrectionists as still racially white, Landaluze leaves the door open for their possible return to the Spanish fold.

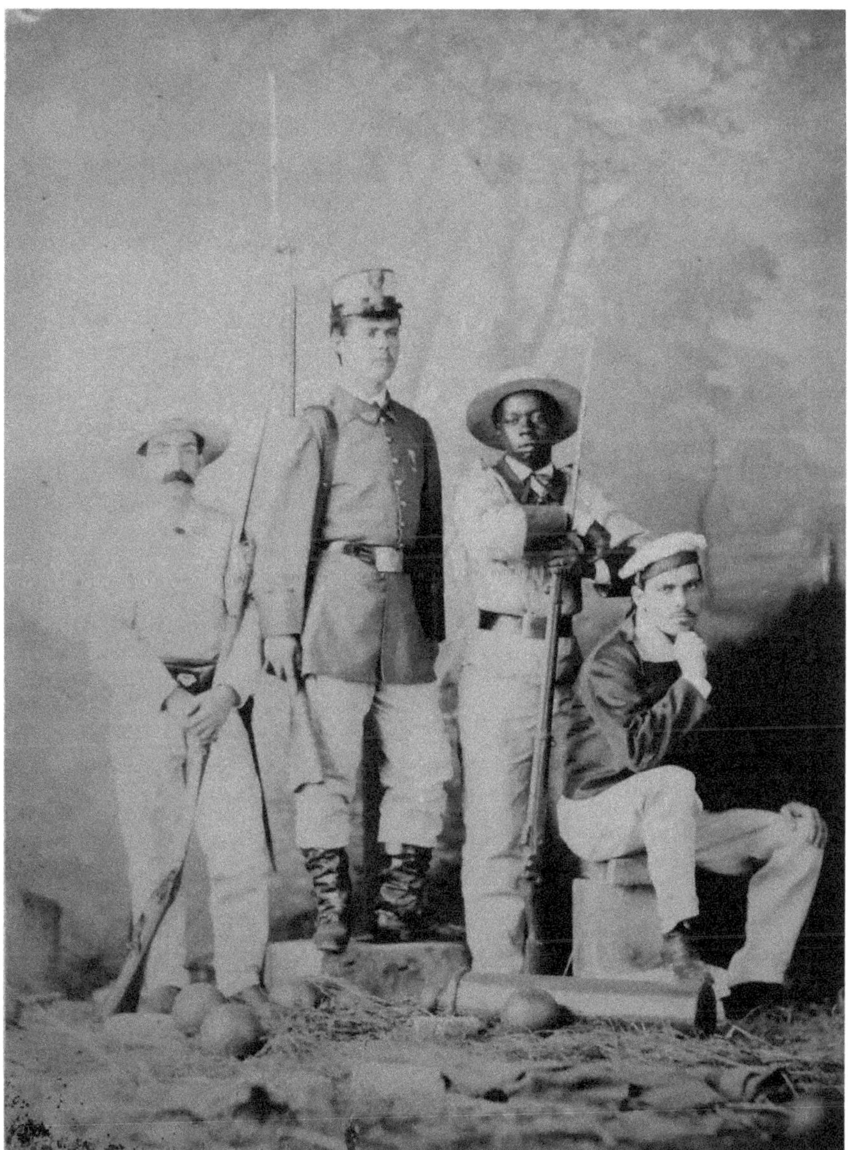

Figure 2.3. Gil Gelpí y Ferro, *Defensores de la integridad nacional* (*Defenders of National Integrity*), 1872. Photography Collection, Miriam and Ira D. Wallach Division of Art, Prints and Photographs, The New York Public Library, Astor, Lenox, and Tilden Foundations.

Landaluze's *Corte de Caña* and Emancipation

Historians of the Ten Years' War frequently point out that it first broke out at Carlos Manuel de Céspedes' sugar mill, La Demajagua, on October 10, 1868. His first act was to free his slaves and invite them to participate in the insurrection to "conquer liberty and independence" for Cuba.[13] Despite the leading insurrectionists' tempered embrace of emancipation during the early phases of the Ten Years' War and their shifting views on racial equality, Céspedes' actions and the many acts of emancipation that followed symbolically drew a line in the sand. These acts clearly expressed the insurrectionist camp's views on the relationship between slavery and independence. Slavery and sugar wealth were Cuba's golden handcuffs; they maintained prosperity at the expense of national freedom. It is for these reasons that Céspedes' first act on his plantation at the outbreak of insurrection was so powerful. Given the charged significance of a specific sugar plantation within the narrative of the Ten Years' War, it is surprising that Landaluze's plantation scene *Corte de caña* (*Cutting Sugar Cane*, Plate 5), painted amid the insurrection in 1874, has never been discussed in relation to the war. For not only does the painting represent a type of location intimately tied to the birth of the insurrection, it also portrays actively laboring slaves at a time when emancipation was a key issue that led to war.

Like Landaluze's Epiphany scene, *Corte de caña* captures familiar aspects of and personages in daily Afro-Cuban colonial life. The scene takes place under a bright blue sky in a verdant tropical landscape. In the far distance, one finds three actively burning smokestacks, echoed by a pair of iconic palm trees, and sugar mill buildings where cut cane is ground, processed, and packaged. In the foreground and midground of the painting is a wide range of figures involved in sugar cultivation. Toward the right middle ground, the *mayoral* (overseer) is distinguished by his black cape and superior vantage point as he sits astride a horse. His Afro-Cuban *contramayorales* or assistants also wear or stand near black capes. The *mayoral* holds a whip in his hand and actively directs the labor of the male and female slaves who surround him. To his right and left, various groups of slaves load harvested cane onto an oxcart or actively use machetes to cut cane under the burning sun. At the center of the composition stands an elderly slave with a jar on her head that holds water to be distributed to the laboring slaves. Next to her stands a young female child; she and the elderly woman are the only two Afro-Cubans not directly involved in the cane harvest. This pair represents a common practice on Cuban plantations: elderly female slaves were devoted to caring for young slave children until the children could labor themselves.[14] Behind and to the right of this pair stands a young boy who has already begun field work. Like the enslaved men who surround him in the field, this young male slave holds a machete in his hand.

A scene of such orderly agricultural production gives no indication of the painting's wartime context, and poses the question of why Landaluze chose to depict a productive plantation *despite* the war. In my estimation, it is precisely this fact that makes *Corte de caña* so resonant with the Ten Years' War period. From one perspective, the scene's visible productivity may relate to the condition of plantations in the western part of the island, where Landaluze lived and worked throughout his life in Cuba. Historian Rebecca Scott has shown that sugar production in the western region increased during the war, in part due to the persistence of slavery and planters' adaptations to the changing times.[15] In a war marked by regionalism—the theater of war was confined to the eastern part of the island—Landaluze's painting could very well represent a plantation in the western part of the island, where no destructions of property took place. That *Corte de caña* depicts a plantation with three active smokestacks suggests that this picture represents an industrialized mill of the sort that was more prevalent in the west than the east.

Even as Landaluze's scene seems to ignore the insurrection's impact on Cuban plantation life by depicting a stable "western" plantation, the repercussions of the conflict are subtly felt in *Corte de caña*. For even if we accept that plantations in the west remained productive and stable during the insurrection, the category of slave did not. By 1870, in response to the emancipatory acts and rhetoric of the insurgents, Spain was forced to adopt a measure of gradual emancipation. After all, how could the colonial authority maintain order if slaves knew they could gain their freedom by joining the insurgency? Spain also had to appear as a purveyor of freedom. Considering *Corte de caña* against the events and repercussions of the war makes it clear that this image offers a reassuring and stable vision of Cuba's sugar economy, then under direct attack by the insurgency. By picturing slaves peacefully going about their labor, the painting also implies that the nature of interracial relations between Afro-Cubans and whites remained unchanged. However, while the image seeks to render the insurrection powerless, it unwittingly acknowledges the process of historical change the insurrection unleashed. On its face, even as *Corte de caña* depicts a productive plantation, its subtext is the war and its impact on Cuban slavery.

What is striking about this painting is how its pictorial signifiers work against the new meanings the insurrection projected onto plantation life. As discussed earlier, the insurgency's limited resources meant that its participants largely waged a guerrilla war, using everything from machetes to arson, as they were known to torch sugar plantations to disrupt the Cuban colonial economy. These acts of arson were prevalent, known, and often recorded in accounts of the war. One 1870 article called out these incidents as acts of barbarism that would lead to the complete ruin of both sugar and tobacco plantations and ultimately block Cuba's economic prosperity.[16] Historian Louis A. Pérez Jr. has further noted that the destruction of sugar estates in the east was so extensive that the plantation economy there never recovered.[17] Landaluze chose to depict a plantation landscape untouched by these contemporary events. His plantation is not a battlefield, but a productive work site. Furthermore, by prominently including slaves wielding machetes, Landaluze's painting also challenges the use of machetes as armaments on the battlefield. Landaluze's caricatures and other manifestations of Spanish visual culture routinely depicted insurrectionists using machetes. By prominently placing machetes in the hands of slaves cutting cane, Landaluze re-signifies or returns the machete to its original agricultural context, negating its wartime purpose.

Landaluze's choice of subject and compositional arrangement also underscores the enduring power of the plantation. Landaluze chooses to portray a plantation during the *zafra*, the harvesting season when cane was at its most critical, optimal stage. During this period, harvested cane had to be processed within forty-eight hours of being cut, or risk spoiling.[18] By depicting slaves dependably laboring at this pivotal time, Landaluze presents a reassuring image of stability when it is most needed. In doing so, he reinforces an expectation that sugar profits will indeed follow and the Cuban economy will prosper. The hierarchical race relations envisioned in the picture support this positive outlook. The *mayoral*, as the only white person in the entire painting, stands as a racial minority, yet he commands a troop of slaves who labor under his whip. His power is buttressed by his placement in the composition; he is silhouetted against the three buildings in the distance—the location where cane is processed and refined. The slaves, alternatively, are silhouetted against the land itself; they appear bound by the land upon which they labor and never visually break through the horizon line. Even the Afro-Cuban *contramayorales*—who in assisting the *mayoral* operate in a kind of midzone between slavery and the discipline of the plantation—are also visually associated with nature: they stand in front of the cut cane on the oxcart.

Depicting a sugar plantation as a powerful institution that shaped slave life, however, was not new. Frédéric Mialhe and Éduoard Laplante, two French artists who lived temporarily in Cuba, created many lithographs depicting Cuban plantations as stable and prosperous enterprises. Some of Mialhe's images from his 1840s series *Album Pintoresco de la Isla de Cuba* (*Picturesque Album of the Island of Cuba*) focused on less-developed plantations and evoked specific aspects of the sugar cultivation process, such as grinding cane. Laplante's lavish 1857 book *Los ingenios* (*The Sugar Plantations*) was a survey of sorts of the major plantations in western Cuba.[19] His book juxtaposed views of plantations with detailed productivity profiles of each site, which itemized number of slaves, quantity of sugar production, and acreage of each plantation. Laplante's often-panoramic portrayals of large plantations practically render slaves as black specks in the landscape, almost imperceptible within the vast scene. Laplante's bird's-eye perspective and accompanying productivity snapshot sought to offer a thorough view of each plantation in his series, and the images essentially functioned as estate portraits.[20] It is the plantation itself—its inner workings, its monumental size, and, by implication, its economic value—that is the focus of Mialhe's and Laplante's works.

Landaluze flips this equation and slave labor itself becomes the main subject of his painting. This is not only implied by the slaves' prominent compositional placement in the foreground, but also by the title of the painting. While *Corte de caña* is often translated as "The Cane Harvest," the more common word used in Cuba to describe the harvest was *zafra*.[21] The *zafra* lasted from the winter to early spring and encompassed several steps: cutting, collecting, grinding, extracting, and boiling cane, followed by the packaging of processed cane for sale and transport.[22] Landaluze's painting focuses on the first two steps in this process, the cutting and collection of cut cane. Considering the entire harvesting process, I believe it is more accurate to translate *Corte de caña* as "Cutting Sugar Cane." This translation emphasizes the act of cutting cane, which relied on slave labor. Landaluze's choice of wording, coupled with the prominent placement of figures in the painting, suggests that his subject was the slave labor that made the harvest possible.

If we take the subject of the painting to be slave labor, then here, too, Landaluze's image stands apart from the related works that preceded it. For while Landaluze's imagery of laboring male and female slaves coincides with previous depictions of slave plantation life, the inclusion of children in his scene is extraordinary. While images of children of color are common in nineteenth-century Cuban art and visual culture, such as in the *Día de Reyes en La Habana*, what is unique about *Corte de caña* is that children are depicted on the plantation work site itself—in some cases, laboring alongside adult slaves. As already noted, the painting depicts a young male child on the right who holds a machete and has started his work as an unfree laborer. That he wears an oversized straw hat also worn by the adult male slaves implies that, despite his youth, his life as a full-fledged slave has begun. Toward the center, a younger female child accompanies an elderly female figure. What is fascinating about this imagery is that by the time this painting was executed in 1874, the categories of child and elderly slave had undergone dramatic and symbolic transformation.

In response to the insurrectionists' strategic emancipation of slaves on the eastern part of the island, the Spanish colonial authority sought to usurp the moral upper hand by promulgating the Moret Law of 1870. Viewed as a preparatory bill for the gradual abolition of slavery, the law—which came to be known as the "Free Womb Act"—granted freedom to children born to slaves after September 1868, who were nevertheless required to remain under the tutelage of their former masters until they reached eighteen years of age. The law also granted freedom to slaves who had reached the age of sixty. While Cuban planters resisted and obstructed the law, on paper it dramatically shifted thousands of enslaved adults and children to a new freed status. In other words, after the Moret Law, no Afro-Cuban child was technically born a slave. Considering this shift, my attention is drawn to the female child in red in Landaluze's painting, who appears so young (probably under six years of age) that she may indeed fall into the category of those children "born free" after 1868. Her inclusion alongside an elderly slave also freed by the Spanish act of gradual emancipation conjures the two major categories of enslaved workers directly impacted by the Moret Law.

Rather than serving as harbingers of freedom, Landaluze's depiction of children in *Corte de caña* signifies the stability of life on Cuban sugar plantations. At first glance, the female child's vibrant red dress singles her out, highlighting her difference from the slaves who surround her. Her singularity is quickly undermined by the fact that her red dress reverberates with that of a female slave cutting cane in the distance. Like the color-coded black cape of the *mayoral* and his assistants, we could read a relationship between the "freed" child and the female slave who also wears red. Furthermore, the female child also holds and bends a stalk of cane, as if rehearsing her future manual labor. This implies that, like the young boy to her right, she too is growing into her future role on the plantation. Her status as a freed slave, therefore, does not seem to affect her future labor. In this way, the painting follows the letter of the law, as the Free Womb Act required that freed children labor for their former masters until adulthood. Therefore, while considered legally free, this young girl is provisionally captive. Considering Landaluze's nuanced representation of slave labor, *Corte de caña* represents a reassuring image in a time of change. Despite the war and the instigation of gradual emancipation, the painting envisions the dependability of black labor and a traditionally hierarchical slave plantation.

In many ways, the peaceful labor scene captured in *Corte de caña* was an omen. After ten long years of fighting, the insurrection ended in February 1878 with the Pact of Zanjón. The treaty granted the colony administrative and political rights (like the right to organize political parties) and unconditional freedom to all slave and indentured Chinese combatants still in the rebellion. Even as the insurrection was successful at fomenting a new language of multiracial Cuban citizenship, disrupting the Cuban plantation economy in the eastern part of the island, and securing emancipation for slaves who participated in the rebellion, it ultimately did not achieve its main goals: Cuban independence or complete and immediate emancipation. Yet peace after Zanjón was elusive. Immediately following the signing of the treaty, the *mulato* General Antonio Maceo and his supporters protested the agreement and continued to fight in Oriente province through June 1878. In August 1879, another war, the so-called *Guerra Chiquita* (Little War), broke out and lasted close to a year. Between the 1880s and 1893, Spanish colonial authorities uncovered five new independence plots.[23] If peace was fragile and intangible, the impact of the war was far more enduring. In its ultimate failure, the insurrection nevertheless had several achievements. It helped set the stage for the complete emancipation of slavery that would finally be achieved in 1886. It ushered in a new political leadership beyond the traditional planter class from the west, which included Afro-Cubans who had distinguished themselves on the battlefield. In addition, the insurrection broadly defined—its leaders, its language of multiracial Cuban citizenship, and even the social and economic unrest that would follow in the 1880s—helped set the stage and tenor for the second major battle for independence between 1895 and 1898, a war that Landaluze, who died in 1889, would not live to see.

Even as I have interpreted Landaluze's paintings as manifestations of Spanish colonial discourse during the 1870s, they could also be read against the grain. *Día de Reyes en La Habana* undoubtedly constructs a reproachful picture of Afro-Cuban spiritual and performative traditions; yet, as numerous scholars in multiple contexts have argued, carnival events themselves allowed for the symbolic and actual reversal of colonial authority.[24] Furthermore, in Cuba, Christmas tips collected during Epiphany could buy the freedom of the still-enslaved. We can also acknowledge that Landaluze's depiction of a multigenerational group of both enslaved and legally freed Afro-Cubans in *Corte de caña* captures, however unintentionally, the process of historical change in Cuba. The painting registers competing impulses—the desire to deny change in a world that was already irrevocably altered. For emancipation, however slowly it unfolded in Cuba, had already begun. Landaluze's depiction of children as post-emancipation tropes could also invite multiple interpretations. Yes, his images of Afro-Cuban children could signify the endurance across generations of disdained African culture or the reliability of Afro-Cuban labor during the decline of slavery; however, to slaves themselves, children born after the Moret Law could also signify freedom. Along these lines, one nineteenth-century account suggests that following the Moret Law, a baby boom took root on many plantations, which he attributed to slave mothers' perceptions that their newly born children would be free.[25] For slaves, children could indeed be harbingers of freedom.

Moreover, Landaluze was not immune to direct responses from critics during his lifetime. Among the insurrection's most significant legacies was the way it ushered a host of new and vocal anticolonial protagonists into the Cuban public sphere. One such protagonist was Doña Emilia

Casanova de Villaverde, wife of the famed Cuban novelist and political activist in exile Cirilo Villaverde, who wrote *Cecilia Valdés* (the definitive edition of which was published in 1882). Working out of their base in New York City, Casanova became a leading fundraiser for the insurrection, and a virtual "first lady" of the Republic in Arms.[26] President Ulysses Grant received her several times at the White House, and she actively courted prominent figures such as Victor Hugo and the Venezuelan President Antonio Guzmán Blanco, asking them to support the rebellion publicly. So well-known were her activities that Landaluze mocked her in caricatures published in *Don Junípero* and other journals like *La Sombra*. In one 1869 caricature titled "Serenata al D. Quijote de la Junta Cubana," Landaluze represented Casanova serenading one of her activist colleagues in exile.[27] The image is in keeping with Landaluze's topsy-turvy approach to depicting the insurrectionist camp. In this case, he reverses traditional gender roles, depicting Casanova in the position of a male suitor, likely a pun on her last name and indirect comment on her "un-feminine" activities in the political realm. From abroad, Casanova caught wind of these offensive caricatures and wrote several letters to the captain general of Cuba at the time, Domingo Dulce, denouncing the breach in decency exemplified by individuals she described as the "Spanish literati." Citing the names of several journals affiliated with Landaluze, she characterized these representations as "indecent and brutal attacks by the Peninsular press in Cuba."[28] In Casanova's brazen letters to the captain general, she inverted notions of civilization that the Spanish colonial authority had long used to malign the insurrection.

As much as Landaluze directly ridiculed these new protagonists, his representations also served as a record of their impact on history. We can thus read into the omissions in Landaluze's version of history. I find it striking that in all of Landaluze's political caricatures about the insurrection—many of which represent actual historical individuals—none appears to represent Antonio Maceo, the most prominent nonwhite insurrectionist, who rose up the ranks to become a leading general of the rebellion. Even Arsenio Martínez Campos, the commander of the Spanish Army in Cuba toward the end of the insurrection, called Maceo "one of the [war's] most famous combatants."[29] Why this absence? One could only assume Landaluze's logic: to represent Maceo, even with the goal of deriding him, would acknowledge his agency and impact on the fate of the Cuban colony. Despite the historical realities of the Ten Years' War,

Landaluze apparently could not bring himself to represent Afro-Cubans beyond images of cultural degeneracy, ridicule, and subservience.

Notes

1. Lázara Castellanos, *Víctor Patricio de Landaluze*, 51.

2. In this chapter I use the term "Afro-Cuban" to refer to a variety of racialized subjects and representations. Although this term emerged in the first half of the twentieth century and is associated with the development of Cuban ethnography and the often-exotic tendencies in vanguard Cuban visual art, poetry, and literature, I use it as an imperfect composite term that could encompass several racial designations that circulated in the nineteenth century. During this time, Cubans used a variety of racialized terms to refer to people of African descent, including *pardo/a*, *negro/a*, *moreno/a*, *mulato/a*, *gente de color* (people of color), and *negro criollo* (Cuban-born black). To employ this complex nomenclature to describe every instance of Landaluze's racialized representations would prove cumbersome and, more importantly, subjective.

3. See Fernando Ortiz, "Dos 'diablitos' de Landaluze"; David Brown, *Santeria Enthroned*; and Judith Bettelheim, "Caribbean Espiritismo (Spiritist) Altars."

4. The art history literature on Landaluze is extensive yet limited, in that it does not sufficiently contextualize his work in its political context of the nineteenth century. With some exceptions, earlier studies in the discipline of art history and beyond often present Landaluze's works as transparent picture windows into the past. More recent works by Vera Kutzinski and Jill Lane approach Landaluze and racialized representations in Cuban visual culture more generally, from a much more critical perspective, especially in relation to issues of race and gender. Key studies include Jorge Mañach, "La pintura en Cuba"; Guy Pérez Cisneros, *Características de la evolución de la pintura en Cuba*; Anonymous, *La pintura colonial en Cuba*; Loló de la Torriente, *Estudio de las artes plásticas en Cuba*; Anonymous, *Víctor Patricio Landaluze (1830–1889)*; Lázara Castellanos, *Víctor Patricio Landaluze*; Guillermo Sánchez Martínez, "Landaluze"; José Antonio Portuondo, "Landaluze y el costumbrismo en Cuba"; Adelaida de Juan, *Pintura y grabado coloniales cubanos*; Jorge Rigol, *Apuntes sobre la pintura y el grabado en Cuba*; and Jorge R. Bermúdez, *De Gutenberg a Landaluze*. See also Vera M. Kutzinski, "Caramel Candy for Sale"; and Jill Lane, "Smoking Habaneras."

5. For almost thirty years, Landaluze served in *Los Voluntarios* and related military forces stationed on the western part of the island, which saw little to no armed battle during the Ten Years' War. What is important to emphasize, however, is the steady and ongoing presence of the military—dedicated to the defense of *Cuba española* (Spanish Cuba)—throughout Landaluze's life. It can also be surmised that Landaluze's military career afforded him a certain level of stability that allowed him to pursue his artistic interests. Details about Landaluze's military career are gleaned from his *Hoja de Servicios* found in the Archivo General Militar de Segovia in Spain.

6. Current scholarship has not sufficiently addressed Landaluze's patronage or his nineteenth-century exhibition history. Documentary evidence regarding these aspects

of his career is either nonexistent or difficult to locate. It is likely that elite Cuban and Spanish residents living on the island purchased his paintings. Nineteenth-century Cuban visual culture—including photography and Landaluze's paintings themselves—often depicts elite, domestic spaces populated with paintings hanging on walls. Plantation owners in other parts of the Spanish Caribbean commissioned estate portraits that included representations of African slaves and their descendants. For example, in 1885, the Spaniard José Gallart commissioned Puerto Rican artist Francisco Oller to depict one of his thriving *ingenios* (sugar mill complexes). It is also possible that Landaluze's works existed as series. Interestingly, some of his costumbrista canvases, including *Corte de caña* and *Día de Reyes en La Habana*, share the same dimensions, suggesting a sequence of images. Published nineteenth-century articles that discuss related pairs of Landaluze paintings support this possibility. For more on Oller's estate portrait and one example of a nineteenth-century account of Landaluze's works, see Richard Aste, "Art of the Spanish American Home"; and Pascual de Riesgo, "Costumbres cubanas."

7. The ideas presented here draw on my doctoral dissertation, which deals with Landaluze's career as a caricaturist, painter, and illustrator in Cuba from the 1850s until his death in 1889. See Evelyn Carmen Ramos-Alfred, *A Painter of Cuban Life*.

8. People of African descent were demographically a large part of Cuban colonial society. Cuban census figures from 1846 place Afro-Cubans (including both enslaved and free people of color) at 52.6 percent of the total population. In 1862, that figure dropped to 43.7 percent of the total population. The bulk of Afro-Cubans resided in rural areas, where plantations dominated. Urban slavery did exist and often paved the way toward freedom. Most free people of color lived in towns and urban environments, where they worked in a variety of domestic, professional, and semi-professional trades. For more on the slave and free populations of color and select census data, see Gloria García Rodríguez, "Introduction," in *Voices of the Enslaved in Nineteenth-Century Cuba*; and Rebecca Scott, *Slave Emancipation in Cuba*, 6–8.

9. *Cabildos* were mutual aid societies sanctioned by the Spanish government, which allowed slaves of the same African cultural group to meet and gain emotional sustenance and financial support during times of need.

10. This figure dons what appears to be a feather headdress, an accoutrement long associated with allegories of the Americas as an indigenous woman. Variations on this allegory prevailed throughout the Spanish empire from the early colonial period. Cuba also had a mid-nineteenth century indigenist, proto-nationalist literary movement known as *Siboneyismo*. For more on the literary movement, see Instituto de Literatura y Lingüística, "Siboneyismo."

11. Ada Ferrer, *Insurgent Cuba*, 76–79.

12. See Jan Nederveen Pieterse, *White on Black*, 216.

13. Ferrer, 15.

14. See Louis A. Pérez Jr., *Slaves, Sugar, and Colonial Society*, 110.

15. These changes included the increased mechanization of the mills and the use of indentured Chinese labor. For more on this period, see Rebecca Scott, "Adaptation, 1870–1877," in *Slave Emancipation in Cuba*, 84–110.

16. "Incendio de un ingenio en Cuba."

17. Pérez, *Cuba: Between Reform and Revolution*, 127.

18. Scott, 24.

19. Facsimiles of Laplante's book have been published on several occasions. See Justo G. Cantero and Eduardo Laplante, *Los ingenios.*

20. For more on estate portraits in the Americas (specifically North America), see Angela D. Mack, "Introduction," in Angela D. Mack and Stephen G. Hoffius, eds., *The Landscape of Slavery*, 1–5.

21. This was the English translation used in the exhibition catalogue *Cuba: Art and History from 1868 to Today*. See Bondil, ed., *Cuba*, 57.

22. Scott, 25.

23. Ferrer, 93.

24. Key scholars associated with these ideas include Mikhail Bakhtin and Victor Turner, as well other scholars who have focused on carnival traditions in the New World. For some of these latter references, see Brown, *Santeria Enthroned*, 43–44.

25. See Scott, 68.

26. Ana Cairo, "Emilia Casanova y la dignidad de la mujer cubana."

27. See Víctor Patricio de Landaluze, "Serenata al. D. Quijote de la Junta Cubana," *Don Junípero* 4, no. 51 (October 17, 1869), 3.

28. Cairo, 239.

29. Ferrer, 66.

Bibliography

Anonymous. "Dos Diablitos—El Día de Reyes en la Habana—Costumbres de la Isla de Cuba." *La Ilustración Española y Americana* (January 20, 1867).

Anonymous. "La Fiesta de los Negros en la Habana." *La Ilustración Española y Americana* (December 25, 1869): 7, 8, 12.

Anonymous. *Los ñáñigos, su historia, sus prácticas, su lenguaje*. Havana: Imprenta La Correspondencia de Cuba, 1882.

Anonymous. *La pintura colonial en Cuba: Exposición en el Capitolio Nacional, marzo 4 a abril 4 de 1950*. Havana: Corporación Nacional del Turismo, 1950.

Anonymous. *Víctor Patricio Landaluze (1830–1889)*. Bilbao: Museo de Bellas Artes de Bilbao, 1998.

Aste, Richard. "Art of the Spanish American Home at the Brooklyn Museum." In *Behind Closed Doors: Art in the Spanish American Home, 1492–1898*, edited by Richard Aste, 40–44. New York: The Monacelli Press, 2013.

Bermúdez, Jorge R. *De Gutenberg a Landaluze*. Havana: Editorial Letras Cubanas, 1990.

Bettelheim, Judith. "Caribbean Espiritismo (Spiritist) Altars: The Indian and the Congo." *The Art Bulletin* 87, no. 2 (2005): 312–30.

Bettelheim, Judith, ed. *Cuban Festivals: A Century of Afro-Cuban Culture*. New York: Garland Publishers, 1993.

Bondil, Nathalie, ed. *Cuba: Art and History from 1868 to Today*. Montreal: Montreal Museum of Fine Arts, 2009.

Brown, David. *Santeria Enthroned: Art, Ritual, and Innovation in an Afro-Cuban Religion*. Chicago: University of Chicago Press, 2003.

Cairo, Ana. "Emilia Casanova y la dignidad de la mujer cubana." In *Mujeres latinoamericanas: Historia y cultura—siglos XVI al XIX*, Vol. 2, edited by Luisa Campuzano, 231–41. Havana: Casa de las Américas; Iztapalapa, Mexico: Universidad Autónoma Metropolitana, 1997.

Cantero, Justo Germán, and Eduardo Laplante. *Los ingenios: Colección de vistas de los principales ingenios de azúcar de la Isla de Cuba*. Madrid: Centro de Estudios y Experimentación de Obras Públicas, 2005.

Castellanos, Lázara. *Víctor Patricio Landaluze*. Havana: Editorial Letras Cubanas, 1991.

Crespo y Borbón, Bartolomé José. *Fiestas con motivo de la llegada del Exmo. Sr. Don José de la Concha*. Havana: Spencer y Compa, 1854.

Cueto, Emilio. *Mialhe's Colonial Cuba: The Prints That Shaped the World's View of Cuba*. Miami: The Historical Association of Southern Florida, 1994.

Cruz, Mary. *Creto Gangá*. Havana: UNEAC, 1974.

de la Torriente, Loló. *Estudio de las artes plásticas en Cuba*. Havana: Úcar García, 1954.

de Riesgo, Pascual. "Costumbres cubanas." *La Ilustración Española y Americana* 18, no. 3 (1874): 42–43, 45.

Ezponda, Eduardo. *La mulata: Estudio fisiológico, social y jurídico*. Madrid: Imprenta de Fortanet, 1878.

Ferrer, Ada. *Insurgent Cuba: Race, Nation, and Revolution, 1868–1898*. Chapel Hill: University of North Carolina Press, 1999.

García Rodríguez, Gloria. *Voices of the Enslaved in Nineteenth-Century Cuba*. Chapel Hill: University of North Carolina Press, 2013.

Gelpí y Ferro, Gil. *Álbum histórico fotográfico de la Guerra de Cuba*. Havana: Imprenta La Antilla, 1872.

Gilman, Sandler. "Black Bodies, White Bodies: Toward an Iconography of Female Sexuality in Late Nineteenth-Century Art, Medicine, and Literature." *Critical Inquiry* 12, no. 1 (1985): 204–42.

Harvey, Eleanor Jones. *The Civil War and American Art*. New Haven: Yale University Press/Smithsonian American Art Museum, 2012.

Instituto de Literatura y Lingüística, Academia de Ciencias de Cuba. "Siboneyismo." In *Diccionario de la literatura cubana*, 266–67. Havana: Editorial Letras Cubanas, 1984.

Juan, Adelaida de. *Pintura y grabado coloniales cubanos: Contribución a su estudio*. Havana: Instituto Cubano del Libro, 1974.

Kutzinski, Vera M. "Caramel Candy for Sale." In *Sugar's Secrets: Race and the Erotics of Cuban Nationalism*, 43–80. Charlottesville: University Press of Virginia, 1993.

Lane, Jill. *Blackface Cuba*. Philadelphia: University of Pennsylvania Press, 2005.

———. "Smoking Habaneras or a Cuban Study in Racial Demons." *Social Text* 104 (2010): 11–37.

Mack, Angela D., and Stephen G. Hoffius, eds. *The Landscape of Slavery: The Plantation in American Art*. Columbia: University of South Carolina Press, 2008.

Mañach, Jorge. "La pintura en Cuba, desde sus orígenes hasta 1900." *Cuba Contemporánea* 36, no. 141 (1924): 5–23.

Menocal, Narciso G. "An Overriding Passion—The Quest for National Identity in Painting." *Journal of Decorative and Propaganda Arts* 22 (1996): 186–219.

Moore, Robin. *Nationalizing Blackness: Afrocubanismo and Artistic Revolution in Havana, 1920–1940*. Pittsburgh: University of Pittsburgh Press, 1997.

Moreno Fraginals, Manuel. *Cuba/España, España/Cuba*. Barcelona: Crítica, Grijalbo Mondadori, 1995.

Ortiz, Fernando. "Dos 'diablitos' de Landaluze." *Bohemia* 44 (1953): 36–38, 99–101.

Pérez, Louis A., Jr. *Cuba: Between Reform and Revolution*. New York: Oxford University Press, 1988.

———. *Slaves, Sugar, and Colonial Society: Travel Accounts of Cuba, 1801–1899*. Wilmington, DE: Scholarly Resources, 1992.

Pérez Cisneros, Guy. *Características de la evolución de la pintura en Cuba*. Havana: Dirección General de Cultura, Ministerio de Educación, 1959.

Pieterse, Jan Nederveen. *White on Black: Images of Africa and Blacks in Western Popular Culture*. New Haven: Yale University Press, 1992.

Portuondo, José Antonio. "Landaluze y el costumbrismo en Cuba." *Revista de la Biblioteca José Martí* 1 (1972): 51–83.

Ramos-Alfred, Evelyn Carmen. *A Painter of Cuban Life: Víctor Patricio de Landaluze and Nineteenth-Century Cuban Politics (1850–1889)*. PhD diss., University of Chicago, 2011.

Rigol, Jorge. *Apuntes sobre la pintura y el grabado en Cuba*. Havana: Editorial Letras Cubanas, 1982.

Sánchez Martínez, Guillermo. "Landaluze." *Universidad de la Habana* 180 (1966): 83–92.

Scott, Rebecca. *Slave Emancipation in Cuba: The Transition to Free Labor, 1860–1899*. Princeton: Princeton University Press, 1985.

Wood, Peter, and Karen Dalton. *Winslow Homer's Images of Blacks: The Civil War and Reconstruction Years*. Houston: The Menil Collection, 1988.

3

Colonial Art and Its Afterlife

Visualizing the Nation Then and Now

Alison Fraunhar

Much like the writing of the nation in nineteenth-century Latin American literature that Doris Sommer has so insightfully called foundational fictions, the visual culture—primarily graphics and fine art—of nineteenth-century colonial Cuba established an image of the nation and its sense of national identity ahead of actual nationhood.[1] It did so through the deployment of European colonial visual conventions and ways of seeing applied to the specific conditions of Cuba. In contrast with South and Mesoamerica, where colonists built upon existing complex civilizations and drew from millennia-old art and craft traditions, Cuba, like other Caribbean islands, was sparsely populated and had not developed sophisticated architectural and artistic traditions. Although the colony was established at the turn of the sixteenth century, the local production and consumption of art, with very few exceptions, did not begin in earnest for 300 years, until the early nineteenth century. Early colonials preferred to import their decorations from Europe, privileging metropolitan style over visual self-invention.

Notwithstanding the delayed development of a national style in Cuba, artists employed three categories to envision the nation in images produced during the colonial era, or, we could say, foundational *visual* fictions of places, people, and events. The first is the representation of the island—through the map and depictions of the landscape and built environment; the second category is the representation of people and identity, especially as viewed through the screen of *costumbrismo* (the depiction of local or regional customs) and the invention of Cuban types; and third is the representation of Cuban history (and geography), the visual story of the island nation that it tells itself. These categories have provided crucial and enduring codes for understanding and consuming Cuba, both within the island and abroad. From the late colonial through the republican era, representations of the island, its people, and its history were developed and deployed as a visual language to articulate and shape national identity. The first part of this chapter is principally concerned with the late nineteenth century, the last fifty years of Cuba's colonial existence, when independence loomed ever larger on the horizon (although, like a phantom limb, the colony retains a ghostly presence that haunts Cuba to this day). I begin with an image from even earlier, a map from 1762, to establish a way of seeing Cuba, that is, through the map. I then turn to an exploration of the afterlife of colonial visual culture as it is reimagined, refracted, and refashioned by contemporary Cuban artists.

The Map

Although Cuba had been a Spanish possession since 1492, it figured on maps and nautical charts produced not only in Spain, but also France, England, the Netherlands, and the United States. For example, this map (Plate 6) was produced for a magazine for the British public during the eleven-month period of British occupation of Havana in 1762. It was not intended as a nautical chart or as a marker of territorial control or imperial knowledge, but it served to reflect the maritime and imperial control that England wielded in the decades before the American Revolution first challenged global British dominance.

In addition to the Caribbean islands, bodies of water, and geographic coordinates, the map shows and names currents, prevailing winds, and sailing routes, situating Cuba and neighboring islands within the archipelago, sea, and islands dominated at that time by the British navy. Apart from islands and water, it features detailed depictions of (presumably) British ships patrolling the Antilles, the Caribbean, and the Gulf of Mexico. In the top left corner is a cartouche with a magnified view of Havana's harbor and bay, and in the center at the bottom an elaborately framed text explains that "an Officer in the Navy" drew the map, depicting the seas and islands surrounding Cuba.

Although this map proclaimed high cartographic accuracy, it was intended for a popular audience, and not as a navigational or strategic chart. Maps such as this were meant to be scientific documents, as well as preeminent visual tools of imperial knowledge, control of spatial and human geography, and mobility. Ostensibly scientific, rational, and objective, the map reminds us of the ideological and political nature of geography by what it includes and excludes, emphasizing certain features over others. The date and Britain's brief control of Cuba also remind us that the control and command the map conveys were not as stable or enduring as the authority it projected. Colonizers and governments come and go, and shifting economic interests require different kinds of maps.

Published in a popular magazine, this map was both an official instrument of visual control and measurement and a popular visual entertainment. In the nineteenth century, maps and mapping appear in another form of popular visual culture, the tiny *marquilla cigarrera*, the small, illustrated papers in which bundles of cigars were sold domestically. Marquillas were one of the most plentiful and productive sites of Cuban visual cultural production; through their wide circulation (and collectability) and enormous inventory of subjects, marquillas educated, informed, and entertained consumers. Cigar companies' lithography departments, featuring state-of-the-art presses and color processes, drew widely from graphic sources, including geographic and cartographic series, for content. Marquillas are a significant archive of nineteenth-century Cuban visual culture not only for the encyclopedic range of subjects they depicted, as literally thousands of marquillas were produced during the mid-to-late nineteenth century, but also for their proliferation, as the paper-wrapped bundles of cigars were inexpensive, sold across the island, and consumed among all social classes. Due to this wide diffusion, they had tremendous power to establish visual conventions for Cuban identity, to inform, and to influence people's expectations and perceptions.

The central image (*escena*) of this marquilla, produced circa 1870, is a map of Cuba (Plate 7). In the border on the left side of the map stands an allegorical native wearing a feather headdress. The *escena*, bracketed by a decorative border like a theatrical curtain and framed by text, looks much like a miniature proscenium, a stage upon which characters enact national identity. It is topped by a banner bearing the grand title "Real é Imperial Fábrica" (Royal and Imperial Factory) and includes coats of arms, an elaborate monogram, and a message both proclaiming gratitude for the privilege of using the royal arms and asserting dominion over the territory depicted.[2] The Indian maiden in the border holds a bow and an animal skin, and is wearing a feather-decorated loincloth. Exotic palm fronds, a feather headdress, a quiver of arrows, and a parrot complete the visual signification of pre-Columbian Cuba. The woman steps on a snake, a complex symbol alluding to both the triumph of good over evil and the power of life.

This imaginary Caribbean native privileges a tropic (as well as tropical) European vision of the inhabitants of the Caribbean: since the indigenous Arawak people who lived on the island had been reduced to small isolated groups in the first decades of European conquest, little first-hand evidence could contradict this representation. Instead, the image complies with a long history of depictions of an imaginary America by Europeans (many of whom had never been there), beginning with the sixteenth-century Flemish engraver Theodor de Bry, who depicted a hemisphere more faithful to European expectations than to actual features of the American landscape or human inhabitants. Indeed, the reification of this imaginary, the control of optics and epistemology, are among the paradigmatic features of the global colonial enterprise. Map, metropolitan authority, and the "authentic" (defunct) native authorize the exotic and noble history of the island transformed into the new, imperial colony. This marquilla illustrates one of the foundational fictions that defined colonial Cuba: the central image is a map of the island bearing the authority of Spanish imperial geo-control and knowledge; the left border depicts an imaginary tropical paradise populated by a voluptuous, docile native (female, of course); and to the right are emblems and trademarks of capitalist production, commerce, and metropolitan authority. Even on a tiny, ephemeral scrap of paper, Cuba's proto-national visual imaginary drew (as did that of most of colonial Spanish America) upon Thomas More's *Utopia* (1516) to authorize the vision of Cuba as a pure, uncontaminated tabula rasa. The marquilla follows a classic cartographic strategy of including visual data on flora, fauna, and population surrounding the map. Thus, as the 1762 British map entertained and informed the British public that consumed it in the pages of a popular magazine, so the marquilla similarly informed and entertained the popular Cuban customers who consumed marquilla-packaged cigars and collected the marquillas a century later.

As Denis Cosgrove, Henri Lefebvre, and others have argued, the idea of landscape is grounded in social relations.[3] How land is seen and used, by whom, whose interests are served, and whose are elided are crucial if latent elements in the optics of land and landscape. Far from representing a "pure" wilderness, images like the border of the marquilla conformed to a social vision, arranged to fulfill hegemonic agendas. From the earliest days of the colony, the reality of conquest and colonial exploitation clashed with the utopian image of the uncorrupted natural state, a crucial piece of visual propaganda for conquest and colonial exploitation. In Cuban colonial art, both the natural and built environments figured prominently as signs of the nation. By the nineteenth century, the colony had congealed into what has been called a plantation—or rather, Plantation—so deeply embedded was the pervasive economic, social, and spatial logic of the plantation mode of production.

The well-known and often-quoted depiction of the Ingenio Buena-Vista is one of a series produced for a privately commissioned and printed volume of views of prominent sugar plantations in the Valley of Yumurí in Matanzas, Cuba.[4] The lavish book *Los ingenios*, purchased exclusively through subscription, had very limited circulation when it was first published, but has subsequently entered into the visual heritage and "national essence" of Cuba through the reproduction of its iconic scenes. The idealized representations of *ingenios* (sugar mills) and their literary equivalent, novels, travelers' accounts, and memoirs that emphasized *las delicias del campo* (the delights of the countryside), predominated in the proto-nationalist imaginary. The views of the ingenios and their operation visualize the plantation as an idealized, rational place of order and harmony, an utter disconnect from the grim and brutal reality of life on the plantation. The view of the Ingenio Buena-Vista, anchored by small figures in the foreground serving as surrogates for the viewer, with trees and hill framing a distant view of the ingenio, was a common way of depicting the optics of the island (Plate 8). The ingenio itself is presented as an orderly, spacious, and tranquil place integrating agriculture, the built environment, and human activity seamlessly into the majestic natural setting. The tiny figures of slaves populating the center of the scene walk in an orderly row in the cane fields; they barely register as human, so insignificant and disempowered do they appear in this visualization of the Plantation imaginary.

In images from *Los ingenios*, the built environment takes center stage; like the natural one, the operation of the ingenio conveys or constructs an idealized view of colonial industry. The plantation house in Ingenio

Buena-Vista was a "shining city upon a hill," bearing all the biblical self-justification and antidemocratic implications of that phrase. In another image from the book, the *casa de calderas* or boiler room is a modern, scientific, rational space of capitalist production. The crisp, detailed view of the boiler room disavows the fiery heat and grueling, dangerous labor it took to run it; the few human figures depicted are isolated and almost relaxed amidst the coolly functioning machinery.

The exquisitely illustrated and minutely detailed depictions of *Los ingenios* made their way from the exclusive volume into the popular imaginary through their reproduction on marquillas. The ingenio was quoted as a central image on a marquilla, with the wide dissemination of this and other images taken from *Los ingenios* and their subsequent absorption into the visual DNA of the nation. Through the movement from the large, exclusive volume to the tiny wrapping paper, the ingenio became part of the Cuban heritage.

In the latter part of the nineteenth century, painters invoked the utopian colonialist imaginary, depicting, as in the border of the previously seen marquilla, an idyllic, idealized space of abundant natural beauty and docile subjects in harmony with nature and with one another. The shimmering idealization of the colony was produced during a time of growing unrest; from the middle of the century until independence, active rebellion and dissent belied the fantasy. Most artists in Cuba were of European origin and were patronized by landowners and merchants who comprised the colonial elite: patronage dictated subject matter, style, and ideology. Cuba had a robust culture of periodical illustration, satire, and caricature, mostly directed at social customs, not cast as a critique of political repression.

Cuban artists, including Esteban Chartrand (1840–84) and his brothers, and European artists like Eduardo Laplante and Frédéric Mialhe, referenced European trends and traditions in landscape painting while extolling the island's singularity. Many of them subtly reinforced the colonial order through images that consistently presented "nature" as immanent, a state of potential awaiting European exploitation, and human activity as tranquil and naturalized. The colonial mentality, looking ever toward the metropolis, sought to institute European conventions, epistemologies, and forms of living on the island; architecture, governance, social customs, and educational systems (including the San Alejandro Academy, the first art academy in Cuba) were implemented. The constant influx of European settlers, adventurers, and entrepreneurs brought European ways of seeing and being to the island; among them were artists who not only trained Creole students in the academy, but also sketched and painted imaginary and actual landscapes, scenes, and people on the island. The apparently natural and unmediated scenes they depicted followed prevalent if slightly passé (by European standards) styles, particularly Romanticism. Stylistically linked to nineteenth-century landscape painting, the *cambio de siglo* style bracketed both Cuban independence and the turn of the century. This style incorporated romantic and realist elements and applied them to conditions of island topography and light. As Manifest Destiny spread the logic of divine right across the continental United States, so the rhetoric of paradise and notions of the New Jerusalem underwrote colonial expansion in Cuba. Throughout nineteenth-century painting, these impulses were projected triumphantly, as evidence of the natural and God-given bounty of the island. This harmonious sense of natural grace and the harmonious implementation of human will aligned with God's will wove its way through nineteenth-century landscape painting and graphic images such as those in *Los ingenios*.

In Chartrand's *Paisaje con vacas* (*Landscape with Cows*, 1882), cows roam the pristine countryside. These animals were introduced on the island in the seventeenth century for meat and hide production as Cuba's original agribusiness. The small skiff with a solitary fisherman in the right foreground anchors the composition through the human presence. Cattle, fisherman, and lush vegetation—nature's splendor is activated by its bounty and utility. The romanticized view of the landscape projects a timeless, idyllic scene at odds with the reality of rural isolation and exploitation.

It is perhaps through paintings and graphics depicting Cuba's unique social landscape that we get a clearer sense of the consequences of colonial racialized, gendered, and economic policies. Through scenes depicting people and their activities in the appropriate settings, colonial systems of knowledge projected the classification and codification of space, place, and people. The societal unrest and contestation inherent in the colonial system of conquest and slavery from its inception found their way into paintings and graphic arts by the mid-nineteenth century through satire, caricature, and stereotyping; the stylistic convention of costumbrismo created racialized, gendered, and classed subjects that were soon taken as signifiers of identity. Costumbrismo, concerned with the appearance and activities of people, was a popular literary and visual style in the middle decades of the century throughout Latin America. Literary costumbrismo made up for its reliance on superficial and stereotypical narrative trajectories and characters in its dazzling detail, becoming an invaluable document of customs and mores. In popular graphics and painting, visual costumbrismo tended more toward a one-liner that focused the viewer's attention on one parodic situation or exaggerated action, rather than the more multilayered scenarios in literary costumbrismo.

Costumbrista "observations" of race, class, and gender ostensibly reinforced dominant values of white patriarchy, but by their sheer repetition, revealed the anxiety, brutality, and instability of the colonial system. Colonial anxieties and the failure of their suppression were expressed onstage, in print, in illustrations in newspapers, on marquillas, and in paintings. Many of these deployed satire, always ready to poke fun at both the high and mighty and the lowly. This sense of humor was interpreted as the Cuban tendency not to take things too seriously, to see the funny side of things, but it always had an edge, a sharp slap following the laugh at the expense of another. Ultimately, this mode of satire, colloquially known as *choteo*, became identified as expressive of the Cuban temperament. It ran through Cuban culture in a Rabelaisian contretemps to the simultaneously rigid and oddly porous social order that dominated the nineteenth century.

Mialhe, the French-born Cuban immigrant painter and lithographer, produced some of the most iconic works of nineteenth-century Cuban art, including scenes like *Día de Reyes*. The latter depicts a performance that took place on Three Kings Day or Epiphany, the only day of the year when African slaves and free people could freely and publicly express their ancestral, geographical, and spiritual identities. Faithful to costumbrista style, Mialhe recorded precise details of dress that authenticated his view, but he exaggerated the dancers' gestures. Both the unfamiliar African costumes and castoff European finery flaunted by the African bystanders would have looked ridiculous and barbaric to European viewers, and although familiar to Mialhe's Creole elite, would have reinforced Europeans' sense of superiority over the slaves and African free people who surrounded them. Adriana Méndez Rodenas suggests a counter-reading, however: in the repressive colonial episteme of nineteenth-century Cuba, the performance of *Día de Reyes* represents an act of resistance or transgression of the established social order.[5] If we endorse such a reading, we

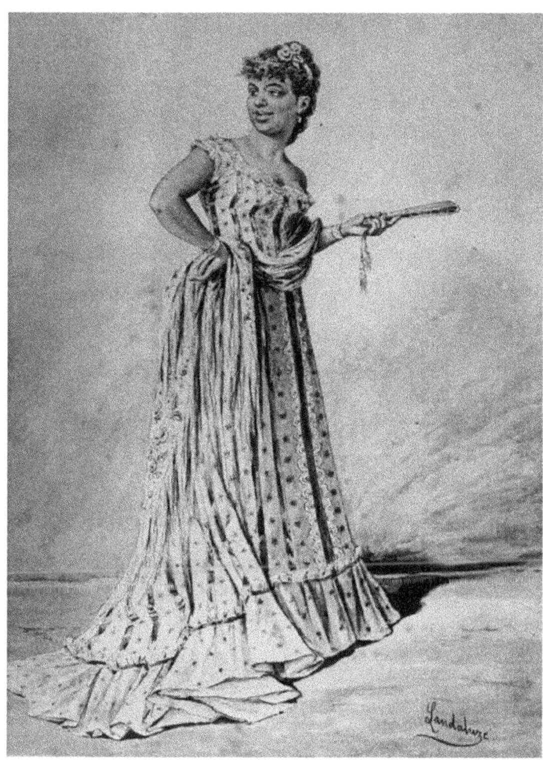

Figure 3.1. Víctor Patricio de Landaluze, *La mulata de rumbo*, 1881. In *Colección de artículos: Tipos y costumbres de la isla de Cuba, por los mejores autores de este género*. Fototipia Taveira. Havana: Miguel de Villa.

can locate the thrill of the spectacle in both the enactment of alterity and its threat.

One of the masterworks of Cuban costumbrismo is the volume *Tipos y costumbres de la isla de Cuba*,[6] with illustrations by the Basque immigrant Víctor Patricio de Landaluze. In *Tipos y costumbres*, Landaluze illustrates scenes of Cuban life at mid-century in costumbrista style, depicting occupations and activities: the fireman, the country doctor, the midwife, and more. Although Landaluze was a well-known loyalist to the Spanish Crown, he is nevertheless considered the foremost observer of nineteenth-century Cuban life. Although some critics have drawn a line between his political and military activities and his scenes of daily life, the acuity of these scenes, like those of Laplante and Mialhe, emphasizing the natural and built environment and scenes of festivities respectively, served to reinforce and legitimate the colonial status quo, thus embedding the colonial worldview within the incipient nation.

One of the most famous images from *Tipos y costumbres*, the lithograph *La mulata de rumbo* (Figure 3.1), depicts a young woman with frizzy hair, deep skin tone, round nose, and full lips. Her body fills the vertical plane of the image, from the hem of her dress touching the lower left corner, to her head in the top center, and her arm holding the *abanico* (fan) reaching to the center right edge. She stands in ¾ profile, gazing over her right shoulder at an unseen admirer, full lips slightly parted in a seductive, knowing smile. Her face is animated but not pretty: her features lack delicacy. The self-awareness in the gaze, smile, and posture of the protagonist, as well as the stage-like setting, point to the performativity of this figure. She embodies a stereotype that had become, by then, congealed: a young woman who is desirable, graceful, sexually available, materialistic, flirtatious, shallow, and vain. This image consolidates an image of sensuality, seduction, and *cubanidad* (Cubanness) that reverberates throughout nineteenth-century Cuban visual culture, literature, and theater.[7]

The mulata's full face and lips and rounded limbs project carnality and physical presence lacking in the depictions of white women in the nineteenth century; her smile is bold, drawing a marked contrast with conventional depictions of white women that foreground delicacy and refinement of affect. She leans to the left holding a fan in her left hand, while her right hand rests on her hip, elbow cocked in a pose both jaunty and sinuous.

Wearing a pretty dress trimmed with lace and a ruffled *bata de cola* (tailcoat) hem swirling on the ground, she has a fringed shawl draped loosely around her waist in a graceful but insouciant style. The shawl, rather than modestly covering her shoulders, reveals more of her neck, décolleté, and arms than a "proper" white woman would have shown in public. Nor would a white woman ever appear alone in public, while the nameless mulata is posed in front of what appears to be an exterior wall and sidewalk, smiling at an unseen spectator. The lack of detail in the setting that would otherwise legitimate or situate the figure as either an individual (a person with a specific identity) or as a social actor (through her occupation) reinforces the starkly staged and denaturalized air of the composition. This manner of dress, her body language, location, and features all combine to flaunt her "not-quite-ness"—not quite white, not quite black. This tension becomes the central paradox and the core of Cuban identity, what Vera Kutzinski calls "the erotics of Cuban nationalism."[8]

The lithograph's multivalence is predicated on the interplay of visual and textual signs in the title and the image. The first meaning of *rumbo* is course or direction, suggesting that the mulata de rumbo is a girl on the move, confident, bold. Rumbo also refers more colloquially to the street, the disreputable public space off-limits to proper white ladies, suggesting that it is the proper place for the disreputable mulata. To this definition, very much in keeping with the costumbrista descriptions that gave rise to the mulata and other archetypal figures of the era, I would add a note concerning rumbo. Although generally translated as "loose," "cruising," having to do with being in/of the street, rumbo also makes explicit reference to the *rumba*, the musical/dance form that developed around Havana and Matanzas in the nineteenth century. *Rumba* was a secularized dance derived from sacred dance forms brought from Africa to Cuba by Yoruba people. Like the mulata, it was a source both of national identity, as a uniquely Cuban dance, and of social concern, as it was considered indecent and lascivious. Hence, this denomination acknowledges African roots, the central importance of motion, mobility, and a fluid, rhythmic gracefulness, in addition to public visibility and sensuality and social danger. The image of the erotic, indolent, graceful, visible, and available mulata belied the realities it masked: that free mulatas were also extremely limited by the oppressive conditions of colonial Cuba, as well as occasionally being savvy economic operators, amassing property, status, and control. Additionally, they were crucial workers in a variety of occupations, and invaluable mediators between the races. Finally, rumbo/rumba is slang for party: the smiling mulata is a party girl.

The various meanings of rumbo all converge as defining attributes of the mulata. The mulata is presented as if onstage in front of an imaginary audience, proclaiming the performance of *mulataje* (mulata-ness) as a set of embodied codes performed in time and space that animate the figure. This effect is reinforced by the smile directed to a spectator located within the diegetic space but out of the pictorial plane. At the time *La mulata de rumbo* was published in 1881, this was hardly a new way of envisioning the mulata: her eroticization in verse had been going on for a long time. As early as the seventeenth century, the mulata's desirability was immortalized in verses like these from the *guaracha* (popular song) titled "La mulata":

Es más dulce que el azúcar,
Cuando quiere una mulata

Entre todas las mujeres
Sin duda es la flor y nata
Es un sabroso bocado[9]

This anonymous *guaracha* equates the mulata with the consumption of delicious, if not nutritious, delicacies (sugar and cream), and sets the tone for signification of the mulata as the archetypal figure of desire and as a comestible linked to sugar, the most important agricultural industry in Cuba, the engine of its economic history. *La mulata de rumbo* is an iconic image, reproduced and referenced extensively since its publication; but rarely has it been analyzed as a symptom of the persistence of colonial relations of knowledge—one that was ostensibly (but not actually) overcome by the Cuban Revolution.

Beyond Landaluze's iconic figure, the mulata was a privileged site of national invention in the most renowned novel of nineteenth-century Cuba, *Cecilia Valdés*, and countless songs and poems; the desirable but ultimately tragic figure is featured in several marquilla series, including "Historia de la mulata." Reminiscent of William Hogarth's *A Harlot's Progress* (1732), the series illustrates the rise and fall of a beautiful mulata. In one scene, the young mulata, bracketed by her Spanish storekeeper father on the left and her African mother in the distance to the right, is seduced by two ne'er-do-well white suitors, thus inaugurating her tragic trajectory.

History Painting

Before independence was won in 1902, history painting, or more broadly the representation of historical events, was one of the most underdeveloped of art genres in Cuba. It was not important until the final years of the colony, when the *cambio de siglo* style encompassed both Cuban independence and the turn of the century. This style incorporated romantic and realist elements and is linked to nineteenth-century painting in both style and subject matter. I push the closure of the colonial period forward into the early days of the republican era with Armando G. Menocal's *La muerte de Maceo* (*The Death of Maceo*, 1908). Although Menocal's romantic style was academic and outmoded, his revolutionary politics were impeccable; he was known as the *mambí*[10] painter for his participation in the last war of independence and advocacy of independence, along with his many canvases depicting scenes from the war.[11] Menocal (1863–1942) enjoyed a long and successful career as an academic painter and teacher; his conservative style was out of step with the modernist *vanguardistas* dominating the Cuban art scene in the early republic, but quite popular with bourgeois audiences and patrons. Two of Menocal's other history paintings hang in the Cuban Building of the Museo Nacional de Bellas Artes (National Museum of Fine Arts) in Havana. One depicts the expulsion of Columbus by the Spanish Governor Bobadilla, and the other, the immolation of Hatuey, the Taíno chieftain who led the first rebellion against Spanish colonizers in the hemisphere, martyred for his resistance to Spanish colonialism. These works conflate a curious set of ideological positions: a foundational episode in colonial history, a foundational episode in nationalist history, and a symbolic gesture against colonial violence and repression, suggesting a seamless teleological arc rather than isolated yet interconnected moments of trauma and rupture.

La muerte de Maceo presents a romanticized view of Maceo's death, framed as a tragic event in the manner of religious painting. As befits mythology, the painting is historically inaccurate, but it facilitated a postcolonial détente among the bourgeoisie who benefitted under the colonial system, disenfranchised subjects, and other constituents seeking to achieve greater social justice through political independence and representative government. *La muerte de Maceo* stands as an iconic painting of an iconic figure from Cuban history, one of the few such pictorial documents of Cuban history. This historical template dominated the national visual imaginary throughout the republican era, right up to the 1959 revolution.

Post-Fall

After the triumph of the Cuban Revolution, the colonial past was of little interest to Cuban artists (and, indeed, counter to revolutionary ideals) for several decades until the fall of the Berlin Wall in 1989 and the collapse of the Soviet Union in 1991, the moment when global events converged to exert a seismic impact on Cuba. Prior to these events, the revolutionary Cuban government and its cultural directives sought to build a revolutionary future, not to reiterate the queasy delights of nostalgia. Until the 1990s, most Cuban artists deployed aesthetic and conceptual strategies of modernism linked to anti-capitalist Third World solidarity.

The onset of the so-called Special Period in 1990 unmoored Cuban society from its dubious complacency, freeing intellectuals and artists, in the direst possible way, to research, reexamine, and interrogate pre- and postrevolutionary Cuban history to critical ends. Now, young Cuban artists—dubbed *mala hierba*, or weeds, by art critic Gerardo Mosquera for their resilience and adaptability—often alluded to the visual and material codes of the colony to reference contemporary conditions.[12] They did so through unpacking, appropriating, and re-inscribing key scenes and icons of Cuban national identity. Increased exposure to the art world beyond the island introduced artists to the posts of the contemporary globalizing era—poststructuralism, postcolonialism, and postmodernism—which they implemented in artwork that displayed an acute awareness of the political and economic reality of Cuba and its historical arc. Artists including Los Carpinteros, Sandra Ramos, Pedro Álvarez, Elio Rodríguez, José Bedia, Carlos Garaicoa, Armando Marino, and Glexis Novoa began to unpack Cuban tropes to recontextualize them as meta-critiques of ideologies ranging from the colonial through the revolutionary, as well as to advance the subjective perspective often absent from artwork after the Revolution.

In key works from the 1990s through the present, Ramos (b. 1969) explores the more complex relationship among nation, island, home, diaspora, body, and ideas of gender, geography, and identity through the deployment of both a map of the island and an avatar, a Cuban Alice in Wonderland in the dress of a *pionera* (a member of a youth organization that replaced the Scouts in 1961), who is both witness and voluntary/involuntary participant in the historical process. In work such as the lithograph *La maldita circunstancia del agua por todas partes* (*The Damned Circumstance of Water Everywhere*, 1993), Ramos addresses the despair of the Special Period, when, in the wake of economic catastrophe and ideological disillusionment, Cubans dreamed of the world but found themselves trapped on the island. Although this figure seems to be a personal reference to Ramos's Cuban feminine identity, the artist deploys these well-known signs as part of a larger social discourse. She has claimed, "art has always been a great document for understanding the country," situating her work as both personal and social.[13] The title of her painting comes from a 1943 poem by the Cuban poet and playwright Virgilio Piñera; the sense of being isolated and trapped was hardly a new phenomenon of the Special Period, but the Revolution's promise to overcome the isolation, alienation, and boredom of island life, and the extent to which it failed to accomplish this, created a sharp disconnect between reality and imaginary.

Ramos exemplifies the turn from the visual rhetoric of the heroic revolutionary state, the planned economy, and the Soviet orbit toward a more overt critique and interrogation of it. As artists became increasingly able to connect with the world beyond the island's shores, they began to reflect on themselves as Cubans, as global citizens, and as racialized, gendered subjects. Ramos's substitution of a recumbent woman for the map of the island is a pointed reference to the colonial (and Spanish linguistic) association between land and the female body, passivity, conquest, and domination, a privileged site for feminist and postcolonial critique. The island/woman floats in an undefined sky/sea. Cuban women are trapped within the contours of the island as Cuba itself lies in waiting, for centuries forced into the role of the passive paramour of successive empires: Spain, Britain (briefly), the United States, and finally the Soviet Union. The Revolution may have temporarily broken old dependencies, but newer ones did little to dislodge centuries of habits.

Revisiting the ingenios of the valley of Yumurí 150 years after *Los ingenios* was published, the art collective Atelier Morales (Juan Luis Morales, b. 1960, and Teresa Ayuso, b. 1961) photographed the sites of the formerly triumphant sugar mills in their present dilapidated and forlorn state. Bearing no resemblance to the tidy if idealized state of the colonial sugar mill, the site is currently an almost entirely abandoned post-agricultural place, ironically retuned to the cows that preceded the ingenio as a prime industry in Cuba's colonial history. Only a rusted tank and a rustic fence speak to the erstwhile human activity.

The complicated history of sugar in Cuba has occupied a central role in Cuban identity and Cuban thought since the nineteenth century; while the Revolution initially sought to liberate the economy from dependence on sugar and reduce acreage under sugarcane cultivation, market forces and relations with the Soviet Union led to intensified if inept sugar production. This led to the disastrous *Zafra de los Diez Millones*, the failed campaign for a ten-million-ton harvest in 1970. Thus, Atelier Morales's project speaks to several moments of crisis in Cuban history precipitated by the sugar industry. Artists and filmmakers have recently begun to unpack this history, moving beyond representations of the barbaric

Plantation of the colonial period, the capitalist machine of the republic, and the phantasmagoric failure of the Revolution, to the slow-motion decomposition of the present.

After the widespread shortages of the Special Period exacerbated fifty years of neglect, and Havana crumbled around and on top of its citizens, Carlos Garaicoa (b. 1967) photographed decrepit buildings around Havana and "restored" them with colorful overdrawings that called attention to their dilapidated present reality and the gap between this reality and the always deferred ideal. Garaicoa's imaginary infrastructure perfectly captures the zeitgeist of the Special Period chronicled in 1990s fiction, particularly the essays and poetry of Antonio José Ponte. It now became possible for artists to interrogate (obliquely) revolutionary narratives that placed the blame for all economic, social, political, and diplomatic hardships on *el bloqueo* (the U.S. embargo), and neglected Cuba's prerevolutionary history and heritage, including its architectural and infrastructural archive.[14]

Referencing the marquilla's pungent humor, the art collective Los Carpinteros (the recently separated artistic duo of Marco Antonio Castillo Valdés, b. 1969, and Dagoberto Rodríguez Sánchez, b. 1970), played with the proverbs, jokes, and puns of *choteo* and the popular visual form of the marquilla, flipping the marquilla's externalized European optics for self-portraits: race and gender as seen from within. Los Carpinteros, as befitting their name, reintroduced traditional artisanal woodworking and craftsmanship to fine art, bringing the social practice of repairing furniture with which the collective began into their subsequent fine art production.

In *One* from the series *The Romantic Dollarscape* (2003), Pedro Álvarez (b. 1967) deploys a realist academic painting style, referencing both the training he received under the socialist system and the colonial history of representation. He juxtaposes iconic images from Cuban and hemispheric popular visual culture in a "pile-up of signs" (to paraphrase Tyler Stallings),[15] including the *mulata de rumbo* and other victims of colonialism, among symbols of the U.S. one-dollar bill, anathema of the Revolution, reintroduced into the Cuban economy during the Special Period. A collision between the winners and losers in the implacable creep of colonial exploitation and capitalism, Álvarez's image critiques a "green and fertile neocolonialism"—a system that remained latent during the Revolution but was never overcome, and erupted in full carnivalesque grotesquerie in the post-fall new world order.

From the generation of artists who came of age on the verge of change in the Special Period in the early 1990s, successive waves of artists synced the subjective experience of everyday life with formal concerns and approaches fostered by ever-increasing circulation in the wider world. Almost twenty years on, the young Cuban artist José Manuel Mesías (b. 1990) sets out to "correct" the errors in Menocal's painting of the death of Maceo through his invented archive of historical data and objects in *Rectificaciones a la obra de Armando Menocal "La muerte de Maceo"* (*Corrections to the Work of Armando Menocal "The Death of Maceo,"* Plate 9).

In this recent installation work comprised of paintings, sketches, sculptures, photographs, and objects, Mesías takes as his overarching subject the battlefield death of General Maceo, an important event in the mythology of Cuban independence. Mesías engages with the painted "documentation" of it by the artist and revolutionary hero Menocal. The works in the exhibition flaunt the fictitious nature of the historical record and of Menocal's version; Mesías's historical revision is yet another constructed version of the official historical record. Through his research and documentation, a wholly constructed set of fabricated documents, photographs, objects, artifacts, and even taxidermy, Mesías creates a meticulous world of parallel history—and in so doing calls attention to the constructedness of the "official" historical record. It is an ambitious reconsideration of the "foundational fictions" of Cuban colonial art and reminds us that the historical record is always/already fabricated, as meticulously as Mesías's artifacts. Among contemporary Cuban artists, Mesías is the one most interested in the "official" historical record, gleefully and painstakingly de- and reconstructing its narratives and its relics.

Cuban colonial art established some of the key elements of national identity and the national imaginary. These images were often revisited during the republican era, but then passed into a sort of no-go zone for the first three decades of the Revolution. For artists of the 1990s generation and beyond, the colonial and republican eras have provided a repertory of images that help us connect the present to different moments of the past, and not fall into the trap of ahistorical thinking, or analyzing present conditions exclusively as the result of what immediately preceded them.

Notes

1. Doris Sommer, *Foundational Fictions.*

2. Agraciada especialmente por S.M.C. con el uso de sus reales armas.

3. Daniel E. Cosgrove, *Social Formation and Symbolic Landscape*; Henri Lefebvre, *The Production of Space.*

4. Justo G. Cantero, *Los ingenios.*

5. Adriana Méndez Rodenas, *Cuba en su imagen*, 219–22.

6. *Colección de artículos: Tipos y costumbres de la isla de Cuba.*

7. Alison Fraunhar, *Mulata Nation*, 36–37.

8. Vera M. Kutzinski, *Sugar's Secrets.*

9. English translation:

When you love a mulata
It's sweeter than sugar
Among all women,
She's the cream of the crop, without a doubt
A delicious mouthful
From Anonymous, *Guarachas cubanas.*

10. The term *mambí* refers to the soldiers of the Cuban independence wars against Spain fought between 1868 and 1898.

11. Antonio Álvarez Pitaluga, "La caída de un héroe y el secuestro de un mito."

12. Mosquera, "An Indescribable Adventure."

13. *Cuban Art News*, "Sandra Ramos."

14. See Fraunhar, "The Ruins of Modernity and Imaginary Havana."

15. Tyler Stallings, ed., *The Signs Pile Up.*

Bibliography

Álvarez Pitaluga, Antonio. "La caída de un héroe y el secuestro de un mito." *Calibán: Revista Cubana de Pensamiento e Historia* 13 (2012). Accessed March 22, 2019. http://www.hraices.uh.cu/index.php/HorR/article/view/8/8.

Anonymous. *Guarachas cubanas: Curiosa recopilación desde las más antiguas hasta las más modernas.* Havana: Consolidada de Artes Gráficas [1882], 1963.

Cantero, Justo G., and Eduardo Laplante. *Los ingenios: Colección de vistas de los principales ingenios de azúcar de la Isla de Cuba.* Havana: Litografía de Luis Marquier, 1857.

Colección de artículos: Tipos y costumbres de la isla de Cuba, por los mejores autores de este género. Fototipia Taveira. Havana: Miguel de Villa, 1881.

Cosgrove, Denis E. *Social Formation and Symbolic Landscape.* 2nd ed. Madison: University of Wisconsin Press, 1998.

Cuban Art News. "Close-Up: *Índice de imágines* [*sic*] at Factoría Cubana." Accessed September 28, 2017. https://www.cubanartnews.org/news/close-up-indice-de-imagines-at-factoria-habana/6226.

———. "Sandra Ramos: 'Art Has Always Been a Great Document for Understanding the Country.'" Accessed September 28, 2017. https://www.cubanartnews.org/news/sandra-ramos-art-has-always-been-a-great-document-for-understanding-the-cou.

Fraunhar, Alison. *Mulata Nation: Visualizing Race and Gender in Cuba*. Oxford: University of Mississippi Press, 2018.

———. "The Ruins of Modernity and Imaginary Havana." *Revista Estudios* 40 (2014): n.p.

Kutzinski, Vera M. *Sugar's Secrets: Race and the Erotics of Cuban Nationalism*. Charlottesville: University of Virginia Press, 1993.

Lefebvre, Henri. *The Production of Space*. London: Wiley, 1992.

Méndez Rodenas, Adriana. *Cuba en su imagen: Historia e identidad en la literatura cubana*. Madrid: Verbum, 2002.

Mosquera, Gerardo. "An Indescribable Adventure: The New Cuban Art." *Transition* 10, no. 3 (2001): 124–36.

Piñera, Virgilio. "La isla en peso." *Calle B: Revista Cultural de Cumanayagua*. March 5, 2013. Accessed September 28, 2017. http://www.calleb.cult.cu/index.php/autopista-sur/426-obra-literaria-de-virgilio-pinera/1841-la-isla-en-peso-.

Sommer, Doris. *Foundational Fictions: The National Romances of Latin America*. Berkeley: University of California Press, 1991.

Stallings, Tyler, ed. *The Signs Pile Up: The Paintings of Pedro Álvarez*. Santa Monica, CA: Smart Art Press, 2007.

4

Cuban Painting at the Turn of the Century (1902–1930)

The Nexus between Traditional and Vanguard

Anelys Alvarez

Cuban historiography has usually associated the first half of the twentieth century with the emergence of modern art—the entrance and assimilation within the Cuban art scene of avant-garde trends mainly imported from Europe. Without undervaluing the Cuban exhibition *1927: Exposición de Arte Nuevo* (*1927: Exhibition of New Art*),[1] in updating the repertoire of visual languages, the emergence of the avant-garde generation on the island forms part of a more complex process of transition. For many years, the history of Cuban art in the early decades of the last century revolved around the juxtaposition between *academia* (the academy) and *vanguardia* (the vanguard)—traditional vs. modern. Such a linear perspective that explains history through an evolutionary succession of events has left very little room for a synchronous view, to appreciate the contribution of artists, languages, and initiatives that are relevant to a comprehensive approach to Cuban art.

This chapter assesses the art production of the first decades of the twentieth century from a perspective of plurality and inclusion. In contrast with other periods that enjoy substantial criticism, studies of Cuban art have usually overlooked the decades before the beginning of the Modern movement (1930). From art history professor Adelaida de Juan to illustrator and professor Jorge Rigol, studies of the generation that preceded—and in many cases coexisted with—the avant-garde are very scarce. Now that the still relatively recent turn of the twenty-first century has awakened the desire to look at the past and review the origins of modernism in different latitudes, it seems pertinent to read Cuban art through the lens of its own time and circumstances and not in comparison with later or even foreign productions.

Early in the first decade of the current century, Cuba's National Museum of Fine Arts (MNBA, its Spanish acronym) and the University of Havana (UH) showed interest in rethinking prevailing notions about what has been called the "turn of the century." Professionals from both institutions shed light on an extensive list of forgotten artists such as Pastor Argudín (1880–1968?), Federico Beltrán Masses (1885–1949), Esteban Domenech (1886–1960), Hipólito Canals (1892–1969), and María Josefa Lamarque (1893–1994), to name just a few.

The concept of the "turn of the century" (1893–1930) comes from the new Spanish historiography currently interested in the revision of the origins of modernity in Spain. By incorporating this terminology in 2001, the MNBA issued a wake-up call about the need to retrace the evolution of Cuban art during the first half of the twentieth century. More than the intention to add a new term to an already long and complicated historiographical vocabulary, the appropriation of this notion drew attention to a period that needed reassessment beyond the constraints of any aesthetic formula. Under that umbrella, a new museography gave autonomy to little-known artists and trends, while suggesting a smoother transition between tradition and innovation.

Motivated by the MNBA, the Department of Art History at UH became interested in the study of this period as well. The essay "Aquel cambio de siglo" ("That Turn of the Century," 2002) by Luz Merino Acosta was probably the starting point of what later became my own research. As a professor in the Department of Art History and Assistant Director of the MNBA, Merino played an important role in identifying the urgency of reevaluating the *entresiglos* (in-between centuries) from a more inclusive and less reductionist perspective. She tried to place the term "turn of the century" within the island's coordinates, paving the way to further analysis of the period, its peculiarities, actors, and contributions. I was Merino's student when I first read this text in 2003, and I accepted the challenge to take it a step farther.

I started to question the exclusive perspective prevailing in the literature on Cuban art. From the foundation of the San Alejandro Academy (1818) to the Exhibition of New Art (1927), the history of the arts in Cuba was usually seen as a monolithic block without many nuances. The art production within this chronological window was cataloged as "academic," a word that often carried a negative connotation. "Academic" stood for everything attached to the romantic and naturalist traditions; it worked as a stigma to describe stagnant production devoid of renewal.

The decades preceding the avant-garde movement suffered the consequences of such an exclusive interpretation. In a period of nearly thirty years, Armando G. Menocal and Leopoldo Romañach (1862–1951) monopolized the historiography of Cuban art. Their long careers as professors, as well as the social demand for their work, contributed to the establishment of their names as representative of a particular tradition. Most scholars thus highlight their significance in the evolution of Cuban art. However, a lack of information prevails concerning other, coexisting artists—some of them mentioned earlier—who are fleeting names in the specialized literature now in circulation.

The arrival of the 1930s Generation explains in part this unequal treatment, but it has more to do with the critical discourse built around the avant-garde. Writers and art critics were more aggressive and opposed to the past than was the artistic practice itself. To explain these contrasting attitudes between critics and promoters of the avant-garde and the artistic production per se, it is instructive to compare the review of the 1927 show by Spanish-born, Havana-based writer Martín Casanovas with the observations of Alfred H. Barr Jr., the director of the Museum of Modern Art (MoMA) in New York, in 1944. While Casanovas situates the exhibition on the platform of change supported by the *Revista de Avance*, Barr observes how Cuban artists managed to combine past and present, local themes with foreign influences.

Speaking on behalf of his generation, Casanovas writes: "We fully condemn and negate the art of the nineteenth century . . . [T]he highest aspiration of young artists is to forget all that has existed, forget all the museums they have visited, and forget all the genial pyrotechnics of the luminaries of past art. It's about starting anew."[2] Almost twenty years later, and with a calmer, more ecumenical spirit, Barr describes the artists' works from a more conciliatory point of view, stating, "Paris and Mexico, the Italian Renaissance and Baroque masters have all contributed to modern Cuban painting but these foreign influences have been fused to a remarkable extent with native Cuban elements . . . [including] fighting cocks, sugar cane cutters, guanábanas, barber shops, bandits, nudes, angels, or hurricanes."[3]

In Cuba, as in many other Latin American countries, the emergence of the Modern movement had political overtones. The avant-garde was identified with nationalist discourse—and was therefore an alleged antecedent of the 1959 Revolution; in contrast, the turn of the century was associated with the republican period. It is not hard to understand why after 1959 many critics and art historians from the island adopted an unfavorable stance toward production developed outside the orbit of the avant-garde.

Spanish historiography has faced a similar situation, in which opposition instead of continuity has traditionally explained Modern art. Writing about the exhibition *Arte para un siglo* (Centro de Arte Reina Sofía, 2002), Francesc Fontbona de Vallescar—a professor at the Royal Catalan Academy of Fine Arts of Sant Jordi—addressed a recurrent problem in the historiography of the period:

> If we follow the manuals that tell us the history of the art of the last century, we will reach the conclusion that the century began practically as an avant-garde, because almost from its inception, the Fauves changed the face of painting, and a little later, the Cubists definitely broke with tradition. . . . But what the manuals tell us, with rare unanimity, is one thing, and what the day-to-day of the art dictated is something else, especially in the peripheral art centers compared to Paris, the city that served as a framework for the incipient avant-garde; the Paris in which, on the other hand, many other types of visual expressions continued to enjoy good health, many of which were not particularly avant-garde and about which we now know very little.[4]

For a long time, two equally exclusive approaches prevailed: that of the traditionalists—for whom modernity meant the death of art—and the linear conception of history. According to this point of view, a continuous succession of "isms" characterized the second half of the nineteenth century. However, the reality is always more plural than what any of those perspectives allows us to appreciate. The turn of the century coincided internationally with an atmosphere of change, including the effects of industrial development, scientific invention, and the transformation of the art system. During this period, the modern channels of art circulation (i.e., cultural magazines, fine art salons, and art criticism, among others) were consolidated and systematized.

Fortunately, recent decades have witnessed a recurrent interest in questioning the official discourse of art history to reevaluate forgotten names and trends. Spain seems to be a pioneer in revisiting this period, as demonstrated by initiatives carried out by institutions and/or individual voices. Both the Thyssen-Bornemisza Museum and the Museo Nacional Centro de Arte Reina Sofía (Queen Sophia National Museum Art Center, or MNCARS in its Spanish acronym) have embraced the turn of the century as a moment of coexistence of seemingly conflicting aesthetic ideas. MNCARS' incorporation of the terminology of *cambio de siglo* ("turn of the century") responded to a reevaluation of its institutional collections and the need to show their values instead of forcing the collections to recreate the "official" history of art.

The desire to spring the molds in which the art history of the twentieth century has been confined led to a cooperation agreement between MNCARS and the Spanish Confederation of Savings Banks (CECA in its Spanish acronym). As part of this agreement, four exhibitions were held between 2002 and 2006 under the generic title of *Arte para un siglo* (*Art for a Century*). Those traveling exhibitions visited more than a dozen cities, showing about 15,000 works from the museum's holdings that, for reasons of space, had not been displayed previously.[5] *Turn of the Century (1881–1925)* inaugurated the cycle, calling attention to the need to rethink artistic production preceding the avant-garde. Under a title that seemed merely a chronological and organizational demarcation, the exhibition presented an overview of the coexisting artists, languages, and trends of those decades. Postimpressionists, naturalists, modernists, *noventayochistas*, idealists, and *noucentistas* testified to the plurality of tastes that characterized a period of transition as "a lot more varied, richer, and more valuable than what was called the procession of the isms."[6]

As mentioned, the MNBA of Havana decided to adopt the curatorial proposal from MNCARS for the reopening of the institution in 2001. That inclusion gave autonomy to artists and works from the permanent collection that had never been shown before or had only been presented under the generic term of "academia." For the first time, this group was classified as a separate collection, as a link between the nineteenth-century tradition and the Modern movement of the 1930s. This new museography pluralized the discourse about Cuban art, offering a polyphony of voices that had frequently been ignored. The exhibition of paintings and drawings spanned approximately 1893 to 1927, taking as a starting point *Embarque de Colón por Bobadilla* (*The Expulsion of Columbus by Bobadilla*) by Menocal. The well-known names of Menocal, Romañach, or Domingo Ramos (1894–1956) shared gallery space with works by Antonio Rodríguez Morey, María Capdevila, Beltrán Masses, and Manuel Mesa, among others. This proposal pointed to the emergence of a vast generation of artists whose heterogeneous proposals are impossible to categorize under a single generic adjective.

Cuban writer and critic Jorge Mañach offers a thought-provoking assessment of the artistic production of the first thirty years of the twentieth century. In his essay "La pintura en Cuba desde 1900 hasta el presente" ("Painting in Cuba from 1900 to the Present"), the author pursues an organizational objective and breaks down the art of the first two decades of the century into three different generations, including an intermediate generation between Menocal and Romañach and the generation of Eduardo Abela (1889–1965) and Víctor Manuel García. Mañach identifies this intermediate generation as *la llama de la transición libertaria* (the flame of the libertarian transition), a transition that in his estimation emerged around 1910.

By 1910, Havana was a fertile arena for changes. In the last quarter of the nineteenth century, the town turned into a cosmopolitan city, as the demolition of the city walls, the construction of new neighborhoods, and the incorporation of technological and industrial innovations accelerated the transformation of the capital and favored cultural development in its various expressions. In the arts arena, a major turning point happened in 1878 when José Miguel Melero (1836–1907), then director of the San Alejandro Academy, introduced significant changes in the teaching and appreciation of art, among them the opening of artistic teaching to women, the creation of the Landscape Department chair, and an emphasis on painting directly from nature.[7]

The last decades of the nineteenth century are highly fragmented and hard to organize: the unexpected deaths of several young painters—i.e., Miguel Ángel Melero (1865–87), José Arburu Morell (1864–89), and Juana Borrero (1877–96)—and the Spanish-Cuban and Spanish-American wars affected artistic production. There was a pause until 1902, when, under new circumstances of stability, art production would reveal a new orientation. The republic and the new century came almost at the same time. Although it has been a point of contention, the establishment of the republic generated a climate of renewed expectations and recovery. The free movement and clash of ideas that had suffered a paralysis in the context of the war (1895–98), as well as the first U.S. military intervention (1898–1902), were rearticulated under the new sociopolitical order.

It is often said that the republic began with a sense of frustration because Cuba gained only partial sovereignty; however, at least in the first thirty years of the twentieth century, a good portion of the artistic production shared a sense of satisfaction, republican culture, and non-colonial modernity. As the country prepared to assert itself as an independent nation, many artists and writers contributed to the island's gradual recovery and modernization through their practice. As a result, the art and culture circulation system was consolidated and enhanced. Several cultural magazines, such as *Arte* (1914–18), *Revista de Bellas Artes* (1918), and *Gaceta de Bellas Artes* (1923–28), appeared in Havana. Those communication channels served as a platform for the young intellectual elite and contributed to shaping an audience for cultural and artistic matters.

As far as exhibition spaces, several places in Havana included art shows as part of their programming, among them El Ateneo, the Spanish regional centers, the newspaper *Diario de la Marina*, the Sevilla Hotel, and the National Academy of Arts and Letters. However, exhibiting art was not their main social objective, but a collateral or alternative function. In 1916, Cuban painter and intellectual Federico Edelman y Pinto (1869–1931) created the Salón de Bellas Artes (Fine Arts Salon), with the intention of stabilizing the promotion of art through annual exhibitions. This initiative had the double purpose of stimulating artistic development and keeping the public informed about local and foreign art trends. After the first Salón, Edelman y Pinto created the Asociación de Pintores y Escultores (Association of Painters and Sculptors), which assumed responsibility for organizing the salon every year until 1934, when the Directorate of Culture created the Salón Nacional de Pintura y Escultura (National Salon of Painting and Sculpture).

Edelman y Pinto was not an isolated figure. During this time, artists became more and more interested in actively participating in both sides of the artistic realm: production and promotion. They assumed the promotion of art as part of their historic mission. The names of these artist-intellectuals not only appeared on the lists of participants at certain events, but they were also part of the organizing teams; served on juries for art contests; delivered art lectures; and functioned as editors and/or critics, as museum directors, and so on. In his book *La pintura y escultura en Cuba a través de la Escuela de Bellas Artes de San Alejandro*, Esteban Valderrama mentions some of the collateral activities of his contemporaries, who spanned the spectrum from being illustrators and caricaturists to directing prestigious cultural institutions.

In the first decades of the twentieth century, the art market started to take shape as well. La Paleta, La Venecia, El Pincel, and El Arte were some of the art supplies stores that simultaneously engaged in selling works of art and crafts. For many artists, those spaces were key to ensuring that their works were marketed to a vast buying public. Such was the case of Juan Gil García (1879–1932), the Spanish painter established in Havana who became popular for his still life paintings. While his participation in the 1916 and 1917 Fine Art Salons probably contributed to the growing demand for his paintings, his contract with El Arte was also fundamental in his career.

Located at Calle Galiano, No. 506, in Central Havana, El Arte was founded in 1907. In its window displays, this unique shop presented buyers with an array of items, including art supplies, works of art, and handcrafted objects. Gil García worked from this platform at a fever pitch, producing paintings featuring the two themes that defined his career: landscapes and still lifes. In particular, his still life compositions of flowers and fruits became the decoration of choice for dining rooms and other spaces in Havana homes. Executed around 1918, *Frutas* (*Fruits*) is a great example of his personal signature: Gil García preferred to paint tropical fruits. The variety and freshness of the Cuban cornucopia—ranging from coconuts, pineapples, and bananas to sugar, apple, mameyes, oranges, and cashews—turn into praise for the island's fertility as well as a metaphor for the heights of opulence and progress to which the young republic aspired (Plate 10).

In contrast to the sobriety of baroque still lifes, Gil García's painting is devoted to voluptuousness; not satisfied with showing fruits' external appearance, he opens them to expose the inner pulp—bright, appetizing—that invites the viewer to savor it. Gil García defined and systematized a genre whose precedents in the country were very rare. His work typifies a form that must wait until the late 1930s to experience a new transformation in the poetics of Amelia Peláez. Despite the success he achieved, Gil García's style and contribution would later be attacked and condemned to ostracism as the embodiment of an obsolete academicism.[8]

Other genres also suffered from being evaluated from the perspective of the avant-garde instead of their own horizon of references. Reverting this process, the production that precedes Modern art can be seen as a link between nineteenth-century tradition and the new propositions that characterized Cuban art after the 1930s. Landscape painters such as Eduardo Morales (1868–1938), Rodríguez Morey, and Ramos initiated a new way of representing the Cuban countryside. This genre favored a dialogue with the modern languages and offered a wide repertoire of possibilities by incorporating a vast spectrum of trends, ranging from naturalism to symbolism. Ramos was among the artists who generalized the realistic representation of light, initiated by the nineteenth-century painter Valentín Sanz Carta (1849–98). Instead of depicting the sunrise and sunset as in the romantic tradition, Ramos preferred to capture moments of greater luminosity, becoming an expert in painting the reverberation of tropical light. *Paisaje con mogotes* (*Landscape with Hills*, 1925) is one of the many works that the artist executed, taking as his motif the geography of the west of Cuba. Obsessed with the hummocks of the Valley of Viñales in Pinar del Río, he painted them again and again, sometimes with a naturalist brush and other times with his peculiar expressionism, in which light predominates over color (Plate 11).

Portrait painting increasingly focused on the psychology of its models and not just on the description of their social position, as in the nineteenth century. The plurality in the representation of women was another contribution to portraiture during the turn of the century. Valderrama's peasant and chaste women coexisted with the aristocratic and exotic femmes fatales of Beltrán Masses, whose style—strongly informed by symbolism and Art Deco—was very peculiar among his contemporaries. Despite the amplification of the spectrum of models and the gradual interest of artists in the background of the composition—which increasingly stopped being a neutral panel to contribute to the characterization of the portrayed individual—the theme of portraits changed only moderately. More than proposing a radical rupture with tradition, this genre describes a storyline that connects the style of Menocal and Romañach with the work of Jorge Arche (1905–56) during the 1930s and 1940s, as well as Canals, Manuel Vega (1892–1954), and Valderrama (1892–1964).

Painters showed a special interest in ornament and decoration, in the recreation of scenographic atmospheres to approach different topics better, whether portraits or scenes of everyday life. Even history and religious subjects, sometimes difficult to classify according to the formal subdivision of art history genres since the two often overlapped, functioned more as a *menu* than as a canon. Such is the case of *Procesión en La Habana* (*Procession in Havana*, 1930) by Manuel Mesa. Putting aside the formalities and sacredness of the religious subject, Mesa took advantage of the language of expressionism to resolve the center of the composition. The artist chose a combined style: a naturalist appearance for the background and a freer expression to represent the fervent crowd. The brightness of the blue and red, the expressiveness of light in the main part of the procession holding the Virgin Mary aloft, and the sketchy brushwork give this work a modern look, while blurring the boundaries among religious, history, and genre painting (see Plate 12).

In the works of Capdevila, Ramón Loy (1894–1936), Ramos, and others, the depiction of elements and symbols of identity was recurrent. Musical instruments, national flora and fauna, architectural symbols—such as the Morro Castle or the Cathedral of Havana—daily life in the Cuban countryside, and the exuberance of tropical fruits, among other typical elements of Cuba, were highlighted as part of a sense of belonging that was taken to another level of discussion and complexity by later generations of modern painters. A devoted educator, Capdevila was one of the artists who used landscape painting to explore notions of identity and belonging. Expanding the repertoire of visual languages from Impressionism and Expressionism to timid but evident dialogues with abstraction, *Paisaje de Trinidad* (*Trinidad Landscape*, ca. 1921) recreates the beauty and serenity of the Cuban landscape. This way of representing the Cuban countryside, particularly the peasant, would be picked up at the end of the following decade in the work of Abela (see Plate 13).

Cuban painting of the turn of the twentieth century should be considered as a bridge connecting tradition and innovation. More than a unique style, the art of these decades experienced a communion of diverse trends that favored the gradual transition to another idea of modernity. As a group, the artists gave their successors other enduring legacies, such as the desire to insert art into the context of contemporary culture, the aspiration to continuous innovation, the freedom to choose from different trends or apply them simultaneously, and the desire to establish a fluid communication with the public. A reinterpretation of the past shows that there was no abrupt rupture between the academic style and the subsequent renewal of Cuban art.

The turn of the century was a significant period in the formation of a national style. If, after the 1930s, the concept of art shifted due to changes not only in Cuba but also around the world, the previous decades had paved the way for such a transformation. It is still a period under review. Only systematic research will continue to shed light on the fragmented biographies of each of these artists and their contributions. Although condemned to the realm of the unknown by later Cuban historiography—in part because of the change in the artistic paradigm, and because many of these artists left the island after 1959—the decades preceding the avant-garde deserve to recover their place within the continuum of art in Cuba and beyond its borders.

Notes

1. *Revista de Avance* (1927–30), the main platform for the artistic and literary avant-garde in Cuba, organized this exhibition. Opening at the Association of Painters and Sculptors on May 7, 1927, the Exhibition of New Art showcased a new generation of artists, including Eduardo Abela, Rafael Blanco, Antonio Gattorno, Gabriel Castaño, Carlos Enríquez, Víctor Manuel García, and U.S. artists Alice Neel and Adja Madlein Yunkers. See Lori Cole, "Reproducing the Avant-Garde."
2. Martí [*sic*] Casanovas, "Nuevos rumbos," 99.
3. Alfred H. Barr Jr., "Modern Cuban Painters," 4.
4. Francesc Fontbona de Vallescar, "Arte español a caballo entre dos siglos," 25.
5. María José Salazar Herrería, "Arte para un siglo."
6. Salazar Herrería, 31.
7. Hortensia Peramo Cabrera, "Un derecho conquistado."
8. Anelys Alvarez, "Juan Gil García (1879–1932)."

Bibliography

Alvarez, Anelys. "Juan Gil García (1879–1932): The Painter of Flowers, Fruits, and Landscapes." Lecture, Cernuda Arte, Miami, April 14, 2014.

Barr, Alfred H., Jr. "Modern Cuban Painters." *The Bulletin of the Museum of Modern Art* 11, no. 5 (1944): 2–7.

Casanovas, Martí. "Nuevos rumbos: La exposición de '1927.'" *Revista de Avance* 1, no. 5 (1927): 99–100.

Cole, Lori. "Reproducing the Avant-Garde: The Art of Modernist Magazines." In *The Aesthetics of Matter: Modernism, the Avant-Garde, and Material Exchange*, edited by

Sarah Posman, Anne Reverseau, David S. Ayers, Sascha Bru, and Benedikt Hjartarson, 187–93. Berlin and Boston: Walter de Gruyter, 2013.

Fontbona de Vallescar, Francesc. "Arte español a caballo entre dos siglos (1881–1925)." In *Cambio de siglo (1881–1925)*, Vol. 1, edited by Carmen Fernández Aparicio, 24–31. Vigo, Spain: Sala Fundación Caja Vital Kutxa, 2002.

Mañach, Jorge. "La pintura en Cuba desde 1900 hasta el presente." *Cuba Contemporánea* 12, no. 142 (1924): 105–25.

Merino Acosta, Luz. "Algo para recordar." *Arte Cubano* 1 (1999): 57–61.

———. "Aquel cambio de siglo." *La Gaceta de Cuba* 3 (2002): 27–31.

Peramo Cabrera, Hortensia. "Un derecho conquistado: Aprender a pintar." *Opus Habana*, March 4, 2009. Accessed May 31, 2017. http://www.opushabana.cu/index.php/articulos/1542-.html.

Salazar Herrería, María José. "Arte para un siglo." In *Cambio de siglo (1881–1925)*, Vol. 1, edited by Carmen Fernández Aparicio, 19–21. Vigo, Spain: Sala Fundación Caja Vital Kutxa, 2002.

Valderrama, Esteban. *La pintura y la escultura en Cuba a través de la Escuela de Bellas Artes de San Alejandro*. Havana: Lex, 1952.

5

The Cuban Avant-Garde and the International Art Community

Ramón Cernuda

The subject of this chapter is the consolidation of Cuban art in the first half of the twentieth century. I have chosen to focus on the word *consolidation* and to dwell on the historical process that brought about a very uncommon phenomenon: an artistic movement from a peripheral area far from the dominant art centers of the world, from an island that had recently become a nation, unquestionably located in the outer delineations of the Modern art movement, unexpectedly found its arts—paintings, sculptures, and works on paper—recognized and consolidated in a period of just thirty years.

This near-miracle takes place from 1927, the chosen birthplace of the Cuban *vanguardia* (avant-garde), to the late 1950s, when, for political reasons and because of social disruptions, the Modernist art movement in the country found itself in disarray, dispersed and disconnected from its main international platform of support, the United States, and, to a lesser extent, from other Latin American countries. To further comprehend the exceptional nature of this occurrence, consider that Cuba's population in 1927 was only 3.8 million, and by 1959, 6.8 million souls.[1]

This movement, the Cuban vanguardia, or, as Alfred H. Barr Jr. and others have also called it, the School of Havana, consists of two generations of artists. The first generation of twentieth-century modernists in Cuba included artists born in the last decade of the nineteenth century and up to circa 1905. They erupted collectively onto the art scene of Havana on May 7, 1927, as part of the Primera Exposición de Arte Nuevo (First Exhibition of New Art), at the Association of Painters and Sculptors, and under the auspices of the *Revista de Avance*.[2]

This exhibition coalesced a movement and the vanguardia became a reality. It was a small and loose band of artists—young, rebellious, and determined to advance the cause of modernity in the arts in Cuba and elsewhere. They were nationalistic in their desire to contribute to the shaping of a national identity, but they were neither isolationists nor chauvinists. On the contrary, they were humanists and internationalists pushing for a new, modern, and revolutionary attitude toward the arts; and further, they set out to promote radical changes in culture and society in general. To be a modern artist in Havana in the 1920s, one had to be blessed with a sort of priestly calling; vows of poverty were all but demanded. The scorn of traditional painters was assumed; the extremely limited exhibition opportunities were unavoidable.

Throughout the following years and decades, the key artists of this movement emerged as recognized and important creators. The most successful in the accumulation of accolades and distinctions, the most acquired in public and private collections, could very well be the twelve names I am about to mention. I acknowledge that art *marchands* are usually arbitrary and capricious, and I am no exception (Plate 14).

My list of the top twelve of the first-generation vanguardia painters follows:

1. Víctor Manuel García, in deference to him being the precursor—the first one to present a one-person show of modern art in Cuba—even before the *Revista de Avance* exhibition in 1927.[3]
2. Carlos Enríquez (1900–57)
3. Amelia Peláez
4. Fidelio Ponce de León (1895–1949)
5. Eduardo Abela
6. Antonio Gattorno (1904–80)
7. Marcelo Pogolotti (1902–88)
8. Alberto Peña (1897–1938)
9. Arístides Fernández (1904–34)
10. Jorge Arche

11. Domingo Ravenet (1905–69)
12. Last in my list, but most important, is Wifredo Lam (Plate 15).

This first generation of Modern Cuban artists was well prepared for the venture. They were aware of the various languages of Modernism, Impressionism, Post-Impressionism, Cubism, Fauvism, Futurism, Surrealism, Abstraction, and Expressionism. They had read, they had studied, and many had traveled, searched, and researched. They carved their own formative path by changing the route of their education; after Havana and mostly the San Alejandro Academy, their preferred destination was Montparnasse and the School of Paris, not Madrid and the San Fernando Academy, as their teachers at San Alejandro had done before them. The young ones went to Paris; they lived, learned, and painted alongside the top artists of the School of Paris in the 1920s and 1930s—Picasso, Matisse, Chagall, Bonnard, Modigliani, Mondrian, Kandinsky, Soutine, and others. These were their neighbors and peers.

The first-generation vanguardia artists soon saw reinforcements coming, and a second generation of artists strengthened and invigorated the movement, continuing the essential goals of the first generation, but expressing themselves through their own distinctive vocabularies and thematic preferences. This second generation was not at all imitative, derivative, or subservient to the older group. It was very different from, for example, the Uruguayan experience of Joaquín Torres García with his atelier and disciples.[4]

The second generation of Cuban vanguardia artists turned out to be just as strong and creative as the first. These artists were aware of the central objectives of the movement:

1. To contribute, define, affirm, and divulge a national identity.
2. To elevate modernist artistic discourse to a higher level of international recognition.

The Marxist intellectual and poet Juan Marinello best stated this duality of purpose, the "national and international," when he wrote at the very beginning of the movement in 1925, "Cubanization of art requires a process of artistic integration in which artists learn to view the indigenous with the eyes of the foreigner and the foreign with the eyes of the Cuban, resulting in the universalization of Cuban artistic themes."[5]

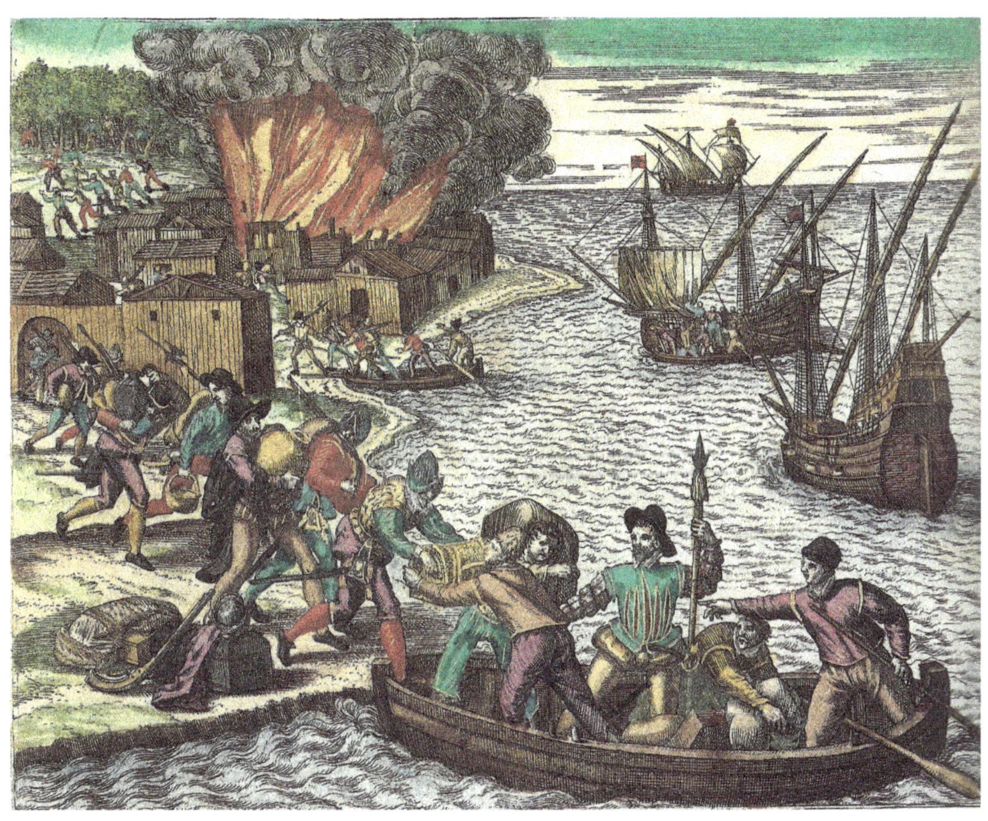

Plate 1. Theodor de Bry, *Americae pars quinta* (*The Fifth Part of America*), 1595, *Galli Chioreram vrbem occvpant, praedantur, and tandem, ob incolarum perfidiam, igne absumunt*. Frankfurt.

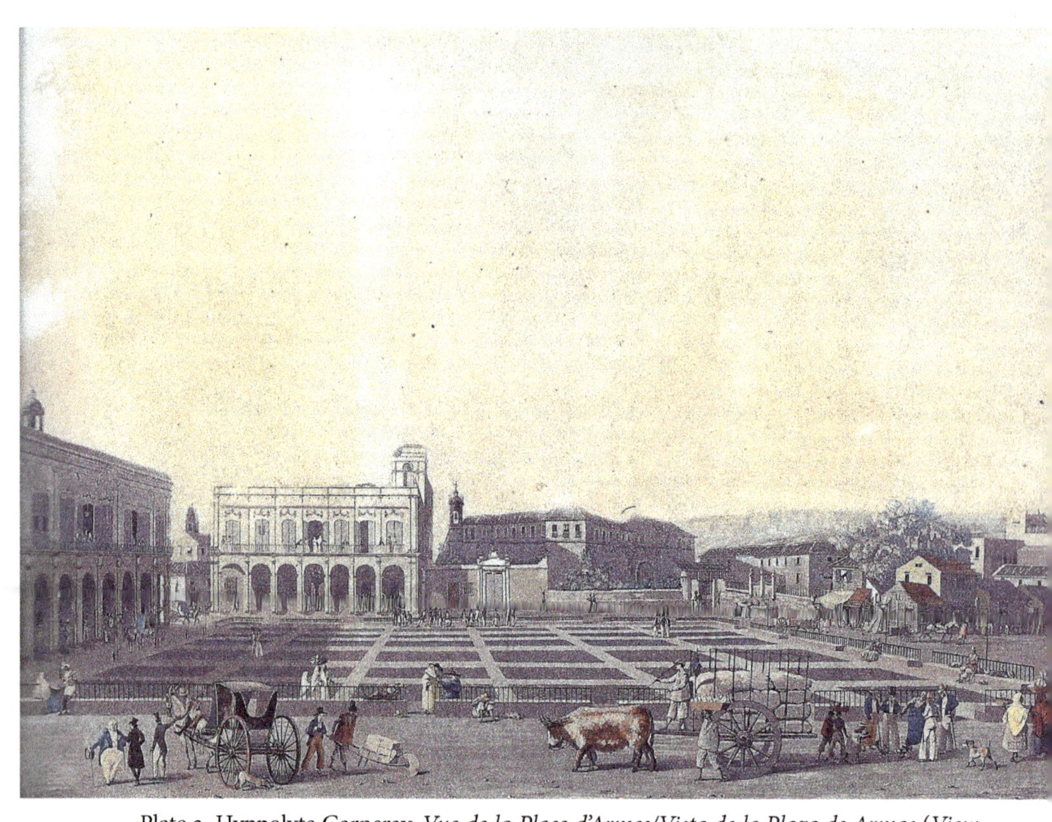

Plate 2. Hyppolyte Garneray, *Vue de la Place d'Armes/Vista de la Plaza de Armas* (*View of Arms Square*), ca. 1835. Paris: Goupil.

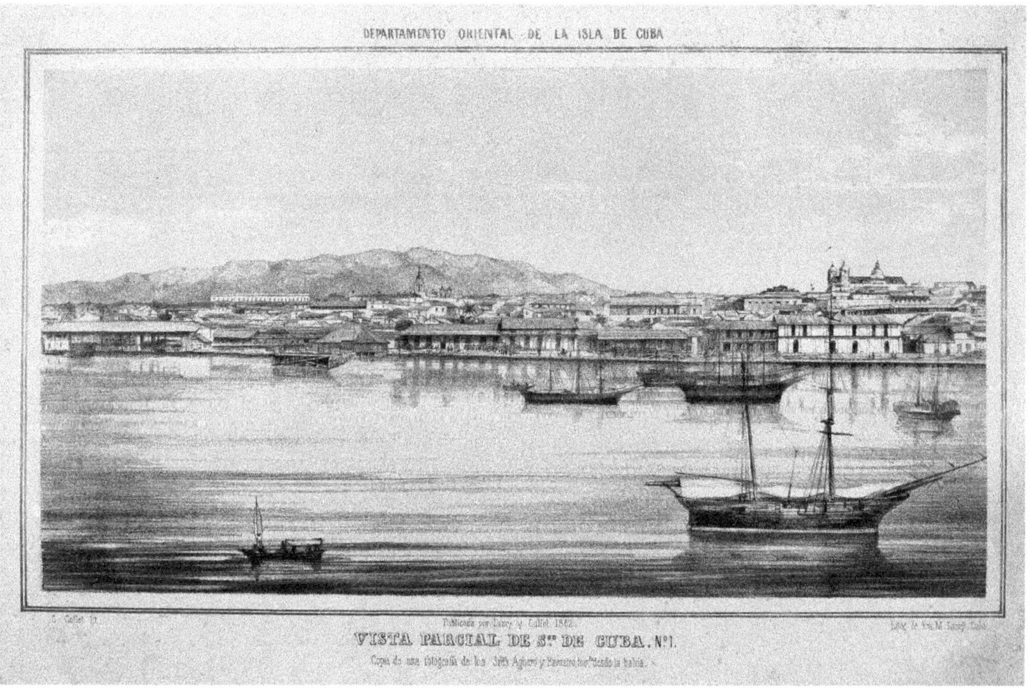

Plate 3. Charles Collet, *Vista parcial de Stgo. de Cuba No 1* (*Partial View of Santiago de Cuba No. 1*), ca. 1862. Santiago de Cuba: Lamy.

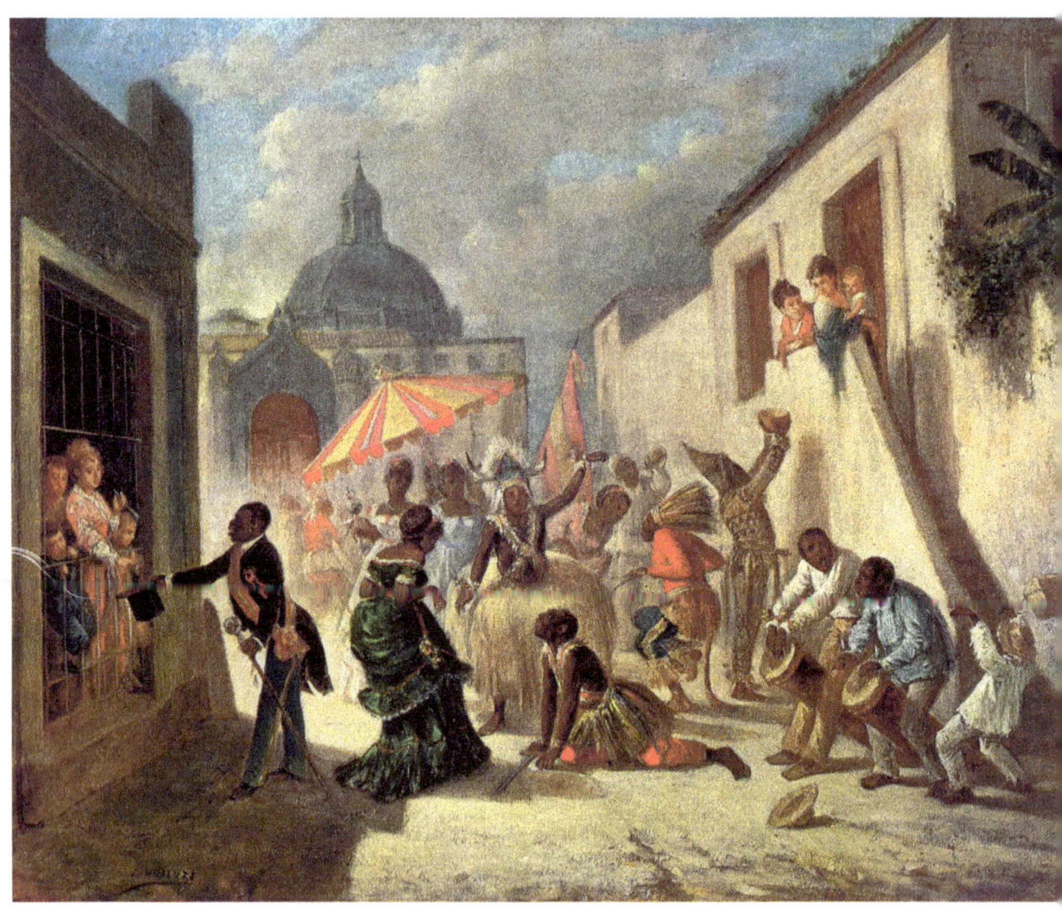

Plate 4. Víctor Patricio de Landaluze, *Día de Reyes en La Habana* (*Three Kings Day in Havana*), ca. early 1870s. Oil on canvas, approximately 20 × 24 inches. Collection of the National Museum of Fine Arts, Havana, Cuba.

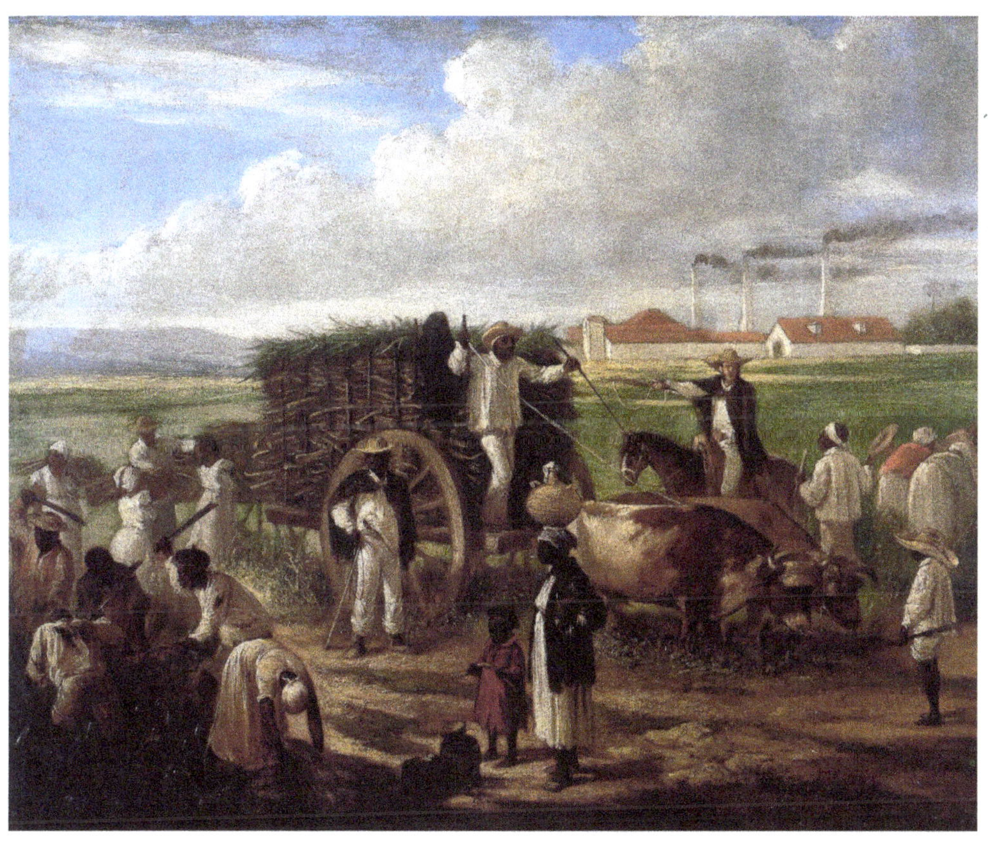

Plate 5. Víctor Patricio de Landaluze, *Corte de caña* (*Cutting Sugar Cane*), 1874. Oil on canvas, approximately 20 × 24 inches. Collection of the National Museum of Fine Arts, Havana.

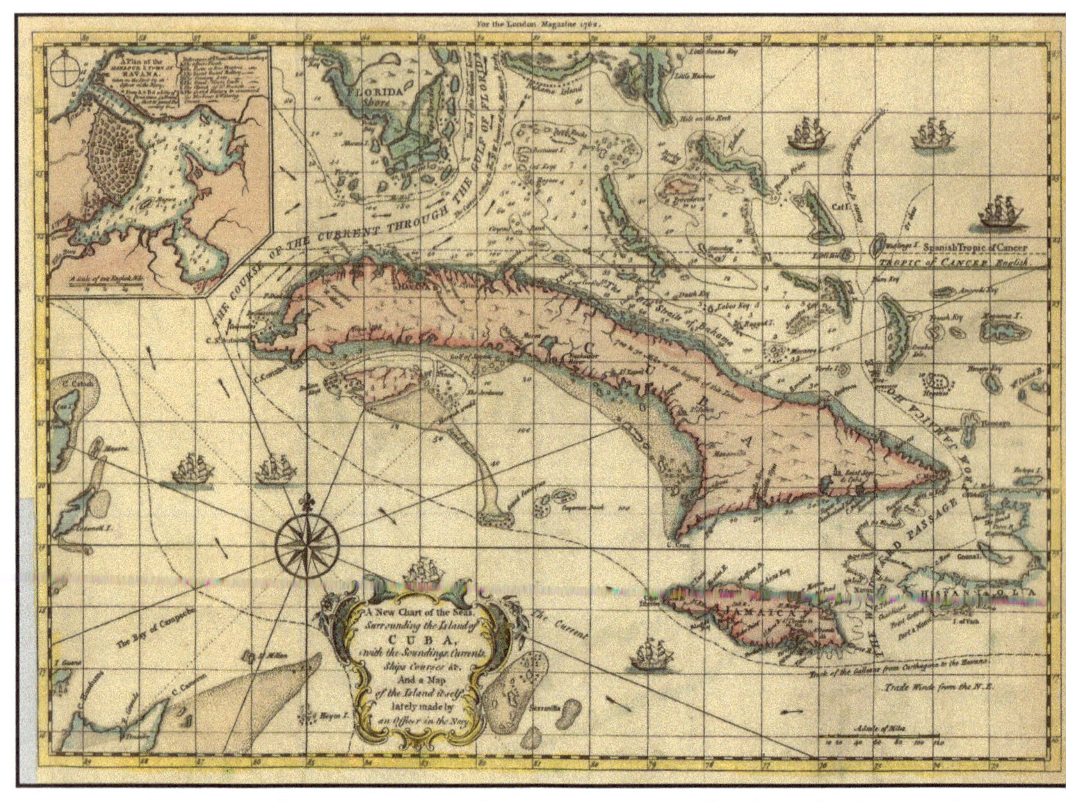

Plate 6. Map of Cuba. *New Chart of the Seas Surrounding the Island of Cuba . . . and a Map of the Island Itself, 1762*. Williams Ethnological Collection, John J. Burns Library, Boston College.

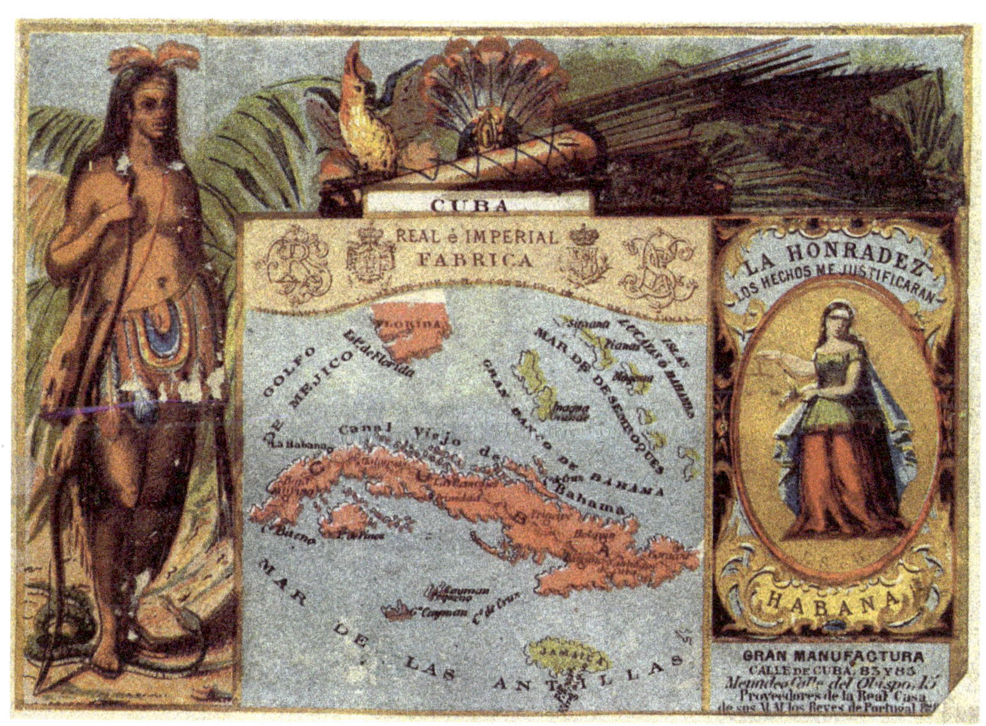

Plate 7. *Marquilla cigarrera cubana* (Cuban Cigar Pack), *La Honradez*, n.d.

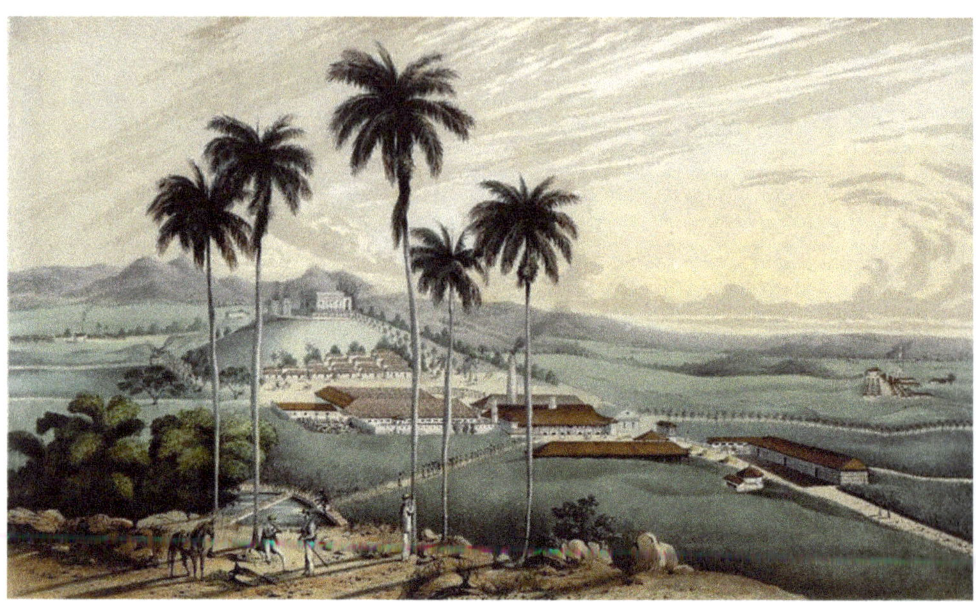

Plate 8. Eduardo Laplante, *Ingenio Buena-Vista* (*Buena-Vista Sugar Mill*), 1857. In Justo G. Cantero and Eduardo Laplante, *Los ingenios: Colección de vistas de los principales ingenios de azúcar de la Isla de Cuba*. Havana: Litografía de Luis Marquier, p. 87.

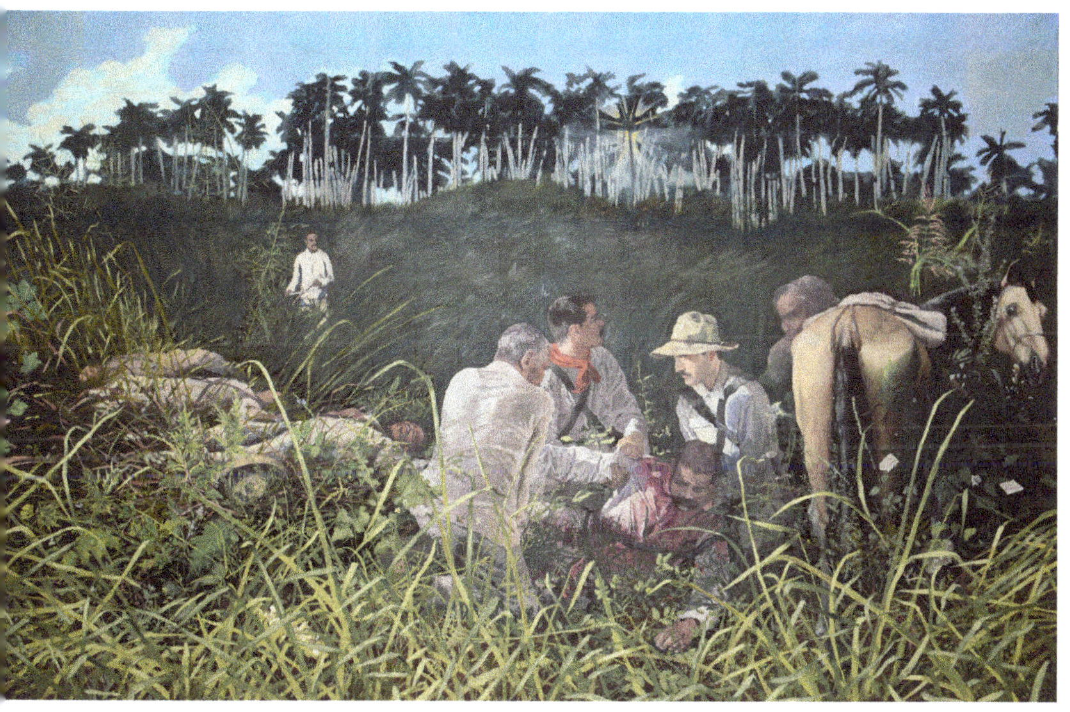

Plate 9. José Manuel Mesías, *Rectificaciones a la obra de Armando Menocal "La muerte de Maceo"* (*Corrections to the Work of Armando Menocal "Death of Maceo"*), 2012–17. Oil and waxed thread on canvas, 109½ × 167⅓ inches. National Museum of Fine Arts, Havana.

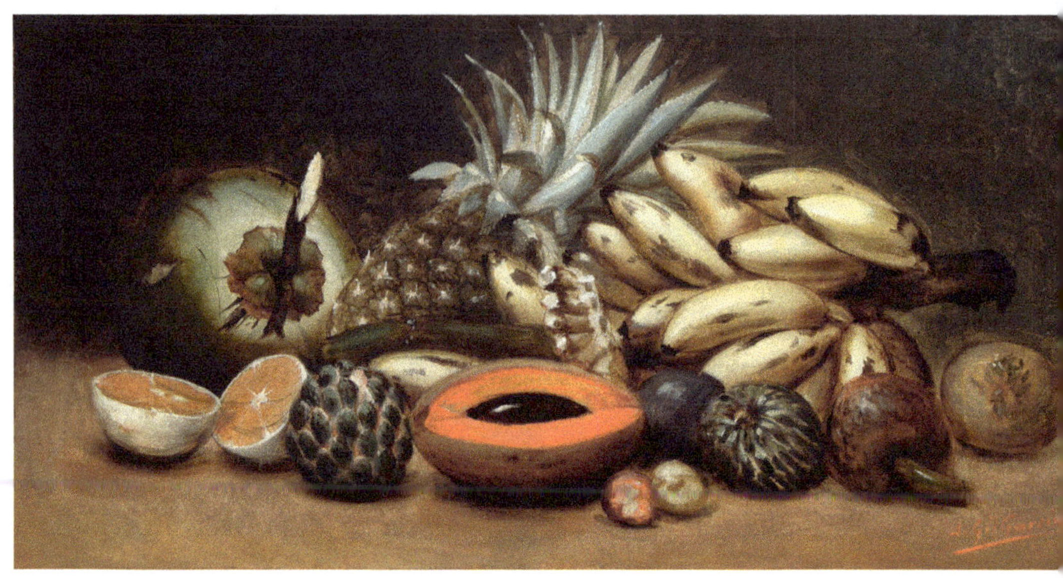

Plate 10. Juan Gil García, *Frutas* (*Fruits*), ca. 1918. Oil on canvas, 14¾ × 28½ inches. Collection of Ramón and Nercys Cernuda, Miami.

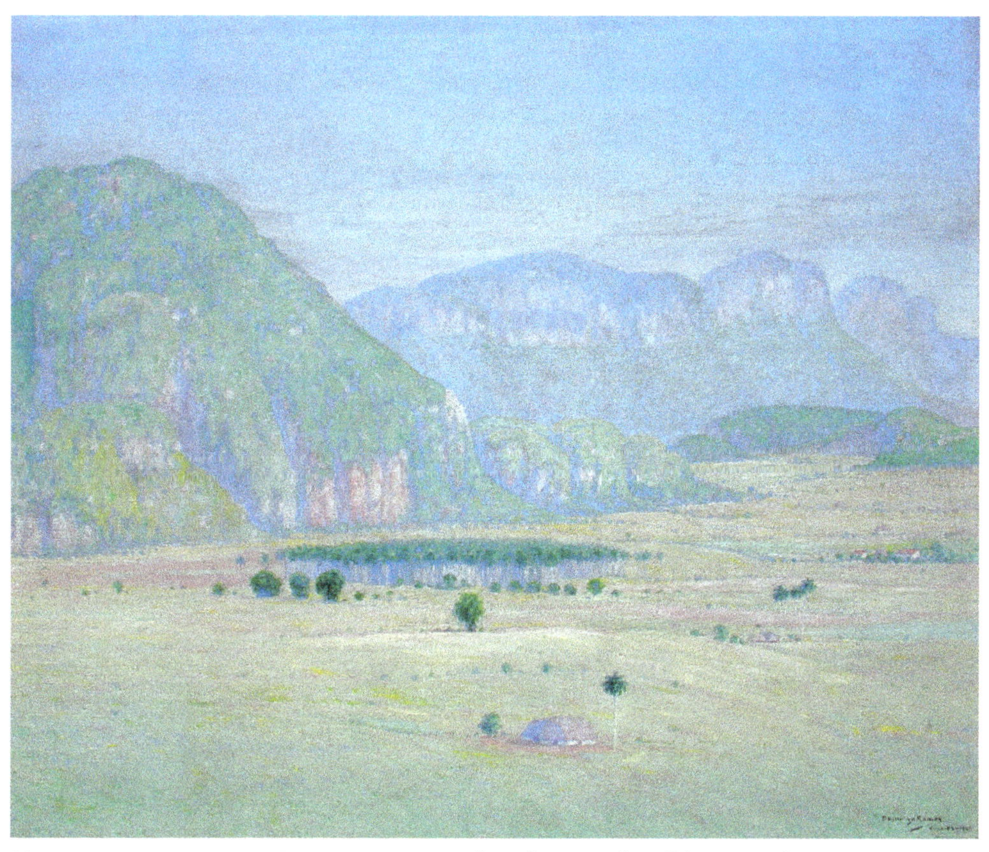

Plate 11. Domingo Ramos, *Paisaje con mogotes* (*Landscape with Hills*), 1925. Oil on canvas, 34 × 39 inches. Collection of Ramón and Nercys Cernuda, Miami.

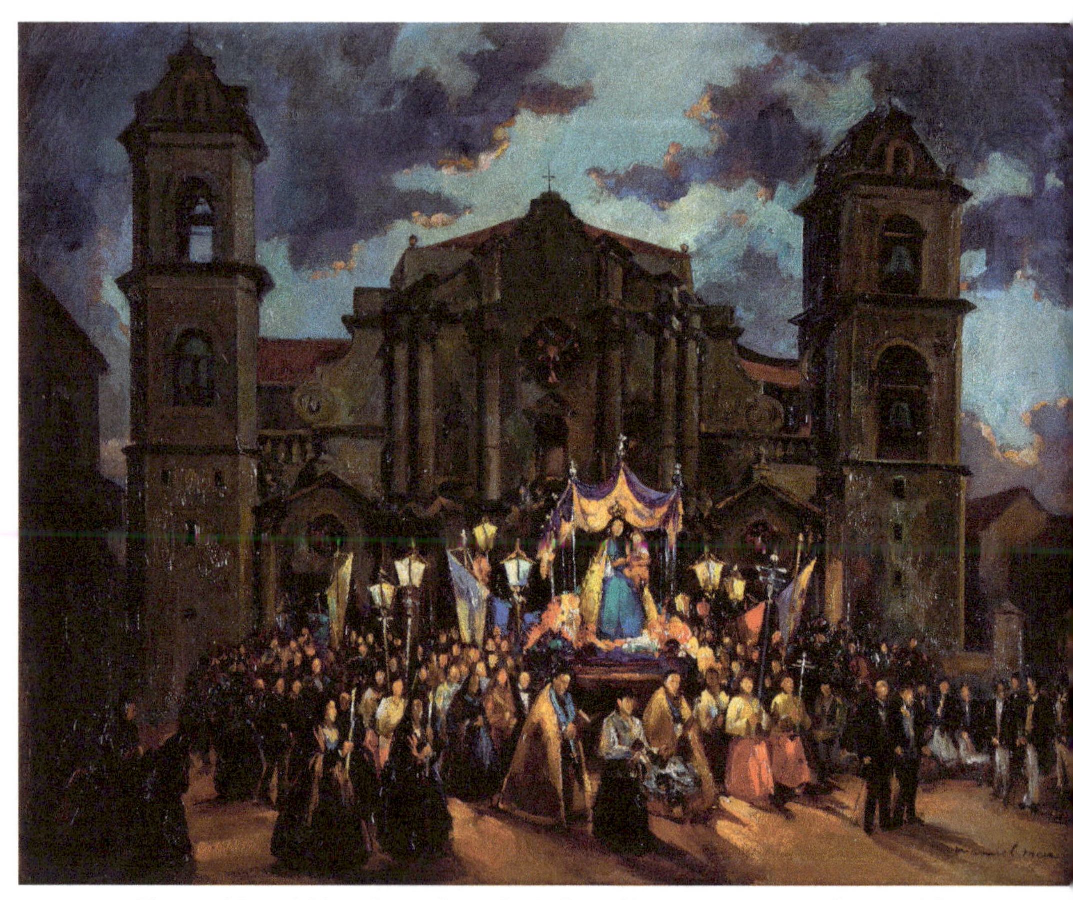

Plate 12. Manuel Mesa, *Procesión en La Habana* (*Procession in Havana*), 1930. Oil on canvas, 16 × 20 inches. Darlene M. and Jorge M. Pérez Art Collection at FIU, Frost Art Museum, Miami.

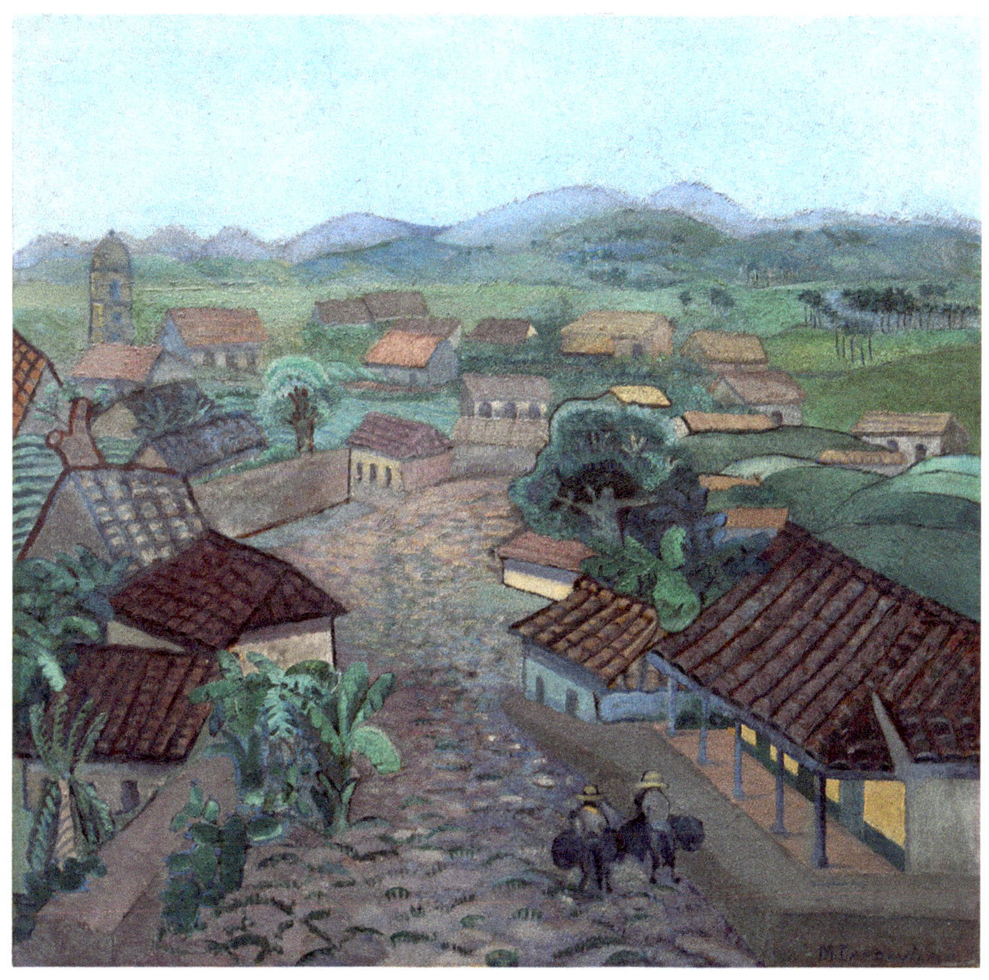

Plate 13. María Capdevila, *Paisaje de Trinidad* (*Trinidad Landscape*), ca. 1921. Oil on board, 27 × 27½ inches. Collection of Ramón and Nercys Cernuda, Miami.

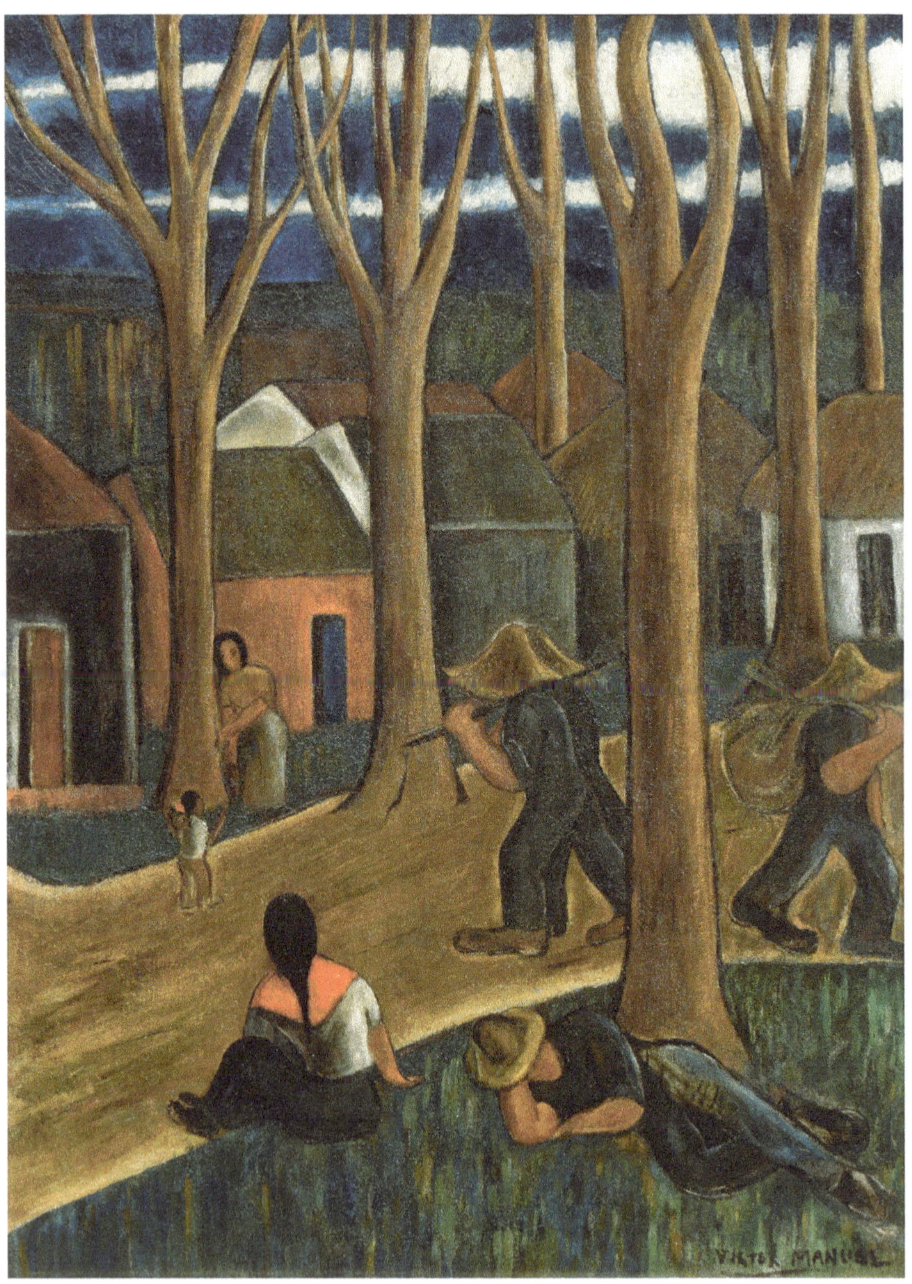

Plate 14. Víctor Manuel García, *Campesinos regresando del trabajo* (*Peasants Returning from Work*), 1935. Oil on canvas, 31 × 23 inches. In Cernuda Arte, *Important Cuban Artworks*, Volume 14. Miami: Cernuda Arte, 2016.

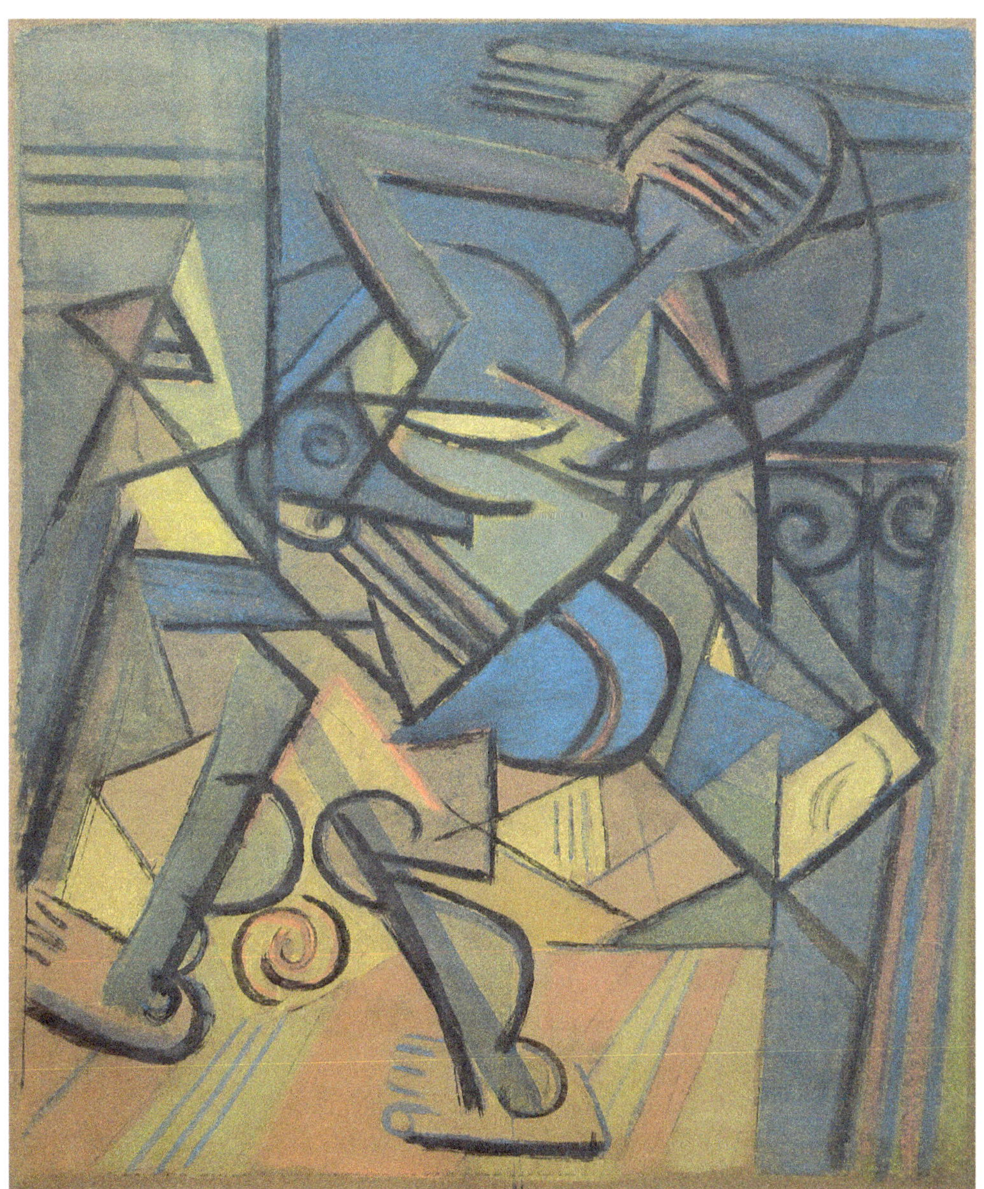

Plate 15. Wifredo Lam, *Sin título (Figura en el balcón)* (*Untitled* [*Figure on a Balcony*]), ca. 1942. Mixed media on heavy paper laid down on board, 38¾ × 31½ inches. In Cernuda Arte, *Important Cuban Artworks*, Volume 14. Miami: Cernuda Arte, 2016.

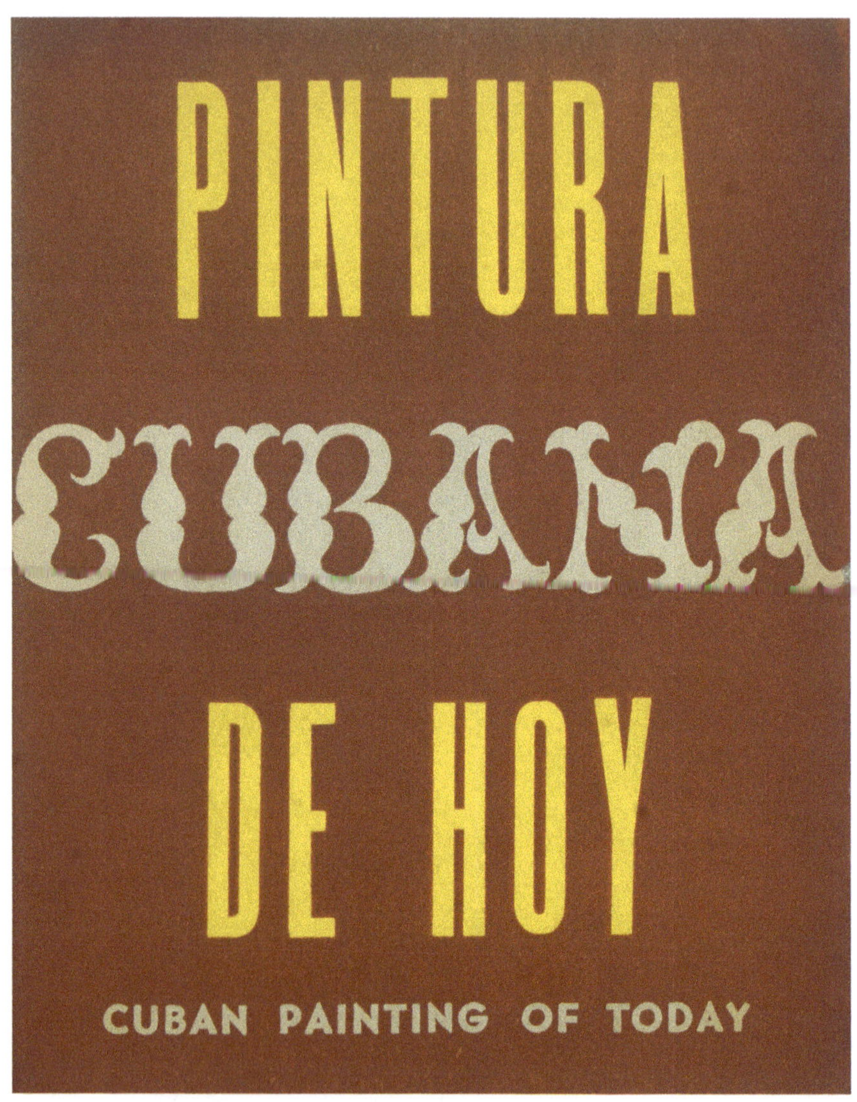

Plate 16. Cover of *Pintura cubana de hoy* (*Cuban Painting of Today*), by José Gómez Sicre, in coordination with María Luisa Gómez Mena, for the 1944 MoMA show. In Cernuda Arte, *Important Cuban Artworks*, Volume 14. Miami: Cernuda Arte, 2016.

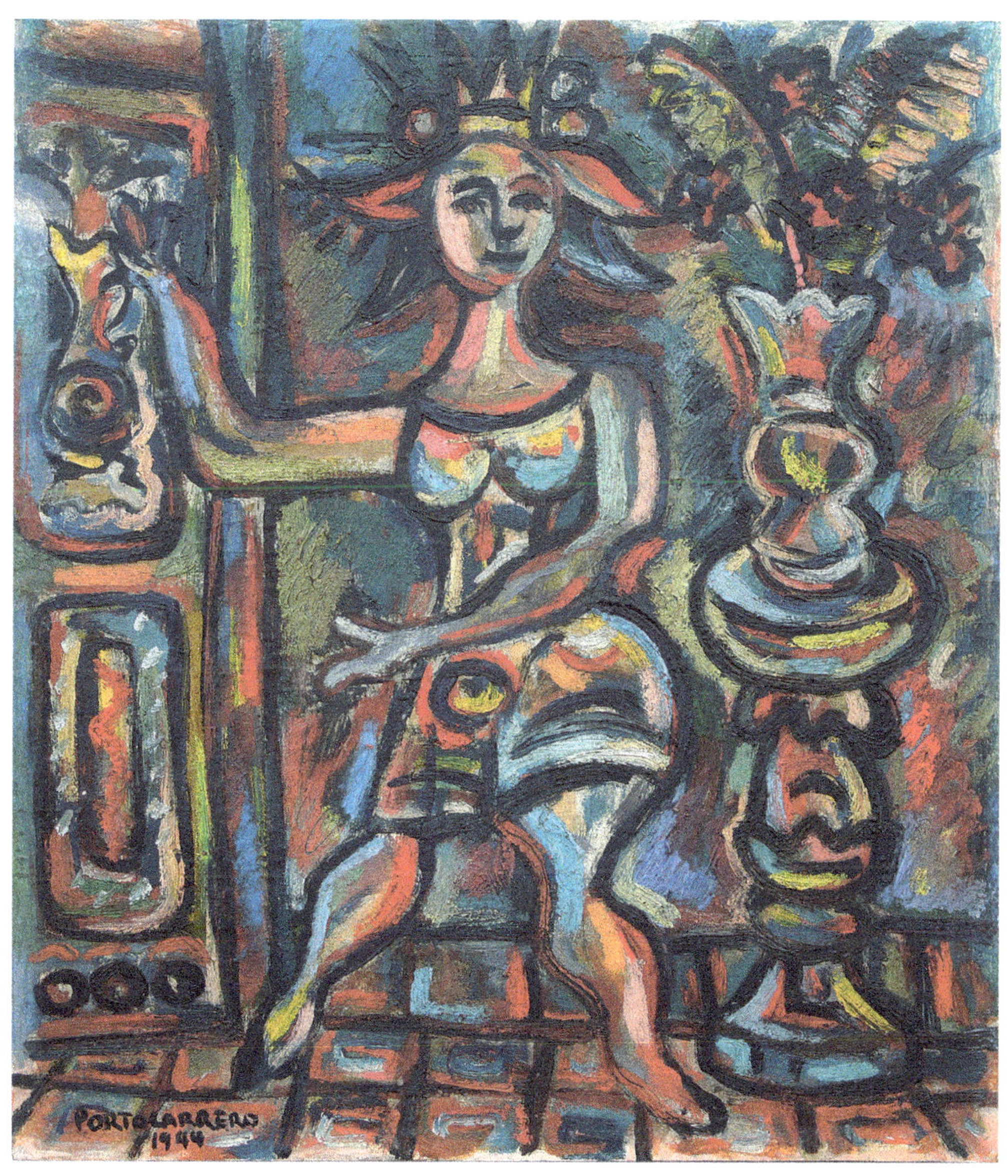

Plate 17. René Portocarrero, *Interior del Cerro con figura danzante* (*Cerro Interior with Dancing Figure*), 1944. Oil on wood, 18 × 15⅝ inches. In Cernuda Arte, *Important Cuban Artworks*, Volume 14. Miami: Cernuda Arte, 2016.

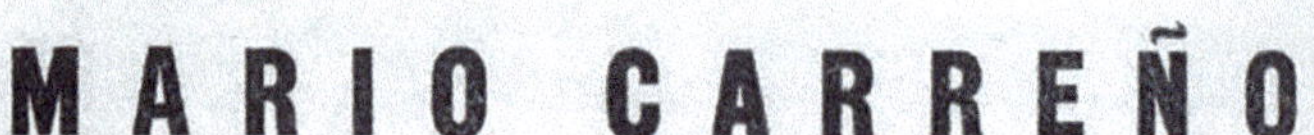

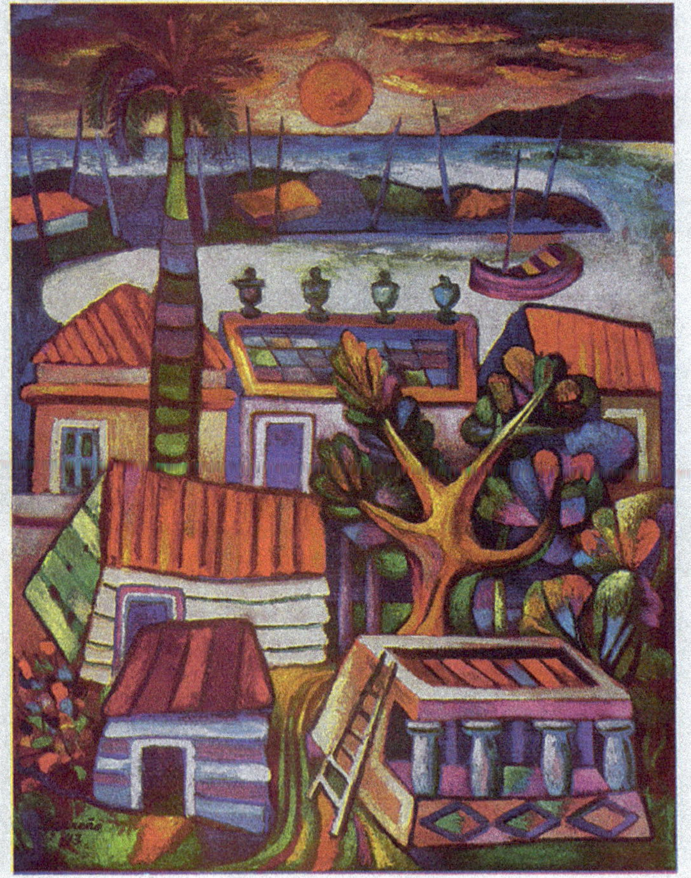

Plate 18. Cover of *Mario Carreño*, 1941. Catalogue for a one-person exhibition at Perls Galleries, New York, March 13 to April 15, 1944. In Cernuda Arte, *Important Cuban Artworks*, Volume 14. Miami: Cernuda Arte, 2016.

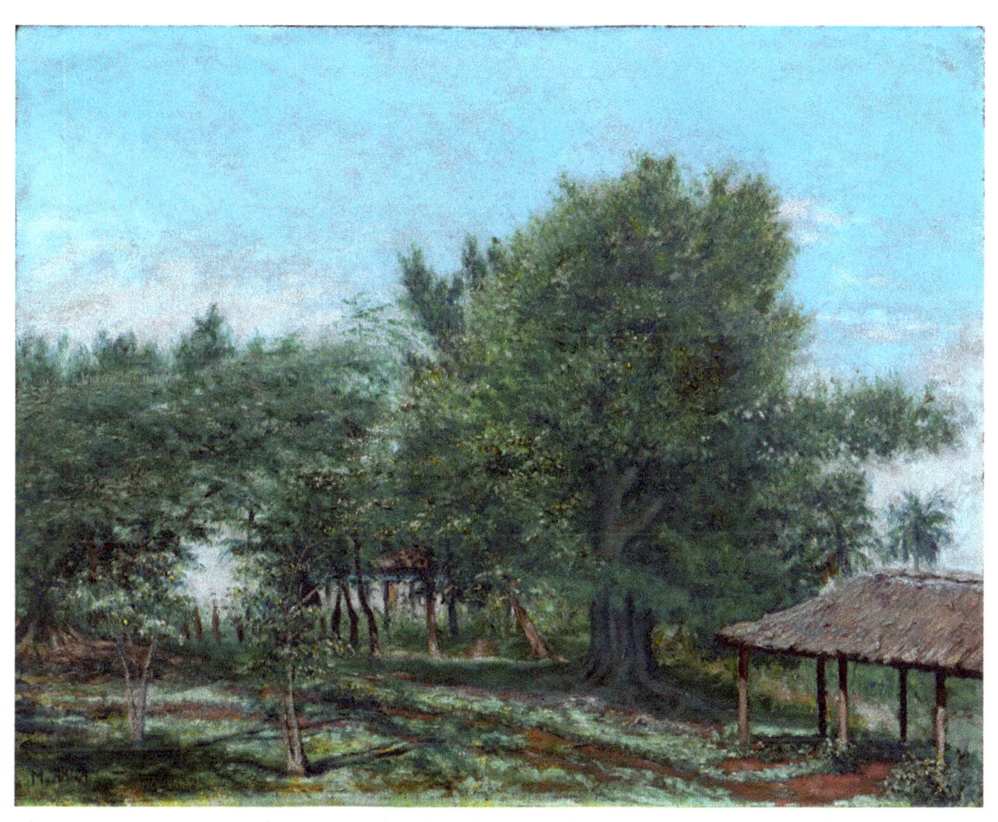

Plate 19. María Ariza y Delance, *Patio* (*Backyard*), 1931. Oil on canvas, 16¾ × 20¼ inches. Courtesy of Cernuda Arte, Coral Gables, FL.

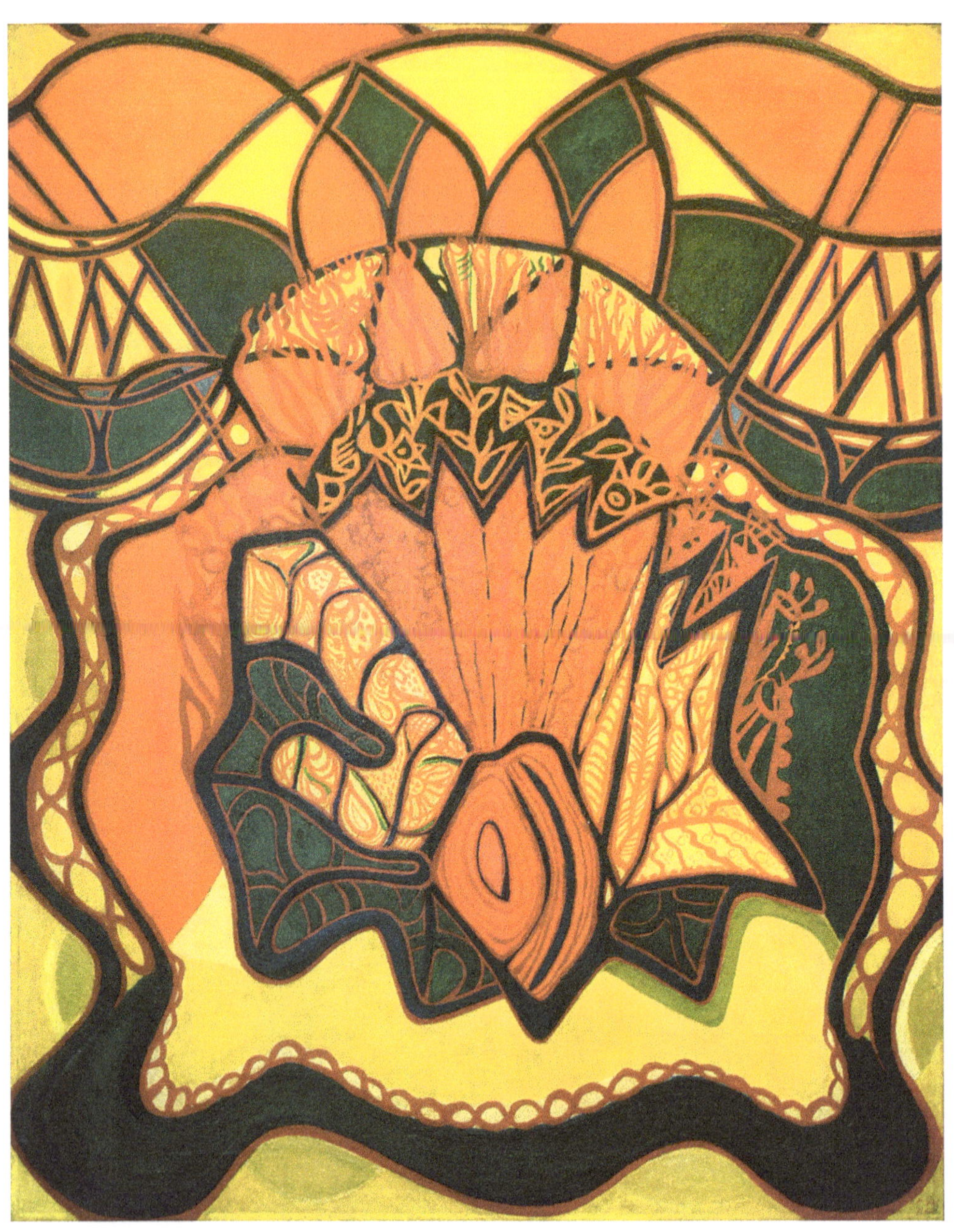

Plate 20. Amelia Peláez, *Sin título* (*Untitled*), 1950. Oil on canvas, 45 × 34¾ inches. Private collection, Coral Gables, FL.

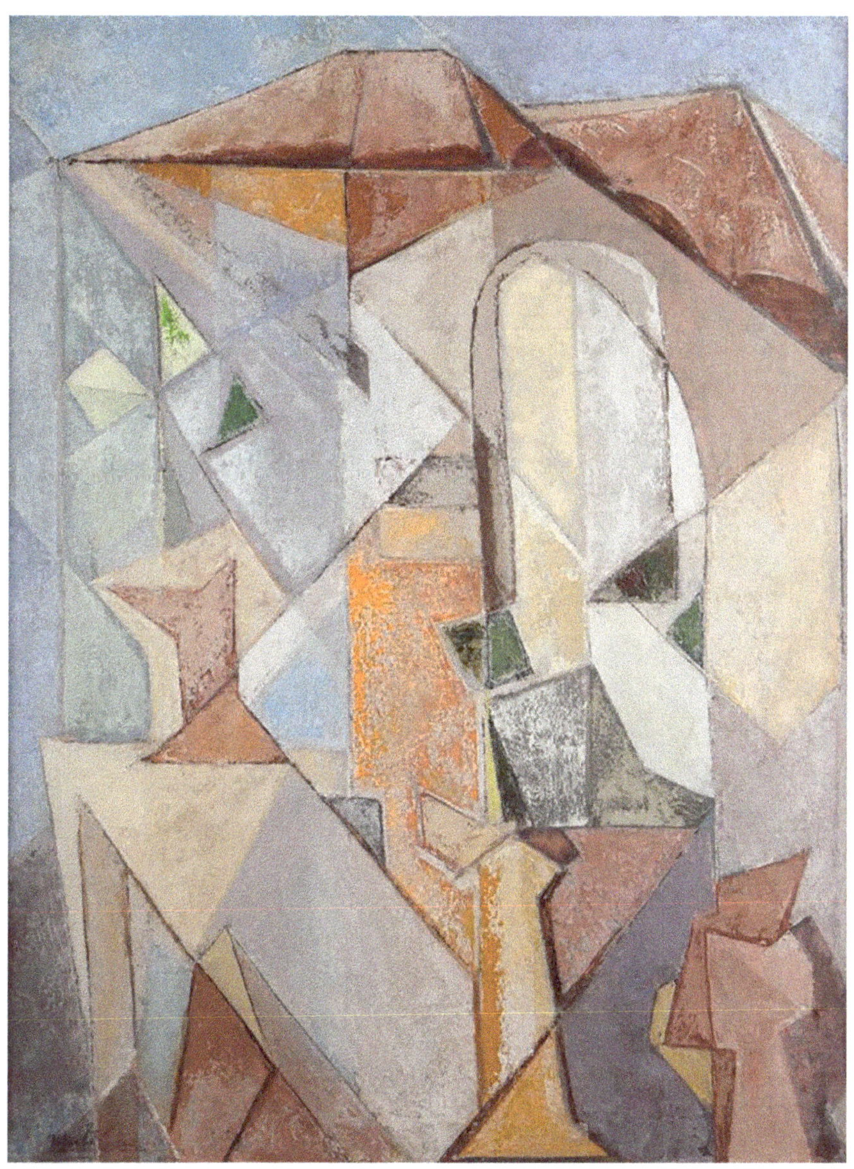

Plate 21. Mirta Cerra, *Balcón* (*Balcony*), 1953. Oil on canvas, 33 × 25 inches. Darlene M. and Jorge M. Pérez Art Collection at FIU, Frost Art Museum, Miami.

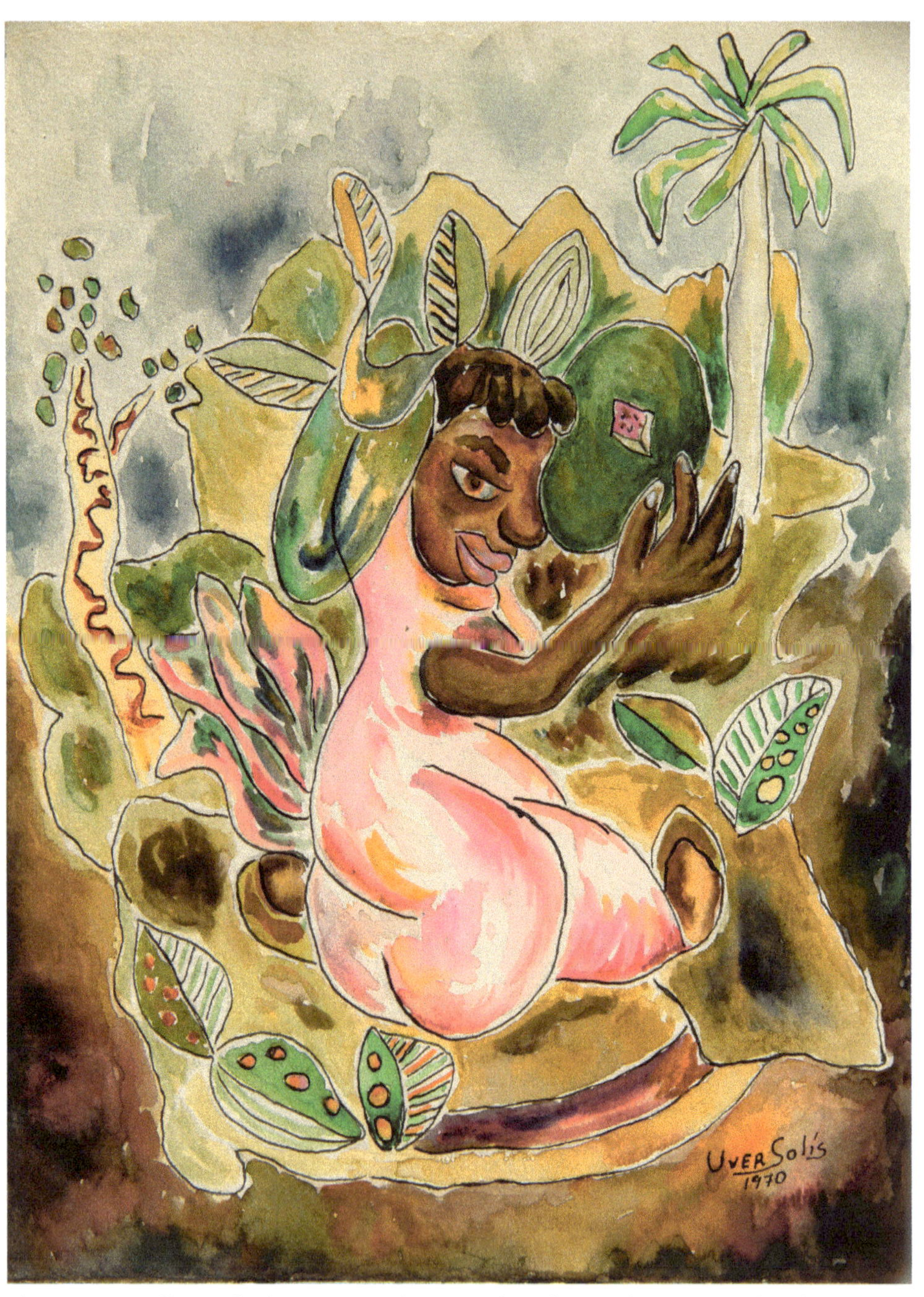

Plate 22. Uver Solís, *Muchacha con mango* (*Young Lady with Mango*), 1970. Mixed media on heavy paper laid down on board, 13½ × 9¾ inches. Private collection, Coral Gables, FL.

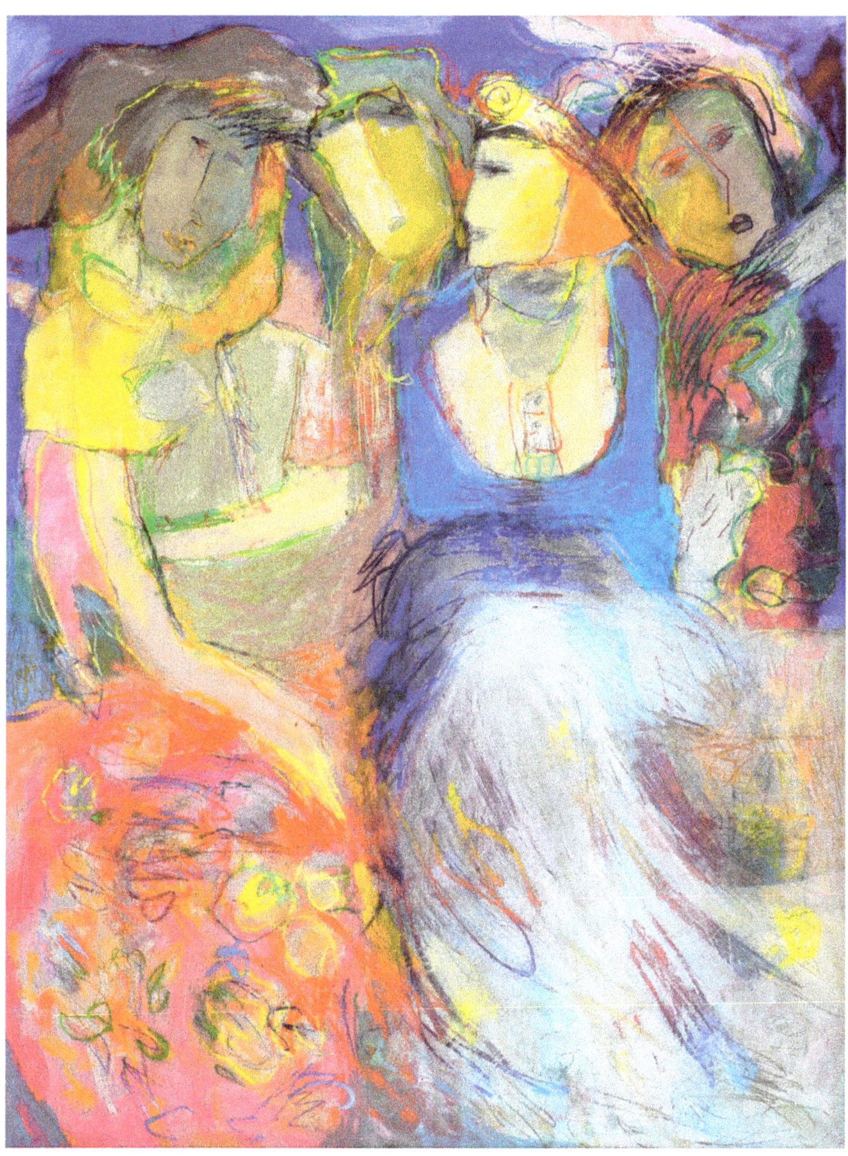

Plate 23. Gina Pellón, *Manipulaciones sin fronteras* (*Manipulations without Borders*), 1986. Mixed media on canvas, 74½ × 55 inches. Courtesy of the Gina Pellón Estate.

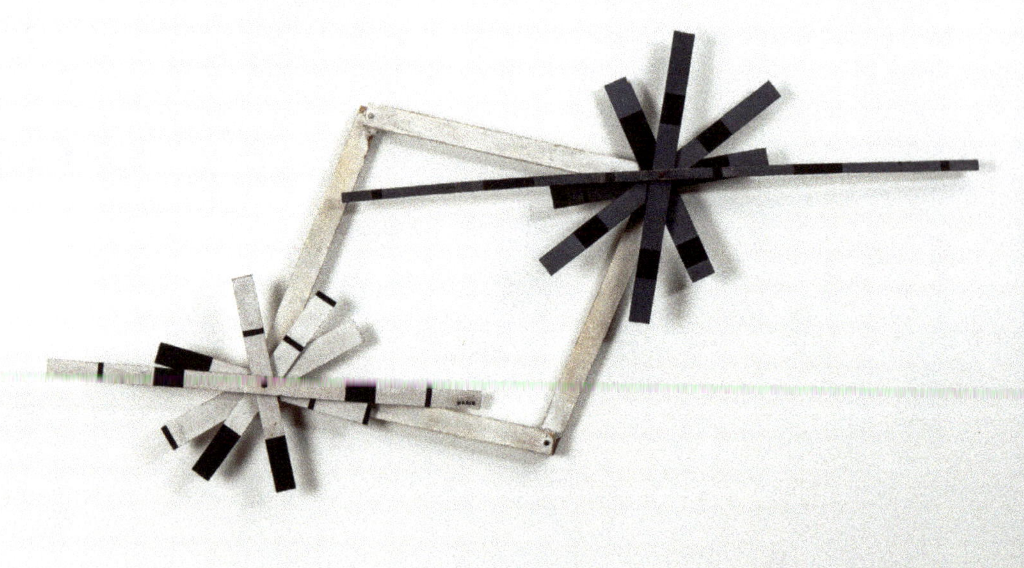

Plate 24. Sandú Darié, *Untitled, Estructura transformable* (*Transformable Structure*), ca. 1950s. Mixed media. Variable measurements, approx. 38 × 31 inches. Location unknown.

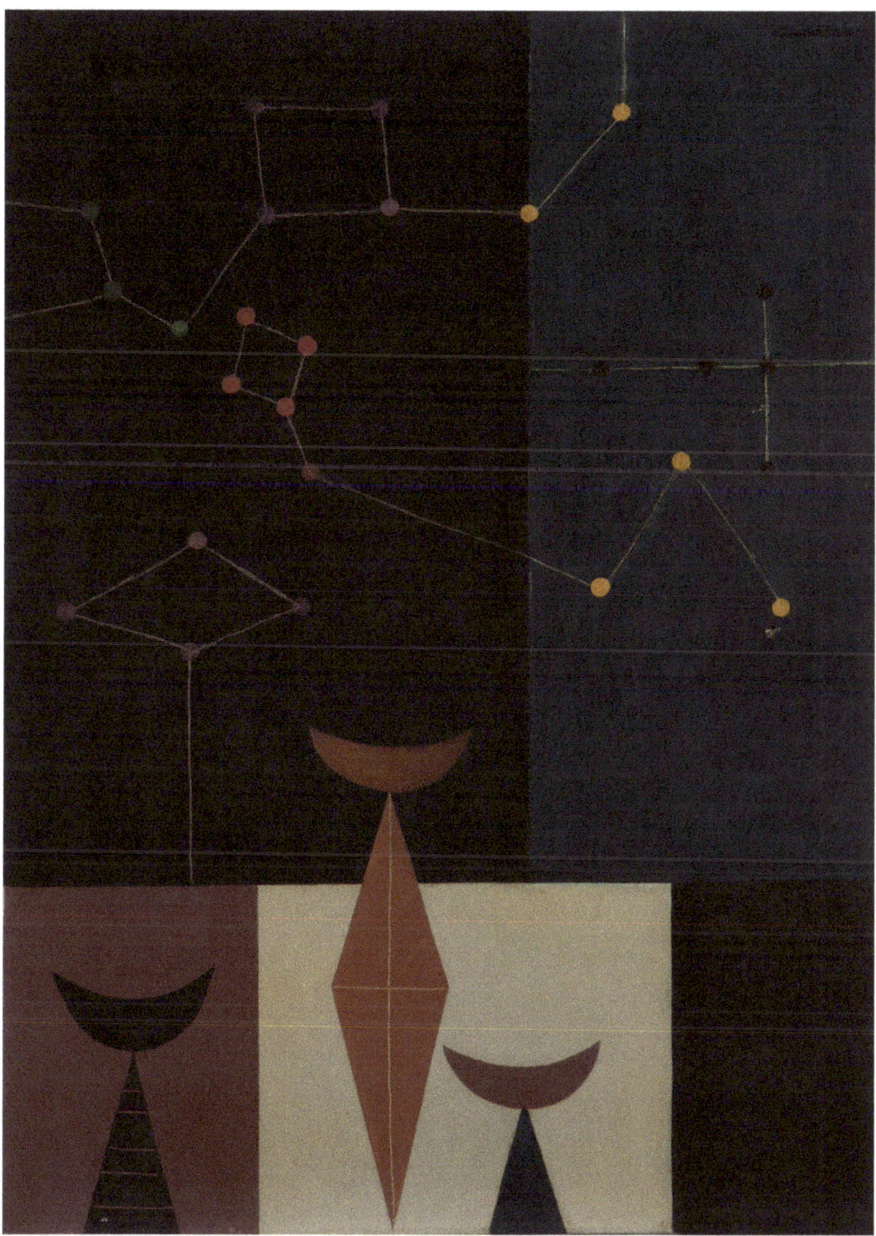

Plate 25. Mario Carreño, *Cielos del sur* (*Southern Skies*), 1950. Oil on canvas, 34 × 24 inches.

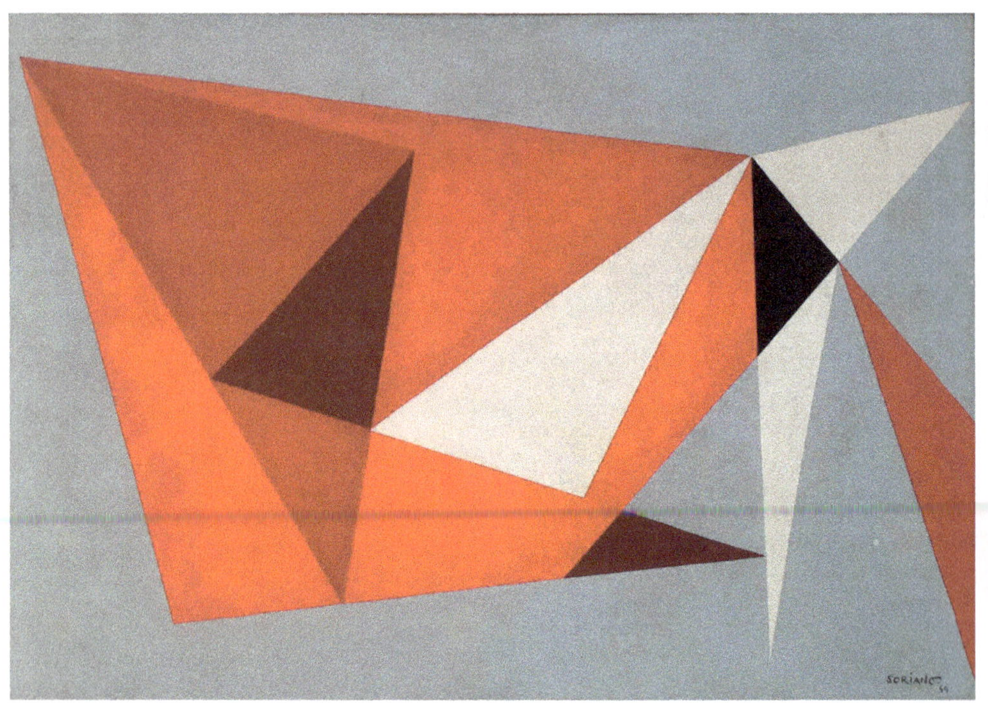

Plate 26. Rafael Soriano, *Composición* (*Composition*), 1959. Oil on canvas, 28⅕ × 39½ inches. The Brillembourg Capriles Collection.

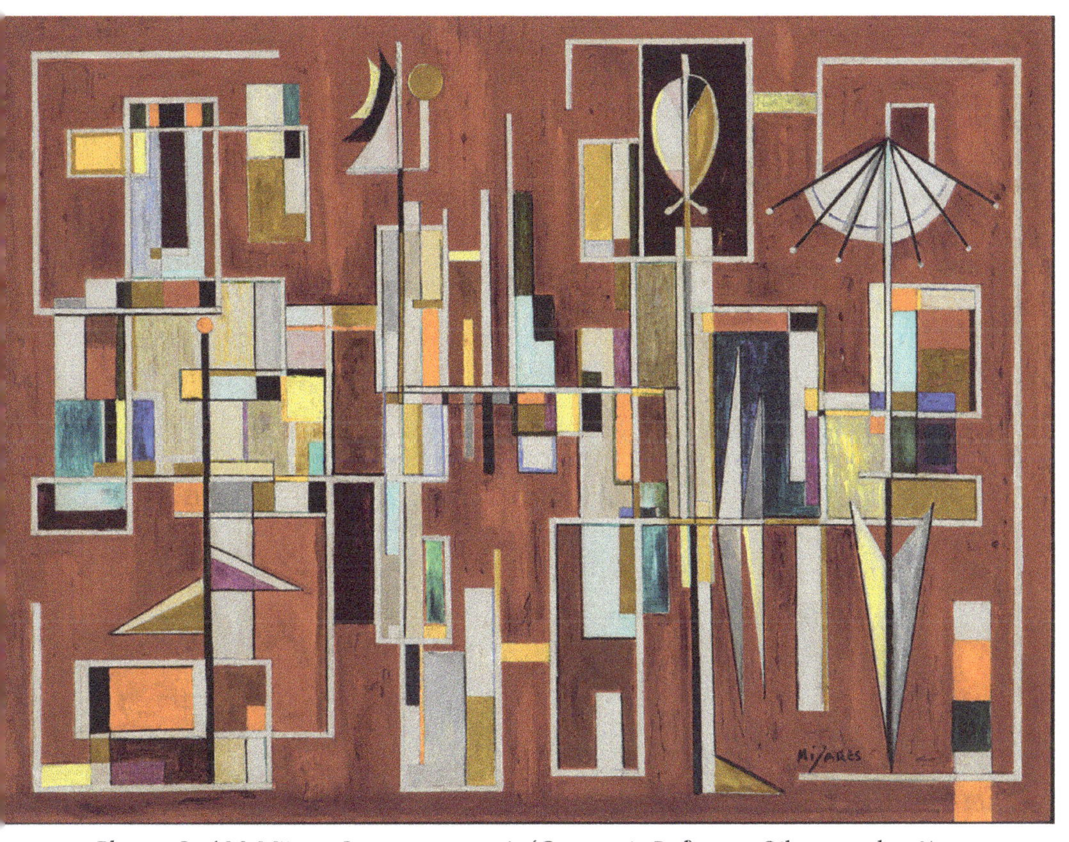

Plate 27. José M. Mijares, *Lo concreto en rojo* (*Concrete in Red*), 1954. Oil on wood, 26¾ × 35 inches. Eigier Collection, New York.

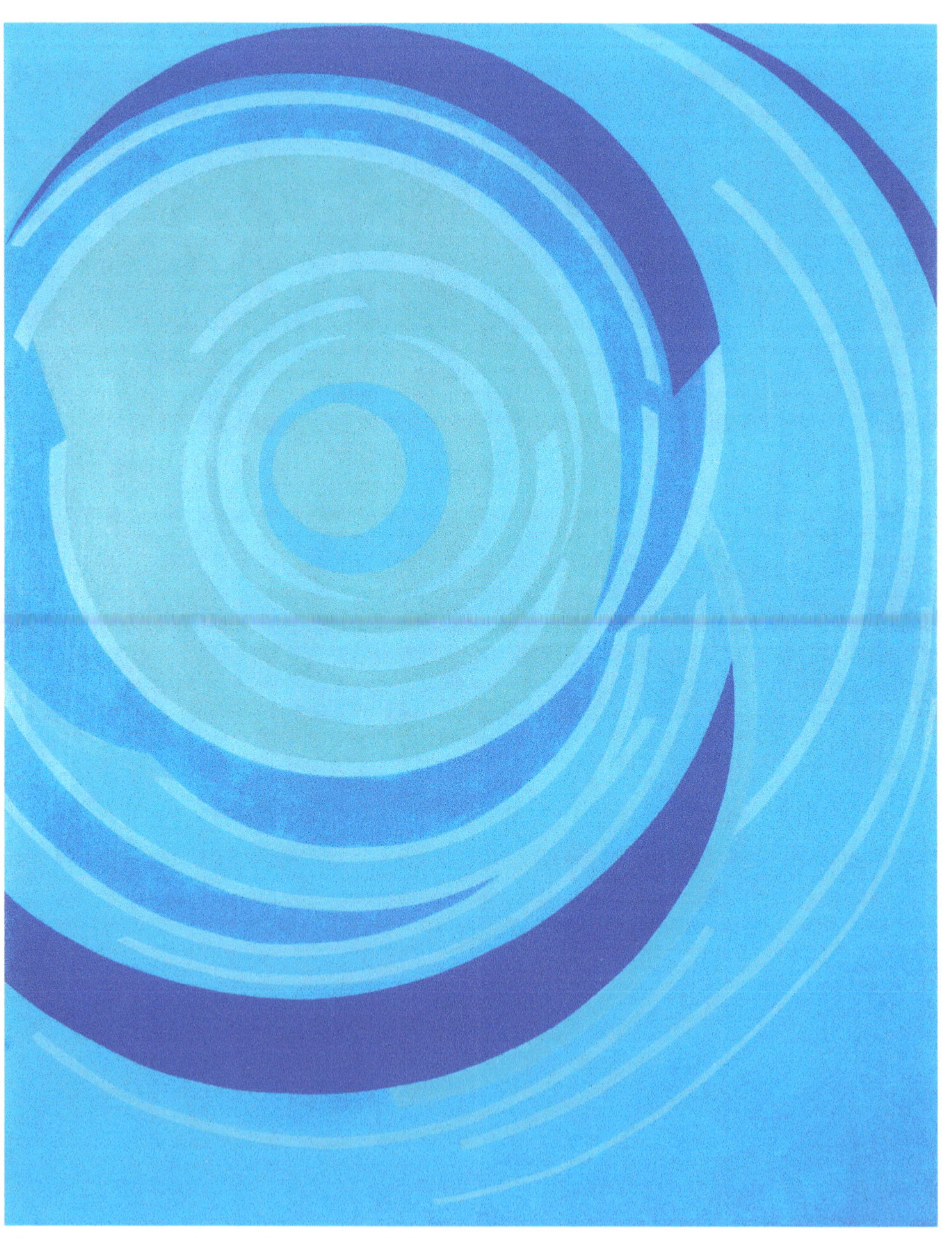

Plate 28. Luis Martínez Pedro, *Untitled*, from the series *Aguas territoriales* (*Territorial Waters*), 1964. Oil on canvas, 40 × 31 inches. Location unknown.

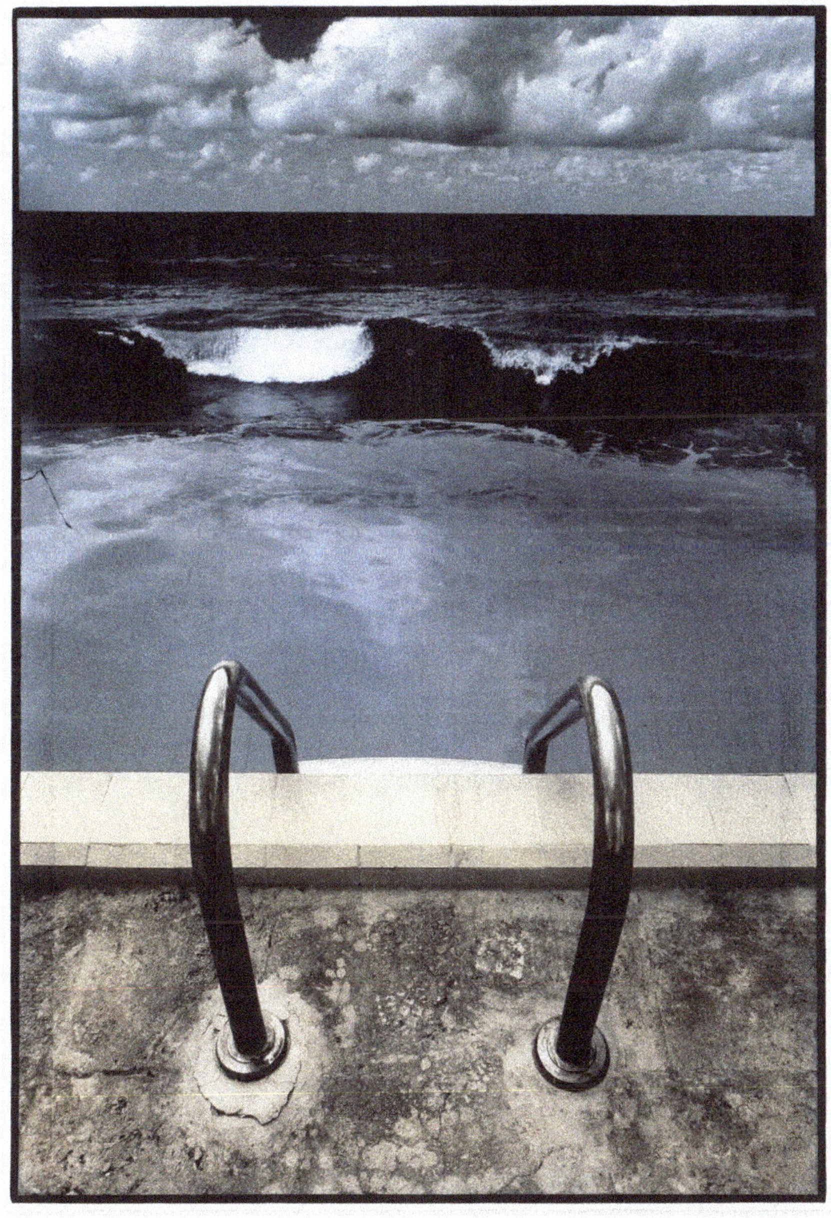

Plate 29. Rogelio López-Marín (Gory), from the series *It's Only Water in a Stranger's Tear*, 1986–2001. Toned gelatin silver print. Courtesy of Lehigh University Art Galleries.

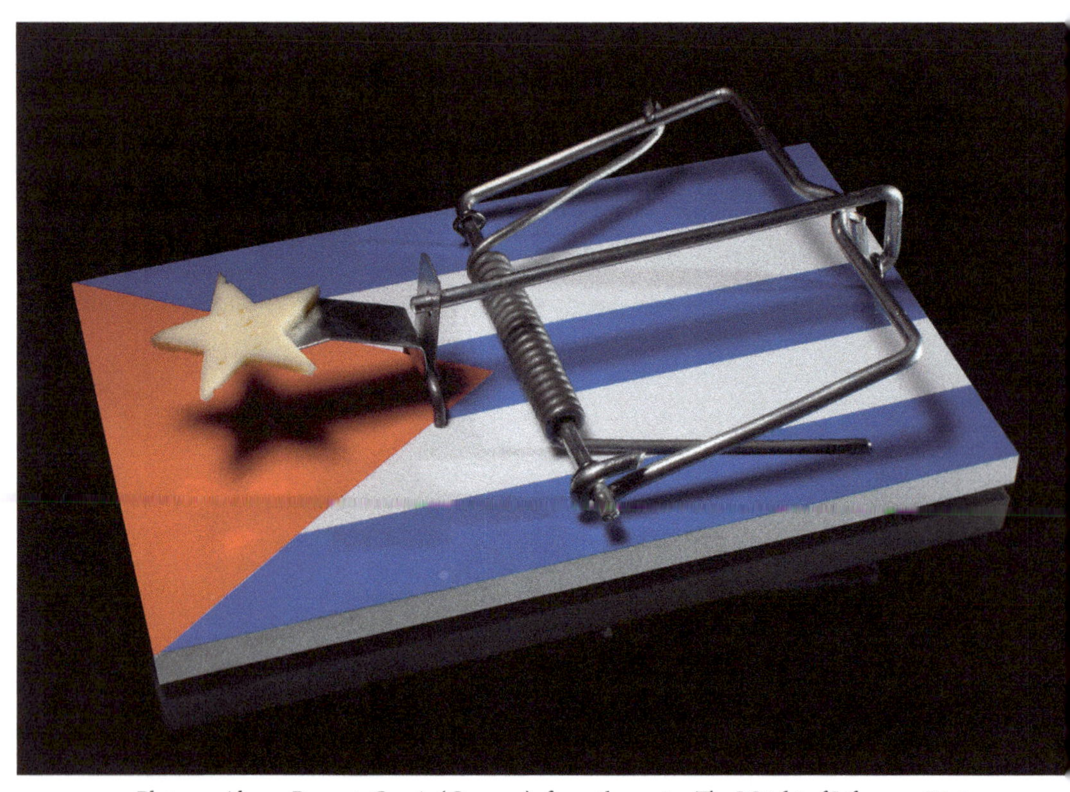

Plate 30. Alvaro Brunet, *Coraje* (*Courage*), from the series *The Weight of Life*, 2011. Digital print. Courtesy of the artist.

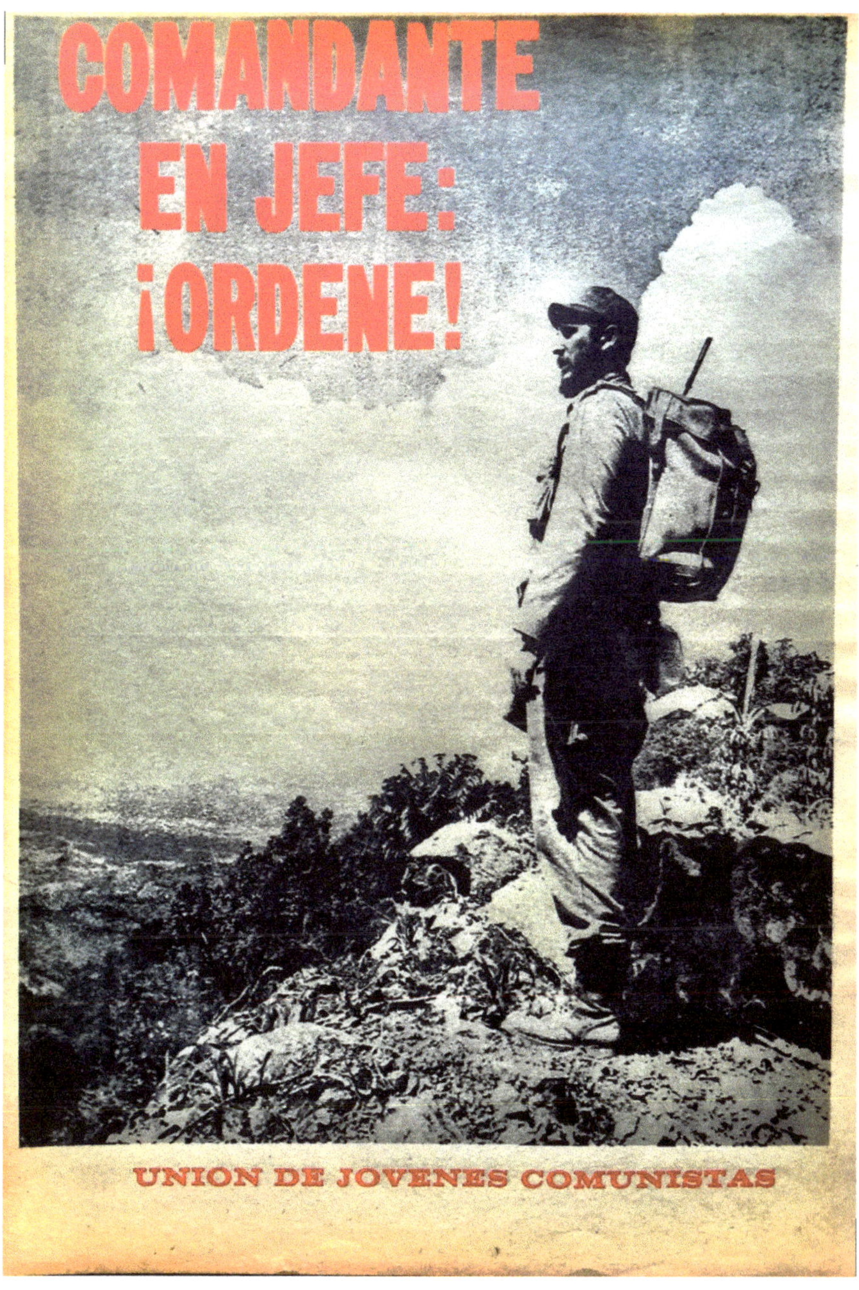

Plate 31. Juan Ayús, designer, *Comandante en jefe: ¡ordene!* (*Commander in Chief, Give Your Orders!*), photograph by Alberto Korda, 1962. Poster designed for the Young Communists Union. Ramiro A. Fernández's revolutionary ephemera collection. Photograph courtesy of Ramiro A. Fernández.

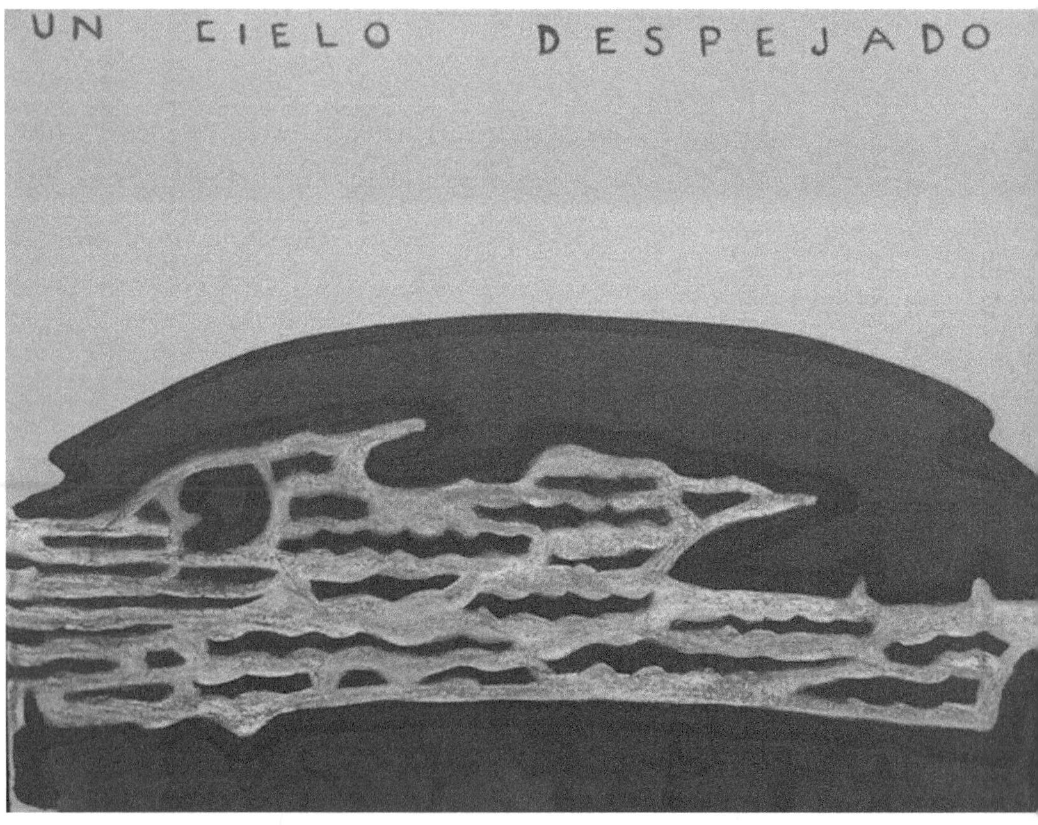

Plate 32. Carlos Rodríguez Cárdenas, *Un cielo despejado* (*A Clear Sky*), 1988. Acrylic on canvas, 16 × 20½ inches. Photograph courtesy of Carlos Rodríguez Cárdenas.

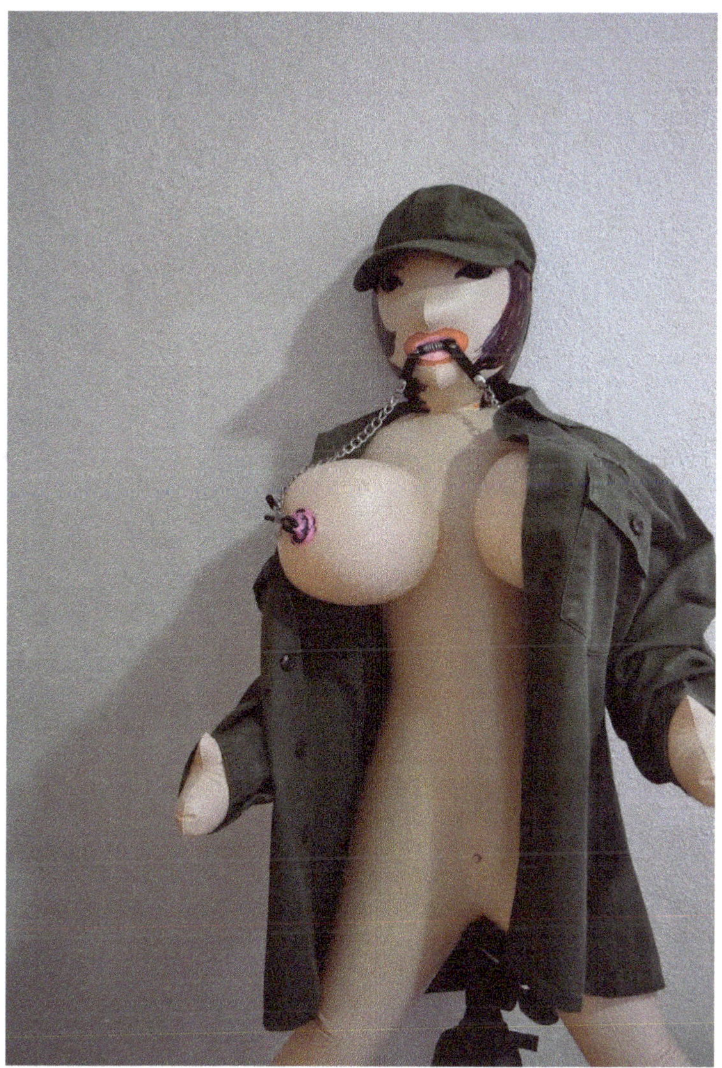

Plate 33. Aldo Menéndez, visual documentation of a performance, 2015. Posted in the blog *Castor Jabao*. Photograph courtesy of Aldo Menéndez.

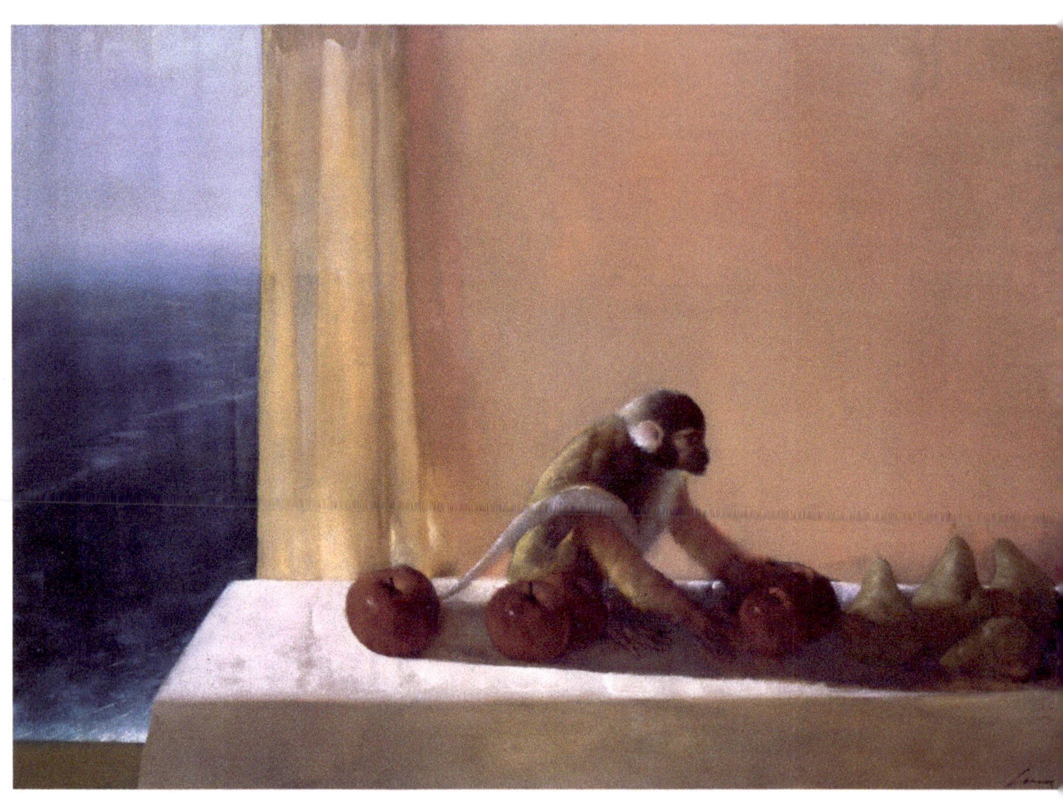

Plate 34. Julio Larraz, *The Intruder*, 1977. Oil on canvas, 44 × 60 inches. © 1989 Julio Larraz. Reproduced with permission of the Saskia Larraz Collection.

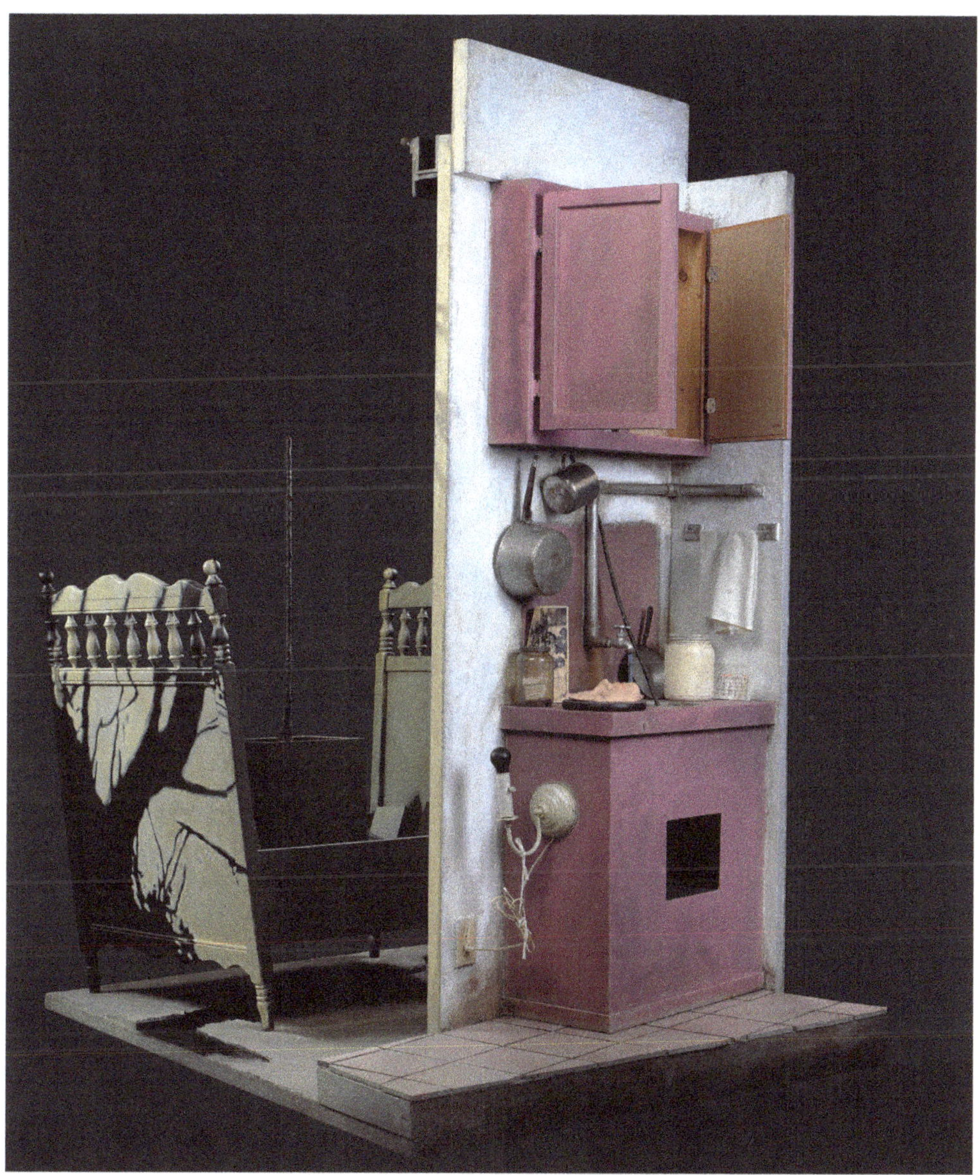

Plate 35. María Brito, *El patio de mi casa* (*The Backyard of My House*), 1990. Mixed media including acrylic paint, wood, wax, latex, gelatin silver prints, and found objects, 95½ × 68¼ × 65 inches. Smithsonian American Art Museum, Museum purchase through the Smithsonian Institution Collections Acquisition Program, Washington, DC.

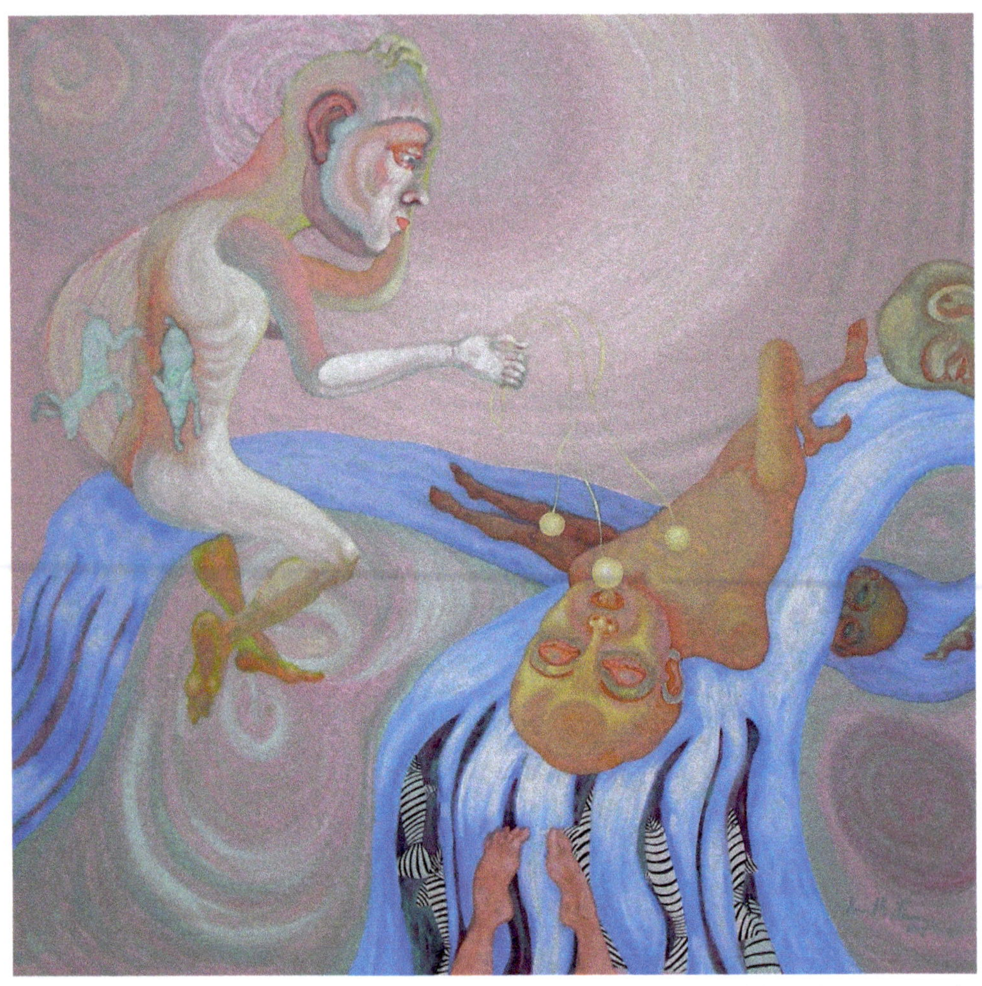

Plate 36. Ana Albertina Delgado, *La coronación del cuerpo* (*The Coronation of the Body*), 2009. Acrylic on canvas, 40 × 40 inches. Courtesy of the artist.

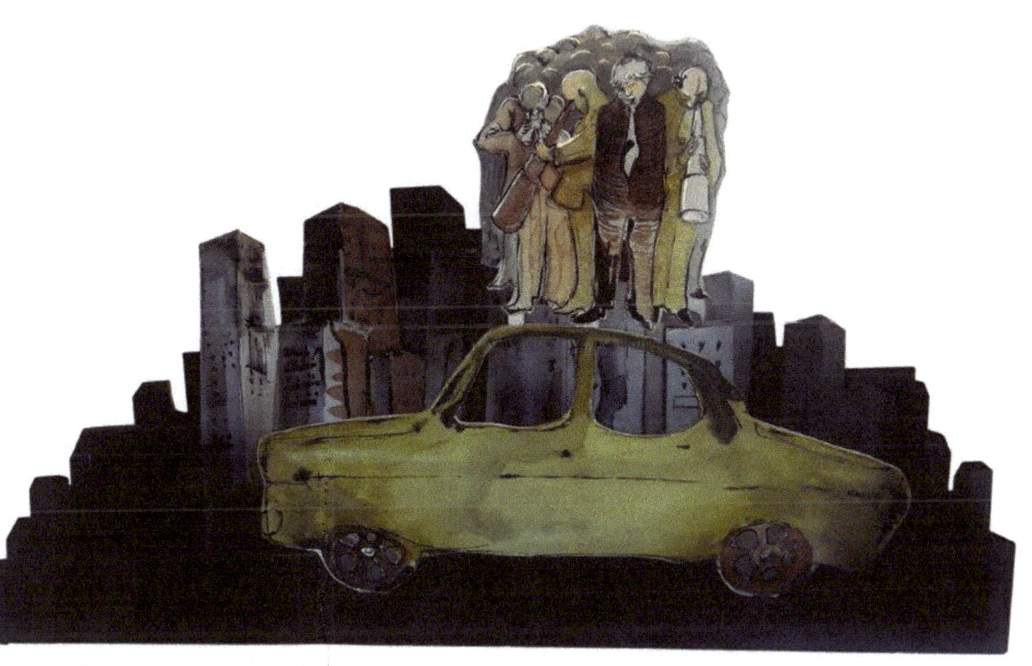

Plate 37. Rigoberto Rosales Jalil, *Where Are You, My Love?*, 2016. From the series *Sirena de tierra adentro* (*Mermaid from Inland*). Acrylic paint and Cuban coffee on wood, 19½ (h) × 31½ × 7½ inches. © Rigoberto Rosales Jalil. Courtesy of the artist.

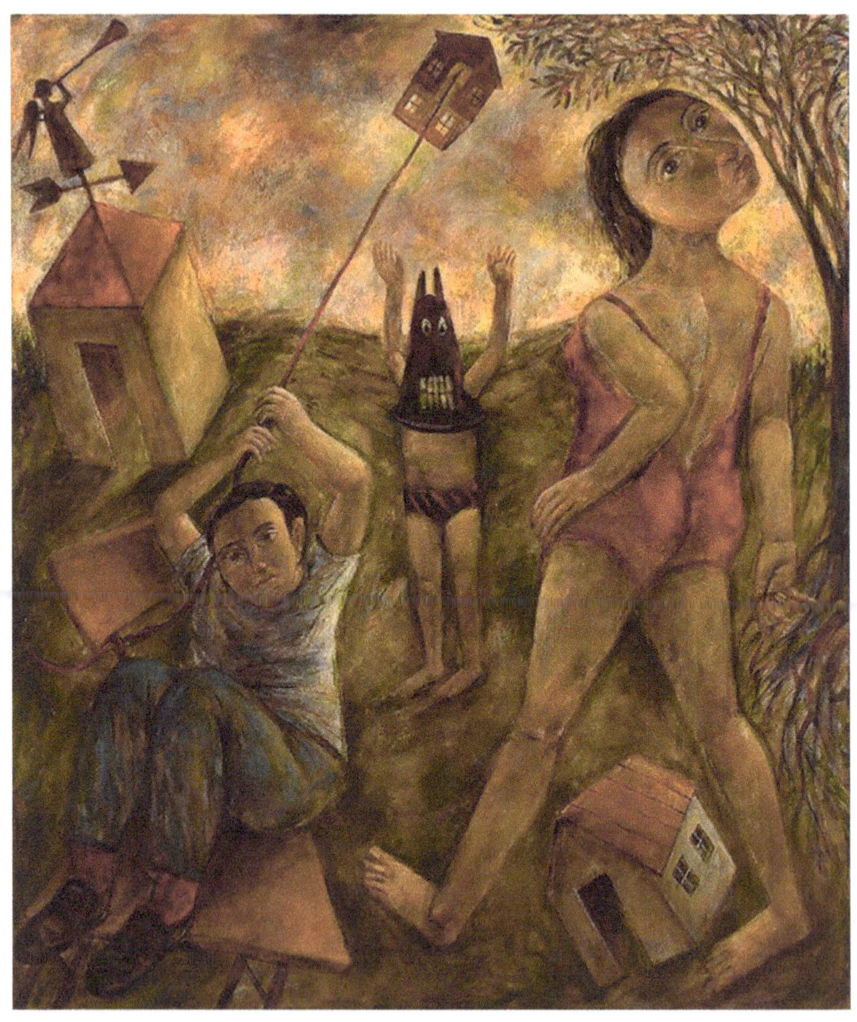

Plate 38. Arturo Rodríguez, *Sin título* (*Untitled*) from the series, *La tempestad* (*The Tempest*), 1998. Oil on canvas, 62 × 38 inches. Smithsonian American Art Museum, Washington, DC.

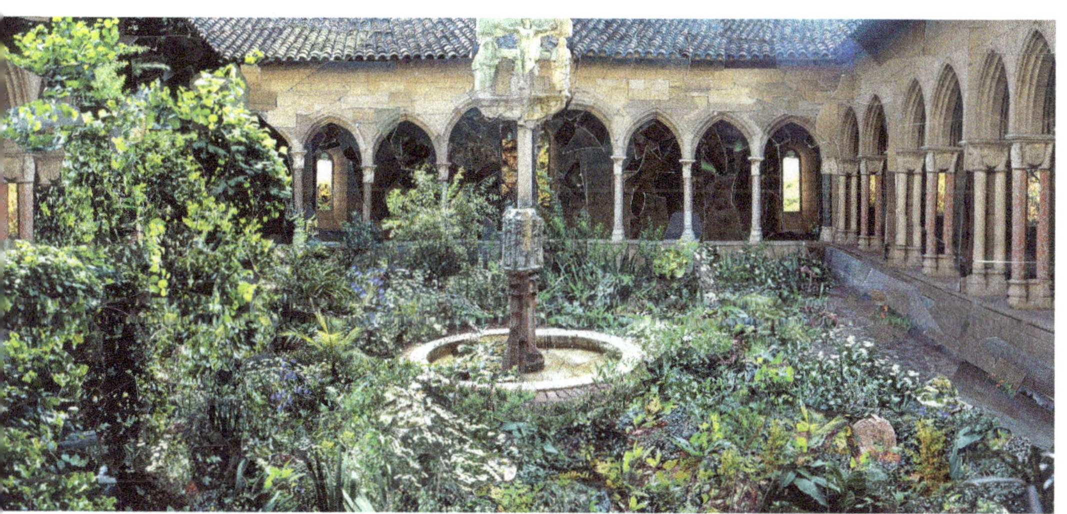

Plate 39. Jake Fernandez, *Trie Garden Cloisters 3*, ca. 2000. Collage, 7 × 15 inches. Private collection. © 2017 JakeFernandez.

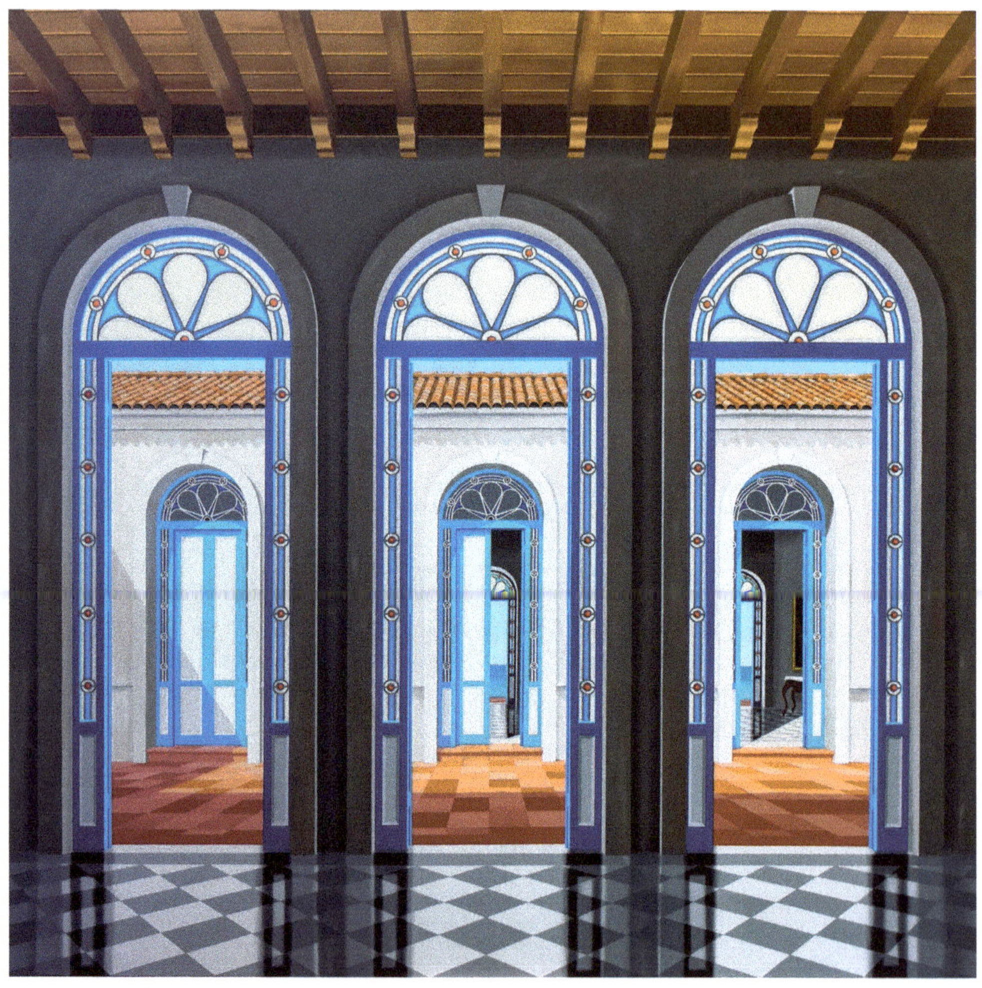

Plate 40. Humberto Calzada, *La tradición* (*Tradition*), 2017. Acrylic on canvas, 60 × 60 inches. Courtesy of the artist.

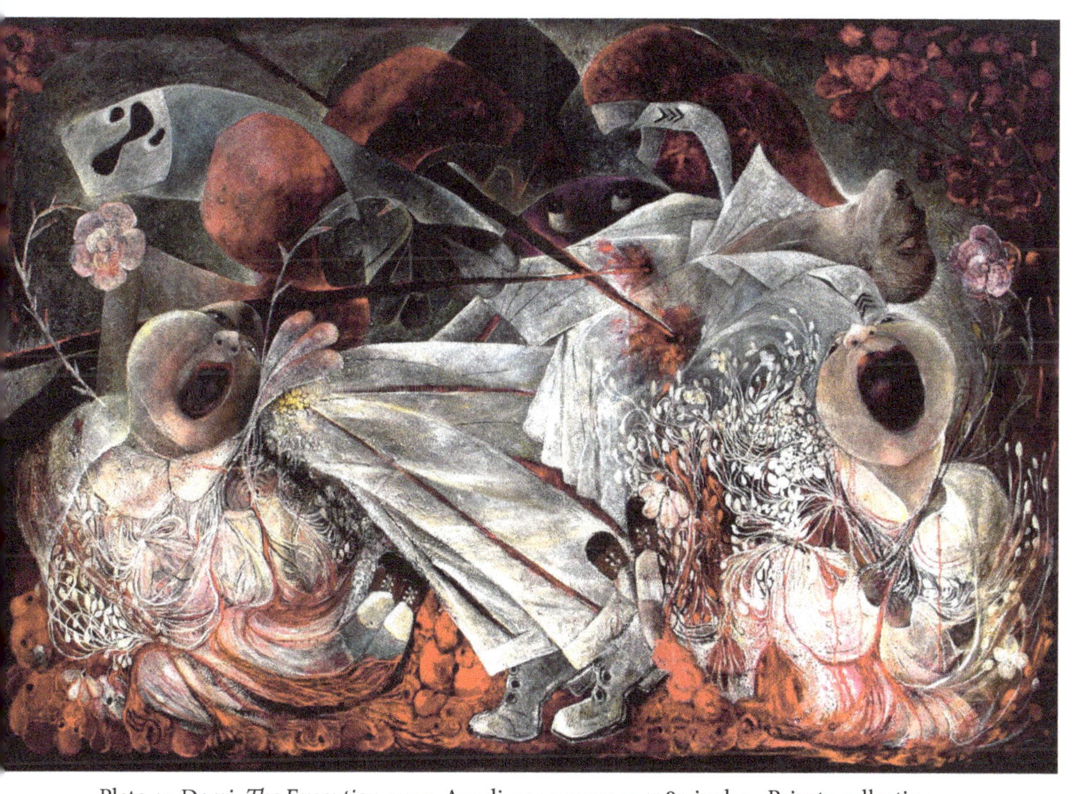

Plate 41. Demi, *The Execution*, 2014. Acrylic on canvas, 55 × 80 inches. Private collection.

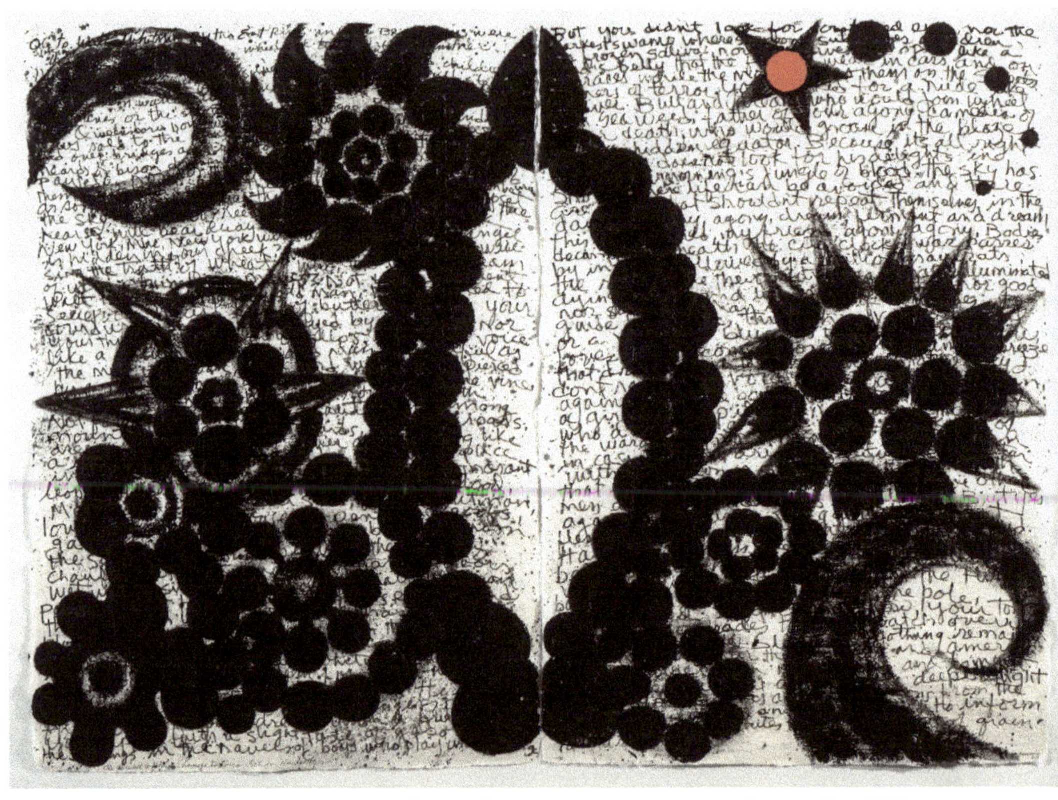

Plate 42. Mario Bencomo, *Ode to Whitman, Homage to Lorca, Poet in New York*, 2013. Acrylic and ink on paper, 38 × 50½ inches. Ms. Ana Bermúdez Collection. Photograph courtesy of Don Queralto.

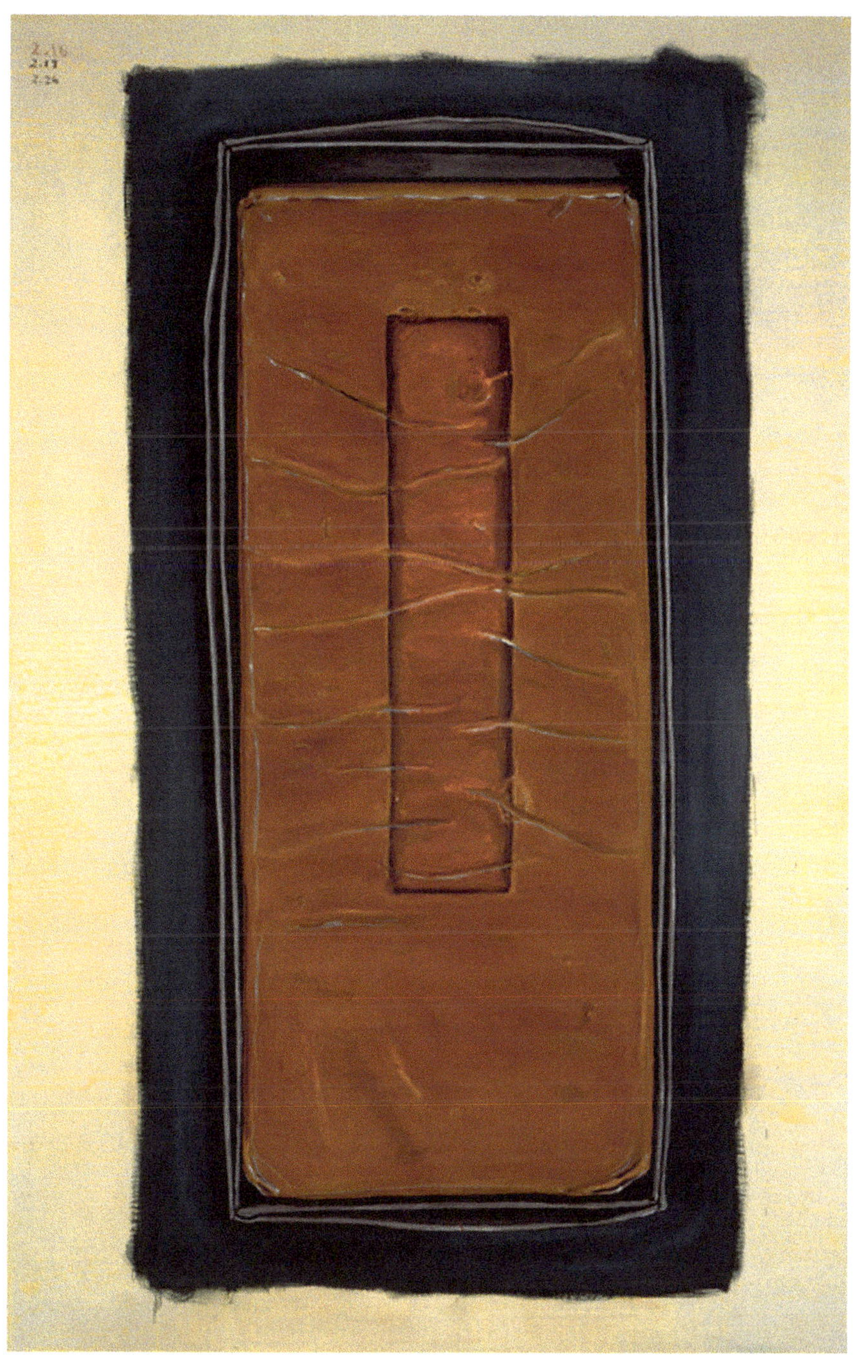

Plate 43. Alberto Rey, *Icon Series: Ancel Guava Paste*, 1993–95. Oils on plaster, 96 × 48 × 4 inches. Fort Lauderdale Museum of Art, Fort Lauderdale, FL.

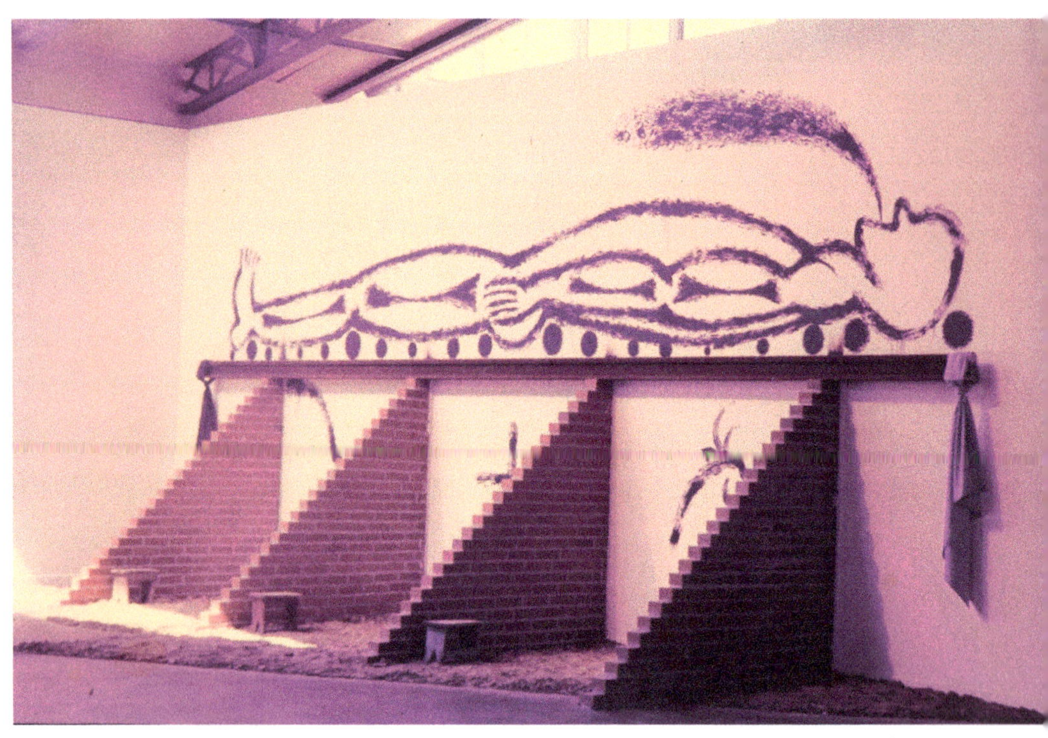

Plate 44. José Bedia, *Vive en la línea* (*He Lives on the Railroad Line*), 1989. Artist's collection. Courtesy of the artist.

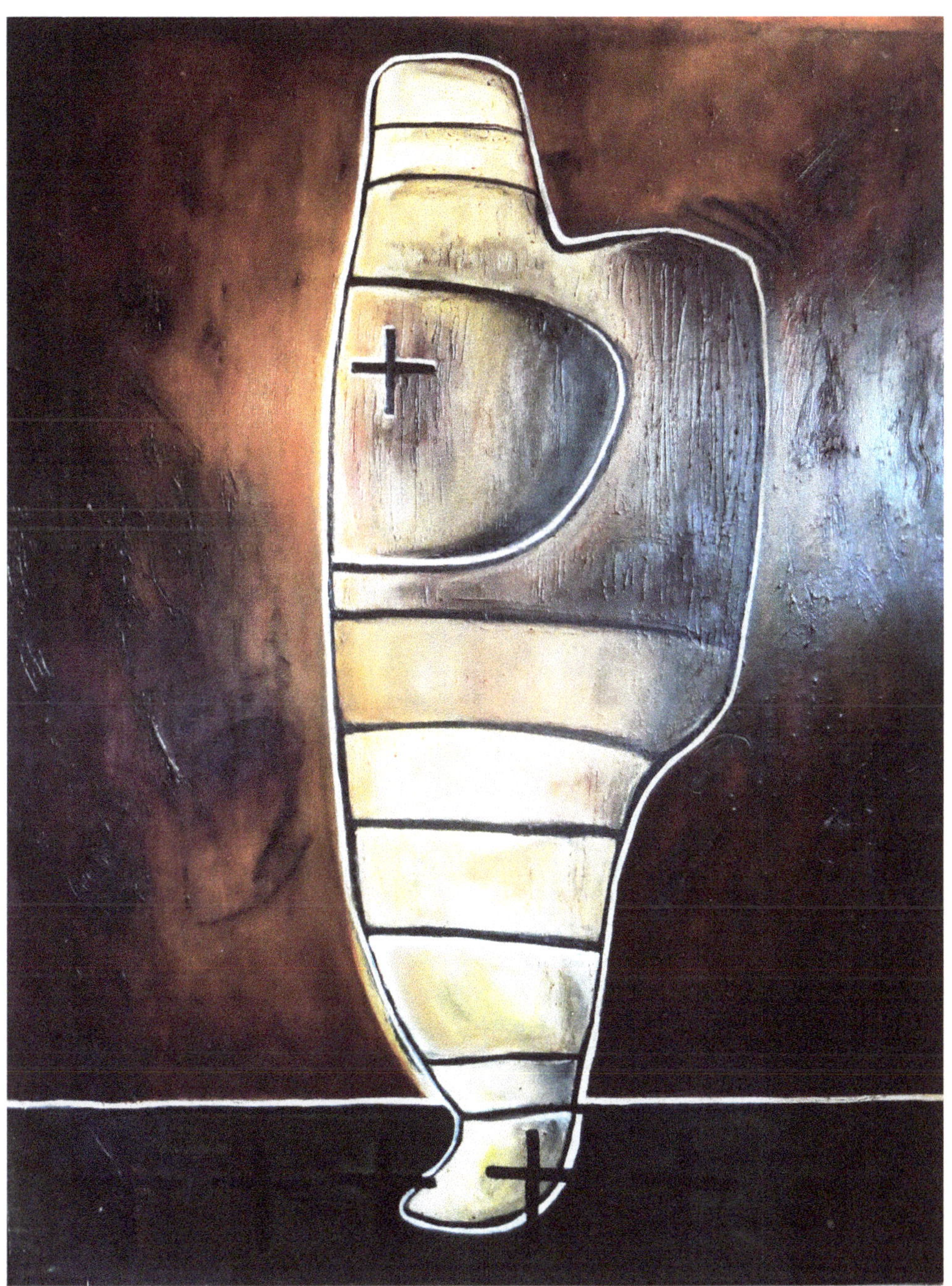

Plate 45. Angela Valella, *Deminan*, 1999. Private collection. Courtesy of the artist.

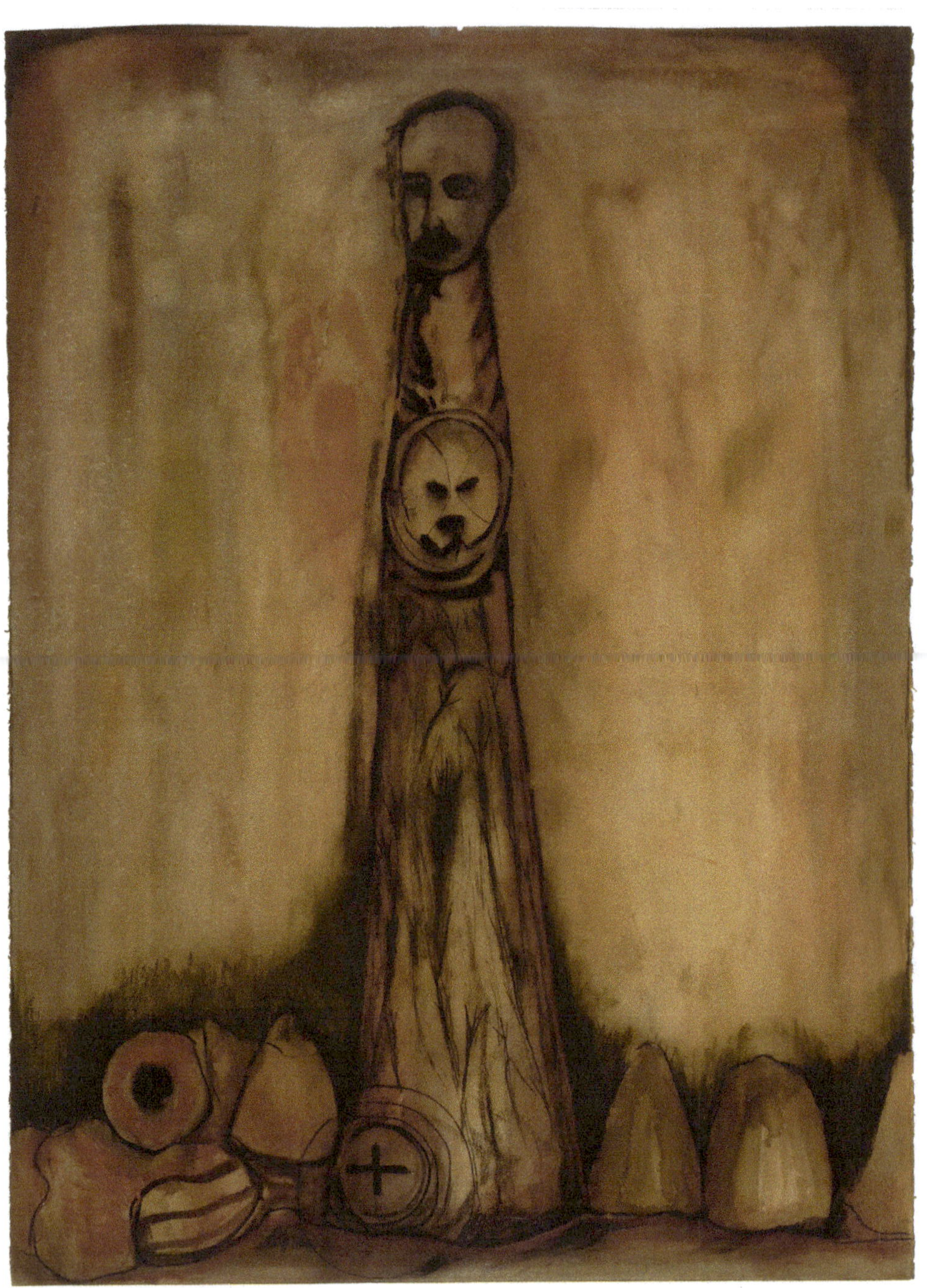

Plate 46. Angela Valella, *The Idol*, 1999. Private collection. Courtesy of the artist.

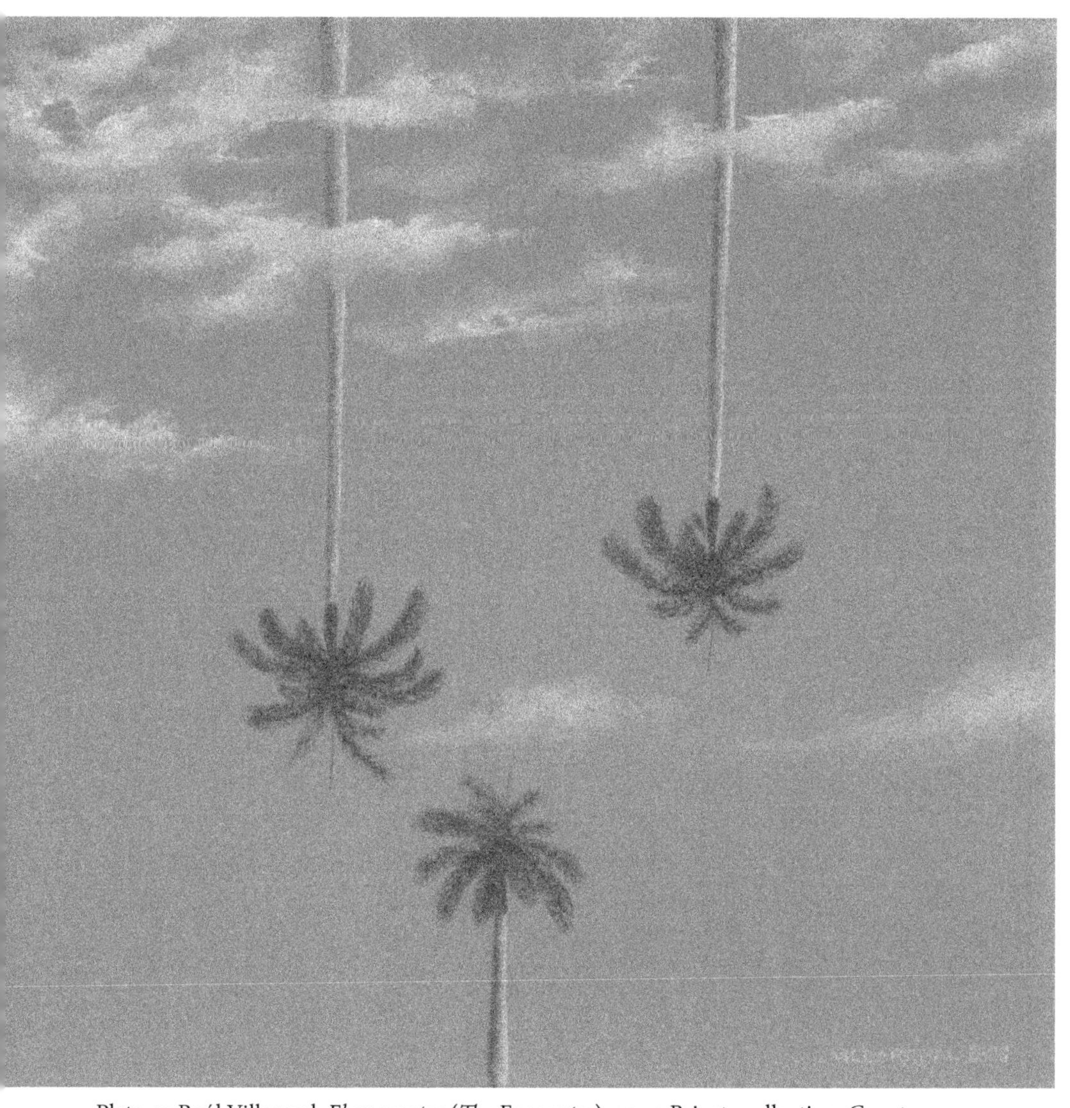

Plate 47. Raúl Villarreal, *El encuentro* (*The Encounter*), 2005. Private collection. Courtesy of the artist.

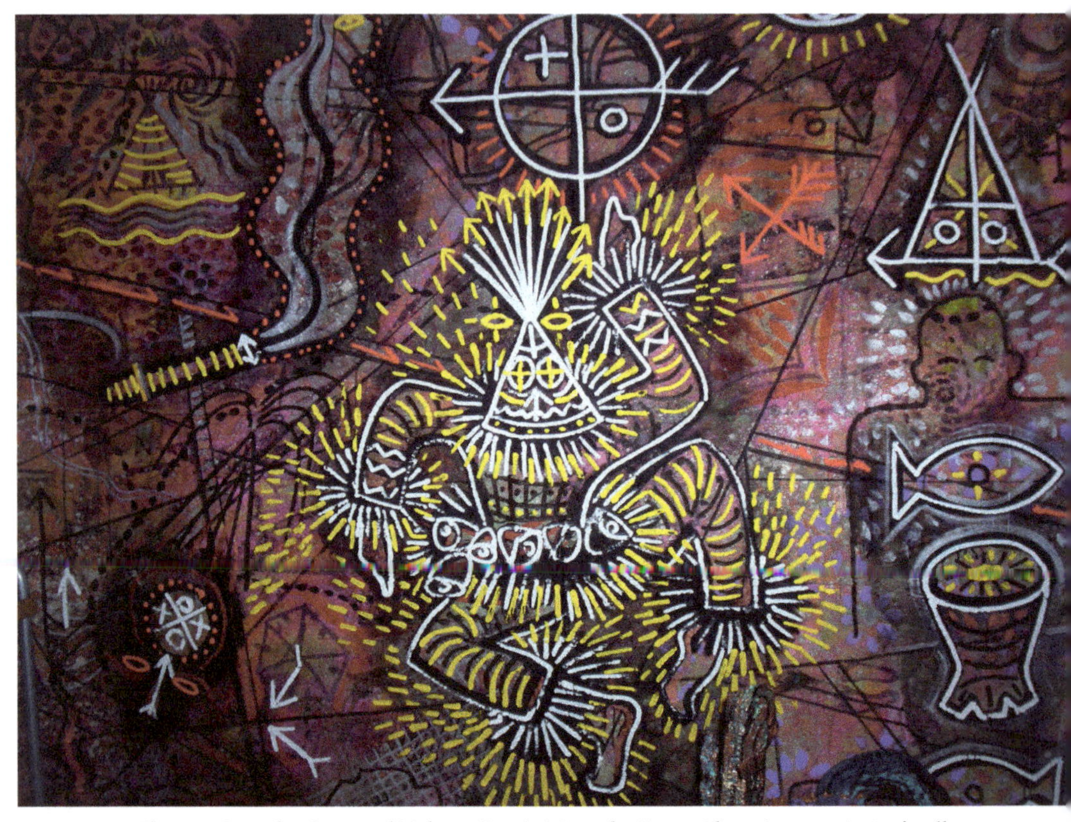

Plate 48. Leandro Soto and Nelson García Miranda, *Ireme Abacuá*, 2005. Artists' collection. Courtesy of the artists.

Allow me to express my preferences regarding the painters and sculptors of this generation, and to list my top twelve creators from this group:

1. Mario Carreño
2. Mariano Rodríguez (1912–90)
3. René Portocarrero
4. Cundo Bermúdez
5. Luis Martínez Pedro
6. Alfredo Lozano (1913–97)
7. Raúl Milián (1914–84)
8. José Mijares (1921–2004)
9. Roberto Diago (1920–55)
10. Roberto Estopiñán (1921–2015)
11. Mirta Cerra
12. Felipe Orlando (1911–2001)

These second-generation Cuban avant-garde artists were born between 1910 and 1921. They arrived at the scene at a moment when, fortunately, Modern art had tenuously secured a foothold in Havana, thanks to the groundbreaking efforts of the first generation. The formative process of the younger artists was somewhat different: less formal schooling at the San Alejandro Academy (except for Mijares, Cerra, Diago, and Estopiñán, who completed their studies at the academy); more self-study and observation of the creations of the prior generation; familiarity with European artistic output, but less travel to the war-torn continent; curiosity about the Mexican Renaissance and trips to that country to study the experience.

Their presentation in Havana's artistic circles was gradual, and not as dramatic as the 1927 event. Some of the young ones were introduced alongside their elders in the 1937 First Exhibition of Modern Art (Portocarrero, Martínez Pedro, Bermúdez, and Orlando).[6] The following year, the Second National Exhibition of Painting and Sculpting in Old Havana included Cerra, Carreño, and Lozano,[7] while most others joined in the 1940 show, *300 Years of Art in Cuba*, at the University of Havana,[8] or the 1941 *Exhibition of Contemporary Cuban Art*.[9]

The modernist movement also had the support of the Cuban intelligentsia, including its writers, poets, and critics. Two notable critics, José Gómez Sicre and Guy Pérez Cisneros, not only explained the substance of the art to the national audience, but also went farther by presenting the Modern art of Cuba in the international arena, thereby facilitating the second objective of the movement. These two art critics and promoters, along with Domingo Ravenet, a painter and art enthusiast, were principally responsible for the organization of most of the art exhibitions in Havana and those that traveled from Cuba to other countries in the late 1930s and 1940s. In securing the material resources and artworks for these events, they exerted a decisive influence on determining which creators would be identified with and recognized as the preeminent Cuban Modern artists in the local and international markets.

In the 1940s, Cuban Modern art exhibitions took place in Stockholm, Moscow, Guatemala City, Buenos Aires, Lima, Port-au-Prince, Mexico City, and Paris.[10] Since Modern art was still in its infancy in some countries, host museums often received these exhibitions as special events and attracted large crowds.

The alliance between the two generations of painters culminated on March 14, 1944, when the Museum of Modern Art (MoMA) in New York City inaugurated the exhibition *Modern Cuban Painters*. Then as now, MoMA was considered the Vatican of international Modernism in the arts. Its director and the show's lead curator, Alfred H. Barr Jr., was idolized as the pope of modernism, and by sponsoring it, he elevated Cuban art to the heavens of legitimacy.[11] Barr traveled to Cuba in 1942 in the company of Edgar Kauffman Jr. to survey the island's artistic movement personally. He then acquired a substantial group of Cuban paintings for MoMA's permanent collection, and upon his return to New York City, he enthusiastically proposed the show to the museum's board, defended its merits, and later organized the exhibition.

Barr's commitment to Cuban art went farther. He wrote the introduction to the exhibition brochure, in which he validated the art of the island by stating:

> There are things about Cuba which surprise you. . . . Modern Cuban painting, for instance—though we need not feel so embarrassed by our ignorance in this field, since the modern movement in Havana is very young, in fact has taken on a consistent and recognizable character only within the past four or five years. It has something of the brashness, but even more of the virtues, of youth—courage, freshness, vitality, and a healthy disrespect for its elders. . . . [12]

MoMA not only put together this exhibition, whose catalogue included a total of thirteen artists and seventy-five artworks.[13] The museum went even farther by offering the show to museums in other cities in the United States. A slightly edited version of MoMA's *Modern Cuban Painters* exhibition, composed of sixty-six works, traveled immediately after the New York show closed. From 1944 to 1945, museums featured this exhibition in twelve other cities throughout the United States, including at the National Gallery of Art in Washington, DC, the San Francisco Museum of Art, and the Seattle Art Museum.[14]

The MoMA show featured four first-generation and seven second-generation Cuban Modern artists, plus two Spanish-born naïve artists, Rafael Moreno (1887–?) and Felisindo Iglesias Acevedo (1889–?). A 200-page book, *Cuban Painting of Today*, written by Gómez Sicre, accompanied the exhibition in New York and in its other venues.[15] The impact of these events totally altered the dynamics for Cuban Modern art. The international art market began to pay attention (Plate 16).

The 1944 MoMA exhibition had several distinguishing curatorial elements. According to *The New York Times* critic Edward Alden Jewell, it was quite large: more than eighty [*sic*] works by thirteen painters were displayed. Most of the artists were relatively young, in their early thirties. Despite their individual differences in style, the painters shared "a joyous use of brilliant color." The works evidenced the influence of the School of Paris, but most adapted and absorbed this influence, so that the "native product" "looks Cuban." Jewell was impressed with the work of the two "Cuban 'primitives'"—self-taught artists Moreno and Iglesias Acevedo—which appeared first in the sequence arranged by the museum's staff.[16]

Prior to 1943, the painters of the Cuban Modern art movement had an extremely limited collecting market for their creations. On the island, few art sales, at very low values, took place, almost exclusively in Havana, Cuba's capital and center of culture. The provinces rarely saw shows of importance, much less art-related commercial transactions. They were barren wastelands for art collecting. Upper-class Cuban families, known for their artistic sophistication, did not regard the Cuban avant-garde worthy of consideration. The Cuban vanguardia—young, rebellious, iconoclastic, anti-dictatorial, and leftist—was best kept at a distance. These families of hereditary rank, some aristocrats, others of newfound wealth, did not pay much attention to Cuban art, whether from the colonial period or early republican period, and certainly they had no interest in the "craziness" of the vanguardias. They concentrated their attention elsewhere[17]—outside the island and its autochthonous cultural output.

Some well-known upper-class art collectors in Havana from the 1930s to the 1950s included the following:

1. The Fanjul family collected Joaquín Sorolla, Mariano Fortuny, Goya, and other Spanish and French nineteenth-century and older European masters.
2. Julio Lobo collected nineteenth-century French art, Greek art, and Napoleonic memorabilia.
3. Mario García Menocal collected Auguste Rodin, French art of the nineteenth century, Jean-Baptiste Corot, and others.
4. Oscar B. Cintas collected old European masters, including El Greco, Rembrandt, van Dyck, Frans Hals, Rubens, Murillo, and others, thus gathering the most important collection of old European master paintings in Latin America during his lifetime.[18]
5. The Count of Lagunillas (Joaquín Gumá) collected Greek, Roman, and Egyptian art, assembling the most important collection on these cultures in all Latin America.[19]

The list of upper-class Cuban collectors could include a few more names, but not many. All of them disregarded Modern art from the island. One exception was María Luisa Gómez Mena, who should be the subject of a separate conversation.[20]

In the 1920s, 1930s, and early 1940s, the vanguardia painters sold few of their works. Artists lived in poverty or near-poverty, barely surviving through support from various sources:

1. Limited family assistance, or frugally managed inheritances, as was the case for Peláez,[21] Enríquez,[22] Gattorno, Bermúdez, and Pogolotti; or
2. Bartering their paintings for food, lodging, or medical attention, as Ponce,[23] Víctor Manuel García, and Mijares did; and in other cases
3. Taking on temporary additional jobs, as Portocarrero,[24] Abela, and Martínez Pedro did.

In the early years, the few collectors who paid something for these artists' works were mostly members of the professional middle class—physicians, attorneys, architects, university professors, diplomats, and small business owners. Some names come to mind: architect Manolo de la Torre, Dr. Ramón Osuna, Dr. Guillermo de Zéndegui, Dr. Raúl Chibás, Dr. Carlos Ramírez Corría, Dr. Héctor de Ayala, and Dr. Jorge Mañach.

It was not until the international modern art community opened to the vanguardia, starting in the mid-1940s, that these artists found the financial support that permitted their better development and enhanced their artistic productivity. I will quote from José Rodríguez Feo, a very significant intellectual, writer, literary critic, and translator who cofounded the cultural magazine *Orígenes* (1944–56) and later directed *Ciclón* (1956–59) in Havana. A dear friend of the Cuban avant-garde, he published the following in *Bohemia* magazine on May 28, 1961:

> When I met Portocarrero, in the year 1944, I was surprised by the difficulties that he had in selling his works in Cuba, and how, from the very beginning, the majority of his paintings ended up in the hands of foreigners, who were great admirers of his art. It is because of this that with Portocarrero, as well as with the other great painters of his generation, there are more works in foreign galleries and foreign private collections than there are in our own country.

Rodríguez Feo continues: "The group that Portocarrero created with other painters, such as Wifredo Lam, Víctor Manuel, Mariano, Amelia Peláez, Ponce, Carlos Enríquez, and others, is now considered the most important and valuable among the arts in Hispanic America, along with the group of Mexican muralists."[25] It was an ironic twist of events that the international art establishment, especially in the United States, decisively embraced Cuban Modern art before that art reached a high level of recognition in its own country (Plate 17).

The aura of the MoMA show and the arrival of the Cuban avant-garde in the United States had other ramifications. The following is a list of major New York galleries that signed, directly represented, and exhibited Cuban artists in the United States in the mid-1940s:

1. The Pierre Matisse Gallery, the number one New York Modern art gallery of the 1940s, featured Lam in at least six one-person shows and more than twenty group shows from 1942 to 1982. It also sold *La jungla* (*The Jungle*, 1943), Lam's iconic work, to the MoMA for $3,000.[26]

2. The Julian Levy Gallery, New York, organized a one-person show for Portocarrero in 1944, plus various group shows from 1945 to 1949. This gallery sold many works by Portocarrero throughout the United States, including at least three to the San Francisco Museum of Art, and exhibited his work alongside paintings by Dalí, Magritte, Giacometti, other Surrealists, and artists from the School of Paris.
3. The Feigl Gallery, New York, featured Mariano Rodríguez from 1945 to 1951 and presented four one-person exhibitions of the artist.[27]
4. The Perls Galleries, New York, represented two artists from Cuba—Carreño and Martínez Pedro. Carreño had one-person shows in 1941, 1944, 1945, 1947, 1948, and 1951, in addition to various group shows (Plate 18). Martínez Pedro had two individual exhibitions at Perls and extensive group show participation.
5. The Passedoit Gallery, New York, exhibited works by Gattorno in a solo show in 1944.[28]

These and other U.S. galleries significantly contributed to assembling a base of U.S. collectors of Cuban Modern artists. Most important, the galleries did not present these artists as "Ricky Ricardo Cubans," but as legitimate international modernists, in conjunction with other well-known modernist masters. Furthermore, other U.S. collectors frequently went to Havana to meet the artists and choose their preferred works.

Some of the better-known international collectors of that time were:

Ernest Hemingway: Gattorno[29]
John Dos Passos:[30] Gattorno, Manuel
Nelson Rockefeller: Lam, Portocarrero, Teodoro Ramos Blanco (1902–72)
Alfred Hitchcock: Ponce
Meyer Lansky: Abela
Albert Miller: Carreño, Peláez, Bermúdez, and others
Joseph Cantor: Lam, Portocarrero, Milián, Peláez
Girón Cerna, from Guatemala: Ponce, Manuel, Enríquez
David Harriton, from New York: Peláez, Carreño
James Amos Porter, a professor at Howard University in Washington, DC: Afro-Cuban artists, Roberto Diago, Lam, Carmelo González (1920–90), and Estopiñán

Ben Wolf, from Boston: Portocarrero
Robert Altman, from Paris: Peláez, Portocarrero, Lam
Joseph Shapiro, from Chicago: Lam, various works of whose were later donated to the Museum of Contemporary Art in Chicago
Maurice de Young, from Haiti: Enríquez, Portocarrero, Bermúdez, Peláez, Martínez Pedro, Orlando, and others

By the end of the 1940s, Modern Cuban art had reached a level of consolidation that foretold its continued ascendancy in the international art arena. Let us review what *The New York Times'* principal art critic of the 1940s, Edward Alden Jewell, wrote in his newspaper column of September 7, 1947, after a two-week sojourn in Havana. There he met with several of the Cuban artists who participated in the 1944 MoMA show, and visited the studios of Peláez, Portocarrero, Mariano Rodríguez, Bermúdez, and Martínez Pedro. Jewell wrote, "I found a modern art movement of considerable range and robustness . . . That there is a Cuban school, recognized as such, could scarcely, I should say, be missed . . ." Jewell continued:

> Most empathetic is the impact created by its nativeness, allied with high color and a certain impetuous, uninhibited zest in brushwork . . . gouache has become a medium possessing peculiar appeal for the Cuban artists, who swing it and make it sing for all it's worth. Gouache seems the happy preference of the modern Cuban artist. . . . [31]

Barr continued to support the Cuban Modernist movement, and by the late 1940s had recommended Gómez Sicre and helped him secure the position of Chief of the Visual Arts Section of the Pan American Union (later renamed the Organization of American States [OAS]), in Washington, DC. Gómez Sicre had officially been recognized as a consultant to the MoMA 1944 exhibition, but it was known that he had played a much larger role in putting the show together. Now Barr returned the favor, to the benefit of the Cuban avant-garde.

Gómez Sicre continued to push for the advancement of the arts of his country from his new position of authority in Washington, and from 1947 through 1959, he presented eleven Cuban art shows of importance in the U.S. capital. Some of these exhibitions were:

1. *Cuban Modern Paintings in Washington Collections*, December 1946. The participating artists were Bermúdez, Carreño,

Enríquez, Mariano Rodríguez, Peláez, Ponce, Diago, Portocarrero, Víctor Manuel, and others.

2. *Felipe Orlando*, August 1947
3. *Cundo Bermúdez: Oils and Gouaches*, April 1948
4. *Luis Martínez Pedro*, one-person show, September 1951
5. *Seven Cuban Painters*, group show, August 1952[32]
6. *Roberto Diago*, September 1953
7. *René Portocarrero and Raúl Milián*, October 1956

The Pan American Union/OAS exhibitions contributed to canonizing the curatorial choices of the 1944 MoMA show. Gómez Sicre especially promoted the work of Modern Cuban artists like Peláez, Carreño, Portocarrero, Martínez Pedro, and Bermúdez, and progressively incorporated younger artists like Estopiñán, Servando Cabrera Moreno (1923–81), and Rolando López Dirube (1928–97) in his collecting efforts. According to the renowned art historian Alejandro Anreus, Gómez Sicre preferred Enríquez, Ponce, and Peláez as the most original exponents of the first generation of Cuban modernists, and considered Carreño and Bermúdez the best examples of the second generation.[33]

Many of the OAS exhibitions were not only cultural but also commercial events, open to acquisitions of artworks by interested collectors, while all funds paid from sales went to the artists. This was a common practice in many U.S. museums in the 1930s and 1940s, intended to help artists survive during the difficult years of early Modernism.

Thanks to the generosity of our dear friend, Alejandro Anreus, we have in our own files not only a copy of the exhibition catalogue of the OAS show of 1952, *Seven Cuban Painters*, but also an extremely rare copy of the price list for the works in that show. This document sheds light on the pricing of works by Cuban vanguardia artists eight years after the seminal MoMA exhibition. The 1952 show included works for sale by Carreño, Bermúdez, Peláez, Portocarrero, Diago, Martínez Pedro, and Orlando. For example, four large-size gouaches on paper executed by Peláez from 1943 to 1945 were offered at $350 each. Adjusted for inflation, $350 in 1952 would represent $3,232 today. In May 2017, a Peláez gouache on paper[34] sold at an auction in New York for $475,500.[35] The OAS document shows similar pricing of works for other vanguardia artists. Bermúdez's oils were sold for $400; Portocarrero's for $250; Carreño's for $500. Despite the valuation enhancement that the 1944 MoMA show brought to Cuban art, eight years later, prices were still accessible to many collectors.

In conclusion, by the end of the 1950s and before the Cuban Revolution, Modern Cuban Art, the movement initiated in the 1920s in Havana, had consolidated in the country and secured a distinguished level of recognition in the international art community. The two generations of Cuban vanguardia artists had achieved the movement's initial objective of contributing to the definition of a national identity and promoting a Cuban ethos that reinforced the spiritual values of its people. Ironically, these achievements would not have been possible without the enthusiastic support of the U.S. art community. The lifeline of U.S. art collections, critics, museum exhibitions, and galleries allowed this art movement—initially ignored by the Cuban upper class—to survive, and gave it the economic, intellectual, and artistic backing needed to earn it respect on the world scene. By 1959, at the advent of the Cuban Revolution, the vanguardia had succeeded in its objectives, principally due to the talent and tenacity of a group of artists who kept on creating and believing despite all obstacles. Cuban Modern art had arrived and secured its place in the international art conversation.

Notes

1. Jan Lahmeyer, *CUBA: Historical Demographic Data of the Whole Country*.

2. Martí [*sic*] Casanovas, "Nuevos rumbos," 99–100, 108–9.

3. Juan A. Martínez, *Cuban Art and National Identity*, 5–6, 155–56. Martínez asserts Víctor Manuel's place as the precursor of Modern art on the island, because he was the first to present a one-person show of Modern art in February 1927, followed closely by Antonio Gattorno in March 1927.

4. Cecilia de Torres, "Taller Torres-García."

5. Juan Marinello, "Nuestro arte y las circunstancias nacionales," 303; my translations throughout. Martínez also notes this argument in *Cuban Art and National Identity*, 42.

6. Municipio de La Habana, *Primera Exposición de Arte Moderno*, 41–45. The exhibition catalogue includes a list of all participating artists, as well as each of the artworks they exhibited. The exhibition ran from March 23 to April 8, 1937 at the Salones del Centro de Dependientes (Shop Clerks' Center) under the auspices of the Administration of the Mayor of Havana, Dr. Antonio Beruff Mendieta. The catalogue featured opening commentaries by Carlos Girón Cerna and Heriberto Portell Vilá, among others.

7. José Veigas-Zamora et al., *Memoria*, 381. The Second National Exhibition of Painting and Sculpting took place in 1938 in Havana. The exhibition opened on June 18 at the

Castillo de la Real Fuerza, organized under the auspices of the Municipal Secretary of Education.

8. Instituto Nacional de Artes Plásticas, ed., *300 años de arte en Cuba*, 43–70. The exhibition catalogue includes a list of all participating modern artists, as well as each of the artworks they exhibited. The exhibition opened on April 18, 1940 at the University of Havana, organized by the National Institute of Visual Arts and the National Tourism Corporation of Cuba.

9. Domingo Ravenet et al., *Exposición de arte cubano contemporáneo*, 11–16. The catalogue includes a list of all participating artists, as well as each of the artworks they exhibited. The exhibition opened in November 1941 at the Salón de los Pasos Perdidos (Salon of the Lost Steps) of the National Capitol Building in Havana. The National Cuban Committee for Intellectual Cooperation organized the show, in conjunction with the Second American Conference of National Committees for Intellectual Cooperation.

10. Veigas-Zamora et al., *Memoria*, 387–402. *Memoria* lists most of these exhibitions: Port-au-Prince, January 18–April 2, 1945; Moscow, March 1945; Buenos Aires, July 2–25, 1946; Mexico City, June 1946; Stockholm, October 29–November 27, 1949; Paris, February 28–March 1951.

11. Alice Goldfarb Marquis, *Alfred H. Barr Jr.*, 212. In a 1945 letter, MoMA Board Chairman Stephen Carlton Clark wrote Barr, "You occupy a unique and very distinguished place in the world of art and if you go on as you are now going you will leave behind you a reputation as the foremost art critic of our time."

12. Alfred H. Barr Jr., "Modern Cuban Painters."

13. Museum of Modern Art Archives, "Checklist for Exhibition of MODERN CUBAN PAINTERS." This original document includes a list of all participating artists and a short bio on each one, as well as descriptions of all works exhibited.

14. Museum of Modern Art Archives, "Modern Cuban Painting." This document, obtained directly from the MoMA archives, includes a checklist of the artworks exhibited in the traveling exhibition, organized by artist, as well as shipping costs and the travel itinerary, including twelve museums, from 1944 to 1945.

15. José Gómez Sicre, *Pintura cubana de hoy*. This book includes texts by Gómez Sicre, as well as biographies of the artists and color and black-and-white plates of the work exhibited at the MoMA show.

16. Edward Alden Jewell, "Cuban Paintings on Display Today."

17. Luis de Soto y Sagarra, *Escuelas europeas*. This exhibition took place at the University of Havana and was organized by the National Institute of Visual Arts, under the auspices of both the university and the National Tourism Corporation of Cuba. The exhibition catalogue features opening commentaries by Mariano Brull and Luis de Soto y Sagarra and sheds some light on the extent to which the Cuban upper class collected European art.

18. Luis Lastra, "Cuadros de la Colección Cintas." This article announces the establishment of the Cintas Foundation for the arts and details the old European master works that were auctioned off following the death of Oscar B. Cintas.

19. Guillermo de Zéndegui, *Sala de arte antiguo: Egipto, Grecia, Roma.*

20. Museum of Modern Art, "Exhibition of Cuban Painting Opens at Museum of

Modern Art." This press release acknowledges "the generous collaboration of Señora María Luisa Gómez Mena of Havana, the leading patron of modern Cuban painting" (2).

21. José Seoane Gallo, *Palmas reales en el Sena*, 5. Seoane Gallo describes Amelia Peláez as having grown up in a household that "oscillated between the petite bourgeoisie and the relative resources of the so-called 'labor aristocracy.'"

22. Martínez writes, "By and large, Carlos Enríquez benefitted tremendously from his family's privileged social class and from their tight family unit. It afforded him the best education in Havana and Philadelphia, provided him with an economic safety net, gave him a strong sense of fidelity and confidence, and even sparked his artistic interest." Martínez, *Carlos Enríquez*, 26.

23. Martínez, *Fidelio Ponce de León*, 49–50. Martínez describes a partnership the artist had with Hortensia Lluch de Berg, which provided him with basic necessities in exchange for his work.

24. Veigas-Zamora et al., *Memoria*, 349. Listed under "Professional Activity" is a period in 1943 in which Portocarrero served as a Professor of Free Drawing at the Havana City Jail.

25. José Rodríguez Feo, "Los pintores cubanos," 149; originally printed in *Bohemia* on May 28, 1961.

26. Helena Benítez, *Wifredo and Helena*, 82: "La Jungla was shown at the second exhibition of Wifredo's work at the Pierre Matisse Gallery from June 6 to 24, in 1944. On May 5, 1945, James Johnson Sweeney used $3,000 from the Inter-American Fund to purchase La Jungla for the Museum of Modern Art (MoMA) in New York."

27. Dannys Montes de Oca Moreda, *Mariano (1912–1990)*, 224–25. Mariano Rodríguez traveled to the United States to exhibit at the Feigl Gallery, New York, in 1945, 1946, 1948, and 1951.

28. Sean M. Poole, *Gattorno*, 45–46. Gattorno had a one-person show at the Passedoit Gallery in New York City on October 2, 1944, following his exclusion from the 1944 MoMA show.

29. Ernest Hemingway, *Gattorno*. Hemingway's enthusiasm for Gattorno's work is evident in the opening commentary of this monograph on the artist, featuring thirty-eight reproductions of his work and critiques by John Dos Passos, Ramón Guirao, Alejo Carpentier, and E. Avilés Ramírez. Only 460 copies of this book were printed.

30. Dos Passos, in Ernest Hemingway, *Gattorno*. As cited above, Dos Passos wrote a short commentary on Gattorno's work, dated January 6, 1935.

31. Jewell, "Modernism in Cuba."

32. Pan American Union, *Seven Cuban Painters*. The Pan American Union organized this exhibition, which took place at the OAS building in Washington, DC, from August 15 to September 20, 1952. The catalogue and price list were part of Gómez Sicre's personal archives, graciously provided by Alejandro Anreus for use in this chapter.

33. See Abigail McEwen, *Revolutionary Horizons*, 121–23; Anreus, "Historical Close-Up."

34. Christie's New York, "Latin American Art," 52–53. Peláez's *Naturaleza muerta en un interior* (*Still Life in an Interior*, 1948) is listed as Lot #20 in the catalogue for this sale.

35. Christie's, "Sale 13256: Latin American Art." The auction results list published online states that Lot #20 sold for $475,500, including the buyer's premium.

Bibliography

Anreus, Alejandro. "Historical Close-Up: Modern Cuban Painters at MoMa, 1944." *Cuban Art News*, April 1, 2014. https://www.cubanartnews.org/2014/04/01/historical-close-up-modern-cuban-painters-at-moma-1944/.

Barr, Alfred H., Jr. "Modern Cuban Painters." *Museum of Modern Art Bulletin* 11, no. 5 (1944): 1–14.

Benítez, Helena. *Wifredo and Helena: My Life with Wifredo Lam, 1939–1950*. Lausanne: Sylvio Acatos, 1999.

Casanovas, Martí. "Nuevos rumbos: La Exposición de '1927.'" *Revista de Avance* 1, no. 5 (1927): 99–100, 108–9.

Christie's. "Sale 13256: Latin American Art. New York," May 24–25, 2017. Accessed May 26, 2017. https://www.christies.com/Results/PrintAuctionResults.aspx?saleid=26533&lid=1.

Christie's New York. "Latin American Art: Wednesday 24 and Thursday 25 May 2017." *Christie's Latin American Art Sale*, New York, May 24–25, 2017, 52–53.

de Soto y Sagarra, Luis. *Escuelas europeas*. Havana: University of Havana, 1940.

de Torres, Cecilia. "Taller Torres-García." N.d. Accessed June 1, 2017. http://www.ceciliadetorres.com/taller.

Gómez Sicre, José. *Pintura cubana de hoy/Cuban Painting of Today*. Edited by María Luisa Gómez Mena. Translated by Harold T. Riddle. Havana: Úcar, García y Cía, 1944.

Hemingway, Ernest. *Gattorno*. Havana: Úcar, García y Cía, 1935.

Instituto Nacional de Artes Plásticas, ed. *300 años de arte en Cuba: Exposición de arte en la Universidad de La Habana*. Havana: La Verónica, 1940.

Jewell, Edward Alden. "Cuban Paintings on Display Today: Outstanding Exhibition to Be Seen at Museum of Modern Art Through May 7." *The New York Times*, March 17, 1944, 15.

———. "Modernism in Cuba: Work by Artists of the Island Reveals Both Native and Outside Influence." *The New York Times*, September 7, 1947, X8.

Lahmeyer, Jan. *CUBA: Historical Demographic Data of the Whole Country*. November 11, 2003. Accessed June 1, 2017. http://www.populstat.info/Americas/cubac.htm.

Lastra, Luis. "Cuadros de la Colección Cintas." *Boletín de Artes Visuales* 11 (1963): 107–13.

Marinello, Juan. "Nuestro arte y las circunstancias nacionales." *Documents of 20th-Century Latin American and Latino Art*. Houston International Center for the Arts of the Americas at the Museum of Fine Arts. February 18, 1925. Accessed June 1, 2017. http://icaadocs.mfah.org/icaadocs/THEARCHIVE/FullRecord/tabid/88/doc/1125430/language/en-US/Default.aspx.

Marquis, Alice Goldfarb. *Alfred H. Barr Jr.: Missionary for the Modern*. Chicago: Contemporary Books, 1989.

Martínez, Juan A. *Carlos Enríquez: The Painter of Cuban Ballads*. Edited by Ramón Cernuda. Miami: Cernuda Arte, 2010.

———. *Cuban Art and National Identity: The Vanguardia Painters, 1927–1950*. Gainesville: University Press of Florida, 1994.

———. *Fidelio Ponce de León: A Cuban Original*. Forthcoming.

McEwen, Abigail. *Revolutionary Horizons: Art and Polemics in 1950s Cuba*. New Haven: Yale University Press, 2016.

Montes de Oca Moreda, Dannys. *Mariano (1912–1990): Tema, discurso y humanidad*. Seville: Escandón Impresores, 2002.

Municipio de La Habana. *Primera Exposición de Arte Moderno: Pintura y Escultura*. Havana: Administración del Alcalde Dr. Antonio Beruff Mendieta, 1937.

Museum of Modern Art. "Checklist for Exhibition of MODERN CUBAN PAINTERS." New York: The Museum of Modern Art Archives, 1944.

———. "Exhibition of Cuban Painting Opens at Museum of Modern Art." New York: The Museum of Modern Art Archives, 1944.

———. "Modern Cuban Painting [MoMA Exh. #255, 17 March–7 May, 1944]." Records of the Department of Circulating Exhibitions II.1/49(3). New York: The Museum of Modern Art Archives, 1944.

Pan American Union. *Seven Cuban Painters: Bermúdez, Carreño, Diago, Martínez-Pedro, Orlando, Peláez, Portocarrero*. Washington, DC: Pan American Union, 1952.

Poole, Sean M. *Gattorno: A Cuban Painter for the World*. Miami: Arte al Día International American Art Corporation, 2004.

Ravenet, Domingo, Rafael Suárez Solíz, and Guy Pérez Cisneros. *Exposición de arte cubano contemporáneo*. Havana: Comisión Nacional Cubana de Cooperación Intelectual, 1941.

Rodríguez Feo, José. "Los pintores cubanos." In *Todo sobre Portocarrero: Compilación de textos críticos, 1936–2010*, edited by René Vázquez Díaz, Axel Li, and José Veigas, 149. Havana: Fundación Arte Cubano, 2014.

Seoane Gallo, José. *Palmas reales en el Sena*. Edited by Esther Toribio. Havana: Editorial Letras Cubanas, 1987.

Veigas-Zamora, José, Cristina Vives Gutiérrez, Adolfo V. Nodal, Valia Garzón, and Dannys Montes de Oca, eds. *Memoria: Cuban Art of the 20th Century*. Los Angeles: California/International Arts Foundation, 2002.

———. *Memoria: Cuban Art of the 20th Century*. CD-ROM. Los Angeles: California/International Arts Foundation, 2002.

Zéndegui, Guillermo de. *Sala de arte antiguo: Egipto, Grecia, Roma. Colección Conde Lagunillas, Palacio de Bellas Artes*. Havana: Instituto Nacional de Cultura, 1956.

6

Women Not Successful Here

Cuban Women Artists, from San Alejandro to the *Vanguardia*

Carol Damian

The history of Cuban art must begin at the San Alejandro Academy and in the Cuban art education system that emerged from the free school of the preeminent portrait painter Vicente Escobar. In the first decades of the nineteenth century, Escobar established a studio for students from the Cuban aristocracy and merchant classes to introduce them to European academic methods and produce art that was acceptable to the new bourgeoisie: a fine art that was elevated above that of the craft of the past. In the climate of the 1812 Cádiz Constitution and enlightened absolutism in Spain, the French Academy was certainly one of the most important schools of art, with its specific curriculum and path to success and respectability, and the best model.

First established by the Royal Patriotic Society and the Royal Consulate of Havana, the Free School of Drawing and Painting under Escobar's leadership quickly advanced. As the necessity for a more traditional academic system became evident, the French painter Jean-Baptiste Vermay (1786–1833) was named to organize and direct an acceptable curriculum. In 1818, the new school, now officially sanctioned as the San Alejandro Academy, was named in memory of Alejandro Ramírez, director of the Economic Society of Friends of the Country, which had appointed Vermay as the first director. Located in the San Agustín Convent in Havana,[1] the teaching curriculum took as its model the French Academy and the European formal system of art education. Vermay, who arrived in Cuba at the age of thirty-one when the Bonaparte empire collapsed, was a pupil of Jacques-Louis David (1748–1825) and familiar with David's rigorous and stern Neoclassicism, and he used copies of David's work as models. As its first director, Vermay introduced San Alejandro to the French Academy's very conservative approach to the creation of art, which suited the bourgeoisie's sentiments in late nineteenth-century Cuba. The academic curriculum was used in Europe to impose official standards and principles of taste through an orthodoxy of aesthetic and artistic doctrine and procedures that focused on technical expertise and theoretical constructs. In Cuba, the San Alejandro Academy soon became the foundation of modern Cuban painting and increasingly popular and respected. It attracted students from throughout Cuba to Havana, and entrance was extremely competitive.

Early records indicate that in 1865, San Alejandro had twenty-six students, increasing to 141 in 1866, and maintained approximately that number throughout the nineteenth century.[2] Its rigorous curriculum was taught in classes that included drawing, printmaking, and painting, and that were led by professors who were themselves professional artists, many of whom are well known in Cuban art history (Juan Francisco Cisneros, Víctor Landaluze, Esteban Chartrand, Leopoldo Romañach Guillén, and Armando G. Menocal, among those in the early years). They espoused realist and representational works, drawing from classical sculpture and live models, and local landscapes. Other trends adopted a more modern European language that was less conservative and included a more naturalistic approach to depicting the environment, and images that reflected the romanticism of the people and places of Cuba. Although these strict academic beginnings are often challenged as too narrow and rigid, the San Alejandro Academy, like its contemporaries in Paris, Madrid, and Rome, helped create a respect for the importance and significance of the arts as serious symbols of a European-inspired national culture.[3] Because of the Academy's prestige and influence, the makeup of its student body is a critical point in the discussion of women artists and their ability to compete and gain the skills necessary to succeed in the Cuban art world of the time. Without the Academy, women were placed in a difficult position, with little opportunity to participate in major exhibitions and in the art market—always dominated by men. Not surprisingly, women excelled as teachers and administrators, and were often recognized as competent artists in their day, but forgotten in the history books.

Until 1879, San Alejandro admitted only male students (the French academy allowed a limited number of female students). The application process was as rigorous as the curriculum. Students had to exhibit a high degree of technical skill, and most had already received art lessons and came prepared for the exams. Scholarships and other opportunities to study in Europe were also limited; without European experience, artists could not progress in the modern world. Women were at a disadvantage if they were unable to receive either private lessons or school instruction in art, or travel alone to art schools abroad. Director Miguel Melero Rodríguez took over the Academy in 1878 and initiated reforms, including the admission of women as full matriculating students, but very few women were accepted, and most who were admitted had connections to influence their acceptance. While the men enjoyed the prestige of a San Alejandro education and the exhibitions that were part of the curriculum, women who tried to pursue a career in the arts at the end of the century were limited by the constraints placed on them by family and society. Women were expected to be "Sunday painters" working in the privacy of their home studios and without the benefits of interaction and exposure so important to a developing student.

The end of the third Cuban War of Independence (1895–98) brought about the island's transition from colony to republic, which had a profound effect on art education and its responsibility to help create a distinctive national identity. Artists returned from abroad, many to join the faculty of San Alejandro and instruct the next generation about new styles and techniques.[4] Women also participated as faculty in the early years of the twentieth century, perhaps becoming better known as teachers than as artists in their own right. Very few were part of the avant-garde, which challenged the institution's rules and encouraged the move toward Modernism.

This chapter addresses numerous questions about the women artists who worked in the first half of the twentieth century in Cuba and their relationship with San Alejandro: Who were they? How many were admitted? Who continued to practice and achieve recognition? Reviewing the record of art exhibitions during this period, it becomes evident that some women enjoyed success and were active participants in the Academy, yet most of their work and story has been ignored or lost to history, or at most given minimal recognition. This is a typical story in art history—women were denied the same educational opportunities as men, which were limited by number and competition; then women were left out of the history books, even if they experienced success during their lifetimes. They were artists who ranged from the most conservative and academic to the folkloric to the independent and the avant-garde. They represent numerous trends and were popular with private clients (who commissioned portraits and landscapes in particular). Many of these forgotten artists participated in exhibitions, solo and group, in Cuba and beyond. They received scholarships and prizes and were recognized in their day. So why do we not know their names? Why do so few of them appear in the literature about Cuban art history? The goal of this chapter is to reintroduce them and their work in the context of early twentieth-century Modernism, leading to the *vanguardia* (avant-garde) period in Cuban art that followed the domination of San Alejandro and changed the course of art on the island.

My research focused on women born before 1930 who worked into the 1990s. Almost all of them were associated with San Alejandro, as students, teachers, and administrators. My list includes María Ariza y Delance (1880–1959); Concepción Ferrant (1882–1968); Luisa Fernández Morell (1897–1952); Amelia Peláez (1896–1968); Mirta Cerra (1904–1986); Rita Longa (1912–2000); Uver Solís (1923–70); and Gina Pellón (1926–2014). Upon reading the original paper that I presented at the Cuban Art and Cultural Identity Conference at Florida International University in June 2017, several collectors shared a few more names and references that I will include as an addendum at the end of this chapter. Given as a PowerPoint presentation, my paper originally contained over forty images. For this essay, I have included only five representative illustrations.

I found my eight featured artists in books and catalogues that contained hundreds of male artists; how many were remembered or recognized? And many had worked until recently. My presentation of the following artists is arranged from earliest to latest date of birth, and begins with María Ariza y Delance. Homeschooled, as was common for women at the time, she exhibited a precociousness and studied at the San Alejandro Academy in 1895, where she was a student of the renowned artist Leopoldo Romañach Guillén. In 1907, she continued her studies in Paris, where she attended the Académie Julian, a private studio school that offered independent alternative education and training in the arts, especially for students, including women, not admitted to the prestigious École des Beaux-Arts. The school also accepted numerous foreign applicants, as well as women, who participated in the same studies as men, including drawing and painting of nude models. Many artists from Cuba attended the school, which offered women opportunities denied them elsewhere. After Paris, Ariza y Delance continued to reside in Europe, in Spain—where she opened a studio in 1916—Belgium, and Italy. Beginning in 1917, she sent works to Havana for inclusion in the Fine Arts Salon exhibitions. She returned to Havana in 1926, joined the faculty of San Alejandro as a Professor of Art History, and became secretary of the institution in 1931.

Ariza y Delance's painting, *Patio* (*Backyard*, 1931, Plate 19), follows the nineteenth-century Romantic tradition of landscape painting that had evolved in Cuba as artists became aware of the diverse beauty of their homeland and sought to convey the peace and tranquility of the Cuban countryside. Her work betrays the influence of the French landscape style with its plein-air naturalism and the impressionistic brushwork of Spanish painter Joaquín Sorolla y Bastida (1863–1923), which she used to create paintings of her own landscape, continuing one of the most significant categories of Cuban art.

In 1902, the Republic of Cuba was created after a long war with Spain; art was an important contribution to the rise of the bourgeoisie, and continued to be influenced by admiration for France and Spain, as students went abroad to study with scholarships. Their return to Cuba was marked by new ideas that brought the avant-garde to the attention of the public. The new republic opened educational and cultural institutions and art finally moved away from the academy's conservative and formulaic dictates. In 1916, the Association of Painters and Sculptors was formed, and the Círculo de Bellas Artes (Circle of Fine Arts) encouraged the publication of journals and bulletins to disseminate information about various artists and art movements. By 1927, Havana had its first Modernist exhibition and things began to change, with San Alejandro remaining significant and many students returning with new ideas that would change its direction, especially as artists returned as teachers (as many women did).

Concepción Ferrant y Gómez enrolled in the San Alejandro Academy in 1907 and in 1918 received a scholarship to study at the National Academy of Design of New York. She traveled to Italy, France, and Spain, where she developed her pictorial skills as an accomplished portraitist. Her ability to capture the personality of her subjects in lively colors and bright lighting effects earned her praise and numerous awards. She returned to

Havana in 1926 to become a professor of painting at San Alejandro. She published an important treatise on art anatomy and other literary works.

Amelia Peláez was known as a quiet student at San Alejandro, where she studied in 1916–24. Her teacher, Romañach, introduced her to outdoor painting and Impressionism; she enjoyed the new sensation of observing the world around her, and began exploring landscape painting, with Impressionist overtones. In 1924, she studied at the Art Students League in New York and then traveled to Paris in 1927. At the École du Louvre and the École des Beaux-Arts, she was introduced to the Paris avant-garde and learned the fundaments of Abstraction and expressive experimentation inspired by the colors of Matisse, Picasso, and Cézanne, and the lessons of Cubism. Each of these renowned artists, among others in Paris, would contribute to the development of her unique style. Coupled with experience working on stage design with Russian artist Aleksandra Exter (1882–1949) and an introduction to Russian Futurism, Peláez explored new perspectives and new approaches to Abstraction while developing what would become her Cubist-Futurist-Fauvist style. Upon her return to Cuba in 1934, her Havana neighborhood of La Víbora offered ideal and personal subjects for her powers of observation to interpret in paint.[5] Inspired by architecture, stained glass, wrought iron, flowers, and interior decorative elements, she was among the first to bring the lessons of Paris home successfully. Her work gives a view into her world, a domestic paradise adorned with a baroque aesthetic full of adornments.

Peláez's painting *Sin título* (*Untitled*, 1950, Plate 20) contains all her signature components. It includes the decorative elements associated with her home in Havana, with its stained glass, iron details, lace cloths, flowers, and heavy contours describing the brilliant colors of the tropics. The style is flat, with highly abstracted color areas, deconstructed in the manner of Cubism, which she understood from her years in Paris, and brought back with her to Cuba, advancing Modernism in the country and contributing to the rise of the vanguardia painters beginning in the 1930s. Their consistent interest in expressing a national ethos and their choices of subjects that reflected the homeland, its environs, and its people, would resonate in her work and in that of an entire generation.[6]

Mirta Cerra studied at San Alejandro between 1928 and 1934, before going to the Art Students League in New York in 1935–36. She participated in exhibitions in Havana, Washington, DC, and New York, and was highly regarded in her day for popular images of the people of Cuba, done with a keen sense of color and sentimentalism. Her work quickly evolved to Cubist-inspired flat planes of color and extreme forms of abstraction. In *Balcón* (*Balcony*, 1953, Plate 21), a street scene is transformed into flat planes of color and abstract elements in keeping with Cubist stylistic techniques practiced during this time at home and abroad. The image is meant to remove any references to reality as it is reduced to a series of geometric elements that eliminate extraneous details and compositional depth.

Rita Longa studied commercial art and later briefly attended the San Alejandro Academy, but she considered herself largely self-taught. In 1937, she joined the faculty of the newly formed Free Studio for Painters and Sculptors in Havana. The short-lived school provided free art lessons and promoted an atmosphere of creative freedom that influenced her career and her independent approach to art. She worked in bronze, marble, and tile, and was one of a few women sculptors to produce large-scale works and receive public art commissions. Her works have a grace and elegance and, even at their most abstract, express an organic quality that relates to nature and the environment. This quality imbues her works, many on a grand scale, with a sensitivity that has made her famous throughout Cuba. One of her most important works is a sculpture of Hatuey that became a nationally recognized symbol for Hatuey Beer, malt, cigarettes, and cigars. Hatuey (d. 1512) was a Taíno cacique (chief) from Cuba's neighboring island of Hispaniola who became a heroic figure for leading his people against invading Spaniards. He fled to Cuba but was captured and executed in 1512. As the first indigenous fighter against Spanish colonialism, he became known as "Cuba's first national hero." His statue is found in one of Longa's most significant projects, the 1964 Taíno Village Reconstruction in Guamá, Matanzas, Cuba, which included twenty-five sculptures of Indigenous people.

Ubernia (Uver) Eduarda Solís Cabrera is perhaps unique among the artists I discuss here. Working in an original and naïve style, she used a simple technique to focus on expressive gestures and actions in paintings that convey the energetic dances, music, and festivals of the Afro-Cuban community in her hometown of Jovellanos in Matanzas Province. Described as "Cuban Antillean," her works were some of the most popular of her time, and she participated in exhibitions of the vanguardia in Cuba and beyond, including at the Fine Arts Palace in Mexico City in 1946, where Diego Rivera acquired one of her works and praised her unique style that merged Spain, Africa, and Asia.[7] She studied drawing at the School of Education in Havana under Domingo Ravenet and had her first individual exhibition in 1945. A free spirit, Solís captured the energy and spirit of the Afro-Cuban people. *Muchacha con mango* (*Young Lady with Mango*, 1970, Plate 22) is a delightful painting, characteristic of Solís's work with its loose, spontaneous, and fluid brushwork. Solís is often described as a folk artist, creating playful images of everyday life without the constraints of academic directives. Her work is instinctive and personal with a fresh originality.[8]

Gina Pellón graduated from San Alejandro in 1954 and taught at the Vedado Polytechnic Institute until 1957. In 1959, she went to study in France and overstayed her visa, fleeing Fidel Castro's dictatorship. She remained in France until her death and became an active member of the Paris school. Her style of abstract expressive brushwork and strong colors is reminiscent of CoBrA (Copenhagen, Brussels, Amsterdam), a group active in the 1940s and 1950s in Paris and other cities in Northern Europe. Her work has their same sense of immediacy and spontaneity that may appear almost childlike but is very sophisticated. Most of her images are of women, and she treats them as painterly subjects through which to explore the properties of color with brash gestural strokes that give each one a vibrant personality. In *Manipulaciones sin fronteras* (*Manipulations without Borders*, 1986, Plate 23), a group of women of diverse ethnic descriptions gather together for a conversation. Their colorful clothing is styled by vibrant brushwork with costume details reduced to abstract notations. Nevertheless, there is a sense of harmony despite their ethnic differences.

While the above artists have received critical acclaim for their works, others, notable in their lifetimes in Cuba, have long been forgotten. Many of them had numerous exhibitions and were recognized for their work, and most of them were teachers and administrators at San Alejandro, a safe choice for a career, which the making of art was not. The following list was added after I presented the original version of this essay, with the assistance of new information from collectors and rare books on early Cuban art history.[9] I am sure that there are others, and so my detective work will continue, with the goal of publishing a book in which all their names will appear and they will be returned to the story of art in Cuba. This chapter also demonstrates the significance of the San Alejandro Academy to the development of art through its teachings and the opportunities it offered students to study in Europe and the United States. The basic lessons taught at the Academy would contribute to building a strong foundation for future generations of artists who moved beyond its academic strictures to explore new directions of Modernism as the Havana avant-garde, the vanguardia.

Addendum

Adriana Billini Gautreau (1865–1946) was born in Santo Domingo, Dominican Republic, and arrived in Cuba at a young age, later studying at San Alejandro. After completing her coursework, in 1899 she founded El Salvador Academy of Painting and Drawing, where she created her own method of teaching and her salons became famous for their discussions about art and culture at the beginning of the Republic. In 1906, she joined the faculty of San Alejandro and continued to operate smaller schools for drawing and painting on the island.[10] Her work is conservative and skillfully painted, in the best of the academic traditions.

Juana Borrero Pierra (1877–96) was one of the youngest students at San Alejandro and a member of one of Cuba's illustrious literary families. As well as receiving acclaim as a painter, she is considered the most important Cuban female poet of the nineteenth century. She studied art in the United States and died of tuberculosis on a trip to Key West, at the age of eighteen. Her few paintings and poems are her legacy.[11]

Isabel Chappotin y Jiménez (1880–1964) was a distinguished sculptor and teacher. She studied at San Alejandro and became a professor of drawing and sculpture in 1923. She was recognized for her teaching methods and for her paintings, which were widely exhibited.

María Capdevila y Casas (1881–1991) painted in an expressionist primitivist style that reflects the personalities and environs of Cuba. She studied in New York and France and graduated from San Alejandro in 1902. She received a doctorate in education and was a professor of drawing. Aware of modernist developments, she chose to maintain her own style. She left Cuba in 1960 for the United States.[12]

Carmen Loredo López (1886–1933) pursued the study of drawing and painting at San Alejandro and later became a professor known for her excellent techniques. She also studied in New Brunswick, Canada, and New York City, as well as at the University of Havana.

Luisa Fernández Morell (1897–1952) studied at the Academy of San

Alejandro, then in Italy. Upon her return to Havana in 1927, she joined the faculty of San Alejandro, where she shared the newest European techniques of loose brushwork, soft colors, and a tendency toward abstraction. Her works display her love of landscape and local scenery.

Carmen Pasos Carril (1902–?) studied at San Alejandro and became professor of applied visual arts. Known for her work in metals and leather, she exhibited in the United States, Cuba, and the Dominican Republic.

Victoria Nanson González de Gutiérrez (1905–99) was a landscape painter who captured the mountains and valleys of Oriente Province with a loose, modern brush in the tradition of Cézanne. She was a student of Romañach at San Alejandro and traveled to Europe to continue her studies. Upon her return to Cuba, she exhibited her landscapes and portraits to great acclaim.[13]

Modesta Vila Riva (1905–?) was known for her landscape paintings and for her teaching at San Alejandro, where she was professor of painting, drawing, and history of art.

Margarita García Mendoza (1906–?) was a painter, sculptor, and granddaughter of Luis Mendoza Sandrino, the highly respected ex-director, ex-secretary, and professor at San Alejandro. Also devoted to teaching at San Alejandro, García Mendoza exhibited her portraits and genre scenes to a wide audience.

Lucía Alvarez Castellón de Romney (1909–2000) created some of the earliest abstract sculptures in Cuba and is considered the first woman to do so successfully. A graduate of San Alejandro, she was also a painter, but excelled with her works in marble and other materials. Her sculptures are refined and elegant and attest to an early modern interest in organic forms. After leaving Cuba in 1960, she lived in New York before moving to Miami. She participated in exhibitions in New York and Washington, DC.

Silvia Fernández Arrojo (1918–81) graduated with the highest grades from San Alejandro, under Romañach's mentorship, and joined the faculty as a teacher and department chair. Married to artist Oscar García Rivera y Gutiérrez (1914–71), she was highly respected, as was her husband. Her career was unfortunately interrupted in 1959, despite numerous honors and awards, and she never exhibited again, was excluded from exhibitions, and forgotten.[14]

Mirta Díaz Betancourt (1920–96) was the daughter of famed portrait painter José Díaz Salinero (1874–1944) and became a portrait painter herself, even finishing his portraits after his death, and is known for portraits of political figures, including José Martí.

Notes

1. Since 1962, the Academy has been located in Marianao, outside of Havana.
2. Luz Merino Acosta, "Academia de San Alejandro (1818–1900)," 452.
3. Gary R. Libby, "The Rise of a Cuban Style," 14.
4. Zeida Comesañas Sardiñas, *Great Masters of Cuban Art*, 38.
5. Museo Cubano de Arte y Cultura/Cuban Museum of Art and Culture, *Amelia Peláez, 1896–1968*, 37.
6. Juan A. Martínez, *Cuban Art and National Identity*, 49.
7. Martínez, 244.
8. Martínez, 18.
9. I am grateful to the collectors who continue to send me information, and especially to Ramón Cernuda for his expertise and for recommending rare and valuable books on the topic. As we have all discussed, this presentation will make a fine book, and I will continue my research with that as a goal.
10. Esteban Valderrama, *La pintura y la escultura en Cuba*, 171.
11. Comesañas Sardiñas, 144.
12. Comesañas Sardiñas, 242.
13. Comesañas Sardiñas, 168.
14. Comesañas Sardiñas, 82.

Bibliography

Comesañas Sardiñas, Zeida. *Great Masters of Cuban Art/Grandes maestros del arte cubano: Ramos Collection/Colección Ramos*. Daytona Beach, FL: Museum of Arts and Sciences, 2009.

Libby, Gary R. "The Rise of a Cuban Style." In *Cuba: A History in Art*, 10–18. Daytona Beach, FL: Daytona Beach Museum of Art and Design, 1997.

Martínez, Juan A. *Cuban Art and National Identity: The Vanguardia Painters, 1927–1950*. Gainesville: University Press of Florida, 1994.

Merino Acosta, Luz. "Academia de San Alejandro (1818–1900)." In *Selección de lecturas de arte. Cuba colonia: Segunda parte*, edited by Lourdes Rodríguez Betancourt, 450–61. Havana: Editorial Félix Varela, 2004.

Museo Cubano de Arte y Cultura/Cuban Museum of Art and Culture. *Amelia Peláez, 1896–1968: A Retrospective. Una retrospectiva*. Miami: Museo Cubano de Arte y Cultura, 1981.

Valderrama, Esteban. *La pintura y la escultura en Cuba/Painting and Sculpture in Cuba/La peinture et la sculpture à Cuba*. Havana: Lex, 1953.

7

Cuban Architects at Home and in Exile

The Modernist Generation

Victor Deupi and Jean-François Lejeune

Within the last thirty years, the history of modern Cuban architecture has received special attention in Cuba, Latin America, and, increasingly, the United States. The Modernist generation of architects—the so-called *Generación de los Cincuenta* (Generation of the Fifties)—was active from the late 1930s until 1959 in Cuba, and then as architects and educators in exile. Its members sought to combine Cuban identity and traditions with the tenets of international modernism in a country that was late to embrace modernity, increasingly under U.S. influence, and on the verge of revolutionary changes. As noted by the Cuban architectural historian Eduardo Luis Rodríguez, "[t]he high standard of its modern architecture placed Cuba on a par with the newly built works in countries like Brazil, Mexico and Venezuela, where the desire to set the artistic avant-garde had developed long before. The race to catch up with modernity and the attempt to abolish Cuba's undoubted stylistic backwardness rapidly elevated this small island to a privileged position."[1] These architects reinvented their architectural practices within their respective cultural and professional contexts, yet were often also able to spread Cuban culture to countries such as the United States (particularly Florida), Mexico, Puerto Rico, Venezuela, France, and Spain. As the architectural avant-garde in Cuba, these architects represent the transnational and transcultural aspects of mid-twentieth century Cuban architecture around the world.

In the late 1920s, Cuban publications such as *El Arquitecto* and *Arquitectura*, published by the Colegio Nacional de Arquitectos de Cuba (National College of Cuban Architects, or CNAC), started discussing and publishing the works of modern architects such as Le Corbusier, Walter Gropius, and Frank Lloyd Wright.[2] Shortly thereafter, in September 1938, the CNAC initiated the annual *Premio Medalla de Oro* (Gold Medal Prize) to promote excellence in design.[3] In doing so, the organization initiated an intense debate between traditionalists and modernists, often resulting in an Art Deco compromise. The regional expression of modernity—how to be modern and Cuban at the same time—also emerged in Cuban architectural circles during this time, and it was increasingly tested by issues of national identity, particularly Spanish and U.S. influences, but also African roots. At the same time, European modernism began to influence Cuban architects in a more direct manner—figures such as Gropius, José Luis Sert, and Richard Neutra began to visit the island, lecture to students at the University of Havana School of Engineering and Architecture, and take on projects in collaboration with Cuban architects. As in Europe, the United States, and elsewhere, residential design was the natural testing ground for innovative ideas on architecture and modern life.

La Casa Cubana (the Traditional Cuban House)

The modern concept of *cubanidad* (Cuban identity), already present in literary and artistic circles, entered debates on architecture through the writings of Joaquín Weiss and Pedro Martínez Inclán, and later through the private houses designed by architect Eugenio Batista (1900–92).[4] As architects relied on patrons for work (either civic or private—there was little speculative building at the time), the house became the natural testing ground for new ideas of living and building. Batista married aspects of traditional Cuban architecture with abstraction, simplicity, and technological advancements in construction. Having studied at Princeton University from 1928–30, when the school still had a Beaux-Arts traditional curriculum, Batista was a master draftsman. His early studies of Cuban colonial architecture and Japanese vernacular building would remain with him throughout his life as a source of inspiration.[5] With his advocacy of the three "Ps"—*persianas* (wooden louvers), *patios* (courtyards), and *portales* (running arcades/colonnades)—he provided a clear direction for a modernism that would use tradition, history, and adaptation to climate to represent the modernizing national identity of the island.[6] He described these three elements as the "a.b.c." of tropical architecture, and this idea would resonate strongly with subsequent generations of Cuban architects.

The house built for Eutimio Falla Bonet (1939) is one of the best examples of Batista's synthetic approach.[7] Built on First Street in Miramar along Havana's coast, the house is situated around a private courtyard, and sits between a motor court in the front and a rear patio with a pool overlooking the Straits of Florida. The integration of colonial elements with a more modern emphasis is very similar to what Frank Lloyd Wright had been doing in his early career with the Prairie houses. Batista's pinwheel plan around the courtyard is also very much like Wright's approach to the hearth as a centralizing device. Though certainly a tipping point in the history of twentieth-century residential architecture in Cuba, the house for Falla Bonet only received the *Medalla de Plata* (Silver Medal) in the 1940 *Premio Medalla de Oro*.[8] After the Revolution, Batista worked as a professor of design at various schools in the United States, including the University of Oregon (1962–71), where he built a house for his family.[9] His strong regionalist sensibility can be seen in this split-level wood and concrete-block house that sits nestled into the wooded hillside, in the tradition of west-coast bungalows. At the center of the house is the hearth, which replaces the patio as a North American equivalent.

A very different approach to the *casa cubana*—and the most international example of the modern Cuban house—can be seen in the work of Mario Romañach (1917–84), who studied architecture at the University of Havana, graduating in 1945. He found early patronage in the Cueto de Noval family, whose first residence he designed for Julia Cueto de Noval in Cubanacán, earning him a Gold Medal from the CNAC in 1949.[10] The second house, for José Noval Jr., is considered a masterpiece of residential architecture in Havana, even though it was never awarded a prize.[11] Deeply influenced by Romañach's mentor and friend, Gropius, the house adapts the rationalist aesthetics of the Modern Movement to the tropical climate of Havana by incorporating long overhanging eaves, patios, pools, and gardens to increase ventilation and comfort. If any criticism could be made, it is that, as the editors of the U.S. journal *House & Home* noted in a 1952 article:

> the Noval house will have little direct influence upon run-of-the-mill modern architecture: contemporary house architects are not

> often called upon to ponder the problem of pools at the foot of cocktail bars, the problem of how to relate the swimming pool to the reflecting pool, the problem of where to entertain the client's male guests while the client's wife is entertaining her women friends.[12]

More than anything, though, the house demonstrated most convincingly how to make a structure in Cuba that was both functionally and aesthetically exceptional.

Romañach left Cuba in 1959, after which he kept combining both his professional and academic pursuits; he was a visiting critic at Harvard (1959), an associate professor at Cornell (1960–62), and, after 1963, a full professor at the Graduate School of Fine Arts at the University of Pennsylvania, and chair of the Department of Architecture from 1971–74.[13] The family house he designed for a remote site outside of Philadelphia with his daughter María, who joined him in 1975 to form the Romañach Partnership, would have been a Cuban version of Frank Lloyd Wright's Fallingwater (Figure 7.1), but was never built.[14] Situated midway up a gentle slope, and surrounded by trees, the house consists of a masonry core with cantilevered terraces. Retaining walls, terraces, and bridges extend the house into the landscape. Had the residence been constructed, it could very well have eclipsed Wright's masterpiece as the most important modern house built in the United States.

Max Borges Recio (1918–2009), a near contemporary of Romañach, came from a reputable family of architects. His father, Max Borges del Junco, was a notable architect and engineer, building great mansions throughout the city. Borges Recio's brother Enrique was also an architect and would often collaborate with him.[15] Max studied architecture at Georgia Tech and the Harvard Graduate School of Design, and became one of the most versatile designers of residential and commercial buildings in Havana. His own house and studio in Miramar embody the machine aesthetic of Le Corbusier, incorporating such radical elements as ribbon windows, *pilotis* (piers or columns that lift a building above the ground), and an open floor plan to achieve a clear, rational structure.[16] After the Revolution, Borges settled in Falls Church, Virginia, and established a practice with his sons. As noted by the Cuban architect Belmont Freeman in Borges's obituary for *The Architects Newspaper*, "Borges [left] behind the beautiful house that he built for himself and his family in the Lake Barcroft section of Falls Church in 1962. Meticulously detailed in stone,

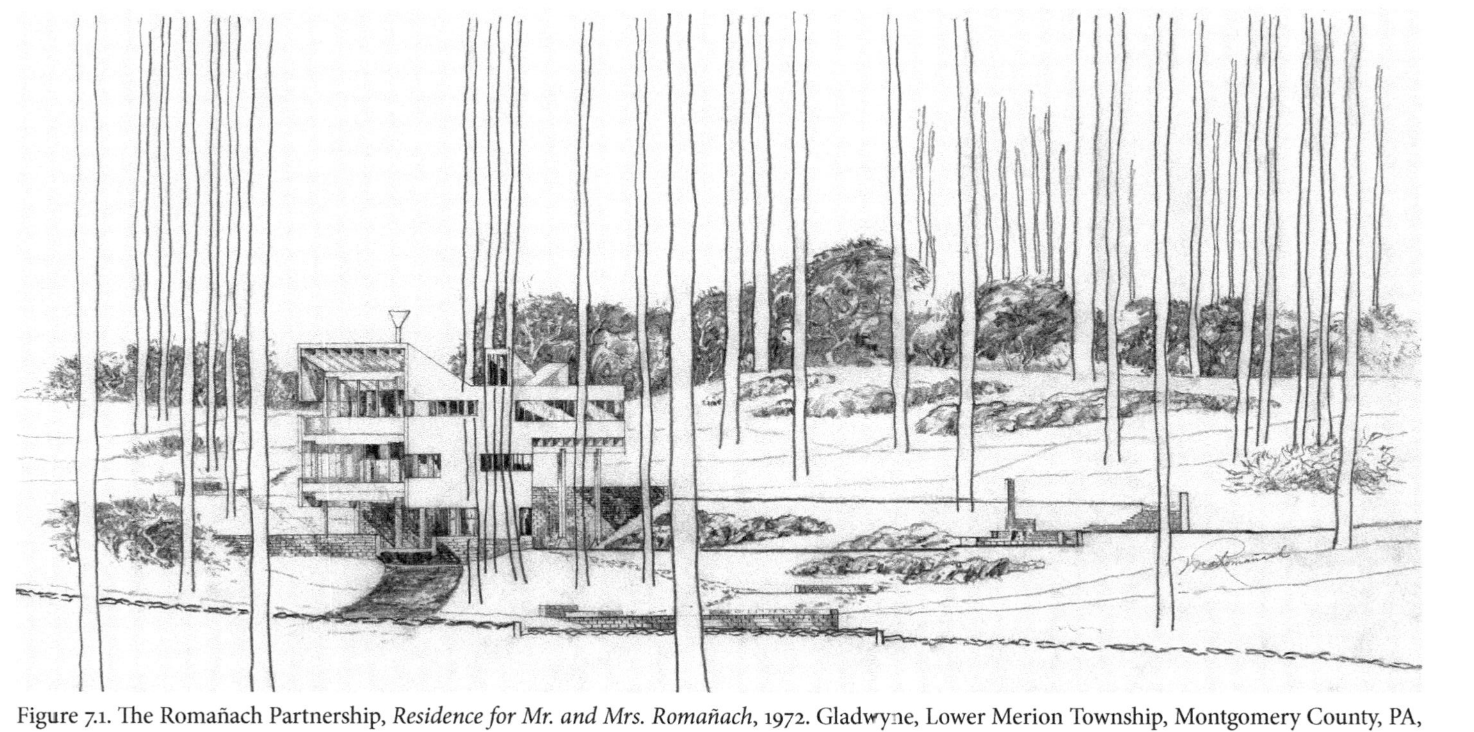

Figure 7.1. The Romañach Partnership, *Residence for Mr. and Mrs. Romañach*, 1972. Gladwyne, Lower Merion Township, Montgomery County, PA, Jan. 12, 1972, Mario Romañach Collection, Architectural Archives, University of Pennsylvania, aaup.048.1.

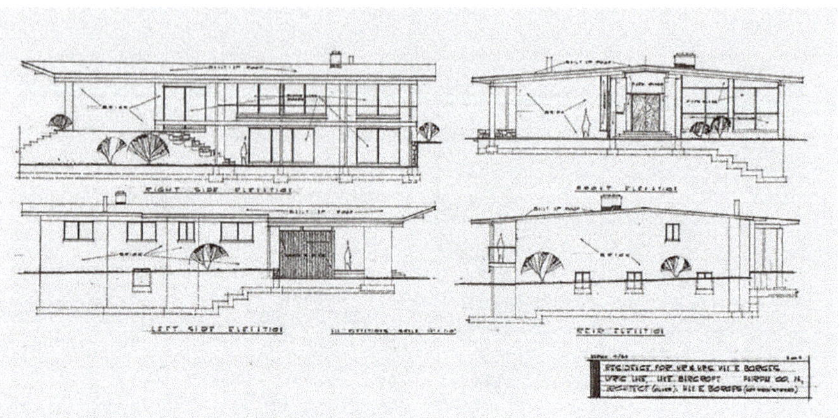

Figure 7.2. Max Borges, *House of Max Borges Recio*, 1963. Elevations, 24 × 36 inches. Max Borges Jr. Collection, Falls Church, VA.

wood, and glass, and filled with plants, it would not be out of place in Marianao or Playa in Havana. It is the only work of true Cuban architecture that he built in the United States" (Figure 7.2).[17]

Curiously, it was not a Cuban architect who designed one of the most important modern houses in Cuba, but rather the Austrian-American Richard Neutra (1892–1970), who made his mark in Southern California. Called to Cuba by the Swiss banker Alfred de Schulthess to design a house in the Country Club district of Havana, Neutra collaborated on the house with a young Cuban architect by the name of Raúl Alvarez (b. 1930).[18] Having graduated from Rensselaer Polytechnic Institute in 1951 and the University of Havana in 1953, Alvarez began his professional career working for Arroyo & Menéndez on the Teatro Nacional project, managing the construction drawings and follow-up.[19] He set up his own practice in Old Havana in 1955, when he was asked to be the architect of record on the Schulthess residence along with Neutra, Roberto Burle Marx, and Hans Knoll; the project received the Gold Medal from the CNAC in 1958. The concrete structure and great projecting eaves allow the walls to be open to the gardens with only the *persianas* mediating between the interior and exterior spaces. The forecourt garden in front functions as a reception area, and the open garden façade and rear terraces open to the garden, extending the interiors to the landscape. This house, perhaps more than any other in Cuba, represents the full synthesis of architecture, landscape, and interior design.

Planning Greater Havana (1925–59)

It was during the presidency (1925–33) of General Gerardo Machado and under the direction of his Minister of Public Works, Carlos Miguel de Céspedes, that the international concepts of modern city planning first appeared in Havana. The French landscape architect and urbanist Jean-Claude Nicolas Forestier (1861–1930) arrived in Havana in 1925 and, with a team of French and local experts, set out on a mission to modernize the city—its overall structure, its streets, and its parks.[20] The goal was to bring the city in line with the modern European and Latin American aesthetics and organization for international business and tourism.

Forestier did not start from scratch, as that same year the Cuban architect and urbanist Pedro Martínez Inclán (1883–1957) published an important book, *La Habana actual* (*Havana Today*).[21] Written between 1919 and 1922, the work was at once didactic, scientific, and highly political, as it read as a thorough denunciation of the general state of the city and the passivity of successive governments concerning urban reform and social housing. Largely influenced by the Civic Art and Park Movements in the United States, Martínez Inclán promoted the beautification of the city through public art and gardens, the renovation of the *Malecón* (the waterfront boulevard), and the construction of parks and neighborhoods for the indigent and working classes. His program, which he labeled as social and patriotic, also promoted the nation's acquisition of unoccupied lands to create land reserves, a program for the construction of schools, the transformation of colonial fortresses into parks and public monuments, and a great park project along the Almendares River. The backbone of his scheme was a system of axes and monuments coherent with the future expansion of the city and with the international theory of urban design of the Société Française des Urbanistes (Society of French Urbanists or SFU), of which Forestier was a founding member in 1911.[22] Martínez Inclán proposed a great circular plaza at the *Loma de los Catalanes* (Catalans' Hill), "bigger than, or at least as big as, the *Place de l'Étoile* in Paris," as the core of a new civic center, from which a radiating system of grand avenues would link with different areas of the city.[23]

Over three trips to Havana from 1925 to 1929 and having flown above the city to understand its regional and geographic context, Forestier developed, refined, and expanded Martínez Inclán's proposals. Even though many of his plans were never realized, Forestier's impact on the city was tremendous and shaped its urban form—and also its "imaginary substance"—for many decades to come: his designs were behind the reconstruction of the Paseo del Prado; the expansion of the Malecón along the colonial center and toward the new suburban neighborhoods of El Vedado and Miramar; the overall master plan of the University of Havana with the monumental staircase that marks its entrance from the city; and the initiation of a system of parks and gardens. From his theoretical perspective of the city as landscape and part of the region, Forestier saw a need to recentralize the metropolis while preserving the colonial center. Logically, the focus of the plan was the civic center located at the *Loma de los Catalanes*, slightly north of Martínez Inclán's original location. Midway between the old city and the district of El Vedado, the proposed new center was to be articulated around a vast T-shaped square. Featuring a central monument to José Martí, it was designed on two levels connected with ramps and terraces; the plan proposed to surround it with fountains and planted malls, as well as with the Museums of Flora and Fauna and the Ministry of Agriculture. From this monumental square, Forestier imagined two perpendicular axes designed as wide parkways or *avenues-jardins* (garden avenues), forming a grand urban cross leading east to a new maritime and train terminal in the bay; south to a new central park, the Gran Parque Nacional; and north to the Castillo del Príncipe, to be converted into a public park, and the new campus of the University.

With the fall of Machado (1933) and the world in crisis, the project for a Civic Center was paralyzed until the early 1950s. The 1930s saw an intense political process that eventually led to the Cuban constitution of 1940. A competition took place for the monument to Martí in 1938, with additional phases in 1942 and 1943. Years went by with a series of debates and political interventions that all but scuppered the project. It was only in 1952, under Fulgencio Batista's dictatorship, that both the Civic Plaza and the monument to Martí were finally constructed. The monument, in the form of a star and almost 300 feet in height, was designed by the third-prize winner of the 1943 competition, Jean Labatut, partner of Forestier in the 1920s and 1930s, with Enrique Luis Varela and Raúl Otero, and Juan José Sicre as sculptor. The highly structured and landscaped urban space proposed as a civic center by Forestier had mutated into a large modernist space. The countryside area of the *Loma de los Catalanes* had been urbanized, but remained to some extent an urban void, populated by the monument to Martí and a series of isolated modernist public structures that reflected the new architectural language of the government.[24]

At that moment, the vision of modern urban planning and architecture in Havana radically changed. In 1939, the Spanish Catalan exile and modernist architect José Luis Sert (1902–83) and his wife spent a few months in Havana preparing for their migration to the United States.[25] There he established important contacts with the new generation of Cuban architects. In 1941, a group of Cuban architects from the Congrès International d'Architecture Moderne (International Congress of Modern Architecture, or CIAM) named themselves the Agrupación Tectónica de Expresión Contemporánea (Tectonic Group for Contemporary Expression, or ATEC), a "nucleus of young minds, inclined to experimentation, investigation, and struggle."[26] They embraced the principles of CIAM, but quickly started to acquire their own identity. In 1943, ATEC set up an innovative exhibition of colonial architecture, *Trinidad, lo que fue, es y será* (*Trinidad, What It Was, Is, and Will Be*), in the heart of Havana. Curated by Emilio del Junco, Eduardo Montoulieu, and Miguel Gastón, the exhibition's message was manifold: it advocated that the urban and architectural qualities of the colonial city of Trinidad be historically preserved, not as a "romantic" expression of Cuban culture and way of life, but rather as an example for the future. The exhibition promoted the recuperation of the city fabric, not as a monument but as a vital and contemporary environment: "Trinidad, in addition to its great archeological value, is a city that . . . is alive; it is potentially a city that can and should revive its splendid glorious past in the 20th century, with the physiognomy of the 20th century."[27] Nicolás Arroyo (1917–2008) and the organizers of the exhibition concluded that Cuban colonial typologies might inform contemporary architecture and progressive urban design.[28] Like in Spain, the relation of modernity to the vernacular and the Mediterranean as a whole was not based only on architecture, but involved the urban milieu in its full complexity. Overall, the exhibition was a definitive demonstration of Eugenio Batista's thesis about the three "Ps."

In this postwar environment, Cuban architects and urbanists were moving away from strict modernist orthodoxy. The low-scale streets of colonial cities were no longer seen as rue-corridors; instead, their traditional patio-based fabric was envisioned as a basic typology for a genuinely Cuban modern city. In 1948, Martínez Inclán published his *Código de urbanismo* (Urban Code), subtitled *Carta de Atenas, Carta de La Habana* (Athens Charter, Havana Charter). The Cuban version of the international Charter of Athens, *Carta de La Habana*, was an important document that followed the structure of its source but added many concepts related to the civic importance of the city and to the need for low-income housing. More significantly, Martínez Inclán inserted two sections. The first, titled "Legislation," outlined the administrative and political components of the systematic planning of the city and the region; the other, "Urban Aesthetics," emphasized the importance of the Cuban manifestations of Civic Art, such as the squares, the streets, and the monuments. In brief, it was a unique document that promoted *cubanidad* in the field of urbanism.[29] This theoretical stand anticipated, to some extent, the upcoming breakup of CIAM and the birth of Team X, a splinter group.

On the legislative side, the Cuban constitution was adopted in 1940. After years of debate about how modernity was to affect the island, its urbanism and architecture, and eventually its identity, the concept of planning—from region to metropolis to town—became a requirement of the new constitution. However, nothing happened until 1955, when the Junta Nacional de Planificación (National Planning Board) was created under the direction of Nicolás Arroyo, architect and Minister of Public Works.[30] In 1953, Arroyo commissioned Sert, Paul Lester Weiner, and Paul Schulz (known as Town Planning Associates) to develop a new plan for Havana.[31] Referred to as the *Plan Piloto* (pilot plan), the idea was to coordinate large areas of urban growth and expansion that extended to Varadero, Trinidad, and Isla de Pinos.[32] Romañach, Nicolás Quintana (1925–2011), and others worked in tandem with Sert and his team. Though praised for their concerted effort to manage growth and expansion, and provide increased parks and green spaces, the *Plan Piloto* received considerable pushback for its design ideas that, although very innovative within the context of CIAM-inspired planning, were eminently destructive, expensive, and ultimately more fantasy than reality.

The plan proposed the widespread demolition of colonial Havana. However, its reconstruction as a mixed-use residential, commercial, and administrative center followed a pattern of streets and blocks superimposed on the colonial grid—every second street was to be widened to accommodate traffic and access to parking. In addition, the plan advocated the use of the "modern patio"—an inner courtyard above parking—at the center of the reconstructed blocks. In accord with the *Carta de La*

Habana, the plan stressed the preservation of the historic fabric around colonial squares. On the seafront, Sert fell prey to U.S. tourist interests as he proposed to block off most of the Malecón from public use by building large hotels directly facing the water and an artificial island to accommodate theaters and casinos. More relevant for the future of the city, whose metropolitan growth was estimated to increase from one to three million residents in twenty-five years, Sert proposed a comprehensive network of urban and suburban neighborhoods, each centered upon a civic center and made up of low-rise high-density courtyard housing. A sophisticated system of parks, directly inspired by Forestier's masterplan of 1925–30, was to connect those new neighborhoods and link them to the historic city. The plan—titled *Plan de enlaces de núcleos cívicos* (Plan to Link Civic Centers)—was a strong reversal of the undifferentiated treatment of green space that distinguished the first CIAM projects. Town Planning Associates proposed to reduce the size of the Plaza Cívica dramatically and transform it into a pedestrian-oriented system of smaller plazas, articulated on different levels and defined by the addition of many public structures.

The main architectural proposal developed within the *Plan Piloto* was that for the Presidential Palace and the adjoining Civic Complex, to be built on the other side of the bay between the Spanish colonial fortresses of El Morro and La Cabaña. The site, accessible by the new automobile tunnel started in 1955 and completed in 1958, was undoubtedly controversial, but the comprehensive project, designed by Sert with Arroyo, Gabriela Menéndez (d. 2008), and landscape architects Sasaki and Walker Associates, was a fascinating proposal. The royal palm dominated the conceptual and formal composition of both palace and gardens. As described in the authors' report, "this symbol of Cuba echoed as well in the architecture of the reinforced concrete umbrella roof that was to give a larger scale and monumentality to the Palace."[33] The umbrella roof—whose concrete columns and funnels were designed by the Spanish exile architect Félix Candela (1910–97) to match the scale and proportions of the royal palm—gave more unity to the diverse constructions that it covered, that is, the presidential offices, the reception areas, the presidential residence, and other services. A large patio planted with palms occupied the heart of the U-shaped palace, whose typology recalled the royal palaces of Madrid, Stockholm, London, and other cities. Under the roof, the architects designed a series of tropical-modern structures, some of which would be lighted by colored stained-glass windows, as was the case in many houses in the colonial center. Gardens with axes of royal palms structured the entire site and connected the palace to two squares, the museums within the fortresses, and the proposed museum of oceanography at the edge of the bay.[34]

At the same time, Nicolás Quintana coordinated the study of the *Plan Piloto* for the resort town of Varadero, fifty miles east of Havana, in collaboration with Sert and Town Planning Associates. Quintana and Sert had met at the CIAM conference in Aix-en-Provence in 1953, and then in Barcelona at the Catalan's invitation. Little material exists regarding the details of the plan, but Quintana's archives contain a colored plan that illustrates the project for this thin peninsula of about ten miles in length, half a mile in width, and bordered by the Straits of Florida on one side and the Bay of Cárdenas on the other.[35] The plan was divided into various zones that ranged from full conservation areas to mid-density beach development and single-family residential islands. Public structures and civic centers, often located within green areas, articulated the fully functional concept of the plan. Overall, the plan for Varadero bore much resemblance to the masterplan for a *Ciutat de Repòs i de Vacances* (City of Rest and Vacation), which Sert and his partners from the Grup d'Arquitectes i Tècnics Catalans per al Progrés de l'Arquitectura Contemporània (Group of Catalan Architects and Technicians for the Progress of Contemporary Architecture, or GATCPAC) had proposed in 1932 for the extensive beaches south of Barcelona toward Castelldefels.[36]

On January 1, 1959, Fulgencio Batista fled Havana, and a new era in Cuban architecture and urbanism began. All planning projects for Havana, East Havana, Varadero, Trinidad, and the Isle of Pines were abandoned. By the end of the decade, Arroyo, Gabriela Menéndez, Romañach, Quintana, Sert, Town Planning Associates, and many more had fled the island. The Plaza Cívica and its gigantic modernist space became the perfect setup for political speeches in front of huge crowds. As in the Rome of Mussolini, and the Berlin of the German Democratic Republic (RDA), modernist planning became a tool of propaganda and politics: a dangerous space for the individual, a perfect theater for the manipulation of the masses.

Modernization and Exile

The 1950s was a decade of intense activity as Cuba experienced major economic changes. While ambitious masterplans were contemplated, modernization impacted the city of Havana on various fronts. The urban center of gravity moved farther to the west along the Malecón and to the entrance to the Vedado district.[37] La Rampa, or 23rd Street, became an important public thoroughfare, the "Broadway of Havana." Its most prominent symbol was the modern Radiocentro Building, built in 1945–47 by Martín Domínguez (1897–1970) in collaboration with Emilio del Junco and Miguel Gastón.[38] The multipurpose structure consisted of two prismatic buildings that reflected their internal functions and included the large Warner cinema, retail spaces, and radio and television studios. A ten-floor rectangular slab building contained the offices and marked a distinct modernist feature of the complex, while a wide two-story arcade along 23rd Street made the connection with the lobby of the theater. Domínguez also designed the pioneering FOCSA residential block nearby, with Ernesto Gómez Sampera and Bartolomé Bestard, the highest structure in Havana.[39] Designed for workers and emerging middle-class families, the thirty-nine-story building, which occupied an entire city block, was conceived as a Corbusian vertical city. The Y-shaped form not only provided views of the Bay of Havana and the Malecón, but was also permeable to the trade winds and sea breezes, while offering maximum resistance to the vortex winds of Caribbean hurricanes.

In the early 1950s, Humberto Alonso (b. 1924), a professor of architecture, established the group Arquitectos Unidos (United Architects), which included Osvaldo de Tapia-Ruano (1930–2014), Enrique (Henry) Gutiérrez (1931–2017), and Hugo Consuegra (1929–2003), to debate current issues in architecture, arts, and politics.[40] In 1953, the group developed the office building for the College of Architects, a structure that blended concrete frame construction with plate-glass windows.[41] With the works of Borges, Antonio Quintana, and Arroyo-Menéndez, the high-rise building became a frequent and architecturally innovative type that, in most cases, adopted environmental strategies to deal with the tropical climate. The last high-rise building in pre-Castro Cuba started as the Banco Nacional, designed by the architect Nicolás Quintana (from a previous scheme by José Pérez Benitoa), but with the Revolution the project changed function and was only completed two decades later as the Hospital Clínico

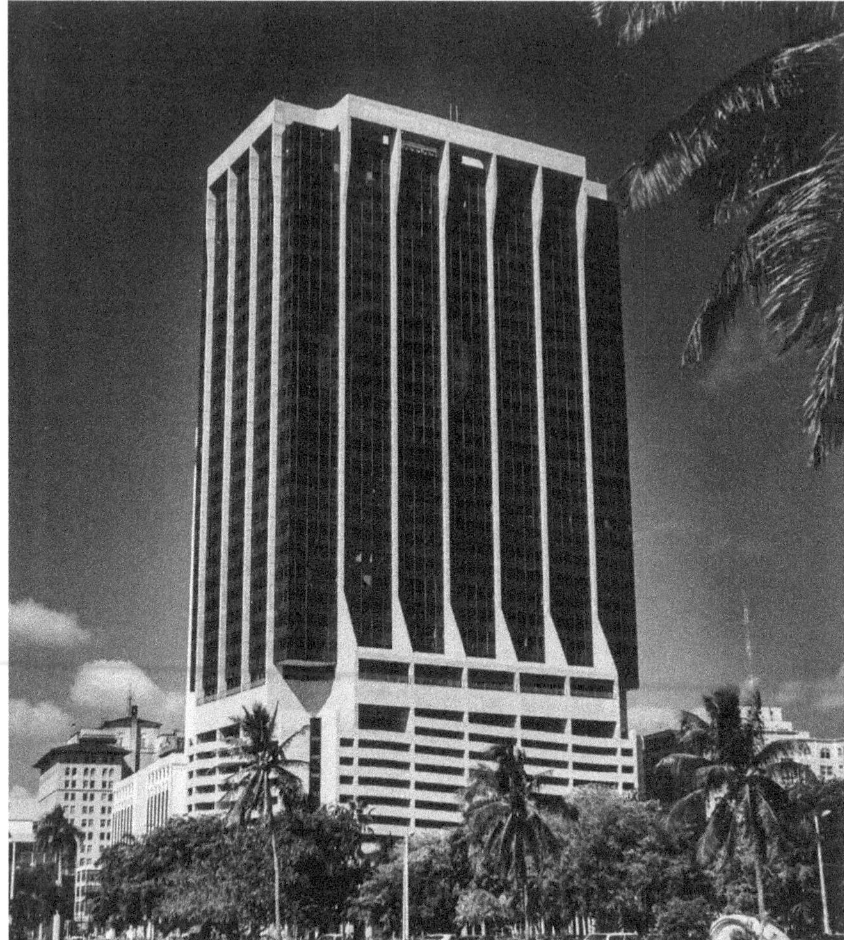

Figure 7.3. Enrique Gutiérrez, Humberto Alonso, Fraga Associates, *First Federal One Biscayne Tower First National Bank*, 1973. Black and white photograph, 10 × 16 inches. Humberto Alonso Collection, Miami.

Quirúrgico "Hermanos Ameijeiras," named after the brothers who were killed fighting against Fulgencio Batista's regime.[42]

Cuban architects would continue to work on high-rise structures outside of Cuba. In 1959, Gropius invited Romañach to come to Harvard as a visiting professor, an appointment that also resulted in Romañach never returning to Cuba.[43] His work in the United States included the design of the Chatham Towers (1959–67), under the firm of Kelly & Gruzen Architects in New York. In Philadelphia, he designed the much-maligned Penn super block with the chair of the school of architecture, G. Holmes Perkins.[44] Henry Gutiérrez joined Raúl Alvarez in 1956 and, two years later, they joined the engineers Sáenz, Cancio, and Martín to create SACMAG, a corporate firm the likes of which only existed in the United States.[45] After the Revolution, Gutiérrez relocated to Puerto Rico, where he continued the firm. His thirty-eight-story One Biscayne Tower (1973), done in collaboration with Humberto Alonso and Pelayo Fraga Associates, was the first modern skyscraper in Miami (Figure 7.3).[46] With large open-floor plates, the building reflected the evolution of the modern office building typology. The tower incorporated dark glass to control heat and glare, and the "glass curtain wall was vertically sliced by sculpted white concrete piers that flared outward where the office tower met the garage."[47] The tower still stands today, though dwarfed by much larger and taller structures.

Another figure to emerge from SACMAG was Hilario Candela (b. 1936), the youngest and one of the last Cuban architects of the Modernist Generation to have practiced in both Cuba and abroad.[48] In 1960, he joined the historic Miami firm of Pancoast-Ferendino-Grafton-Skeels-Burnham. Candela was immediately asked to work on the Miami Marine Stadium Grandstand on Virginia Key, in collaboration with Andrew Ferendino (Figure 7.4). Candela and Ferendino eventually succeeded—with the collaboration of Norman Dignum Associates Engineers of Miami—in demonstrating the prowess of poured-in-place concrete construction. With its paraboloid roof cantilevering sixty-five feet by approximately 300 feet in length, the Grandstand became the only structure in the United States to rival Pier Luigi Nervi's thin-shell work in Europe and the Americas.[49] Candela (with Peter Spillis) was also commissioned to develop the ambitious urban and architectural program of Miami-Dade Junior College (Figure 7.5). Between 1962 and 1967, Candela directed the design of the north and south campuses of the newly established college as a tropical adaptation of international brutalism. The colleges were built as raw concrete structures, clad with prefabricated gravel-washed concrete and ceramic panels. The buildings were connected through a continuous grid of outdoor spaces and covered walkways, suggesting both a "mat-building" strategy and a reinterpretation of Cuban and Latin American plazas.[50] For Candela and his colleagues, it was not Paul Rudolph but rather Le Corbusier and Félix Candela who provided most of the impetus. Concrete, open-air public spaces and circulation, natural ventilation, and solar protection were, for the architects, "a question of civic and cultural responsibility."[51]

Hilario Candela once said that the first rule of exile is survival.[52] The ability to use the possibilities offered by the United States and other countries—and to benefit professionally from them—was not available to all who left Cuba after the Revolution. Those in the world of construction benefitted the most, and had the most possibilities, as Cuban education and practice were more technical than theoretical. As similarly noted by another Cuban-American architect, Raúl Rodríguez, also from Miami,

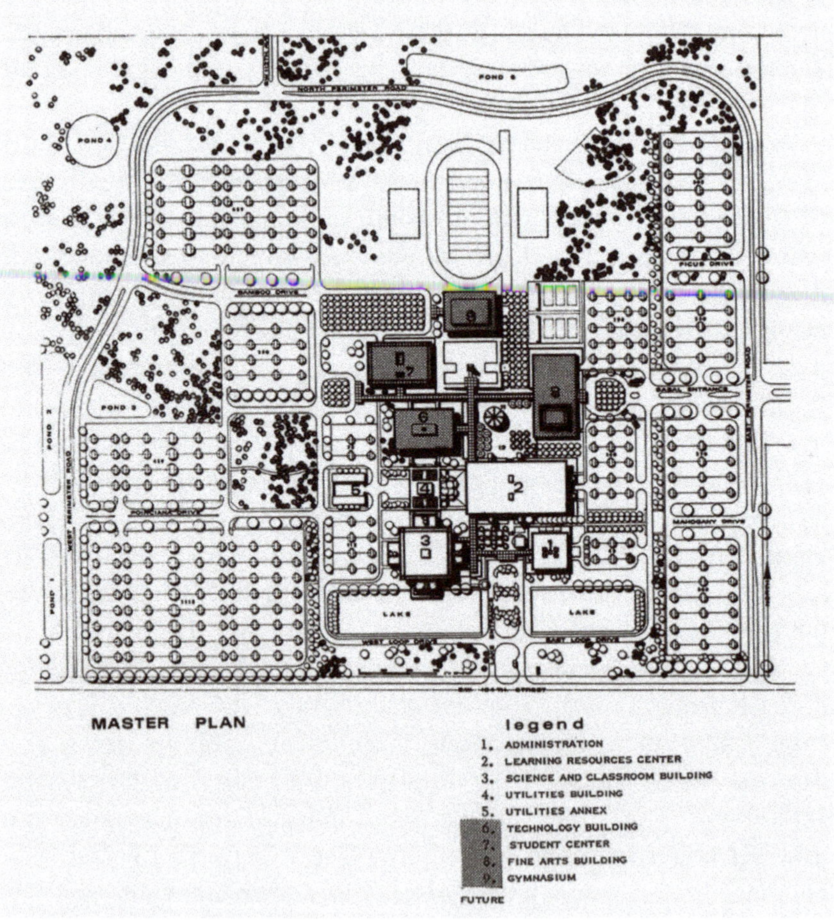

Figure 7.4. Hilario Candela (Pancoast-Ferendino-Grafton-Skeels-Burnham), *Plan of the Miami Dade College South Campus*, Kendall, ca. 1963. Black and white photograph. Miami Dade College Archives, Miami.

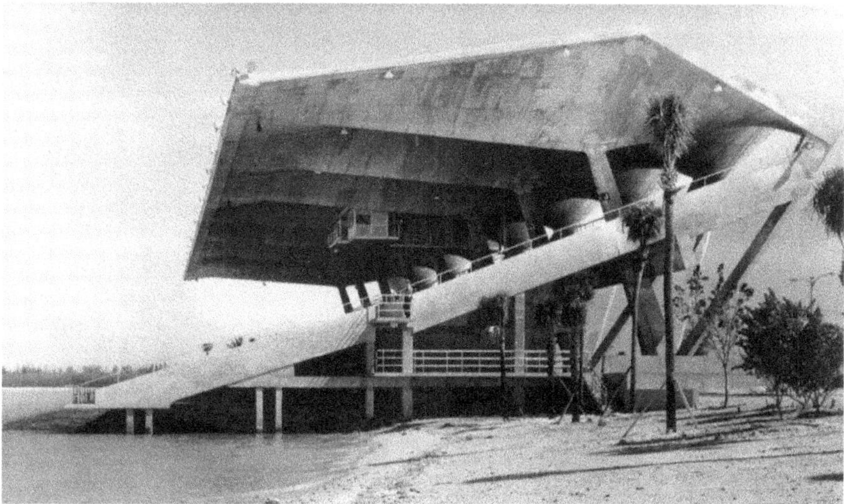

Figure 7.5. Hilario Candela (Pancoast-Ferendino-Grafton-Skeels-Burnham), *Marine Stadium*, Miami, 1962. Black and white photograph. Hilario Candela Collection, Coral Gables, FL.

the Modernist Generation of Cuban architects "left behind an island society with a rich centuries-old tradition of architectural high design and exceptional quality construction. Left behind were established professional practices with clients who functioned more like patrons who built to keep rather than speculate. Left behind, inaccessible to them even to photograph, were their buildings, their lives' work."[53] Ahead lay demanding climate conditions, design methods, and speculative practices that were new to them. The need to intern, license, and practice in a language that was not their native tongue provided new challenges and new beginnings. Yet we should not think of this generation of architects as having two lives. Their creative output at home and abroad should be seen as one, and it belongs to all of us—Cubans on the island and in the diaspora. Their stories are part of the great Cuban patrimony of architecture in the twentieth century.

Notes

1. Eduardo Luis Rodríguez, *The Havana Guide*, vii.

2. Rodríguez, *The Havana Guide*, ix; Francisco Gómez Díaz, *De Forestier a Sert*, 263–75. On the CNAC, see Colegio Nacional de Arquitectos de Cuba, "Historia," http://www.cubanarchitects-naca.org/historia.htm.

3. Gómez Díaz, 275ff.

4. Gómez Díaz, 221–35. See also Rodríguez, *The Havana Guide*, xi–xiii; Carlos Sambricio, "Notas bio-bibliográficas," 57–58, 63.

5. Eduardo Luis Rodríguez, *La Habana, arquitectura del siglo XX*, 240–45; Sambricio, "Notas bio-bibliográficas," 50–51; Gómez Díaz, 230–35. See also the Eugenio Batista Collection, Cuban Heritage Collection, University of Miami Libraries, Coral Gables, FL, CHC 0331.

6. Eugenio Batista, "La casa cubana."

7. "Havana, Cuba: All Rooms in This House Open on Courtyards"; Rodríguez, *The Havana Guide*, 84–85.

8. Rafael de Cárdenas won the first prize for an even more traditional residence in the Country Club neighborhood for Alberto W. Kaffenburg, whose family in the United States owned the Standard Havana Tobacco Company. See *Arquitectura* 89 (December 1940), 314–20; Gómez Díaz, 278–79.

9. See the Eugenio Batista Collection.

10. Rodríguez, *La Habana, arquitectura del siglo XX*, 269–91; Gómez Díaz, 506–59; Sambricio, "Notas bio-bibliográficas," 61; *Arquitectura* 198 (January 1950), 9–15.

11. "Una obra de los arquitectos Silverio Bosch y Mario Romañach," *Arquitectura* 219 (October 1951), 430–31; "Una obra de los arquitectos Silverio Bosch y Mario Romañach," *Arquitectura* 243 (October 1953), 420–23; Rodríguez, *The Havana Guide*, 48–49.

12. "Caribbean Mansion in Havana," 116–19.

13. Felipe Gorostiza, "Mario Romañach," 210–11; G. Holmes Perkins, "The Romañach Partnership," 245–47.

14. See *Residence for Mr. and Mrs. Romañach*, Gladwyne, Lower Merion Township, Montgomery County, PA, Jan. 12, 1972, Mario Romañach Collection, Architectural Archives, University of Pennsylvania, aaup.048.1.

15. Rodríguez, *The Havana Guide*, 250–53; Gómez Díaz, 434–45; Sambricio, "Notas bio-bibliográficas," 53–54; "Construcciones Max Borges [Sr.]," 821.

16. *Arquitectura* 204 (1950), 318; Rodríguez, *The Havana Guide*, 91.

17. Belmont Freeman, "Max Borges, 1918–2009."

18. Thomas S. Hines, *Richard Neutra and the Search for Modern Architecture*; "El Premio Medalla de Oro del Colegio de Arquitectos de 1958," *Arquitectura* 306 (January 1959), 10–18; Rodríguez, *The Havana Guide*, 54–55; Gómez Díaz, 366–70.

19. See *Cuban Architects: Their Impact on the Urban Landscape of Miami*, 15–19.

20. Gómez Díaz, 43ff.; Sambricio, "Equipamientos y vivienda en La Habana, 1925–1950," 23ff. See also Jean-François Lejeune, "The City as Landscape" and "La ville comme paysage," 173–87.

21. Pedro Martínez Inclán, *La Habana actual*.

22. See Fernando Diniz Moreira, *Shaping Cities, Building a Nation*.

23. Martínez Inclán, 200. See also Enrique Montoulieu y de la Torre, "El crecimiento de La Habana y su regularización," *Anales de la Academia de Ciencias de La Habana* (1923), reprinted in Felipe Préstamo, ed., *Cuba: Arquitectura y urbanismo*, 237–55; Gómez Díaz, 43–51.

24. On the Monument to Martí, see Timothy Hyde, *Constitutional Modernism*, 213–52.

25. Josep M. Rovira i Gimeno, *José Luis Sert*; Gómez Díaz, 259.

26. Gómez Díaz, 257ff.

27. Nicolás Arroyo, "La A.T.E.C. y la última exposición de Trinidad," *Arquitectura* (May 1943), 192, quoted in Hyde, 260–61.

28. Sert's influence on these matters was significant. The Catalan architect continued his advocacy of the patio with his important article, "Can Patios Make Cities?"

29. *Código de urbanismo*; see also Hyde, 75ff.; Gómez Díaz, 109–14; and the reprint in Préstamo, *Cuba: Arquitectura y urbanismo*, 437–49.

30. Gómez Díaz, 424–34; Sambricio, "Notas bio-bibliográficas," 49–50.

31. Hyde, 131.

32. Town Planning Associates et al., *Plan piloto de La Habana*.

33. Town Planning Associates et al., 36.

34. Hyde, 253–87.

35. Nicolás Quintana, *Plan piloto: Varadero*, ca. 1958, Nicolás Quintana Papers, Cuban Heritage Collection, University of Miami Libraries, Coral Gables, FL. CHC5314. See also Gómez Díaz, 477.

36. See *A.C. La revista del G.A.T.E.P.A.C., 1931–37*.

37. Gómez Díaz, 167ff.; Joseph L. Scarpaci et al., *Havana*, 127–28.

38. Pablo Rabasco and Martín Domínguez Ruz, *Martín Domínguez Esteban*, 16ff., 80–84; Rodríguez, *The Havana Guide*, 123; Gómez Díaz, 386–89.

39. Rabasco and Domínguez Ruz, 18ff., 91–93; Rodríguez, *The Havana Guide*, 138; Gómez Díaz, 394–98.

40. John A. Loomis, *Revolution of Forms*, 21ff.; Abigail McEwen, *Revolutionary Horizons*, 35ff.

41. Rodríguez, *The Havana Guide*, 137.

42. Scarpaci et al., 279–81.

43. Gómez Díaz, 558–59.

44. Gorostiza, "Mario Romañach," 210.

45. Allan T. Shulman, *Building Bacardi*, 57–59. Hector Tate of Welton Beckett Associates in Los Angeles helped SACMAG structure itself as the largest architectural office in Cuba, providing the full repertoire of architectural and design services (notes presented to Victor Deupi by Raúl Alvarez, March 3, 2016).

46. See "One Biscayne Tower," in Allan T. Shulman et al., eds., *Miami Architecture*, 24–25.

47. "One Biscayne Tower."

48. Hilario Candela was educated at Georgia Tech in Atlanta, where he had the opportunity to hear lectures by Pier Luigi Nervi and Félix Candela (notes presented to the authors on February 9, 2016).

49. See Jean-François Lejeune, "Miami Marine Stadium," 352–59; Lejeune, "Preserving the Marine Stadium (1962–64)."

50. See Lejeune, "William Morgan in Florida," 425–31; Gray Read, "A Center in the Middle of Nowhere," 256–61.

51. Notes presented to Jean-François Lejeune by Hilario Candela, January 25, 2016.
52. Notes presented to the authors, February 9, 2016.
53. Rodríguez, "Architecture."

Bibliography

A.C. La revista del G.A.T.E.P.A.C., 1931–37. Madrid: Museo Nacional Centro de Arte Reina Sofía, 2008.

Balbín Behrmann, Juan Enrique de, and Carlos Sambricio, eds. *Arquitectura en la ciudad de La Habana: Primera modernidad*. Madrid: Electa España, 2000.

Batista, Eugenio. "La casa cubana." *Artes Plásticas* 2 (1960): 4–7.

"Caribbean Mansion in Havana by Architects Silverio Bosch and Mario Romañach Combines Beauty with Climate Control." *House & Home* (August 1952): 116–19.

"Construcciones Max Borges [Sr.]." In *El libro de Cuba: Historia, letras, artes, ciencias, agricultura, industria, comercio, bellezas naturales*, edited by Wifredo Fernández and Emilio Roig de Leuchsenring, 821. Havana: Talleres del Sindicato de Artes Gráficas, 1925.

Cuban Architects: Their Impact on the Urban Landscape of Miami. Miami: Cuban Museum of Arts and Culture, 1985.

Freeman, Belmont. "Max Borges, 1918–2009." *The Architect's Newspaper* (March 4, 2009). https://archpaper.com/2009/03/max-borges-1918-2009/.

Gómez Díaz, Francisco. *De Forestier a Sert: Ciudad y arquitectura en La Habana (1925–1960)*. Madrid: Abada, 2008.

Gorostiza, Felipe, "Mario Romañach." In *The Book of the School: 100 Years, the Graduate School of Fine Arts of the University of Pennsylvania*, edited by Ann L. Strong and George E. Thomas, 210–11. Philadelphia: The Graduate School, 1990.

"Havana, Cuba: All Rooms in this House Open on Courtyards." *Architectural Record* 86 (July-December 1939): 45–47.

Hines, Thomas S. *Richard Neutra and the Search for Modern Architecture: A Biography and History*. New York: Oxford University Press, 1982.

Hyde, Timothy. *Constitutional Modernism: Architecture and Civil Society in Cuba, 1933–1959*. Minneapolis: University of Minnesota Press, 2013.

Lejeune, Jean-François. "The City as Landscape: Jean-Claude Nicolas Forestier and the Grand Public Works in Havana, 1925–1930." *Journal of Decorative and Propaganda Arts* 21 (1996): 150–85.

———. "Miami Marine Stadium." In *Miami Modern Metropolis: Paradise and Paradox in Midcentury Architecture and Planning*, edited by Allan T. Shulman, 352–59. Miami/Glendale, CA: Bass Museum of Art/Balcony Press, 2009.

———. "Preserving the Marine Stadium (1962–64): Tropical Brutalism, Society of Leisure, and Ethnic Identity." *DOCOMOMO-US* (July 15, 2014). http://www.docomomo-us.org/news/preserving-the-miami-marine-stadium-1962-64-tropical-brutalism-society-of-leisure-and-ethnic-identity.

———. "La ville comme paysage: Influences et projets américains à La Havane." In *Jean-*

Claude Nicolas Forestier, 1861–1930: Du jardin au paysage urbain, edited by Benédicte Leclerc, 173–87. Paris: Picard, 1994.
———. "William Morgan in Florida: Tropical Brutalism in the Age of Consensus." *DoCOMOMO* (Proceedings of the 14th International Conference), 425–31. Lisbon: DoCOMOMO, 2016.
Loomis, John A. *Revolution of Forms: Cuba's Forgotten Art Schools*. New York: Princeton Architectural Press, 2011.
Martínez Inclán, Pedro. *Código de urbanismo: Carta de Atenas, Carta de La Habana*. Havana: P. Fernández y Cía., 1949.
———. *La Habana actual: Estudio de la capital de Cuba desde el punto de vista de la arquitectura de ciudades*. Havana: P. Fernández y Cía., 1925.
McEwen, Abigail. *Revolutionary Horizons: Art and Polemics in 1950s Cuba*. New Haven: Yale University Press, 2016.
Moreira, Fernando D. *Shaping Cities, Building a Nation: Alfred Agache and the Dream of Modern Urbanism in Brazil (1920–1950)*. PhD diss., University of Pennsylvania, 2004.
"Una obra de los arquitectos Silverio Bosch y Mario Romañach." *Arquitectura* 219 (October 1951): 430–31; *Arquitectura* 243 (October 1953): 420–23.
Perkins, G. Holmes. "The Romañach Partnership." In *Drawing toward Building: Philadelphia Architectural Graphics, 1732–1986*, edited by James F. O'Gorman, 245–47. Philadelphia: University of Pennsylvania Press, 1986.
"El Premio Medalla de Oro del Colegio de Arquitectos." *Arquitectura* 89 (1940): 314–20; *Arquitectura* 198 (1950): 9–15; *Arquitectura* 246 (1954): 12–19; and *Arquitectura* 306 (1959): 10–18.
Préstamo, Felipe, ed. *Cuba: Arquitectura y urbanismo*. Miami: Ediciones Universal, 1995.
Rabasco, Pablo, and Martín Domínguez Ruz. *Martín Domínguez Esteban*. Ithaca, NY: Cornell AAP Publications, 2015.
Read, Gray. "Miami-Dade Junior College South Campus: A Center in the Middle of Nowhere." In *Miami Modern Metropolis: Paradise and Paradox in Midcentury Architecture and Planning*, edited by Allan T. Shulman, 256–61. Miami Beach/Glendale, CA: Balcony Press, 2009.
Rodríguez, Eduardo Luis. *La Habana, arquitectura del siglo XX*. Barcelona: Blume, 1998.
———. *The Havana Guide*. Princeton: Princeton University Press, 2000.
Rodríguez, Raúl L. "Architecture." In *Cubans: An Epic Journey—The Struggle of Exiles for Truth and Freedom*, edited by Sam Verdeja and Guillermo Martínez, 587–95. St. Louis, MO: Reedy Press, 2012.
Rovira i Gimeno, Josep M. *José Luis Sert: 1901–1983*. Milan: Electa, 2000.
Sambricio, Carlos. "Equipamientos y vivienda en La Habana, 1925–1950." In *Arquitectura en la ciudad de La Habana: Primera modernidad*, edited by Juan Enrique de Balbín Behrmann and Carlos Sambricio, 23–47. Madrid: Electa España, 2000.
———. "Notas bio-bibliográficas sobre los arquitectos de La Habana entre 1925 y 1950." In *Arquitectura en la ciudad de La Habana: Primera modernidad*, edited by Juan Enrique de Balbín Behrmann and Carlos Sambricio, 49–63. Madrid: Electa España, 2000.
Scarpaci, Joseph L., Roberto Segre, and Mario Coyula. *Havana: Two Faces of the Antillean Metropolis*. Chapel Hill: University of North Carolina Press, 2002.

Segre, Roberto. "La Habana: Ortodoxia y digresiones de la Primera Modernidad." In *Arquitectura en la ciudad de La Habana: Primera modernidad*, edited by Juan Enrique de Balbín Berhmann and Carlos Sambricio, 65–? Madrid: Electa España, 2000.

Sert, José Luis. "Can Patios Make Cities?" *Architectural Forum* 99, no. 2 (August 1953), 124–31.

Shulman, Allan T. *Building Bacardi: Architecture, Art & Identity*. New York: Rizzoli International Publications, 2016.

Shulman, Allan T., Randall C. Robinson, and James Donnelly, eds. *Miami Architecture: An AIA Guide Featuring Downtown, the Beaches, and Coconut Grove*. Gainesville: University Press of Florida, 2010.

Town Planning Associates, Nicolás Arroyo, Mario Romañach et al. *Plan piloto de La Habana, directivas generales: Diseños preliminares, soluciones tipo*. New York: Town Planning Associates, 1959.

8

Concrete Cuba

Abigail McEwen

"Touch the painting," Sandú Darié instructed the spectators of his early three-dimensional reliefs (Plate 24). "Turn the axes, dematerialize the line[,] travel through space, in r[h]ythm. Remake the line, like a magician closing his fan—and open it again, if you want to breathe and get away from the dead, from the amorphous line."[1] In his pioneering series *Estructuras transformables* (*Transformable Structures*, ca. 1950s), Darié challenged the fixity of line and color, directing their movement dynamically beyond the frame, implicitly displacing art into life. The morphology of his structures nods to the Neoplastic precedent of Piet Mondrian and his purist abstraction, and yet their shape-shifting forms radically deconstruct the modular grid, spatializing its geometry in ways that resonate with the contemporary work of the Grupo Madí in Argentina and, later, Brazilian Neoconcretism. The prime mover behind Cuban Concretism, the Romanian-born Darié arrived in Havana in 1941, a wartime émigré from Paris. By the start of the 1950s, his work had shed its earlier expressionistic tendencies, and its gravitation toward geometric abstraction matched the maturing modernist project on the island, aligning an emerging generation of Cuban *concretos* with the transatlantic avant-garde. With Mario Carreño, Luis Martínez Pedro, and Loló Soldevilla (1901–71), Darié championed Concretism, creatively redeploying its historical values—rationalism, universalism, utopia—within the unidealized climate of dictatorship under Fulgencio Batista, in power from March 10, 1952 until January 1, 1959, and ultimately within the revolution that followed.

A highly periodized phenomenon, "Concrete Cuba" embodied the national zeitgeist of the decade, leveraging abstraction as a signpost for the country's modernization and cultural cosmopolitanism. Its streamlined geometries blended easily within the built environment of Havana, in which a regional and tropical vernacular merged with newly fashionable International Style architecture, effectively absorbing steel-and-glass abstraction within a familiar national syntax. Cuba's concretos advanced a similar proposition, pitching Concrete art simultaneously in national terms—as the final movement of Cuba's *vanguardia*, which had pioneered modern art since 1927—and, aspirationally, as a measure of the country's synchronicity with advanced art the world over. Concretism in Cuba, as elsewhere throughout Latin America, took interpretive liberties with historical Concrete art, first formalized in Paris around 1930 by the Dutch artist Theo van Doesburg to define works with no basis in the natural world and no symbolic content. Yet if Cuba's cognizance of Concretism was imperfect and idiosyncratic, at times elided with Constructivism and contemporary Op and Kinetic art, the movement embraced the exigencies of its local conditions; indeed, its practitioners strategically positioned their work within the country's social landscape, affirming its transformative potential amid shifting political winds.

The convergence of Carreño, Darié, and Martínez Pedro around abstraction at the start of the 1950s set in motion a series of exhibitions and publication projects that articulated Concrete art within a Cuban context. Central to the cultivation of this progressive, modernist mindset was their editorial collaboration on the magazine *Noticias de Arte*, published monthly over eleven issues in 1952–53, and its richly illustrated reporting on art news across Cuba and around the world. The first arts magazine of its kind in Havana, with an international purview and the ambition "to be a true source of pride for those who care about improving our cultural environment," *Noticias de Arte* served an essential pedagogical role in shaping Cuba's emergent art world. Carreño and Darié penned regular national and international art columns, respectively; distinguished contributors included José Gómez Sicre, the long-serving director of the Visual Arts Section of the Pan American Union in Washington, DC ("La plástica cubana actual"), and Alfred H. Barr Jr., the founding director of the Museum of Modern Art in New York ("¿Es el arte moderno comunista?"). Carreño broached abstraction in a theoretical essay, "El factor moral en la pintura abstracta," introducing concrete art as "an aesthetic corollary of the historical and spiritual needs of our time" that was already anticipated in Cuba's vanguardia past: paintings by Amelia Peláez, René

Portocarrero, and Cundo Bermúdez—eminences of the Havana School, celebrated in the 1940s as the embodiment of modern Cuban art—appeared alongside incipient concrete works by Carreño, Darié, Martínez Pedro, and the younger artist José M. Mijares.[2] If Carreño apprehended Concretism in part in familiarly national terms, *Noticias de Arte* also underscored the transatlantic orbit of these artists and their increasing purchase abroad, highlighted in its coverage of Cuban delegations to the XXVI Venice Biennale (1952) and the II Bienal de São Paulo (1953).

To an initially skeptical public, the internationalization of Cuban art in style and scope called into question the national bona fides of abstraction, which not only departed from prevailing representations of *lo cubano* but appeared elsewhere as a polemic against traditional values of painting and, explicitly, against the Batista regime. Modern Cuban art had trained itself on inculcations of national identity since the rise of the lauded Generation of 1927, led by Víctor Manuel, Amelia Peláez, and Carlos Enríquez, who adapted the forms of Cubism and Surrealism within a regionally inflected iconography of palm trees and *guajiros* (peasants).[3] Similar shadings of the social landscape characterized the next-generation vanguardia, christened the Havana School, whose protagonists—Bermúdez, Portocarrero, and Mariano Rodríguez, among them—became renowned for more painterly, color-driven compositions in the 1940s. Carreño and Martínez Pedro ranked among the celebrated artists of these generations, whose success was consecrated in the landmark exhibition *Modern Cuban Painters*, held at the Museum of Modern Art in 1944. Thus, their wholesale turn toward abstraction and accompanying repudiation of representational art precipitated a calling to account for Cuba's vanguardia at the start of the 1950s. As in Buenos Aires and São Paulo, no less than in Bolshevik Russia, nonobjective art connoted a utopian imaginary, a tabula rasa upon which to construct a new order. In Havana, its geometric austerity and universal projection appeared at first—and to some, forever—incongruous with Cuba's national identity (*cubanidad*). Hence the concretos sought from the outset, through *Noticias de Arte* and in Carreño's column for the popular weekly magazine *Carteles*, to position concrete art as the natural corollary of the modernizing nation and its historical vanguardia. In this regard, their work intersected with that of Los Once (The Eleven), a group of younger artists who radicalized gestural abstraction in Havana across a series of exhibitions from 1953 to 1955 that railed against the Batista dictatorship. Although the concretos demurred from the overt politicizations of the *onceños* and their "so-called Abstract Expressionism," in Carreño's words, they too believed in their work as a medium of social transformation, albeit effected not on the ground but rather in the form and function of the artworks themselves.[4]

The task of acculturating Concrete art within the trajectory of Cuba's vanguardia fell in large part to Carreño, in whose work the gradual geometricization of *lo cubano* served as an early touchstone for the movement. An outstanding colorist, Carreño earned plaudits during the 1940s for his monumental paintings of Cuban and Afro-Cuban life, which condensed the daily rituals and customs of the nation into painterly cadences that mingled classicizing forms within a decorative program. "My humble 'guajiros' followed the geometric trend," he explained of the subsequent flattening and abstraction of his work, seen for the first time in Havana in 1951 following his return from New York, where he had mostly lived since the mid-1940s. "Everything led to the square."[5] His initial Concrete work conveys a new structural clarity, as seen in *Cielos del sur* (*Southern Skies*, 1950), in which warm, verdant tones of dark green, ocher, black, and ivory outline a gridded, nocturnal horizon (Plate 25). To the extent that these geometric elements retain traces of Carreño's earlier iconography—for example, in the triangles and crescent moon, drawn from Afro-Cuban symbology, that form suggestively figural presences—the painting creatively, if unwittingly, muddies the waters of Concrete art, allowing vestigial forms to impinge on the painting's putative autonomy. Such self- and national referencing becomes less legible by mid-decade, however, as seen in the asymmetric eloquence of *Donde empieza la luz* (*Where the Light Begins*, 1956), in which prismatic, complementary colors distill the break of dawn. Carreño decamped to Chile in 1957, weary from his administrative position within Havana's Instituto Nacional de Cultura (National Institute of Culture) as a mediator between the Batista government and Cuba's artists and, as such, a much-beleaguered adjudicator of cultural policy. Although not officially one of Los Diez, Carreño was arguably the most public and authoritative spokesperson for Concrete art in Havana, and his paintings—no less than his considerable writings—set a leading example.

If Carreño trained his focus on the Cuban art world, Darié brought the concretos international exposure and, over the course of the 1950s, emerged as the movement's most sophisticated and inventive practitioner. Darié arrived in Havana in 1941 and, soon after, declared his commitment to "a new pictorial structuralism," stimulated by encounters with historical abstraction—works by Mondrian, Georges Vantongerloo, and Josef Albers, among others—in New York galleries. Through the Greek-American artist Jean Xceron, Darié struck up a correspondence with Gyula Kosice, cofounder of the Grupo Madí, which had stirred the development of Constructivism in Argentina since the mid-1940s. "The existence of Madinemsor is brilliant," Darié wrote to Kosice in 1950. "It is the concern of a group of men who arrive at the same conclusions in the plastic arts, amid the divided aesthetic of our times."[6] That spirit of fraternity and synchronicity with Kosice and the Madí movement, which Darié joined as its sole Cuban representative, anchored Havana's incipient concretos—not least, the triumvirate behind *Noticias de Arte*—within Latin America's postwar avant-garde, opening a meaningful and locally less-traveled circuit to South America. Darié debuted his *Estructuras pictóricas* (*Pictorial Structures*), among his first geometric works, at Havana's Lyceum, a cultural institution long supportive of the vanguardia, in 1950. Like the *Estructuras transformables* (Plate 24), they defied the formalist rhetoric of the "framing edge," positing the extensibility of the grid—and its rationalist utopia—infinitely outward. His numerous collaged drawings from this period experiment further with the perceptual play of positive and negative form (and interior and exterior space), phrasing a pieced-apart grid within a flux of floating, lens-like circles. Darié applied a similar analysis to his major paintings from this period, in which the nodes of the grid are both magnified and dissociated; the fusion of color and line characteristically extend to the painted frame, which mediates between the radiant space of the image and its physical support. Although Darié represented Cuba internationally during this period (notably at the Bienal de São Paulo in both 1953 and 1955), a joint exhibition with Martínez Pedro, held at the University of Havana in April 1955, brought his work—and Concrete art—prominently before the Cuban public for the first time.

Advertised as Cuba's "first concrete exhibition," the University of Havana show also marked a coming-out of sorts for Martínez Pedro, who had reinvented himself as a concrete painter at the start of the decade. The affinities between Darié's and Martínez Pedro's work become clear in an installation photo: suspended within an open frame, Martínez Pedro's canvas floats off the wall, the centrifugal energy of its two folded shapes in playful dialogue with the movable axes of Darié's *Estructuras transformables* (Plate 24). Like Carreño, Martínez Pedro apprehended abstraction through earlier figurative and ethnographic studies, as seen in his excellent pencil drawings; his ongoing work at the advertising agency Organización Técnica Publicitaria Latinoamericana (Latin American Technical Advertising Organization), which he cofounded in 1948, suggests a diversity of graphic sources. In 1953, UNESCO honored his painting *Espacio azul* (*Blue Space*) at the II Bienal de São Paulo as "the most outstanding example of abstract art," and his commitment to Concrete art only increased following travel the next year across Western Europe. Martínez Pedro visited the studios of artists such as Victor Vasarely, Gino Severini, and Jean Dewasne, and held solo exhibitions in Venice, Milan, and Frankfurt. "The true artist of today attempts to order, rather than provoke, chaos," Martínez Pedro declared in 1955, in veiled reference to the political unrest in Cuba. "The Concrete artist exceeds in re-creating that lost equilibrium in his works, in the attempt to express in stylistic terms his desire for order and peace, that peace for which the human spirit is so desperate."[7]

While Carreño, Darié, and Martínez Pedro had the greatest visibility at the beginning of the decade, a slightly younger generation of proto-Concrete artists, led by Rafael Soriano (1920–2015) and José M. Mijares, began to emerge around the same time. For each artist, the path to abstraction evolved out of Cuba's original vanguardia generation—particularly Peláez, but also Roberto Diago—and its post-Cubist handling of faceted color, rather than through the more florid vernacular style of the Havana School. In Matanzas, Soriano created some of the first nonobjective paintings in Cuba, which he arrived at through his progressive condensation of color from an earlier, lyrical ebullience into clarified, planar geometries. In works such as *Composición* (*Composition*, 1959, Plate 26), he folds planes of origami-like color, effectively flattening and triangulating two-dimensional space along a diagonal axis. Mijares similarly came to Concrete art through a process of winnowing out descriptive elements, eventually allowing panes of flat color to articulate geometric space. *Lo concreto en rojo* (*Concrete in Red*, 1954, Plate 27) patternizes panes of color, vitalizing the Neo-Plastic purity of plane, line, and color through kaleidoscopic asymmetry and a near-continuous, framing line that travels in right angles, circumscribing the corners of compositional space. The retention of a strong linear sensibility in his Concrete paintings has a point of origin in the baroque line of Peláez and, more distantly, in the wrought-iron work and stained-glass *vitrales* of colonial Havana. For

Mijares and others, the paths to Concretism were varied and particular, mostly more intuitive than precisely mathematical, and often bearing the displaced remnants of Cuba's vanguardista past.

By mid-decade, the critical mass building around Concrete art received new stimulus with the return of Loló Soldevilla to Havana in 1956, following her diplomatic posting to the Cuban embassy in France. A late-blooming artist, she had immersed herself in the cultural ambience of postwar Paris since 1949, studying at the Académie de la Grande Chaumière and at the Atelier d'Art Abstrait, founded by Jean Dewasne and Edgard Pillet, and she received informal guidance from others, including Vasarely, Robert Jacobsen, and Jean Arp. Numerous collages and metal sculptures from this period record her explorations within Constructivist paradigms, ranging from utopian grids and geometries to transparencies of form, sometimes named in homage to the historical avant-garde (among them Arthur Rimbaud, Kazimir Malevich, and Franz Kafka). The artisanal materiality of many of Soldevilla's mixed-media reliefs calls to mind the early cardboard *Fisicromías* of the Venezuelan Carlos Cruz-Diez. The tactility of the twine and unfinished wood checks an impulse toward pure opticality, instead slowing the pace of viewing and emphasizing the physical space of the structure. Soldevilla cites Malevich in a striking relief from 1955, in which the spatial effects of overlapping color are dramatized in contrasts of scale and shape: along opposing diagonals, the green triangle flies downward and the white rectangle recedes; the brown circle echoes the curving edge of the black ground. Shortly following her arrival in Havana, Soldevilla organized a major exhibition of postwar abstraction, *Pintura de hoy: Vanguardia de la Escuela de París* (*Painting Today: Vanguard of the School of Paris*, March 22–April 8, 1956), with organizational support from Carreño, at Havana's Palacio de Bellas Artes (Palace of Fine Arts). Drawn from the personal collection she had assembled in Paris, the exhibition included forty-six artists at the forefront of Hard-Edge, Op, and Kinetic art, among them Arp, André Bloc, Sonia Delaunay, Serge Poliakoff, Nicolas Schöffer, Michel Seuphor, and Vasarely. In his introduction to the exhibition, Carreño declared that abstraction reflected the "sui generis manifestations" of the modern mechanical age, and the implied relationship between developments in Cuba and the international avant-garde was, for the concretos, a signal endorsement.[8]

Among the artists exhibited in *Pintura de hoy* was Wifredo Arcay (1925–97), who, like Soldevilla, provided a direct link between Havana and Paris. At the Atelier d'Art Abstrait and, beginning in 1953, as a member of the Groupe Espace, formed by Bloc and Félix Del Marle to support the integration of art and everyday life, Arcay oriented his practice around Constructivist models of participatory art and social commitment. Since arriving in Paris in 1949, Arcay had gained practical knowledge of historical abstraction through his practice of serigraphy, a technique he introduced to France. His acclaimed portfolio *Art d'aujourd'hui, maîtres de l'art abstrait* (*Art of Today, Masters of Abstract Art*, 1953) included prints after paintings by such artists as Vasily Kandinsky and Paul Klee; for later editions, frequently in collaboration with the Galerie Denise René, he worked with Arp, Julio Le Parc, and Jesús Rafael Soto. "I find that serigraphy is a means which resembles our day and time," Arcay observed, and no doubt the cooperative, re-creative process of silk screening mirrored the social values he espoused in his painting, particularly as it expanded into architectural space by the late 1950s.[9] Typically executed on a small scale, his paintings share the intense color saturation and hard edges of his prints, equilibrating spatial tensions through chords of color. The collectivist orientation of Arcay's practice, from serigraphy to mural proposals, anticipated the similarly utopian drive of Havana's concretos by the end of the decade, as they affirmed the potential for art not only to inhabit but to positively shape the patterns of everyday life. While he remained in Paris, showing regularly at the Salon des Réalités Nouvelles (1951–54) and with the Galerie Denise René, both leading venues for geometric abstraction, Arcay was also among the regular exhibitors at Havana's Galería Color-Luz.

The establishment of the Galería Color-Luz by Soldevilla and Pedro de Oraá in October 1957, and its incubation of the artists who would declare themselves to be Los Diez Pintores Concretos (The Ten Concrete Painters) in 1959, marked a milestone for the Concrete movement in Cuba. Named after the sculptural *relieves luminosos* (light reliefs) that Soldevilla had developed in collaboration with the Spanish kineticist Eusebio Sempere, the gallery provided semi-permanent exhibition space to the vanguardia and introduced Cuba's concretos firsthand to historical abstraction. Special exhibitions primarily served a didactic purpose (the gallery was not commercially successful); highlights included *Homenaje al pequeño cuadrado* (*Homage to the Small Square*, 1957), a nod to Albers's series *Homage to the Square*, the anthological *El arte abstracto en Europa* (*Abstract Art in*

Europe, July 3–31, 1958), and *El panneau moderno en Cuba* (*The Modern Signboard in Cuba*, August 1–31, 1958), dedicated to new modalities of (mural) painting.[10] The gallery remained open during the last months of 1958 as civil insurrection intensified across the island and the revolutionaries moved westward toward Havana. "For us," de Oraá reflected, the gallery "signified a bastion from which to project an attitude of resistance and a program of action to protect, to the extent of our ability, the artistic values undermined on the one hand by the opportunism of the cultural apparatchiks and on the other, by the partisan dogmatism that failed to recognize those values."[11] In casting their exhibition practice as praxis, the concretos self-consciously correlated their work with radical social revolution, projecting themselves into Cuba's postrevolutionary process.

The inception of Los Diez Pintores Concretos at Galería Color-Luz in November 1959, in the anticlimactic midst of Fidel Castro's revolution, marked the culmination of a decade-long fervor around Concrete art. If the integrative, interdisciplinary initiatives of the Grupo Madí and the Groupe Espace provided discrete points of reference, Los Diez also acknowledged their roots in the local coordinates of Cuba's vanguardia. The group included already established artists (Arcay, Darié, Martínez Pedro, Mijares, and Soriano), as well as a younger cohort cultivated by Soldevilla and de Oraá at the gallery: Pedro Álvarez (1922–97), Salvador Corratgé (b. 1928), Alberto Menocal (1928–2004), and José Ángel Rosabal (b. 1935; the eleventh member of the nominal "ten," he replaced Álvarez). Following their debut exhibition, *10 pintores concretos exponen pinturas y dibujos* (*10 Concrete Painters Exhibit Paintings and Drawings*, 1959), the group's members showed at the Biblioteca Ramón Guiteras in Matanzas in January 1960 and, for the third and final time as a group, at the Galería de Artes Plásticas in Camagüey.[12] They enacted their practice through the print medium as well, publishing two volumes of serigraphs, both produced by Corratgé: *7 pintores concretos* (1960) and *A* (1961), in which the same seven artists interpreted the letter A in support of the national literacy campaign begun that year.[13] As at Arcay's atelier in Paris, the production of multiples was of a piece with the collaborative ethos of the time; many of the *A* serigraphs embraced the revolutionary palette of red and black, though only Martínez Pedro referenced typography and, suggestively, its period relationship to concrete poetry. Los Diez exhibited *A* at the Feria de Arte Cubano (Cuban Art Fair) that accompanied the First National

Congress of Writers and Artists of Cuba (August 1961); their participation marked the last formal activity of the group and followed the quiet shuttering of Galería Color-Luz.

Cuba's concretos ceded the limelight in the early revolutionary moment amid the changing of the cultural guard, and the work produced in the headiness of the 1960s variously bore out the transformational promise that had girded the movement over the past decade. Referencing the Suprematist black circle and square, Soldevilla assumed the task of painting for the revolutionary present: the dialectical austerity of black and white, balanced along a diagonal axis, shapes positive and negative space, casting the future in binary, nonobjective terms. A poet as well as a painter, de Oraá evolved a more subjective geometry, akin to the organic *geometria sensível* of South America and its latent corporeality. Corratgé, an erstwhile architecture student, similarly relinquished the rigid rectilinearity that had once characterized his painting, introducing curved forms that swell and taper in chromatic rhythms. This transition from Concrete painting, laden with the political exigency of the time, toward Hard-edge and proto-Minimalist experimentation, particularly in work by the two youngest members of Los Diez, Rosabal and Menocal, insinuated a shift in orientation from the public sphere to the contemporary subject.[14] "To insert oneself into the world is to be swept up in the social tide," de Oraá later reflected, and the embodiedness of later projects—set and costume designs for the ballet *3 misterios: Lucumí, Abakuá y Ochún* (1962) by Darié and Martínez Pedro; Darié's synesthetic film *Cosmorama: Electro-pintura en movimiento* (*Cosmorama: Electro-Painting in Motion*, 1964)—suggests the entangled agency between the artwork and its postrevolutionary beholder.[15]

The gradual disbanding of the Concrete movement, foretold in the critical haranguing over abstract art in the aftermath of the Revolution, marked an ending as well to the modernist project that it had carried forward through the 1950s. Although the Communist state mostly demurred on an aesthetic hard line, not subscribing to the Soviet model of socialist realism, in practice artistic freedoms were curtailed and abstraction phased into a peripheral place, dimmed (if unfairly) by perceived associations with the prior regime. "The epoch of the fifties was very beautiful, I think romantic for us," de Oraá reflected in retrospect. "At times all we did was cross the desert, but to do that we not only had to see the mirages but also to invent them. I think that the latter was, for us, the essential point."[16] Lastly, deprived of the utopian anticipation long vested in Cuba's historical vanguardia as it had advanced modern art in tandem with the nation, abstraction lost its ideological valence by the mid-1960s, its forms emptied of their earlier critique. As this new reality took hold, the exhibition of Martínez Pedro's extraordinary series *Aguas territoriales* (*Territorial Waters*, 1963–73)—first in Havana and then at the VII Bienal de São Paulo in 1963—resounded as an elegy for Los Diez and the epochal generation they represented (Plate 28). Allegorical images of Cuba's changing cultural geography following the first wave of mass migration, after the Bay of Pigs Invasion (1961) and the Cuban Missile Crisis (1962), the series distilled the territorial and diasporic anxieties of the island into pulsing, concrete curves. The return of narrative, anathema to the pure plasticism of Concrete orthodoxy, renders the series in plaintive, national terms, reaffirming (if in vain) the profoundly Cuban cognition embedded in its cool, geometric forms. A swan song for Los Diez and for Cuba's vanguardia, the works in *Aguas territoriales* reverberate with the historical consciousness of the once and future island, and the rippling effects of its revolution.

Concrete Cuba mostly receded into memory over the intervening years, its protagonists quelled and the art readily diminished as a relic of the prerevolutionary past. The recent excavation of Los Diez comes thus at an auspicious moment, amid dovetailing interests in Cuba and in the midcentury blooming of geometric abstraction across the Americas. As the concretos reclaim their place in the transatlantic passages of Constructivism, the specificity of their history—embedded in Cuba's vanguardia past and conditioned by its revolutionary present—opens new perspectives onto the art of the postwar and the oft-fraught politics of abstraction. If the conjunction of the terms "Concrete" and "Cuba" challenged conventional notions of Cuban art as tropically vernacular and Concretism as purely self-referential, these dualities proved no less than generative for the artists who forged themselves in the crucible of the 1950s and who situated their practices—and praxis—between local and global horizons and beyond narrow aesthetic or political notions of cubanidad.

Notes

A version of this chapter originally appeared in *Concrete Cuba: Cuban Geometric Abstraction from the 1950s* (New York: David Zwirner Books, 2016).

1. Sandú Darié, "Centric Composition in Movement."

2. Darié et al., "Presentación," 3; Carreño, "El factor moral en la pintura abstracta," 14. The magazine *Inventario*, published by Luis Dulzaides Noda between 1948 and 1952, preceded *Noticias de Arte* in its coverage of the arts, but lacked the latter's consistently professional standards of journalism and international reach.

3. The Generation of 1927 launched the oft-declared "critical decade" of modern Cuban art with that year's *Exhibición de Arte Nuevo*, which marked the debut of the young vanguardia artists, many of whom had recently returned from travel abroad. Organized in concert with the cultural magazine *Revista de Avance* and the left-leaning Grupo Minorista, the exhibition brought together modern art and activist politics—here aligned against President Gerardo Machado—and set a precedent for the politically engaged artists who emerged in the 1950s.

4. Los Once exhibited mostly in Havana between 1953 and 1963, repeatedly staging their practice of gestural abstraction in opposition to the Batista dictatorship. While the group affiliated itself with abstract art, in practice its members worked within a range of lyrical, Surrealist, and geometric modes. The group's members included Agustín Cárdenas, Hugo Consuegra, Guido Llinás, Raúl Martínez, and Antonio Vidal. Mario Carreño, "¿Qué es el arte concreto?" 125.

5. Carreño, quoted in Jesús Fernández Torna, *Mario Carreño*, 333.

6. Darié, *Estructuras pictóricas 1950*; Darié, letter to Gyula Kosice, January 30, 1950, trans. Michael Agnew, in Osbel Suárez, ed., *Cold America*, 466.

7. "Entregan cuadro de Martínez"; Martínez Pedro, quoted in Carreño, "Entrevista."

8. Carreño, *Pintura de hoy*.

9. Wifredo Arcay, quoted in Francis Delille, *Je vous écris*, n.p.

10. Pedro de Oraá, "Noticia comentada sobre la Galería Color-Luz," 108.

11. de Oraá, 106.

12. No documentary material pertaining to the exhibition in Camagüey survives. Corratgé and de Oraá confirm that the exhibition took place, but no further details are known to exist.

13. The seven artists who contributed to each portfolio were Corratgé, Darié, Soldevilla, Martínez Pedro, Mijares, de Oraá, and Rosabal.

14. Darié, quoted in Edmundo Desnoes, "1952–1962 en la pintura cubana," 47.

15. de Oraá, "Una experiencia plástica," 119.

16. de Oraá, quoted in Carina Pino-Santos, "Vidal, Corratgé, Oraá," 29.

Bibliography

Barr, Alfred Jr. "¿Es el arte moderno comunista?" *Noticias de Arte* 1, no. 6 (February 1952): 6–7, 15.

Carreño, Mario. "El factor moral en la pintura abstracta." *Noticias de Arte* 1, no. 8 (May 1953): 8–11, 14.

———. "Entrevista: Itinerario de Martínez Pedro." *Carteles*, February 20, 1955.

———. *Pintura de hoy: Vanguardia de la Escuela de París*. Havana: Instituto Nacional de Cultura, 1956.

———. "¿Qué es el arte concreto?" *Carteles*, May 29, 1955.

Darié, Sandú. "Centric Composition in Movement." Sandú Darié Artist File, Archives of the Art Museum of the Americas of the Organization of American States, Washington, DC.

———. *Estructuras pictóricas 1950, del 9 al 20 octubre*. Havana: Lyceum, 1950.

Darié, Sandú, Mario Carreño, and Luis Martínez Pedro. "Presentación." *Noticias de Arte* 1, no. 1 (September 1952): 3.

Delille, Francis. *Je vous écris: Entretiens avec Wilfredo Arcay et Francis Delille*. Paris: Herscher, 1986.

Desnoes, Edmundo. "1952–1962 en la pintura cubana." In *Pintores cubanos*, edited by Oscar Hurtado and Edmundo Desnoes, 39–48. Havana: Ediciones Revolución, 1962.

"Entregan cuadro de Martínez: Ha sido distribuido por la Unesco a sus filiales." *El Mundo* (Havana), January 26, 1955.

Fernández Torna, Jesús. *Mario Carreño: Selected Works, 1936–1957*. Miami: Torna & Prado Fine Art Collection, 2012.

Gómez Sicre, José. "La plástica cubana actual." *Noticias de Arte* 1, no. 11 (October-November 1953): 2.

Oraá, Pedro de. *Visible e invisible*. Havana: Letras Cubanas, 2006.

Pino-Santos, Carina. "Vidal, Corratgé, Oraá: El camino de la abstracción." *Revolución y Cultura* 1, no. 99 (January–February 1999): 23–29.

Suárez, Osbel, ed. *Cold America: Geometric Abstraction in Latin America (1934–1973)*. Madrid: Fundación Juan March, 2011.

9

Cuban Photography after 1959

Shifting Paradigms

Iliana Cepero

Narratives on post-Revolution Cuban photography tend to condense four of five decades of photographic practices in a rectilinear fashion that begins with the renowned images of the guerrillas, then recounts the spirit of labor and workers in the 1970s, continues with the theme of the everyday life of the 1980s, and concludes with the conceptual approaches of the 1990s and 2000s. This is an accurate trajectory; however, alternative works that strayed from the thematic mandates of each period might be overlooked. Understandably, the challenge of dissecting the nuances of more than sixty years of Cuban photography exceeds the extant chronological exhibitions and the few scholarly overviews.

The first question to ponder is how to define the notion of Cuban photography. Is it that practiced by Cubans who live on the island, by those who developed their careers in Cuba before they emigrated, or by Americans of Cuban descent? Does it encompass all? Should it also include foreigners who have photographed Cuba with extraordinary eyes? These broad questions require careful consideration, but keeping them in mind, this chapter will offer some glimpses into a photographic history made by Cubans who lived and produced their most important work on the island before their deaths or eventual exile. They shot their images amidst difficult conditions. Their ability to get assignments and obtain photographic material was contingent upon acquiescing to the political content dictated by official demands. Despite these hurdles, Cuban photographers found ways to subvert that ideological paradigm. This chapter will demonstrate how, in the first two decades following the Cuban Revolution, a period characterized by strong censorship, photographers were able to produce parallel narratives: one that reinforced the mythical and heroic essence of the Revolution, and another that celebrated escapism from the politicization of life. From the late 1980s on, after the government relaxed its tight control over the cultural field, photography on the island gradually undermined the so-called epic and messianic photographic paradigm that the government-controlled media established in the early 1960s. Postrevolutionary Cuban photography has navigated between political and social imperatives and artists' struggle for self-expression.

The irruption of the guerrillas into the Cuban scene in 1959 shook the political, social, and economic foundations of the country. The new government not only issued laws to abolish the old political order, but also set guidelines for the country's future cultural endeavors. Photography endured the most severe of those restrictions. According to official guidelines, images were to be committed to "the service of the Revolution"; in other words, they were to serve propaganda purposes. Photographers needed to be affiliated with the official media to obtain photographic supplies. These stipulations, in place roughly until the mid-1980s, were intended to curtail any artistic initiative that could jeopardize the political content the government expected in its propaganda-driven images.

Cuban photography in the early 1960s displayed the revolutionary fervor of those who supported the new regime established by Fidel Castro. Deeply aware of the power of images in political persuasion, Castro commissioned former fashion and advertising photographers to chronicle his daily political activities, which ranged from visiting a small town in Oriente Province and signing a new law to cutting cane and giving a speech at a rally. In a country that had just toppled Fulgencio Batista, a military dictator, and had longed for the return of democracy, Castro was determined to advertise his public persona in the most positive light, so he could advance his socialist and increasingly dictatorial rule. One image, taken by José (Pepe) Agraz (1909–82) on January 8, 1959, and widely reproduced by the media the following day, exemplifies Castro's use of photography to craft his messianic narrative for Catholic Cubans. In the photograph, taken during Castro's victory speech at Batista's former military headquarters in Camp Columbia, Havana, Castro appears jubilant. He stands in front of an adoring crowd and is surrounded by his bearded commanders. White doves fly around, except for one perched on Castro's left shoulder. As Ernesto Hernández Bustos argues, this dove accomplished its symbolic mission at different levels. People were so impressed by the dove landing right on his shoulder that they spoke of the Holy Spirit and of peace, the theme of that speech at Camp Columbia. (This scene was allegedly a carefully staged spectacle by Castro, with theories ranging from the doves consuming a diet of lead birdshot to prevent them from gaining too much altitude to the application of male dove pheromones to the leader's jacket.) For practitioners of Afro-Cuban religions, the white dove was a symbol of Obatalá, the Chosen One, the Son of God. In other words, people were led to believe that Castro was Christ's messenger, an idea that even the most conservative newspaper of the time, *Diario de la Marina*, could not ignore. Hernández Bustos rightly observes:

> That moment marked two fundamental shifts that went unnoticed in all the photographic glamour. First: it was the moment at which Cubans stopped judging politics based upon facts, and began, instead, to consider it as a regimen of symbols. Secondly, as Norberto Fuentes explains so cogently in his monumental *Autobiography of Fidel Castro* (2010), that moment, in which the dove's chosen one permits himself to joke before the multitudes by disingenuously asking his guerrilla comrade Camilo Cienfuegos if he is doing all right, marks the beginning of the absolute power that Fidel Castro held by force for nearly fifty years, much to Cuba's misfortune.[1]

Images laden with Catholic symbolism and others carrying a message of triumph and ideological consensus dominated the visuals in the media. They helped create the concept of the Cuban Revolution as an epic event, and Castro as the country's modern savior. Those notions were exported abroad in a relentless manner, consolidating the romantic vision that many people around the world hold about the Revolution, a very costly political event for generations of Cubans.

Meanwhile, in the mid-1960s, José Alberto Figueroa (b. 1946), a young photographer at the time, captured his middle-class young friends posing unapologetically next to their Buicks, hanging out in a pool, and smoking and listening to music at house parties. Feeling at odds with the new revolutionary era, these members of the "old and decadent bourgeoisie" were either waiting to leave the country or already experiencing societal marginalization for failing to join the socialist chant. Figueroa also authored

Exilio (*Exile*, 1967), a photograph that depicts his mother walking across the airport tarmac toward her one-way trip to the United States. She waves to him goodbye. *Exilio* encapsulates the tragedy of thousands of Cuban families who after 1959 endured an agonizing split between the two shores of the Florida Straits. The official media never published images of this sort. Furthermore, Figueroa's negatives remained stored until recently, when better political times allowed for their display.

Another interesting series from the 1960s that felt far removed from the political mandates of the time crystallized in Marucha's (María Eugenia Haya, 1944–91) *La peña de Sirique* (*Sirique's Joint*). Shot in 1967 while she was working as a still photographer for Héctor Veitía's documentary on the history of Cuban music genres, the series depicts old black musicians rehearsing traditional songs in a dilapidated warehouse in Havana. They reminisce about the past while the world around them looks forward to the future. The *peña*'s members do not conform to the archetype of the white, young, bearded, cigar-smoking, uniformed, hypersexual, masculine guerrilla fighter endorsed by the mainstream media. Thus, by photographing people with their minds stranded in the past and inhabiting spaces of freedom and longing, Marucha countered the orthodoxy of the Communist Party's discourse.

In the 1970s, a period characterized by political purges and strong Soviet dominance over the island, the government focused on economic matters. Sugar production and industrialization became the top themes for journalistic assignments. One eloquent image by Rigoberto Romero (1940–91) and Leovigildo González (b. 1943) from their 1975 series *Con sudor de millonario* (*With a Millionaire's Sweat*) depicts a sweaty and greasy sugarcane cutter against a tapestry-like sugarcane field in the background. Posing akimbo and confident before the camera, he holds a machete in his right hand. The title of the series alludes to the challenging quotas that some of these cane cutters achieved, which turned them into instant celebrities in the fields. Such images were intended to mobilize the population, so it could join forces in the full-scale economic plans set by the government. Photography in this era also attempted to promote Che Guevara's idea of the "New Man," envisioned as an individual devoid of material pursuits and fully committed to the construction of Communist society.

However, amid these assignments, photographers could save photographic supplies to create more personal work. As Cristina Vives points out, "Throughout those years, the most distinguished photographers shifted the axis of their interests not only in correspondence with the historical-social unfolding of the nation but also in connection with their own individual interests as artists."[2] This explains Figueroa's *Todos nosotros* (*All of Us*), a series originally conceptualized as an anthropological study of Cubans across the island. Exhibited in 1973 at the Vedado Gallery under the new title *Rostros del presente, mañana* (*Faces of Today, Tomorrow*), an unsigned text and a note of apology accompanied the images "for a deficiency—to the working classes who are 'building the new society.'"[3] Figueroa's substitution of ordinary Cubans for portraits of worker-heroes faced disapproval at the time, given the government's obsession with the visual representation of workers, but his images foretold an interest in everyday life that distinguished photographic practices in the following decade.

In 1980, the crisis of the Mariel boatlift forced the government to reconsider some of its policies. In the cultural sphere, the government had created the Ministry of Culture four years earlier, and throughout the 1980s, cultural institutions proliferated. Founded in 1986 under Marucha's guidance, the Fototeca de Cuba (Photographic Library of Cuba) provided a safe space for Cuban photographers to exhibit and promote work that could be divorced from political requirements. In the 1980s, domesticity and life on the streets became a setting for infinite visual possibilities. Interestingly, during those years, women photographers began to emerge. One of them was Gilda Pérez (b. 1954), whose photographs combined satirical juxtapositions, such as one featuring an old American car driving in front of a Havana landmark Art-Deco building called America (Figure 9.1).

Katia García's (b. 1961) series *La boda* (*The Wedding*, 1989) explored the ways in which ordinary families prioritized the celebration of traditional family rituals, regardless of their low incomes. The corners of the everyday sprinkled with humor resulted in iconic series, such as José María (Tito) Alvarez's (1916–2002) *Gente de mi barrio* (*Neighborhood Folks*, 1985), which portrayed vernacular characters: the butcher, the bodega vendor, and the old woman shopping and gossiping. The individual portraits confer dignity on the sitters in the simplicity of their everyday lives, an aesthetic that became popular during this decade. Among this explosion of documentary practices celebrating the ordinary citizen or surreal incidents unfolding in the urban landscape, a major painter of

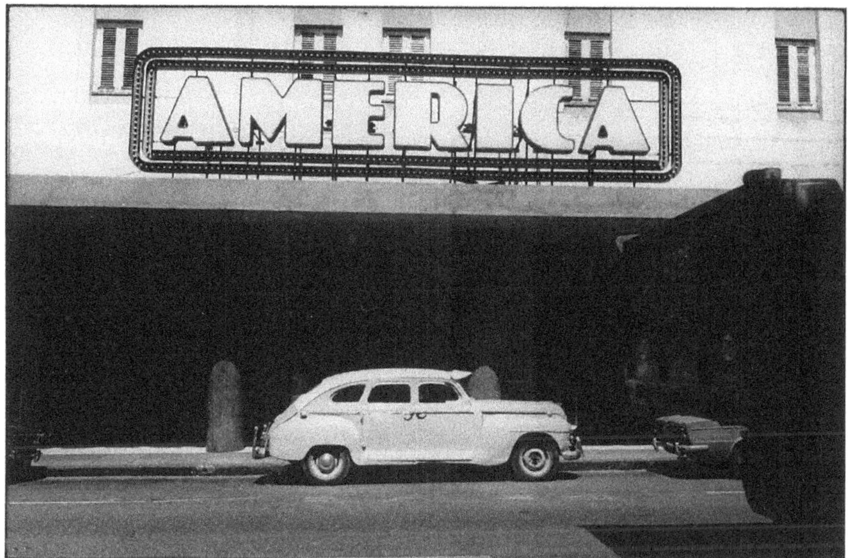

Figure 9.1. Gilda Pérez, *Untitled*, from the *La Habana* series, 1986. Silver print. Courtesy of Lehigh University Art Galleries.

the time, Rogelio López Marín (known as Gory, b. 1953), began to experiment with collages. In his most lyrical series, *It's Only Water in a Stranger's Tear* (1986, Plate 29), Gory juxtaposed the edge of a swimming pool with vistas of the open sea or flooding cities to speak subtly about exile and escape. His poetic imagery of the late 1980s predates the irruption of a more allegorical vision that would typify Cuban photography in the ensuing decade.

In the 1990s, photographers used the camera as a critical tool to document the malaise of Cuban society at the time—a society steeped in scarcity, hopelessness, and isolation during the infamous Special Period, the years that followed the demise of the Soviet Union in 1991. While the government was occupied with finding feasible alternatives to mitigate the crisis, photographers suddenly found themselves with relative flexibility to scrutinize themes considered taboo in previous decades, such as poverty, racism, queer issues, and religion, to name a few. In 1990, the Fototeca de Cuba promoted a new generation of Cuban photographers, who had become members of UNEAC (Unión Nacional de Escritores y Artistas de Cuba, or National Union of Writers and Artists of Cuba), through the exhibition *6 × 6*. The exhibition featured six photographers—Rolando Córdoba, Adalberto Roque, Alfredo Sarabia, Jorge Macías, Sergio

Romero, and Isabel Sierra—and thirty-six images. The words of Cuban art critic Jorge de la Fuente in the catalogue implied the conquest of the so-called epic paradigm, that is, the ways in which Cuban photographers were now zooming in on fleeting and complex slices of everyday life:

> Within the present panorama of Cuban photography, this exhibition represents a turning point both in the cultural practices of local institutions and in the aesthetic value of Cuban photography. . . . The intimist, metaphoric, and paradoxically distant vision of these photographs repositions the photographer as a true producer of images, which have been found from within and not in the unrepeatable exceptionality of the outside.[4]

In this newly inward, allegorical look, what were the new themes? Instead of symbolizing a venue in which to boast about victory, collectivism, or the industrial prowess of socialism, the city turned into the core of chaos and scarcity, a repertoire of geometric forms, a location for nostalgia mixed with urban utopia, as well as a place to *resolver* (literally, to resolve; figuratively, to make do or get by). For example, Carlos Garaicoa (b. 1967) fashioned himself as an "urban archaeologist" who would find a building, photograph it, and then proceed to "intervene" in it. The intervention consisted of making a drawing of the building completely renovated, with futuristic features added. In his work, the ruin became the symbol of the collapse of the socialist dream. Garaicoa used Havana, now turned into a crumbling museum of architectural styles, as a trope to convey the profound nostalgia of Cubans for a prerevolutionary architectural legacy, proud of its variety and stylistic richness. Institutional critique and subversive acts shone through in Garaicoa's works of the 1990s, such as *Sloppy Joe Bar's Dream* (1995), an installation that combined a cast of the famous bar's long counter with black-and-white photographs that showed the neglectful conditions of the then-closed spot.

Ramón Pacheco's (b. 1954) *Convivencias* (*Living Together*, 1990–2000) unveils the pockets of deep poverty in Matanzas, his hometown, where single mothers leave their children alone at night in their apartments so they can prostitute themselves on the street, buildings are surrounded by garbage dumps, young men are unemployed, and people eat their meals at home off cardboard plates. Analyzing this series, Juan Antonio Molina argued, "This is the magic of the marginal: its ability to make us feel that we are facing something unreal. And one ends up enjoying the pleasure of transgression because there is always something forbidden behind that frontier of the unusual."[5]

The 1990s also witnessed the proliferation of photographic conceptual practices. Influenced by the works of Robert Mapplethorpe, Cindy Sherman, Gerardo Suter, Mario Cravo Neto, and Joel-Peter Witkin, Cuban photographers perceived the body as a territory in which to express notions of identity, the complexity of the self, and the psychological conflicts of the individual, all traits standing in contrast to prior representations of the goals of the collective. Disguises, masks, allegorical objects, distorted bodies, and transvestism were part of these photographers' mise-en-scène. Marta María Pérez's (b. 1959) self-portraits reinterpreting Afro-Cuban religious practices eloquently illustrate this trend. Employing natural light and a neutral background, she performs before the camera with objects related to Cuban popular religions, creating simple tableaux with allegorical references to orishas or rituals (Figure 9.2).

René Peña (b. 1957) examines race relations in Cuba, a subject considered taboo because of the government's systematic assertions that the Revolution had eliminated racism. He uses his own body as a medium through which to affirm his black identity and, at the same time, stress racial prejudice on the island. The combination of his black skin and the "white" items he wears evoke the racial education of black Cubans, who have been told from childhood to behave like white people. Disparaging phrases like "black on the outside but a true white on the inside," used to indicate a black person's worth, and "He/she *had* to be black!" emphasizing that blacks not only are expected to err but also are morally flawed by nature, have become customary in Cuba. Eduardo Hernández Santos's (b. 1966) photocollages of effeminate models with their bodies fragmented, bent, distorted, or subjected to physical strain evoke memories of psychological suffering because of years of marginalization and persecution of the LGBT community on the island. According to Hernández Santos, the photocollage provides him with simultaneity, juxtaposition, overlapping, and deconstruction of discourse about psychological aspects of queer sexuality. In *Fragmentos clásicos* (*Classical Fragments*, 1998), Hernández Santos created collages with male models scattered among classical columns and monuments from Greece and Rome. The images conjured up the splendor and hedonism of a distant antiquity.

Cuban photography today, in both its conceptual and documentary approaches, aspires to dismantle the epic paradigm through which the

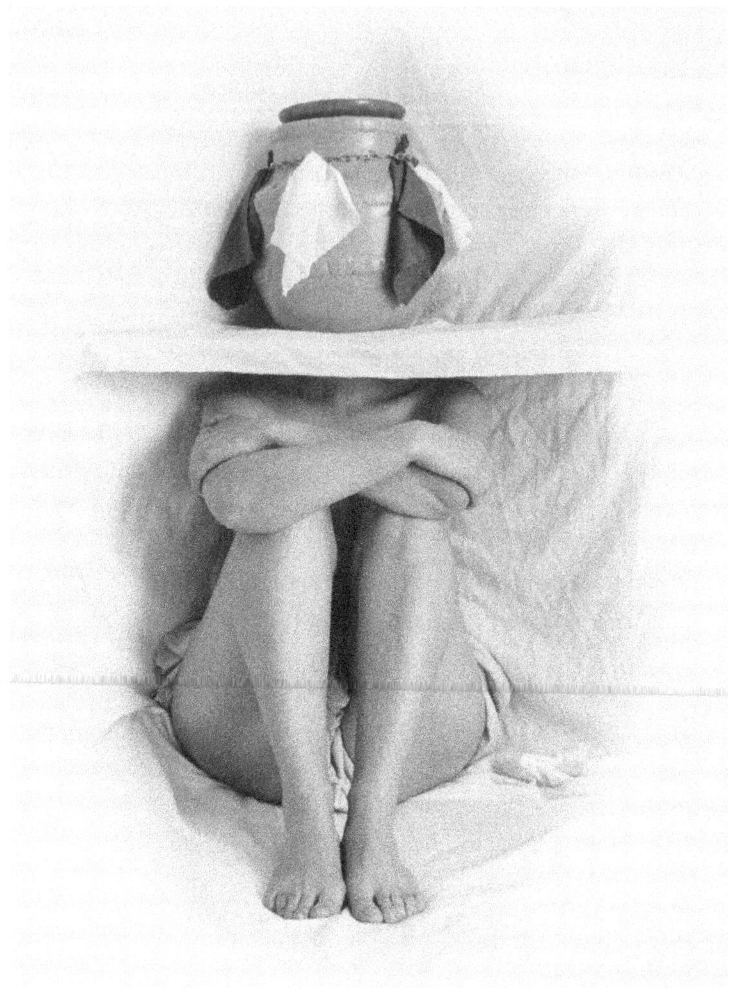

Figure 9.2. Marta María Pérez, *The Stronger They Are, the More They Protect Us . . .*, 1997. Silver print. Courtesy of Lehigh University Art Galleries.

Revolution came to be known as a visual phenomenon. Enjoying less censorship, photographers now dive deeply into politically controversial waters. Alvaro Brunet (b. 1974), an architect and business major from Villa Clara Province, takes advertising-like photographs of everyday objects infused with political connotations. *Coraje* (*Courage*, 2011, Plate 30) shows a profusely lit and colored-enhanced mousetrap. A Cuban flag covers the trap's platform and the hold-down bar is topped with a star-shaped piece of cheese. The work might suggest the alluring traps that the island can pose for gullible tourists, who expect to find a nonexistent socialist paradise on the island.

Documentary practices also thrive and often focus on domesticity and family life. Leysis Quesada-Vera's (b. 1973) color series, *Vista interior* (*Interior View*, 2014), recreates the cluttered domestic interiors of her marginal neighborhood in Havana. The homes display a bizarre arrangement of objects, from Che Guevara's pictures, the Sacred Heart, and plastic dolls to photographs of ancestors, American pre-Revolution film posters, and a Russian television set. Such eclectic choices illustrate not only the mixture of ideological predicaments that have shaped life on the island, but also the nature of the bedraggled material culture that Cubans have created by hoarding objects or spare parts due to the difficulties of purchasing new items. Eduardo García's (b. 1978) *Home* (2016, Figure 9.3) documents the hardships of a man squatting for twenty years in the now-crumbling Campoamor theater in downtown Havana. In arresting black-and-white images, the man is depicted sweeping the large floor, tending to his dog, looking out the window, and storing food among the peeling walls and collapsing ceilings. A somber mood pervades these images of hopelessness and decay.

I would like to conclude with the work of Leandro Feal (b. 1986), a graduate of the Chair of Behavioral Art, formerly directed by the Cuban

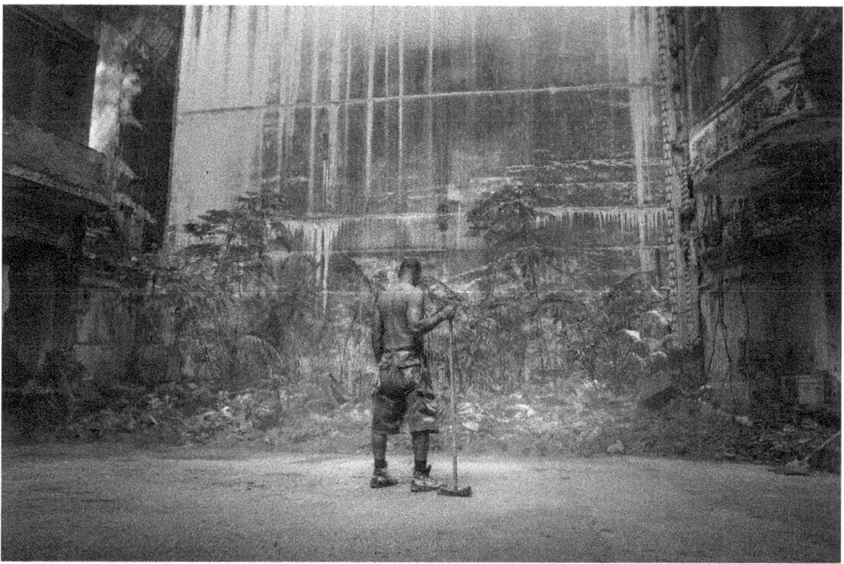

Figure 9.3. Eduardo García, *Home*, 2016. Digital print. Courtesy of the artist.

artist Tania Bruguera, at the Higher Institute of Art (ISA in its Spanish acronym). Swinging between the documentary and the conceptual, and borrowing from the aesthetic of Wolfang Tillmans and William Egleston, Feal's Polaroid-like images capture the flavor of a Cuban counterculture inhabited by punk artists, political activists, and dilettantes. He credits Cuban cinema of the 1960s, specifically the documentary films of Nicolás Guillén Landrián and Santiago Álvarez, as one of his most important influences. Interested in the epic tradition of revolutionary Cuban photography, Feal's colored snapshots, as he claims, are intently devoid of all epic. His images take, in effect, the pulse of the times. Cuban photography today raises the curtain on the unpalatable reality faced by most Cubans. Devoid of transcendental feats, this reality manifests the devastating effects of the regime's political repression coupled with years of failed economic policies.

Notes

1. Ernesto Hernández Bustos, "Revolution, Still Photos," 61–62.
2. Cristina Vives, "Cuban Photography," 108.
3. Vives, 103–4.
4. Jorge de la Fuente, *6 × 6*.
5. Juan Antonio Molina, "Fotografía cubana" (my translation).

Bibliography

de la Fuente, Jorge. *6 × 6*. Havana: Fototeca de Cuba, 1990.

Hernández Bustos, Ernesto. "Revolution, Still Photos: Images and Myths from the Cuban Revolution." *Review: Literature and Arts of the Americas* 44, no. 1 (2011): 59–63.

Molina, Juan Antonio. "Fotografía cubana de los 90: Tirando la piedra y escondiendo la quinta pata." *Loquevenga* 2, no. 1 (1995): n.p.

Vives, Cristina. "Cuban Photography: A Personal History." In *Shifting Tides: Cuban Photography after the Revolution*, edited by Tim B. Wride and Cristina Vives, 82–121. London: Merrel Publishers/Los Angeles County Museum of Art, 2002.

10

Fashioning and Contesting the Olive-Green Imaginary in Cuban Visual Arts

María A. Cabrera Arús

In 2015, the English fashion designer Stella McCartney launched her Resort 2016 collection at a New York City garden party with a Cuba theme.[1] The collection itself bore little resemblance to Cuban sartorial practices or history other than its tropical ethos, but at the premier extravaganza McCartney treated her guests to mojitos, a salsa band, chocolate cigars, and the presence of Fidel Castro and Che Guevara impersonators, clad in military fatigues. The following year, Karl Lagerfeld made history when he presented the Chanel 2016/17 Cruise collection in Havana's Paseo del Prado.[2] The French fashion house combined references to Cuba's midcentury material culture with sartorial elements borrowed from revolutionary imagery, including allusions to Castro's guerrilla. The olive-drab color of the fatigue uniform and Guevara's beret—adorned with zirconia studs in the shape of the Chanel logo instead of a star—gave local allure to the show and introduced Cuba's military chic to the world-renowned tailored universe of haute couture.

These two major events, widely promoted around the world, were by no means the first or only instances of commodification of guerrilla garb since the dawn of the Cuban Revolution. Back in the early days, the 26th of July Movement (M-26-7) was highly successful in associating the anti-Batista insurgency with the olive-drab fatigues and beards of the Sierra Maestra rebels. As historian Michelle Chase observes, the M-26-7's propaganda "romanticized rural rebellion," flaunting the revolutionaries' "beards, uniforms, armbands, and long rifles" to foreign journalists and locals.[3] On February 24, 1957, *The New York Times*' veteran reporter Herbert L. Matthews presented Castro as the "flaming symbol of the opposition" to Fulgencio Batista, describing his style in detail.[4] The M-26-7's propaganda department also lured CBS journalist Robert Taver and cinematographer Wendell Hoffman to the rebels' hideout, where they shot the thirty-minute documentary *Rebels of the Sierra Maestra: The Story of Cuba's Jungle Fighters*, aired by CBS News on May 19, 1957, and covered in photo reportages in the magazines *Life* (in the U.S.) and *Bohemia* (in Cuba).[5]

The M-26-7's publications also indulged before and after the victory in depictions of the guerrilla's sartorial identity. For instance, the comic strip "Julito 26," published during the insurgency in the clandestine newspaper *El Cubano Libre*, edited in the Sierra Maestra, and written and illustrated by Santiago Armada (Chago, 1937–95), introduced the homonymous character as a male guerrilla who wore a campaign uniform and a black beret—elements Stella McCartney and Chanel borrowed sixty years later.[6] Campaign 03C, launched in December 1958, days before the fall of the Batista dictatorship, also acknowledged the contrasting prestige of the insurgent garb vis-à-vis elegant urban dresses.[7] With 03C standing for zero movies, zero shopping, and zero nightclubs, this campaign opposed the frivolity of Christmas shopping to the life-threatening anti-Batista war the fatigue-clad young guerrillas were fighting.

By midnight on December 31, 1958, when Batista escaped to the Dominican Republic and a new era dawned in Cuba, the uniform of the Sierra Maestra guerrilla was widely recognized as a revolutionary symbol, and people took to the streets to celebrate the victory wearing fatigues.[8] U.S. photographer Burt Glinn, who flew to Havana in the early morning hours of January 1, 1959, noted that, at first sight, "it was not clear who was the legitimate rebel and who was not" until the authentic guerrillas arrived.[9] The revolutionary cabinet's first Minister of the Treasury, economist Rufo López-Fresquet, also referred to the prevalent visibility of olive-drab uniforms in the aftermath of the victory, which many associated with Castro's guerrillas, as illustrated by a photograph taken on January 8, 1959, the day Castro and his troops arrived in Havana.[10] The photo features a toddler clad in the uniform of the Rebel Army and wearing a fake beard, a black beret, and a sign that states, *estoy con Fidel* ("I am with Fidel").[11]

Castro and the guerrilla leaders opted not to change out of their uniforms after the triumph, not even to step in to occupy civil positions in the revolutionary cabinet. Castro was sworn in as Prime Minister on February 16, 1959, dressed in guerrilla fatigues, having stated that it was preferable to take the risk of evoking a Latin American military dictator, as one of his advisers had warned him, rather than change his clothes.[12] Luis M. Buch Rodríguez, Secretary of the Council of Ministers at the time, recalls Castro's protest: "*Ah no*; this uniform and this beard represent the rebelliousness of the Sierra Maestra and our Revolution, and I absolutely won't get rid of them; look for another Prime Minister."[13]

As literary critic José Quiroga notes, "the Cuban *comandantes* . . . were, from the beginning, the most aesthetically self-conscious political *nomenklatura* in Latin American history."[14] Moreover, they were interested in the possibilities fatigue uniforms—and their iconoclastic identity in general—offered as a means of reenacting the revolutionary ethos of the Sierra Maestra enduringly in post-1959 daily life, as Castro and Guevara expressed several times.[15] Foreign as this identity was to many of the leaders who, like Castro himself—the son of a wealthy landowner—came from privileged backgrounds, the unpretentious military fatigues also portrayed them as being close to the working class.[16] All in all, the guerrilla identity helped to convey the advent of a new era and the emergence of a new political class.

For that, leaders also counted on the media, both private and state-owned.[17] The printed media, for instance, went to great lengths to establish a hierarchy of sorts that enthroned Castro's guerrilla and its sartorial identity as a symbol of the Revolution, the regime, and, by extension, the country.[18] Magazine covers, postcards, posters, postage stamps, banknotes, book covers, and billboards reproduced epic photographs of the guerrillas, which Cubans rushed to consume, collect, and even display in domestic spaces.[19]

INRA, the magazine of the National Institute of Agrarian Reform, founded in 1960 at Castro's request, published the photographs of principal government officials on the covers of issues 7 through 11 of its inaugural year.[20] These invariably portray the guerrilla leaders clad in their uniforms, with a daydreamer's expression, staring into space as if they were envisioning a bright future. In contrast, President Osvaldo Dorticós Torrado was photographed working in his office, dressed in a formal suit, much like a bureaucrat. The contrast between the epic stature of the guerrillas and the simple administrative position of the presidency is also stressed in the portraits' order of appearance on the magazine's covers, with Fidel Castro, Raúl Castro, and Che Guevara featured before President Dorticós, who precedes only Afro-Cuban *comandante* Juan Almeida Bosque. Implicit in this order is the idea that civilian authority, even presidential, was secondary to the prestige of the principal guerrillas.

Images of Castro clad in guerrilla uniform were also associated with the country's flag and other national symbols in magazine spreads, flyers, and publication covers, as seen in Figure 10.1. In this propaganda illustration, Castro appears above the Cuban flag and the national emblem's Phrygian cap (representing liberty) and olive branch (the symbol of victory and peace). This illustration is not only worshipful of the guerrilla leader but also equates the man with the country's national symbols, giving the former preeminence over the latter. In doing so, this illustration anticipates the idea of a *fidelista* state.[21]

The guerrilla leaders also counted on the collaboration of artists to produce the olive-green fidelista iconography. They created emblematic posters and works of art that, over the years, have identified "the Revolution," as well as, after the critical 1980s, canvases and prints that contested the regime's legitimacy. Political posters, for instance, promoted iconic photographs of the leaders, clad in fatigues. Initially doing little more than conveying their iconoclastic identity through black-and-white photographs, poster designers soon began to explore the expressive possibilities of olive green as a symbol of the regime—at the expense of the red-and-black colors of the M-26-7—and, by the end of the 1960s, of postrevolutionary society in general.

The first poster designed after the revolutionary war, created on January 1, 1959, by Eladio Rivadulla (1923–2011), features one of the photographs Taver and Hoffman took of Castro in the Sierra Maestra, modified to produce a high-contrast black-and-white outline of the leader, clad in fatigues, over a red-and-black background.[22] Three years later, Castro was also depicted in the first photographic poster made after 1959, designed in 1962 by Juan Ayús for the Young Communists Union.[23] *Comandante en Jefe: ¡ordene!* (*Commander in Chief, Give Your Orders!* Plate 31) reproduces a black-and-white photograph Alberto Korda (1928–2001) took of Castro standing on a mountain peak after the rebels' victory. In his campaign uniform and carrying a rifle and a backpack, Castro looks like a classic general or king surveying his domains.[24] The message, in big red typeface, stresses the leader's larger-than-life stature, compelling citizens to surrender to his will: "Commander in Chief, Give Your Orders!"

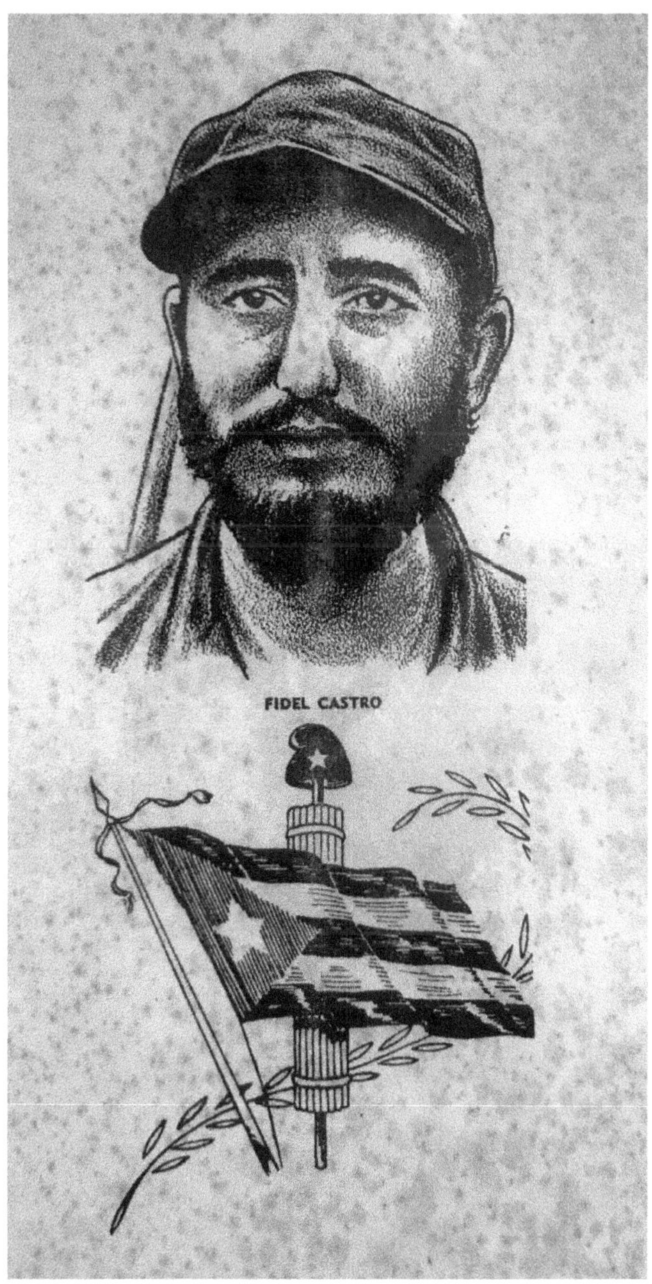

Figure 10.1. Illustration featuring Fidel Castro, the Cuban flag, and the Phrygian cap and olive branch of the national emblem, 1959. Cuba Material Collection. Photograph by María A. Cabrera Arús.

In 1969, Félix René Mederos Pazos (1933–96) designed for the Department of Revolutionary Orientation of the Central Committee of the Cuban Communist Party the poster *1959–1969 Tenth Anniversary of the Triumph of the Cuban Rebellion*, also based on a photograph Taver and Hoffman took in the Sierra Maestra.[25] In it, Fidel and Raúl Castro appear at the front of a group of guerrillas, all holding their rifles up in the air. Mederos Pazos, however, transformed the photograph with a colorful style, painting with psychedelic pink, yellow, and blue the anonymous guerrillas and their weapons, yet leaving untouched the Castro brothers, their uniforms, and the Cuban flag. The special treatment Fidel and Raúl Castro and their uniforms receive in this poster, similar to that observed with the country's flag, leaves no doubt as to the symbolism of both the leaders and their costume.

The use of olive-drab as a symbol of the Revolution and the regime is a constant in Mederos Pazos' work, also observed, for instance, in *Condenadme, no importa, la historia me absolverá* (*Condemn Me, It Doesn't Matter, History Will Absolve Me*), a 1973 silkscreen that features Castro addressing the masses in Revolution Square.[26] At the lectern, Castro wears his olive-drab uniform, with even his boots painted this color. A background of political slogans and a faceless multitude that disappears in a palette of colors surround the leader in this elegiac composition, stressing the political semiotics of olive green as symbol of the fidelista state. And yet, in a way, if only incidentally, this work also denounces the homogenization of the masses under Castro's rule and their lack of political agency.

Literary critic Duanel Díaz Infante has compared the political propaganda built around guerrilla imagery with Snow White's neurotic stepmother, constantly looking at herself in the mirror.[27] And certainly, as in the children's fairytale, the (re)production of the revolutionary ethos in postrevolutionary Cuban society was based on strategies of representation. Yet it was also the result of mechanisms of impersonal rule that sought to mold individual identities and practices after the archetype of the guerrilla leaders, giving shape to a figured world of power centered around the figure of Castro as a larger-than-life revolutionary hero.[28]

The fidelista mechanisms of impersonal rule were laid out in great part through government-sponsored institutions, such as paramilitary mass organizations, which promoted practices and lifestyles associated with the Sierra Maestra guerrilla—e.g., climbing Turquino Peak, Cuba's highest mountain. These institutions also transformed the sartorial identity of

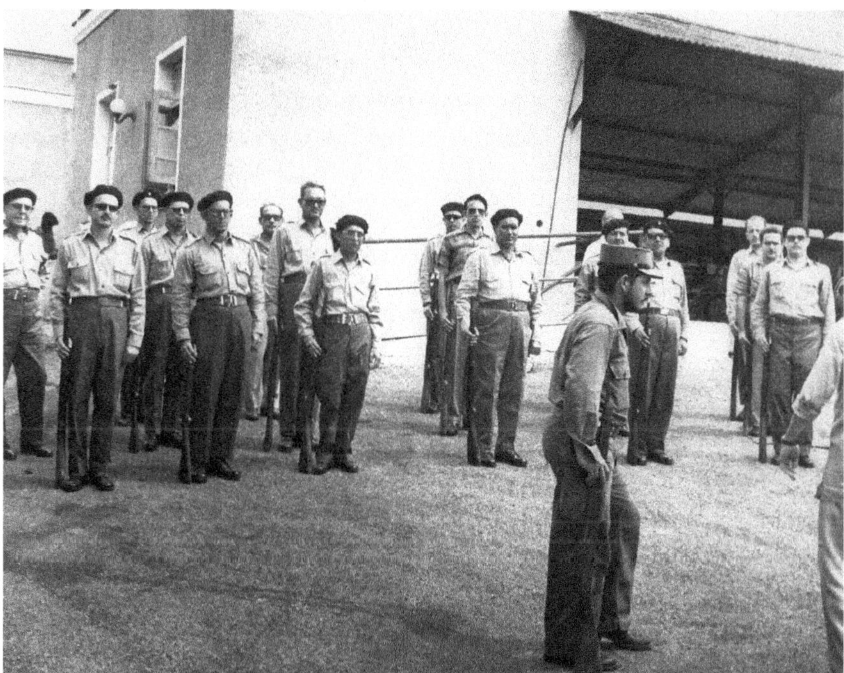

Figure 10.2. Military training of the militias of the medical association in Havana, April 24, 1960. María A. Cabrera Arús family photograph.

the citizenry once workers, students, and intellectuals were drafted, mobilized, and trained in the military or the militias, as Figure 10.2 illustrates.[29]

Just as people recognized and expressed their political allegiances by wearing fatigues, visual artists also used olive green to represent political sympathies. Painter Raúl Martínez (1927–1995) depicted members of Cuba's socialist society with olive-drab complexions in pieces such as *Patria* (*Fatherland*, 1969–70) and *Isla 70* (*Island 70*), the latter painted in the watershed year of 1970, when the government planned to produce ten million tons of sugar to develop the island's economy and, to achieve this goal, mobilized workers and students to harvest sugarcane.[30] Exhibited at Cuba's Museo Nacional de Bellas Artes (National Museum of Fine Arts), this tableau depicts a group of persons, including Martínez himself, along with historical figures such as Vladimir I. Lenin, Ho Chi Min, José Martí, Che Guevara, and Fidel Castro, all painted with olive-green skin, against a background of phallic sugarcane that also includes a sugar mill and the logo of the Committees for the Defense of the Revolution.

The painting, inspired by the national mobilizations for the Ten-Million-Ton Sugar Harvest, represents the society of the time, including the pantheon of heroes (national and foreign, anti-capitalist and anticolonial) the regime then extolled. Notably, Martínez depicted with a bluish complexion a young man whom art critic Ernesto Menéndez-Conde identifies as dissident writer Reinaldo Arenas, stressing the symbolism of olive green in signaling people's support of the regime.[31] But, in Martínez's painting, olive green is more than a symbol or marker of people's allegiances—something external that can be put on (and taken off) at will, like clothes; it also represents the *incorporation* of the fidelista dogma into the biological body and moral self—which would explain why Arenas, the dissident, is depicted with blue skin.

It took more than ten years, over a decade described as bitter and dark in terms of individual liberties, for a new generation of artists finally to approach olive green first as a commentary on postrevolutionary society and eventually as a critique of the fidelista regime.

At the first Havana Biennale in 1984, Leandro Soto (b. 1956) exhibited the series *Retablo familiar* (*Family Altarpiece*), composed of altarpieces made from family photographs, toys, postcards, and other objects from his own childhood, in a nostalgic unearthing of bygone days.[32] According to Soto, he wanted to address through this work criticism from cultural officials who had pointed to his practice of yoga as an ideologically compromised activity, and prove his and his family's long-term commitment to the Castro regime.[33]

Within this series, the wooden altarpiece *La familia revolucionaria* (*The Revolutionary Family*) features a 1962 family photograph in which Soto's mother is wearing a militia uniform, his siblings are clad in the uniform of the literacy brigades, and he, a toddler, wears the uniform of the *pioneros* children's organization—all but the latter being variations on guerrilla fatigues. To have that photograph taken, Soto explains, they walked to a photo studio across town in a political performance of sorts that demonstrated their "revolutionary" credentials.[34] Twenty-two years later, Soto subverted these meanings, and the hierarchy of the fidelista figured world, offering himself and his family as cult objects in lieu of the leader they had previously revered—an attitude typical of the so-called William Tell Generation.[35]

It was not, however, until the late 1980s that a new generation of painters consciously formulated an uncompromising critique of the fidelista regime and its mechanisms of political persuasion and exclusion, based on the olive-green trope. Carlos Rodríguez Cárdenas (b. 1962) is perhaps one of the Castro regime's most vocal and systematic critics among those artists. In *Ahorrando más, tendremos más* (*By Saving More, We Will Have More*), painted in 1988 for his solo show *Artista de calidad* (*Quality Artist*), scheduled to open at the Castillo de la Fuerza, Rodríguez Cárdenas depicts Castro's face, connecting his mouth to a pipeline that discharges fluid into a reservoir.[36] Everything is painted olive green, an unequivocal symbol of the fidelista state, but also, in this case, of the lack of alternatives and diversity the regime offered, whereas the mouth and pipeline allude not so subtly to the uncritical reproduction of *fidelismo* as a dogma.

In the same series, *Come micrófonos* (*Microphone Eater*, 1988) portrays Castro both as a fleshless cartoon-like figure composed of unintelligible words and a character who eats microphones at a podium, painted in olive green.[37] According to the artist, he took inspiration from Castro's fascination with having his words amplified through microphones and loudspeakers.[38] But, like *Ahorrando más, tendremos más*, this painting criticizes the mechanical production and circulation of the fidelista dogma, portraying it as a signifier emptied of meaning, produced by a doodle whose contradictory fate is to consume his own words.

In *Máscara de cocodrilo* (*Crocodile Mask*), another olive-green monochromatic painting from the 1988 series, Rodríguez Cárdenas depicts Castro in his guerrilla uniform, wearing the bracelet of the M-26-7, a pistol, and a rifle, putting on (or taking off) a crocodile mask.[39] Given that the island of Cuba has always been compared to a crocodile in its shape, the overlapping of the silhouettes of Castro and the island in this painting alludes to Castro's nationalistic discourse as a mask. Cuban crocodiles are, moreover, aggressive animals that stalk their prey by blending into their surroundings, a characteristic that Rodríguez Cárdenas would have also implicitly attributed to Castro.

Finally, in *Un cielo despejado* (*A Clear Sky*, 1988, Plate 32), Rodríguez Cárdenas denounces the Castro regime as a deadly *fatum*, suggesting that only with the leader's death would the country have peace.[40] The artist paints Castro's silhouette lying at the bottom of the sea, depicting his drowning as the cause of Cuba's clear sky. The painting also presages the drama endured by thousands of people who fled the country on simple rafts during the 1990s, sailing when skies were clear—meaning good weather—and hoping to reach the United States. Many of them never made it, drowning in the Florida Straits, as the crosses buried at the bottom of the sea in this image might premonitorily indicate, resting inside a Castro-like figure that would have been the ultimate cause of their deaths.

And yet, much like in the elegiac work of Mederos Pazos, Martínez, and Soto some elements suggest a subtler sociopolitical critique, we can detect in Rodríguez Cárdenas's up-front political criticism the underwriting of some of the discourses of legitimation of the Castro regime, notably the postrevolutionary nationalism and Castro's embodiment of the government, the country, and the nation. Regardless, the exhibition *Artista de calidad* never took place; Cuban authorities censored it.[41]

That same year (1988), Glexis Novoa (b. 1964) inaugurated *To Be or Not to Be* at Galería Habana with works from what he called his *etapa romántica* ("romantic stage"), which he describes as a reaction "to the censorship of [artists] Tomás Esson and Carlos [Rodríguez] Cárdenas."[42] Of *To Be or Not to Be*, art critic Rachel Weiss writes that it was "a general mess of an exhibition that meant to, and did, confuse everybody, hung up between critique, repudiation, and acceptance of the ideas that seemed to be in the work."[43] One of the pieces in the show consisted of a text written with sloppy olive-greenish brushstrokes that stated, "this piece was made by a young artist, born and living within the Revolution. Havana. Cuba."[44] As with the Rodríguez Cárdenas series *Artista de calidad*, this was a monochromatic piece with olive green arguably representing the fidelista state, but in this case meanings are not to be found in the canvas or color. Novoa's piece—and the show in general—denounced a cultural policy that privileged art that, first and foremost, was meant to be "revolutionary," that is, aligned with the regime's ideology, even if it were to the detriment of its artistic qualities. Novoa's critique thus rested not in the exhibited pieces, but in the show itself as a denunciation of the ideological restrictions imposed upon art.[45]

The following year (1989), René Francisco Rodríguez (b. 1960) and Eduardo Ponjuán González (b. 1956) inaugurated the show *Artista melodramático* (*Melodramatic Artist*) at the Castillo de la Fuerza, in which they exhibited, for a brief five days before censorship intervened, *Las ideas llegan más lejos que la luz* (*Ideas Go Farther Than Light*, 1989).[46] In this painting, René Francisco y Ponjuán, as the duo was known, represented the Morro fortress—one of the symbols of the city of Havana and part of the colonial military complex that included the Castillo de la Fuerza—painted in green, with the head of Castro in lieu of the lighthouse's beacon. The head emits alternative halos of white and black birds toward a red sea, leaving the city behind in darkness, a not-so-hidden allusion to Castro's Janus faces, which promote a black-and-white discourse of liberty and hope in Communism overseas while ruining the territory he administered.

Five days after the opening of *Artista melodramático*, political commissars took down this painting, along with three other pieces, alleging that they misrepresented the Cuban leader.[47] One of the other banned pieces, *Suicida* (*Suicidal*, 1989), forms Castro's silhouette with small pieces of mirror glued to plywood painted olive green. Reflecting the image of the viewer, the mirror de facto fuses it with—or incorporates it—into the leader's silhouette, making any attempt at destroying the latter an act of self-destruction or suicide, as René Francisco declared in a recent interview.[48] In this work, again, olive green is the substrate, medium, or background, the uterus in which the symbiosis of leader and viewer occurs.[49]

Referring to the artists who emerged in the 1980s, frequently called the Children-of-William-Tell Generation, art critic and curator Gerardo Mosquera argues that they "initiat[ed] and spearhead[ed] a critical consciousness that ha[d] never been publicly expressed in Cuba."[50] Both as a collective and individually, this generation of artists put forth a political critique of the fidelista state articulated, and on occasion concealed, through the olive-green trope. In the post-Soviet era, when the Cuban government introduced a series of political and economic reforms—including the legalization of the U.S. dollar—to keep the Cuban economy afloat and guarantee the stability of the socialist regime after the disappearance of the Soviet Bloc, a new generation of artists worked with the photographic image and actualized the olive-green metaphor within new forms of sociopolitical critique.

Like Rivadulla did in 1959, José Ángel Toirac (b. 1966) drew from the photographic archive of the early postrevolutionary years, recreating iconic images of the radical 1960s more than a decade before it became trendy in Cuban literature and art.[51] Toirac put them in conversation with iconic capitalist commodities, including brands such as Marlboro and Yves Saint Laurent, in a political commentary that denounced guerrilla chic—and the ideology this trope represented—as a global commodity. In the light box *La Maison. Casa cubana de modas* (*La Maison. Cuban Fashion House*, 1995), Toirac reproduced a photograph of a young Castro taken in the mid-1960s by U.S. photographer Lee Lockwood, in which the leader is dressed in military fatigues and wears no shoes, smoking while relaxing in a rocking chair at one of his country houses.[52] By combining this image with the logotype and slogan of the Cuban upscale fashion house *La Maison*, opened in the early 1980s to cater to foreign tourists and diplomats, and transformed in 1994 into a high-end boutique for dollar-holding Cubans, Toirac contrasts the former utopian discourses of revolutionary asceticism with the commoditization of the revolutionary ethos and its imagery in the post-Soviet era.

Toirac's commentary on Cuba's opening to the global market as a means of sustaining and legitimizing the local regime after the disappearance of the Soviet Bloc is not limited only to the combination of capitalist and upscale socialist *brandscapes*. *La Maison. Casa cubana de modas* also alludes to the commodification of the revolutionary myth, in ways that resemble the commercial signs that resurfaced in the public space in the 1990s. All in all, as curator Juan Carlos Betancourt argues, this work suggests that "socialist propaganda and capitalist advertising shared a common goal: to sell compelling images aimed at mass consumption."[53] With fine-tuned sarcasm, this piece denounces the contradictory coexistence of an official rhetoric of sacrifice and material austerity alongside the emergence of state-sanctioned spaces and mechanisms of distinction, mainly restricted to the political elite and dollar-holding foreigners. Also, playing with the domestic setting in which Castro was photographed, the title of the piece, *La Maison* (French for "the house"), demystifies the fidelista epic, portraying the leader as an ordinary man.

With the turn of the twentieth century, the photographic image gained in elaboration in the critique that visual artists put forth of the olive-green figured world of power. In his 2009 piece *Samurai (según Donatello)* (*Samurai [after Donatello]*), a life-size photograph of a naked black man imitating Donatello's David but wearing a corduroy olive-drab cap and a sword, René Peña (b. 1957) merges classical and contemporary referents in a powerful political critique.[54]

Peña's references to the biblical character who faced the giant Goliath with no armor and killed him with a slingshot allude to the triumph of the powerless over the strong—that is, to the victory of courage and determination against the sheer power of force. At the same time and almost contradictorily, the reference in the work's title to samurai, the Japanese medieval warriors who owed absolute loyalty to their feudal lords and were willing to kill themselves for honor, criticizes the obedience the fidelista regime demanded from individuals, in particular black bodies, and the onerous sacrifices—and even death—Castro had asked people to endure to preserve his power. Moreover, Peña's naked David-samurai evokes the sexual objectification of black bodies, frequently dehumanized as mere cogs in Cuba's large military, trapped in the myth of David versus Goliath, which the Castro regime translated in terms of the island's antagonism toward the United States.[55]

A similar critique toward the military apparatus is developed by Adonis Flores (b. 1971), a former student of the Camilo Cienfuegos military school and an Angola war veteran, in this case conveyed through photographic images of (generally) the artist himself, clad in camouflage fatigues. His work *Maleza* (*Undergrowth*, 2005), which literary critic Rachel Price describes as "a large format print that teems with soldiers in army crawl, outfitted in camouflage—all digitally replicated copies of Flores himself," denounces the homogenization of individuals under military institutions. Military training, Flores suggests, turns individuals into identical clones, comparable to an unproductive extension of weeds—undergrowth.[56]

In the series *Camouflages*, which Flores began in 2007, he develops a more general critique of the impact of the militarization of society and the relationship between power and individual identity. Inspired by da Vinci's *Vitruvian Man*, *Canon* (2012), a piece in this series, portrays the archetypical Renaissance man as a soldier dressed in camouflage fatigues.[57] Representing the impossible reconciliation of praetorian and humanistic values, Flores denounces the idea of the soldier as the measure of all human things, a message that arguably alludes to Cuban state propaganda, which presented Castro and Guevara as archetypes to imitate by the generations born after 1959. *Canon*, moreover, might also denounce the spurious, antithetical humanism of the fidelista regime.

In 2009, Tania Bruguera (b. 1968) presented the performance *Tatlin's Whisper #6 (Havana Version)* at the Wifredo Lam Center, during the Tenth Havana Biennale.[58] In that version of *Tatlin's Whisper*, the artist invited members of the audience to express their thoughts at a podium, granting each person a minute to speak, escorted by a young man and woman clad in military uniforms. The fatigues-clad actors also escorted speakers off of the stage when their allotted time was done, and placed a white dove on their shoulders when they stepped in, a nod to Fidel Castro's inaugural speech in Havana after the revolutionary victory. Among the multiple meanings each element of this performance suggests (including some not referred to here), I want to stress the use of military uniforms not just as a representation of power but also as the source of it—Bruguera's collaborators are mostly obeyed because of the uniform they wear. In Bruguera's reenactment of a democratic forum, the uniformed individuals are the authority that guarantees order and, thus, conversation, protecting against others' abuse of their allotted time. In doing so, Bruguera's performance arguably points to the role military authorities are called to play in a democracy, when—as the artist declares on her webpage—people awake to their political responsibility and become the authors and owners of their political lives.[59] In such a scenario, fatigue uniforms are due to become the guarantee of each other's rights and public dialogue.

I will conclude with the work of Aldo Damián Menéndez López (b. 1971), especially the recent protest art of Maldito Menéndez, his alter ego, directly confronting the fidelista regime and its symbols, notably military drab and guayabera shirts.[60] On his blog *Castor Jabao*, an anagram of *abajo Castro* ("down with Castro"), Maldito Menéndez documents his performances of protest, including a 2015 denunciation of his banishment from Cuba and state authorities' decision to send him back to Spain on the same plane on which he had arrived in Havana to participate in an artistic event while visiting his mother.[61] Maldito Menéndez posted pictures of an inflatable sex doll (Plate 33) that he dressed in an army shirt and "adorned" with tools of sadomasochistic sex in an explicit denunciation of the abuse of power the military and political authorities perpetrated against artists and citizens in Cuba.[62] Those pictures address not just the militarization of the Cuban regime, but also the tyrannical power the government exerts against citizens and their bodies, similar to sadomasochistic practices.

Exploring the representation of the olive-green imagery in a group of works of visual art, this chapter has interpreted a diverse repertoire of critical approaches to the Castro regime and the olive-green figured world of power, ranging from praise to uncompromising critique, including more or less tacit conciliations. Whereas in the early postrevolutionary decades Cuban artists often conveyed their hope in and support for the socialist regime, celebrating its symbols, namely through the olive-green trope, criticism eventually emerged targeting the praetorianization of Cuban society, the disproportionate power of its military caste, and the state's intrusion into the private sphere and transformation of family relations, individual identities, and people's daily lives. Unacknowledged by international couture labels, which enthusiastically borrow from the olive-green imaginary to recreate Cuba's long-lost revolutionary ethos, throughout the last four decades Cuban visual artists have deconstructed this history, pulling the military drab imaginary apart.

Notes

1. Alyssa Vingan Klein, "Stella McCartney Brought Cuba to Nolita for Her Resort Presentation."

2. Sarah Mower, "Resort 2017: Chanel."

3. Michelle Chase, "The Making of Fidel Castro."

4. Anthony DePalma, *Myths of the Enemy*, 3. Matthews's coverage, which spawned three articles published on February 24, 25, and 27, 1957, was, in Cuban officials' view, "worth more than a military victory." DePalma, *The Man Who Invented Fidel*, 111.

5. Chase, "The Making of Fidel Castro."

6. Jorge L. Catalá Carrasco, "El humor gráfico revolucionario en Cuba."

7. See the campaign brochure in Chase, "The Making of Fidel Castro" and *Revolution within the Revolution*; Lillian Guerra, *Heroes, Martyrs, and Political Messiahs in Revolutionary Cuba, 1946–1958.*

8. Burt Glinn, *Cuba 1959*; Lee Lockwood, *Castro's Cuba*; Rufo López-Fresquet, *My 14 Months with Castro.*

9. Glinn, 96.

10. López-Fresquet.

11. Ignac90, "La llegada de los barbudos."

12. Luis M. Buch Rodríguez, "El día que Fidel asumió el cargo de Primer Ministro."

13. Buch Rodríguez, my translation. All translations are mine unless otherwise noted.

14. José Quiroga, *Cuban Palimpsests*, 94; see also Iván de la Nuez, "La imagen lo absorberá"; Guerra, "'Una buena foto es la mejor defensa de la Revolución'"; Juan A. Molina, "La marca de su cicatriz."

15. See, for example, Buch Rodríguez; Omar Fernández Cañizares, *Primer viaje del Che al exterior.*

16. Yeidy M. Rivero, *Broadcasting Modernity*, 158; Marifeli Pérez-Stable, *The Cuban Revolution.*

17. Rivero; Pérez-Stable. See also María A. Cabrera Arús, "For Sale"; Chase, "The Making of Fidel Castro."

18. Cabrera Arús, "For Sale."

19. Guerra, *Heroes, Martyrs, and Political Messiahs.*

20. Minerva Salado, *Censura de prensa en la Revolución Cubana. INRA* was accessed online at the Digital Library of the Caribbean of Florida International University, http://www.dloc.com/AA00013449/00001/allvolumes?search=inra.

21. Guerra, *Visions of Power in Cuba.*

22. Chase, "The Making of Fidel Castro."

23. Luis Hernández Serrano, "Cincuenta octubres de un cartel." This photograph also

appeared on lapel pins, bookmarks, stickers, and other media. It was the photo displayed at Castro's wake in November 2016, both by the (empty) coffin and on the façade of one of the buildings surrounding Revolution Square.

24. Hernández Serrano; see also Isabel, "El grafismo cubano en estos años"; Chase, "The Making of Fidel Castro."

25. Shreeya Sihna, "Castro's Revolution, Illustrated." This photograph is also reproduced in the masthead of the *Granma* newspaper, the official organ of the Cuban Communist Party. It was taken atop the Turquino Peak, in the Sierra Maestra mountains, during the production of the CBS documentary.

26. Sihna.

27. Duanel Díaz Infante, *La revolución congelada* and "La revolución es el espectáculo"; Guerra, *Visions of Power in Cuba.*

28. I develop the notion of Cuba's revolutionary figured world of power in chapter 1 of my book in preparation, "Dressed for the Party: Fashion and Politics in Socialist Cuba," after the theory formulated by sociologist Chandra Mukerji in "The Territorial State as a Figured World of Power."

29. María A. Cabrera Arús and Mirta Suquet, "La moda en la literatura cubana"; Guerra, *Visions of Power in Cuba.*

30. "Adiós Utopia"; John V. Alencar, "Raúl Martínez, Island 70"; Rachel Weiss, *To and from Utopia in the New Cuban Art.*

31. Ernesto Menéndez-Conde, "Dos bromas de Raúl Martínez (II)."

32. Carlos Tejo Veloso, *El cuerpo habitado.*

33. Leandro Soto, personal communication, June 23, 2017, Miami; Enrique González Rojas, "'Yo vengo de todas partes y hacia todas partes voy'"; Juan A. Molina, "La marca de su cicatriz"; Weiss.

34. Soto, personal communication.

35. On the William Tell Generation, see Ruth Behar, ed., *Bridges to Cuba*; Betancourt, "The Rebel Children"; José M. Fajardo, "Los hijos cubanos de Guillermo Tell." The musical theme that gave the name to this generation, composed by songwriter and singer Carlos Varela, was first performed in 1989 at the Chaplin Theater in Havana.

36. Carlos Rodríguez Cárdenas, Facebook message to author, July 26, 2017; Weiss.

37. Rodríguez Cárdenas.

38. Rodríguez Cárdenas.

39. Rodríguez Cárdenas.

40. Rodríguez Cárdenas.

41. Weiss.

42. Weiss, 75.

43. Weiss, 73.

44. See GlexisNovoa.com.

45. Weiss.

46. Betancourt, 74; Rose M. Salum, "Adiós a la utopía cubana"; Weiss. *Las ideas llegan más lejos que la luz* is also the title of a previous painting by Rodríguez Cárdenas.

47. Betancourt.

48. Salum; Weiss.

49. In 1986, Glexis Novoa also colored in olive green the background of his paintings *No tengo palabras para expresar mi emoción* (*I Have No Words to Express My Emotion*) and *Martí en el 3er congreso del PCC* ([José] *Martí at the 3rd PCC Congress*). See GlexisNovoa.com.

50. Quoted by Betancourt, 74; see also Behar; Fajardo.

51. Rachel Price, *Planet/Cuba*.

52. Betancourt, 79.

53. Betancourt.

54. Deborah Vankin, "In Havana, Following a USC Museum Director in Search of Great Cuban Art."

55. "'Queloides: Race and Racism in Cuban Contemporary Art.'"

56. Price, 154.

57. "Exhibition Walk-Through."

58. "Tania Bruguera. *Tatlin's Whisper* #6 (Havana Version)"; Taniabruguera.com.

59. Symptomatically, one of the speakers protested against "the militarization of the country." "El susurro de Tatlin #6 (versión para La Habana)," at 2:18.

60. Cabrera Arús, "Tratado de guayatola."

61. Maldito Menéndez, "Cuba, no es país para artistas."

62. Menéndez, "La Vía anal de La Vana."

Bibliography

Alencar, John V. "Raúl Martínez, Island 70." *Pop Art in the Americas, 1965–1975*. Accessed June 15, 2017. http://popinlatinamerica.trinity.duke.edu/exhibits/show/national-identity/raul_martinez_isla_70.

Behar, Ruth, ed. *Bridges to Cuba: Cuban and Cuban-American Artists, Writers, and Scholars Explore Identity, Nationality, and Homeland*. Ann Harbor: University of Michigan Press, 1995.

Betancourt, Juan C. "The Rebel Children of the Cuban Revolution: Notes on the History of 'Cuban Sots Art.'" In *Caviar with Rum: Cuba-USSR and the Post-Soviet Experience*, edited by Jacqueline Loss and José Manuel Prieto, 69–84. New York: Palgrave MacMillan, 2012.

Buch Rodríguez, Luis M. "El día que Fidel asumió el cargo de Primer Ministro (+ Fotos y Video)." *CubaDebate.cu*, February 17, 2017. http://www.cubadebate.cu/especiales/2017/02/16/el-dia-que-fidel-asumio-el-cargo-de-primer-ministro-fotos-y-video/#.WMGwNxjMyRs.

Cabrera Arús, María A. "Dressed for the Party: Fashion and Politics in Socialist Cuba." Unpublished manuscript.

———. "For Sale: Cuba's Revolutionary Figured World." *Age of Revolutions* (blog), January 22, 2018. https://ageofrevolutions.com/2018/01/22/for-sale-cubas-revolutionary-figured-world/.

———. "Tratado de guayatola: Cuba Material entrevista a Maldito Menéndez." *Cuba Material* (blog), April 7, 2015. http://cubamaterial.com/blog/tratado-de-guayatola-entrevista-a-maldito-menendez/.

Cabrera Arús, María A., and Mirta Suquet. "La moda en la literatura cubana, 1960–1970: Tejiendo y destejiendo al hombre nuevo." *Cuban Studies* 47 (2019): 195–221.

Catalá Carrasco, Jorge L. "El humor gráfico revolucionario en Cuba: El camino hacia un arte militante." *Revista Latinoamericana de Estudios sobre la Historieta* 8, no. 29 (2008): 1–18.

Chase, Michelle. "The Making of Fidel Castro: The International Mass Media and the Rebel Army." *Age of Revolutions* (blog), January 16, 2017. https://ageofrevolutions.com/2017/01/16/the-making-of-fidel-castro-the-international-mass-media-and-the-rebel-army/.

———. *Revolution within the Revolution: Women and Gender Politics in Cuba, 1952–1962.* Chapel Hill: University of North Carolina Press, 2015.

Cisneros Fontanals Art Foundation. *Adiós Utopia: Dreams and Deceptions in Cuban Art since 1950 (Traveling–Houston).* Accessed July 26, 2018. http://cifo.org/cifoart/index.php/en/current-exhibitions/794-adios-utopia-dreams-and-deceptions-in-cuban-art-since-1950.

De la Nuez, Iván. "La imagen lo absorberá." *ElPaís.com*, November 26, 2016. https://internacional.elpais.com/internacional/2016/11/26/actualidad/1480195990_770268.html.

DePalma, Anthony. *The Man Who Invented Fidel: Castro, Cuba, and Herbert L. Matthews of The New York Times.* New York: Public Affairs, 2006.

———. *Myths of the Enemy: Castro, Cuba, and Herbert L. Matthews of The New York Times.* Working Paper #313, July 2004, Helen Kellogg Institute for International Studies, University of Notre Dame. https://kellogg.nd.edu/publications/workingpapers/WPS/313.pdf.

Díaz Infante, Duanel. *La revolución congelada: Dialécticas del castrismo.* Madrid: Verbum, 2014.

———. "La revolución es el espectáculo." *Diario de Cuba*, August 11, 2012. http://www.diariodecuba.com/cultura/1344672447_694.html.

"El susurro de Tatlin #6 (versión para La Habana)." *Vimeo*, accessed October 10, 2018. https://vimeo.com/21394727.

"Exhibition Walk-Through: Adonis Flores at Galería Habana." *Cuban Art News* (blog), July 31, 2014. https://www.cubanartnews.org/news/exhibition-walk-through-adonis-flores-at-galeria-habana.

Fajardo, José M. "Los hijos cubanos de Guillermo Tell." *ElPaís.com*, June 19, 2008. https://cultura.elpais.com/cultura/2008/06/07/actualidad/1212789610_850215.html.

Fernández Cañizares, Omar. *Primer viaje del Che al exterior: Aniversario 50.* Havana: Ciencias Sociales, 2010.

Glinn, Burt. *Cuba 1959.* London: Rare Art Press, 2015.

González Rojas, Enrique. "'Yo vengo de todas partes y hacia todas partes voy': Entrevista con Leandro Soto." *Guanaroca del Sur* (blog), August 26, 2013. Accessed February 16, 2018. http://guanarocadelsur.blogspot.com/2013/08/leandro-soto-yo-vengo-de-todas-partes-y.html.

Guerra, Lillian. "'Una buena foto es la mejor defensa de la Revolución': Imagen, producción de imagen y la imaginación revolucionaria de 1959." *Encuentro de la Cultura Cubana* 43 (2006–7): 11–21.

———. *Heroes, Martyrs, and Political Messiahs in Revolutionary Cuba, 1946–1958*. New Haven: Yale University Press, 2018.

———. *Visions of Power in Cuba: Revolution, Redemption, and Resistance, 1959–1971*. Chapel Hill: University of North Carolina Press, 2012.

Hernández Serrano, Luis. "Cincuenta octubres de un cartel." *JuventudRebelde.cu*, October 23, 2012. http://www.juventudrebelde.cu/cuba/2012-10-23/cincuenta-octubres-de-un-cartel/.

Ignac90. "La llegada de los barbudos." *Barbudos* (blog), August 18, 2014. https://losbarbudos.wordpress.com/2014/08/18/la-llegada-de-los-barbudos.

Isabel. "El grafismo cubano en estos años." *Blog Artes Visuales*, December 15, 2016. https://www.blogartesvisuales.net/general/grafismo-cubano/.

Lockwood, Lee. *Castro's Cuba: An American Journalist's Inside Look at Cuba (1959–1969)*. Berlin: Taschen, 2016.

López-Fresquet, Rufo. *My 14 Months with Castro*. New York: World Publishing, 1966.

Menéndez, Maldito. "Cuba, no es país para artistas." *Castor Jabao* (blog), April 4, 2015. https://malditomenendez.blogspot.com/2015/04/cuba-no-es-pais-para-artistas.html.

———. "La Vía anal de La Vana: Entre la espada y la pared." *Castor Jabao* (blog), May 22, 2015. https://malditomenendez.blogspot.com/2015/05/la-via-anal-de-la-vana-entre-la-espada.html.

Menéndez-Conde, Ernesto. "Dos bromas de Raúl Martínez (II)." *Art Experience New York City* (blog), April 4, 2008. http://lapizynube.blogspot.com/2008/04/dos-bromas-de-ral-martnez-ii.html.

Molina, Juan Antonio. "La marca de su cicatriz: Historia y metáfora en la fotografía cubana contemporánea." In *Nosotros, los más infieles: Narraciones críticas sobre el arte cubano (1993–2005)*, edited by Andrés Isaac Santana, 835–45. Murcia, Spain: CENDEAC, 2007.

Mower, Sarah. "Resort 2017: Chanel." *Vogue.com*, May 4, 2016. https://www.vogue.com/fashion-shows/resort-2017/chanel.

Mukerji, Chandra. "The Territorial State as a Figured World of Power: Strategics, Logistics, and Impersonal Rule." *Sociological Theory* 28, no. 4 (2010): 402–25.

Pérez-Stable, Marifeli. *The Cuban Revolution: Origins, Course, and Legacy*. New York: Oxford University Press, 1993.

Price, Rachel. *Planet/Cuba: Art, Culture, and the Future of the Island*. New York: Verso, 2015.

"'Queloides: Race and Racism in Cuban Contemporary Art': A Groundbreaking Exhibition Makes Waves in Pittsburgh." *Cubanartnews.org*, November 9, 2010. https://www.cubanartnews.org/2010/11/09/queloides-race-and-racism-in-cuban-contemporary-art/.

Quiroga, José. *Cuban Palimpsests*. Minneapolis: University of Minnesota Press, 2005.

Rivero, Yeidy M. *Broadcasting Modernity: Cuban Commercial Television, 1950–1960*. Durham, NC: Duke University Press, 2015.

Salado, Minerva. *Censura de prensa en la Revolución Cubana*. Madrid: Verbum, 2016.
Salum, Rose M. "Adiós a la utopía cubana." *LiteralMagazine.com*, March 19, 2017. http://literalmagazine.com/adios-la-utopia-cubana/.
Sihna, Shreeya. "Castro's Revolution, Illustrated." *NYTimes.com*, November 26, 2016. https://www.nytimes.com/interactive/2016/11/26/world/americas/fidel-castro-cuban-posters.html.
"Tania Bruguera. *Tatlin's Whisper #6* (Havana Version)." *Guggenheim.com*, accessed October 10, 2018. https://www.guggenheim.org/artwork/33083.
Taniabruguera.com. Accessed October 10, 2018. http://www.taniabruguera.com/cms/112-0-Tatlins+Whisper+6+Havana+version.htm.
Tejo Veloso, Carlos. *El cuerpo habitado: Fotografía cubana para un fin de milenio*. Santiago de Compostela: Universidad Santiago de Compostela, 2009.
Vankin, Deborah. "In Havana, Following a USC Museum Director in Search of Great Cuban Art." *LATimes.com*, May 26, 2016. http://www.latimes.com/entertainment/arts/la-ca-cm-cuba-curator-20160520-snap-htmlstory.html.
Vingan Klein, Alyssa. "Stella McCartney Brought Cuba to Nolita for Her Resort Presentation." *Fashionista* (blog), June 9, 2015. https://fashionista.com/2015/06/stella-mccartney-resort-2016.
Weiss, Rachel. *To and from Utopia in the New Cuban Art*. Minneapolis: University of Minnesota Press, 2011.

11

Theatricality in the Art of the Cuban Diaspora

The Progression of Tropes

Ricardo Pau-Llosa

I have always believed that tropes reveal patterns of identity that go beyond considerations of style, in the works of individual artists as well as the groups—cultural, gender-based, generational, philosophical, among others—with which they identify or that they can reasonably be identified with. Style is the result of a dialogue between artists and the themes and concerns they inherit from their tradition, be this dialogue participatory or confrontational. Whatever its roots in the creative domain of the unconscious, style is engaged by the artist and analyzed by critics as a public matter; hence its importance in art history analysis. However, tropes, which influence stylistic and other aesthetic decisions, are an expression of the oneiric/creative imagination as the force that shapes visual thought. Hence, understanding tropes and extrapolating concepts from their operation in any of the arts are generally more complicated endeavors than determining questions of style, the most obvious aspects of influence, or extracting explicit or implied aspects of the artist's identity or opinions.

The emergence of Latin American Modernist art gives clear evidence of these complications. Early pioneers of *vanguardias* (avant-garde movements) across the region sought in local imagery or long-suppressed cultural legacies a platform upon which to connect the art of their nations to new developments in Western European art. In doing so, artists such as Rufino Tamayo, Amelia Peláez, Tarsila do Amaral, Joaquín Torres-García, Fernando de Szyszlo, and Roberto Matta, to name but a few, dramatized the power of metaphor to join past and present—thematic, cultural-religious, and aesthetic patterns linked to a cultural past with concerns that were guiding Modernist innovation. Metaphor enabled them to embrace, obliquely but poignantly, the long-held Latin American attitude toward the "present" as a confluence of multiple "pasts," marking a regional break with linear Western European and U.S. attitudes toward temporality and the evolution of ideas. Thus, the Latin American penchant for rescuing regional legacies rather than discarding them, counter to an anti-legacy bias central to the European Modernist rebellion against the evils of nationalism that culminated in World War I, inadvertently generated a divergent Modernism in Latin America. The nature and implications of this divergence are still difficult for critics outside the region, or their acolytes within the region, to understand and appreciate.

Although tropes have always played a role in the visual arts, the reason for their importance in Latin American Modernism marks a key divergence from Western European Modernism. Reduction became the hallmark of most major Modernist movements in Europe, with innovation from one style or movement to the next hinging on what could be removed from the current aesthetic standards or trend to generate a new way of making art. Eliminating the third dimension in painting, a goal intimated by Paul Cézanne, culminated in Cubism. Eliminating references from Cubism led to Constructivism, and so on. Reduction always compels emphasis on another aspect of art—Manet's Velázquez-inspired foregrounding of pigment, Expressionism's placement of psychological turmoil and emotion at the forefront of our apprehension of a painting. The reductionist search was on for greater synthesis and purity in art, a process that was accelerated by the general rejection of bourgeois European values in culture and social life which were believed to be at the root of World War I. All but the Surrealists abjured representation, narrative, and theatricality in painting; they used these aesthetic strategies to produce their own anti-establishment works anchored in psychoanalytical approaches to dream imagery and other expressions of the unconscious.

In general, a suspicion of culture, especially high culture, and its prevailing standards of beauty and meaningfulness, drove Modernism. However, Latin American Modernists, many of them visiting Europe for the first time in the 1920s, did not see legacy as the enemy. On the contrary, they sought to meld the new styles with their own cultural identities—which combined European, West African, Indigenous, and Asian traditions—to rehabilitate these identities after centuries of disparagement. For the Latin Americans, the European Modernist styles would be used to express something radically different from what the creators of these styles intended: the preservation, not the purgation, of cultural legacy and identity. Tropes had been embedded for millennia in European, Ibero-colonial, and pre-conquest Indigenous art of the Americas. Centering their visual thinking on tropes enabled Latin American Modernists to amplify the powers of their art to represent the world and, more importantly, ideas, even if the aesthetic idioms of this endeavor were the mostly anti-representational modalities of European Modernism. Just one among countless examples from the 1960s and 1970s is the kinetic art of Jesús Rafael Soto of Venezuela, with its poetic approach to the infinite as a philosophical concept, as well as allusions to music, language itself, and even Amazonian waterfalls, in contrast to European kineticists (Op artists) Victor Vasarely and Bridget Riley, whose works have been praised for their utterly non-referential, trompe l'oeil effects.[1]

To say that one or more tropes drive a Latin American artist's work, then, is to place our understanding of the sustained value of representation within the regional Modernist program at the heart of our approach to this artist's work. Tropological visual thinking and theatricality also lie at the heart of European Surrealism, as well as the works of figurative artists of the twentieth century in the United States, e.g., Clarence Holbrook Carter, Edward Hopper, and Georgia O'Keeffe. But these U.S. artists were mavericks who kept representation alive and were consequently treated as marginal to the more highly regarded, reductionist Modernist movements of Abstract Expressionism, Pop, Minimalism, Found-Object Art, Conceptualism, and others. Conversely, reduction or its absence played a minor role in the emergence and valuation of Latin American Modernism within the region. In Europe and the United States, a different story has unfolded. The Latin American blending of dissonant European styles—e.g., Constructivism and Surrealism—and the conscious or unwitting embrace of tropes, representation, and theatricality have struck First World art cognoscenti in mostly negative ways. It was not until the 1970s, with the rise of Postmodernism, that this negative view of the region's art began to change somewhat.

Centering visual thinking on tropes while reinventing the values and connotations of stylistic idioms imported from Europe may well have been an inevitable course for the Latin American Modernists. For one thing, tropes are rooted in the syncretic cultures of the region and the art and religious practices that have flourished in it, to say nothing of the nonlinear concepts of time attached to these syncretic cultures. But perhaps as importantly, tropological thinking enabled the region's artists to reassign new values to these metropolitan styles. The styles themselves acquired the semantic content of images and concepts in metaphor, metonymy, synecdoche, and other tropes, so that these expressions of style—originally imagined as ways to bracket or escape traditional representation—could now embody ideas by establishing similarities between referents (metaphor), effecting transferences of connotations and denotations between referents (metonymy), uniting disparate elements into a dynamic context (metonymy), and seeing instances of patterns or contexts as signifiers of broader realities (synecdoche). When combined into complex tropes, these can link action to immediate as well as archetypal realities and dissolve the boundaries between everyday and oneiric awareness—the bases for theatricality in visual art.

The polysemia and non-literalness of all tropes made them ideal for this transgressive and expropriatory use of European anti-representational idioms in the Latin American Modernist agenda, which was grounded in representational, narrative, oneiric, and theatrical aspects of art. Nowhere is this clearer than in the region's most original early Modernist, the Uruguayan Joaquín Torres-García, who took the Constructivist grid (the pinnacle of European abstractionism) and filled it with letters, numbers, and symbols derived from everyday life, and pictographs of his own making. He turned the grid itself into a symbol—a concept born of metaphor—of the infinite, and not just a reductivist expression of geometric imagery for its own sake, then overlaid it with symbols of language, that most human, universal, and quotidian expression of the infinite.[2] A juxtaposition of the two—i.e., a metaphor—generated a very American (in the Western hemisphere sense) Modernist approach to a major theme in all the cultural roots that make up Latin America.

In the case of Cuban Modernism, most of the First- and Second-Generation masters centered their work on particular tropes. First-Generation artists were born in the early twentieth century, or the late nineteenth, and the Second Generation in the 1910s or early 1920s. This single-trope model is important for laying the foundations of a divergence from ideas and concerns in vogue at a given time. Metaphor informs Peláez and René Portocarrero. Metonymy rules Carlos Enríquez and Wifredo Lam. The paintings of two pivotal Second-Generation artists, Mario Carreño and Cundo Bermúdez, would draw on juxtaposition to initiate the theatrical current in Cuban Modernism (more on this later). Synecdoche would emerge prominently in specific movements within the Third Generation, driving the geometric abstraction of the Concretos and the Informalist-inspired Grupo de los Once (the Group of Eleven).

What typifies Third-Generation Cuban art (artists born in the 1930s) is the preponderance of complex tropes—visual thought that simultaneously entertains more than one trope in the conception and execution of images, often reveling in paradox. Synecdochic patterns and the theme of the Infinite are framed in the archetypal, mnemonic symbolism (i.e., metaphor) of architecture in the paintings of Emilio Sánchez. Fusions of metaphor and metonymy depicting the similarities and transferences among machines, armor, and flesh are central to the paintings and drawings of Agustín Fernández. Fusions of synecdoche and metaphor figure prominently in sculptor Rolando López Dirube's hedonistic representation of mathematical concepts in diverse media, from tropical woods to reinforced concrete. Hugo Consuegra—one of the founding members of Los Once—would give Informalist imagery almost sculptural qualities and situate these images in room-like settings. He is the only major Cuban abstractionist painter to incorporate a theatrical dimension into his conception of pictorial space. As a divergence becomes capable of sustaining its identity over three generations, it affirms, in its maturity, the validity of its approach within the broader tradition—in this case, Western Modernism. With maturity, tropes become more complex and subject matter as a signifier of cultural identity and cohesion declines in intensity. Cultural identity and cohesion become a function of deeper patterns in visual thought. For this reason, Cuba's Modernist maturity was reached during the Third Generation of artists, whose culmination coincided with the rise of totalitarianism in 1959 and the internal repression and exile that it unleashed.

Evolution toward complex tropes can only occur within a tradition that values representation in art, something almost all European and U.S. Modernist movements rejected (again, except for Surrealism). One could speak of a Latin American Modernist Secessionism, which embraced representation and saw in tropes a way of broadening, rather than bracketing, its power in the visual arts; Cuba's Modernism was no exception. However different the overall Latin American Modernist attitude toward reference might have been, it remains part of Western Modernism, an aesthetic adventure perfectly capable of sustaining divergence and dissidence.

A two-sided question begs to be addressed: given the complex tropes that dominate Cuban visual thinking from the 1950s to this day, what does theatricality as a theme reveal about congealing diasporic sensibilities—and, conversely, how does diaspora help us understand the theatrical in the works of various Cuban artists? I use "diaspora" to refer to a culture's trans-territorial vitality and evolution resulting from an exile that extends beyond one generation. Exile can only turn into diaspora when a significant cross-section of a nation's population flees intolerable conditions without relinquishing pride in and attachment to the native culture, however complete and even triumphant its assimilation to new cultures might be. This emotional and cultural dual citizenship is managed when diasporic exiles create for themselves an unconscious culture of survival and continuity. Not all exiles evolve into diasporas, but Cuba's epic of displacement (six decades and counting) certainly has. I use "theatricality" to reference the use of scenarios or symbol-based narratives, or both, in representations of action (physical, imagined, historical, or conceptual) that shed light on the poetics of shelter (from time, history, persecution, and other forces).[3]

A diasporic sensibility will tend to approach shelter differently from a native sensibility. One possibility is placing shelter within the framework of theater precisely because the cultural survivalist craves the concepts of "psychical distance" (Edward Bullough) and "willing suspension of disbelief" (Samuel Taylor Coleridge) to reconcile expulsion from native soil with membership in a still-viable epic that interprets and gives transcendent meaning to this predicament.[4] The crux of the matter—and this is an important point given the sociological reductionism so prevalent in the study of the arts in our time—is not merely to identify an artist's stance on particular issues or predicaments, but to understand how tropological thinking shapes the artistic process and the imagined (and/or real) viewer's grasp of the image. Polysemia, so often dismissed in our hermeneutically reductionist time, is inseparable from the creation and apprehension of works of art because tropes are mechanisms of plural signification. They are essentially prismatic, refractive, and only marginally discursive (ranging from the expository to the polemical).

The three tropes that govern this approach to Cuban Modernism and the perpetuation of its central concerns in the post-1959 diaspora are metaphor, metonymy, and synecdoche. Metaphor operates through resemblance, but more deeply, it fuses disparate images and ideas into a new image, often with little dependency on context. Peláez fuses the colonial *vitral* (stained-glass window) with Synthetic Cubism, but the fusion also includes painting and window as referents and concepts.[5] The new image is not presented within an architectural setting but is excised from such settings. For Peláez's coalesced painting-*vitral* to become a new image, metaphor must be free of metonymy. This second trope operates through transmission of meanings or connotations between images in a setting. Metonymy also informs our sense and expectations of setting, in everyday life as well as in theater, movies, literature, and painting. Metonymy, in the art of Carlos Enríquez, enables landscape, figures, action, and multiple emotional states—from the erotic to the violent—to coexist as on a stage or movie screen. Nevertheless, the setting remains present and is, in fact, the imagistic protagonist of the painting. Synecdoche operates by focusing on patterns, usually abstract or geometric, that conceptually continue beyond the physical confines of the work of art. Metonymy and metaphor accentuate the sense of the artwork as a world unto itself, regardless of its references. Synecdoche projects patterns, textures, and gestures outside the physical reality of the painting or sculpture. In Emilio Sánchez, for example, the architectural motif is secondary to the reverberative abstract patterns created by light, shadow, columns, tiles, angles and perspective, streets, roofs, and other referents.

Theatricality is the aesthetic ambition that emerges in Cuban Modernism with the paintings of Cundo Bermúdez and Mario Carreño, two Second-Generation figures who, like Portocarrero and others of their time, sought to link regional imagery to a wider range of European Modernist movements—Surrealism and Expressionism especially. That their work has remained important for Cubans of the diaspora may well be because of their roles as founders of a theatrical sensibility in the nation's Modernist art. For diasporic individuals, catharsis, tragic recognition, empathy, and the use of projection as a vehicle for analysis of events and the alignment of memory with sense of self are all pressing concerns, individually and collectively. In the paintings of Carreño and Bermúdez, overtly theatricalized settings, often with a high level of oneiric content, employ juxtaposition and metonymy. In Carreño's paintings especially, volumetrically modeled representation and flattened, stylized shapes derived from the human figure or objects, such as fruit bowls or architectural elements, share the scene and generate transferences of semantic values associated with the referents. Such transferences almost always occur within scenarios that are explicitly theatrical.

Carreño and Bermúdez are also the two Second-Generation masters who launched the diasporic sensibility. Carreño left Cuba at the end of the Batista era and Bermúdez during the early years of the Communist period; neither one ever returned, and they produced most of their innovative work in exile. Carreño's sense of theater echoes in the paintings of Emilio Sánchez, Gustavo Acosta, and Julio Larraz, to name but three major figures. Larraz (b. 1944), in particular, captures the geometric poetry of architectural spaces but fills them with characters and objects whose sense of transformation is coded by a panoply of textures of light and shadow and wide tonal range that includes satire and the savoring of enigma (see *The Intruder*, 1977, Plate 34).[6] An almost tactile luminosity imbues Larraz's scenes with the fragrance of imminent transformation and, simultaneously, a sense of archetypal, almost monumental immovability. In Larraz's art, theater is not about juxtaposition, but about the sensuality of paradox. The radical present, the immanent moment, and the evoked timelessness of the scene coexist in the viewer's mind.

Larraz is a major figure of the Fourth Generation, those born in the mid-to-late 1940s. Other prominent figures include María Brito, Luis Cruz Azaceta, Paul Sierra, and Ramón Alejandro, all of whom developed styles that employ theatrical contexts. Many Fourth-Generation artists went into exile as teenagers or young adults and would be inspired by Third-Generation masters who, already mature in 1959, constituted a formidable platform for the nation's cultural identity, having discovered deeper and subtler aesthetic patterns and concerns, beyond regionalism, which exemplify Cuban Modernism in terms of visual thought and ideas. As Fourth-Generation innovators took these concerns further, they gravitated toward the theatrical.

An excellent example is María Brito. Primarily a sculptor and perhaps Cuba's finest installation artist, Brito is also an accomplished painter (see *El patio de mi casa* [*The Backyard of My House*], 1990, Plate 35). Like

Larraz, Brito extends the power of theatricality within an oneiric language where archetypal and personal themes converge. Her work of the 1980s and 1990s uses fragments of imaginary rooms, or installations the size of a small house, to draw the viewer into labyrinths of the unconscious. As with Larraz, the personal and the collective coincide with a miraculous clarity that, nonetheless, resists easy translation into univocally constructed interpretations.

The diasporic artist seems compelled to align the personal epic of displacement with the archetypal realm of consciousness in which the theme of exile is prevalent, as evidenced in literature, myth, and art. The personal must become, for these artists, the archetypal, and vice versa. This becomes one of the bases for the new continuity between past and present, and its native language is the theatrical.

Clearly, the theatrical could not function without the multiplicity, or complexity, of tropes. Imagined contexts function as everyday ones, to establish meanings and expectations, the very sense of situation and the temporality that emerges from it. Every space we inhabit—classroom, restaurant, home, hospital, bar, etc.—is identified through metonymy, or how the different elements in that space come together to form a mental context through the transference of meanings among the perceived elements. A syntax emerges, and syntax is metonymic. However, for a context to "mean," it must have semantics, elements whose meanings can be grasped, changed, denied, and so forth. Semantics is metaphoric. These poles of language, explored by Roman Jakobson in the mid-twentieth century, offer insights into visual thinking, especially in traditions that accept the representational power of images as a value instead of a detriment.[7]

Indeed, syntax and context are so important to art that is grounded in reference that jolting that syntax becomes significant, as is the case of Surrealism and other oneiric-based artistic movements. Turning syntax itself—the rule-governed roles each element plays in the context—into the central theme of a work of visual art to expand the ability of context to reflect in a natural, i.e., non-jolting way, the power of the imagination is what theatricality in the Cuban and Latin American Modernist experience is all about. Distinguishing the foregrounding of syntax or the jolting of contextual expectation separates Surrealism from the oneiric theatricality that runs through much Latin American Modernist art. For Cuban diaspora artists, this theatricality might be the alternative provider of sense and order in a world in which not only is one cut off from one's native land, but that homeland itself—its history, identity, customs, and values—has been defamed, dismantled, and despoiled.

I would like to end with comments on three extraordinary artists of the newer generations, the Fifth (born in the late 1950s and early 1960s), and the Sixth (born in the 1970s and early 1980s). José Bedia grew up in Communist Cuba and left the island in the early 1990s. He has attained international acclaim for his paintings, installations, and sculptures, which intersect Western and tribal cultural referents (predominantly West African, whose impact on Caribbean and Latin American identity is pervasive). The theatrical presence is felt throughout Bedia's painting, and not just in his renowned installations. Allusions to buildings, ships, altars, and similar structures are abundant and serve to enshrine theatricality as the metonymic shaper of context and as an image within the dramatized flow. In other words, in Bedia, shelter and theater themselves become part of the semantic/metaphoric vocabulary of a metonymic art that expands the range of ancestral motifs and myth through reflection on contemporary issues, including flight and exile as themes. Patterns often introduce a synecdochic energy into the fusion of metaphor and metonymy in his paintings.

Ana Albertina Delgado (b. 1963) is one of the premier painters of the Fifth Generation and, like Bedia, was part of the exodus of artists and intellectuals during the early 1990s, the "Special Period." In a tradition filled with artists deeply influenced by Surrealism and focused on oneiric imagery, her paintings stand out for their variety and depth, not to mention tonal complexity (see *La coronación del cuerpo* [*The Coronation of the Body*], 2009, Plate 36). All attempts to reduce her images—at once bold and fluid, sensual and aggressive, revelatory and enigmatic—to simplistic interpretations are doomed from the onset. Her aesthetic has affinities with that rapturous yet cerebral Mallarmé of the tropics, José Lezama Lima. Images whose connotations we think we know are caught up and transformed, connected to new semantic life. Metonymy in Delgado alters metaphor, which in turn intensifies the melding, transformative drama of her imaginings.

Rigoberto Rosales Jalil (b. 1976), of the Sixth Generation, is a recent exile, having come to the United States in 2011. His sculpture takes theatricality as its central and abiding theme. Influenced by popular art and various contemporary trends, Rosales Jalil creates dramatic secular *retablos* (altarpieces) in which viewers see themselves reflected in a cacophony of characters (see *Where Are You, My Love?* 2016, Plate 37). They stumble across the stage, back-dropped by the skyscrapers of his new American home, and like many a native, they are not entirely sure of the ground they are walking on. Modernity and postmodernity have become synonymous with the crisis of the individual in a depersonalized social milieu whose changes in values and conditions often outpace those who live in it. However, Rosales Jalil ironically includes angelic beings among the lost in the age of GPS and mass communications. They search with desperately wrong instruments—telescopes—for the truths and deceptions under their noses and feet. They are Pirandellian angels looking for an authorial myth to return them to the common life of socially harmonious beings, and willing to come close and walk away with no cigar. This theatricality has caught up with our condition and gives it back to us, with its troubled meanings and scarred syntax, yet still very much as a stage on which diasporic epic and everyday life unfold.

Notes

1. See Gérard-Georges Lemaire, *Soto.*
2. See Mario H. Gradowcyzk, *Joaquín Torres-García.*
3. For more information on Cuban visual thinking in the diaspora, see Ileana Fuentes-Pérez et al., eds., *Outside Cuba/Fuera de Cuba.*
4. See Edward Bullough, "'Psychical Distance' as a Factor in Art," and Samuel Taylor Coleridge, *Biographia Literaria.*
5. See Ramón Vázquez-Díaz, "Encuentro con Amelia Peláez."
6. See Edward Lucie-Smith, *Julio Larraz.*
7. See Roman Jakobson, *Fundamentals of Language* 2.

Bibliography

Bullough, Edward. "'Psychical Distance' as a Factor in Art and as an Aesthetic Principle." *British Journal of Psychology* 5, no. 2 (1912): 87–117.

Coleridge, Samuel Taylor. *Biographia Literaria; or, Biographical Sketches of My Literary Life and Opinions.* Chapter XIV. London: Rest Fenner, 1817.

Fuentes-Pérez, Ileana, Graciella Cruz-Taura, and Ricardo Pau Llosa, eds. *Outside Cuba/Fuera de Cuba: Contemporary Cuban Visual Artists.* New Brunswick, NJ: Transaction, 1989.

Gradowcyzk, Mario H. *Joaquín Torres-García*. Buenos Aires: Ediciones Gaglianone, 1985.
Jakobson, Roman. *Fundamentals of Language* 2. The Hague and Paris: Mouton, 1956.
Lemaire, Gérard-Georges. *Soto.* Paris: Édition de la Différence, 1997.
Lucie-Smith, Edward. *Julio Larraz.* Milan: Skira Editore, 2003.
Vázquez-Díaz, Ramón. "Encuentro con Amelia Peláez." In *Amelia Peláez en el centenario de su nacimiento: Óleos, témperas y dibujos (1924–1967)*. Havana: Centro Wifredo Lam, 1996.

12

The Cuban-American Exile *Vanguardia*

Toward a Theory of Collecting Cuban-American Art

Lynette M. F. Bosch

This chapter contributes to the growing body of scholarship on Cuban-American art, focusing on the group of artists identified here as the Cuban-American Exile *Vanguardia* (avant-garde). Members of this Exile Vanguardia arrived in the United States between 1959 and 1980, as children and adolescents.[1] They became noteworthy artists in the mid-1970s to late 1980s and worked mostly in Miami, New York City, Chicago, and New Orleans. North and Latin American and European collectors, museums, and public institutions have recognized the Exile Vanguardia's artists individually and as a group.[2] Their subjects and themes explore identity, hybridity, transnationalism, and the emotional and experiential territory of exile. This chapter contextualizes the Exile Vanguardia within the parameters of critical theory to explain the artists' motivation and intentionality and to contextualize them within developments in Contemporary Art.

The members of the Exile Vanguardia came with memories of Cuba before the Revolution, even as they learned to integrate into U.S. culture.[3] Their acculturation paved the way for other children and adolescents who came after 1980. As the Exile Vanguardia's artists began to make art, they joined a history of Cuban art that had sought visual representations for *lo cubano* (Cubanness) since Cuba's postcolonial phase. Additionally, the Exile Vanguardia artists were the first who defined *lo cubano-americano*

(Cuban-Americanness)—their unique contribution to the history of Cuban and American art.

Defining *lo cubano* in the visual arts emerged in the work of nineteenth- and twentieth-century Cuban artists, such as Armando G. Menocal, Leopoldo Romañach, and Antonio Sánchez Araujo (1887–1946), in landscape and *costumbrista* paintings. In the 1930s and 1940s, the artists of the Cuban vanguardia, such as Carlos Enríquez, Fidelio Ponce, Eduardo Abela, and Amelia Peláez, sought to represent *lo cubano* as an identity shared by Cuban-Europeans, Afro-Cubans, and Cuban-Asians (especially Chinese). The vanguardia artists were also social and political reformers, as Juan A. Martínez discussed.[4] Collectors now pay millions for their work, as the vanguardia represents a Golden Age of Cuban art.[5]

In the 1950s, Cuban Modernist artists turned toward abstraction, joining international Modernist trends, including Expressionism, Minimalism, and Surrealism.[6] José Mijares, Rafael Soriano, Baruj Salinas, Eladio González, Antonia Eiriz, Agustín Fernández, Gladys Triana, Cundo Bermúdez, Rolando López Dirube, Gina Pellón, Jorge Camacho, and Enrique Gay García's works reflected Cuba's rapid internationalization. This group became exiles as adults, while the Exile Vanguardia arrived as children and adolescents. With time, the Cuban Modernists became *La Vieja Guardia* (the Old Guard) and they continue producing notable works of art.

The Exile Vanguardia is composed of hundreds of significant, contemporary artists, chronicled by numerous exhibitions of their work. For all, Miami was home or a touchstone for Cuban culture. The Miami group included Mario Algaze, Mario Bencomo, María Brito, Juan González, Humberto Calzada, Emilio Falero, Jake Fernandez, María Lino, Silvia Lizama, Miguel Padura, and Lydia Rubio. Arturo Rodríguez, whose exile began in Spain, later joined the group, when he arrived in Miami in 1973. Demi, Rodríguez's wife, began painting in Miami in 1984. Outside Miami, Luis Cruz Azaceta, Paul Sierra, Alberto Rey, and Ana Mendieta retained connections to the city. As a group, their work manifests the Cuban-American writer Gustavo Pérez Firmat's description of "life on the hyphen."[7]

Unsurprisingly, Miami-based, Cuban-American collectors bought the work of the Exile Vanguardia artists. International collectors eventually bought their work in the Wynwood district, in Coral Gables galleries, and at the annual assembly of Art Basel.[8] Thus, a global group of collectors now appreciates the Exile Vanguardia's stylistic diversity and creative energy.

The Exile Vanguardia's stylistic variety manifests Arthur Danto's argument, in *After the End of Art*, that art finds meaning in diversity. For the Exile Vanguardia, cultural variety includes Cuba's Taíno, Siboney, and Carib, the Spanish, the descendants of African slaves and Chinese and Filipino indentured servants, and other Europeans who came to Cuba, along with a significant Jewish population. The composite national identity of these groups constitutes what Fernando Ortiz identified as the *ajiaco cubano*, a stew composed of Cuba's hybrid population.[9] Thus, the Exile Vanguardia's art incorporates, within its production, what Marwan Kraidy characterized as the mark of a globalized network of culturally allusive and metaphorical "traces of other cultures."[10]

Analogous to Kraidy's "traces" of other cultures manifesting as hybridity is Cuban *neo-Barroquismo*, defined in the critical literature of Alejo Carpentier, José Lezama Lima, and Severo Sarduy, from the 1940s to the 1960s. Cuban neo-Barroquismo was grounded in the cultural hybridity produced by Cuba's admixtures of European and Latin American art, and it incorporated the stylistic diversity characteristic of Cuba's seventeenth century, the baroque foundation for Cuba's architecture. Baroque revivals in modernity recur, as Mieke Bal has indicated in her work, and Cuba's neo-barroquista writers Lezama Lima, Carpentier, and Sarduy (and others) defined Cuba's importance for this cultural stream.[11] In the art of the Exile Vanguardia, the cross-cultural hybridity essential for the emergence and continuity of neo-Barroquismo emerges as a renewed cultural force that functions as a medium of communication among their diverse identities.

To the Exile Vanguardia artists, the cultural accretion of neo-Barroquismo was a natural part of their Cuban cultural inheritance, to which they added their American lives. Such cultural merging situates them within transnational categories, codified by Randolph Bourne (1886–1918). Bourne's categorization of transnationalism as "a new way of thinking about the relationships between cultures" finds a parallel in the Exile Vanguardia's art.[12] Because the Exile Vanguardia retains strong Cuban personal and cultural memories, this retention is analogous to Bourne's argument that the American "Melting Pot" was not the only response, or even the best response, to post-immigrant identity.

The process of making art is an act of memorialization, thus the erasure of any remembered identity is not desirable for the artistic process. In his *Natural History* (Book XXXV.5), Pliny the Elder linked Mnemosyne and painting, recounting how painting began when a young girl traced the shadow of her lover before he went to war. Today, neuroscientists categorize memory into sensory memory, short-term memory, long-term memory, and flashbulb memory (the imprint of dramatic events), all types of memory that Exile Vanguardia artists manifest in their work.[13]

Among the artists of the Exile Vanguardia, Arturo Rodríguez (b. 1956) is a consummate painter for whom the process of painting is an essential, even metaphysical, conduit for his observation of the human condition. Rodríguez is the group's leading artist, who unflinchingly and consistently depicts displacement, alienation, and the trauma of exile. Conversely, he is also a perceptive caricaturist of subtle wit and irony.[14] Rodríguez's work is a benchmark for the Exile Vanguardia: he creates from memory and draws inspiration from his encyclopedic knowledge of global music, literature, and philosophy, and his extensive knowledge of the history of art. Barroquismo appears in his ongoing, painterly, and conceptual dialogue with art's history, from the Baroque to Modern and Contemporary art, and in his absorption of cultural hybridity adapted from the art of Asia, Africa, Europe, and the Americas.

In his work, Rodríguez explores external exile and the internal exile inherent in humanity's solipsistic condition. Toward this goal, he has developed compositional structures that present architecture or landscape in disjointed, segmented areas of spatial discontinuity. The figural distortions of his personages, reflective of pain, anguish, isolation, and longing, augment the fragmentation in his compositions. Figures reach across space (and time?), yet cannot touch or comfort one another. When contact does occur, the twists and turns of bodies deny stability. These images emphasize the limitations imposed by our inability to engage in true intimacy through the insufficient tool of language. Thus, for Rodríguez, who searches for connection through paint, the flow of paint in his work and the lines that define his drawings (Rodríguez is an expert draughtsman) are part of his two-dimensional reification of his phenomenological investigation of the fabric of existence. As Rodríguez has created his visual vocabulary of spatial and figural proxemics, he has consistently explored these sometimes-coterminous states.

Rodríguez's paintings communicate his comprehension of external exile to anyone who experiences the alienation that is part of our solipsistic existence, manifested in the intrusion of alienation, displacement, and disorientation that is a universal experience. Paintings such as *The Tempest* series (1998, Plate 38) employ Rodríguez's visual vocabulary fully. Homes tilt at odd angles that make them uninhabitable, while people float in disjointed isolation. Rodríguez's manipulation of an inconsistent and unstable perspective that shifts from bird's-eye view to *di sotto in su* increases this dissolution of stable architecture and the separate lives of individuals. The resulting instability conveys the internal emotions of exile and alienation.

The impact of Rodríguez's work on the spectator is aligned with the concept of *ostranenie* (defamiliarization), associated with Viktor Shklovsky, the Russian literary theorist, who argued, "The technique of art is to make objects 'unfamiliar,' to make forms difficult, to increase difficulty and length of perception . . . [to make it] an aesthetic end in itself . . . [that] must be prolonged."[15] The prolongation of visual absorption and observation of art, according to Shklovsky, can be best achieved by juxtaposing seemingly disparate elements in individual works of art, in which beauty of color and form can represent or describe a tragic subject. Ostranenie is the disjunction that exists in the gap between attraction and shock. Ostranenie is precisely the intellectual territory owned by Rodríguez, who, through paint, draws the spectator into his mind, even if only to explain that a true union of object, audience, and artist cannot be achieved. Thus, Rodríguez holds the spectator's attention by defamiliarizing the everyday world, even as he beguiles through lush brushwork, lyrical colors, and fluid compositional transitions. In so doing, Rodríguez shocks, amazes, attracts, amuses, and maybe even repels his audiences, by compelling them to rethink reality.

The ostranenie Rodríguez captures in his paintings is also evident in his drawings, an example of which is the suite of drawings composing *The School of Night*, completed in 2014, with the publication of the book that documents the group. The drawings of *The School of Night* are an intimate representation of his life as an artist who creates at night, when life is removed from the noise and light of living.[16] Rodríguez's *The School of Night* draws inspiration from Ingmar Bergman's film *The Hour of the Wolf* (*Vargtimmen*, 1968). Rodríguez records his personal *vargtimmen*, "at home, at night, when the world sleeps and dreams," sometimes alone and sometimes accompanied by his wife, Demi. In the drawings that compose *The School of Night*, surrounded by his collection of masks and his walls of world music, Rodríguez reads, eats, walks, paints, and listens to music, sometimes with Demi. This nightlife is the catalyst for Rodríguez's exploration of the human psyche.

Night is the time of ostranenie because it transforms the familiar into the unknown. Night is when humanity's fears about mortality rise. Night isolates, separates, and displaces individuals. Night is exile from light and from seeing clearly. Night's sleep is a *memento mori*. Rodríguez awakens at night, when he exploits night's ostranenie and distills reality into art. In the *School* drawings, Rodríguez moves among bursts of sporadic lamplight and the deep shadows of his home's unlit corners. Crisscrossing lines form pathways of movement, where his steps provide compositional structure. Seemingly animated masks hang on walls, distorting the familiarity of the human features they display.

Rodríguez's art is a nexus of worlds, cultures, and artistic movements, all studied from his studio in Cuban-American Miami. In Rodríguez's artistic synthesis, Europe meets Latin America, with touches of Africa and Asia, as he is an essentially transnational artist. In paint, Rodríguez talks to William Blake, Pablo Picasso, Edvard Munch, Diane Arbus, Philip Guston, Piet Mondrian, Francis Bacon, Theodore Gericault, Kitagawa Utamaro, Tōshūsai Sharaku, and Giuseppe Arcimboldo. Touches of Dada and Surrealism emerge in Rodríguez's juxtapositions of impossible tableaux of figural contortion, movement, and space. His work takes us from Zurich's Cabaret Voltaire to André Breton's *Surrealist Manifesto*. Music is crucial to Rodríguez's artistic process, and he has an encyclopedic collection of world music. Through music, Rodríguez travels across time and place from Cuba, to Mexico, to the United States, to Spain, to Europe, and to the Renaissance and Baroque that engendered Cuba's Barroquismo. Visionary, mystical, fantastical, and imagined beings change shape, shifting in the art of Rodríguez, the exile from his home country, who understands that everyone is an exile from each other, except when connected through the subconscious universal streams of spirituality and art from which each emerged.[17]

Rodríguez's identity as an exile transformed him into an artist, and its memories inform his work. His intellectual concerns expand his themes and his intercultural and interdisciplinary intellectual program encompasses and transcends the thematic parameters of his generation. In so doing, Rodríguez's oeuvre addresses modernity from a philosophical and experiential base in a deep exploration of existence and perception.

Jake Fernandez is the leading landscape artist of the Exile Vanguardia.[18] Through his landscape and architectural paintings, collages, photographs, and drawings, Fernandez represents his experience of hybridity, identity, and exile, using metaphor and allusion.[19] In reimagining landscape and architecture into color and form, Fernandez reinterprets them into "other" forms that can defy identification, rendering the familiar foreign. The beauty, intrinsic to Fernandez's artistic vision combined with the defamiliarization of forms, is the essential tension of ostranenie. This is how Fernandez's manipulations of visual reality function—as though he has partially opened a door into a familiar reality that quickly closes, leaving in its place screens of form and color remade and reinterpreted into a transcendent surreal.

Through landscape, Fernandez conveys the experience of the bicultural exile, the alienation of the transplanted, the unfamiliarity of the "new," and the assimilation that always leaves raw edges. With dense bands of color and forms, Fernandez interweaves space, topography, and a vegetal chiaroscuro into images that incorporate uneasy transitions and evoke the layering of alternate identities of his bicultural life, which is never seamless. These landscapes create a liminal space, a threshold—a hyphen between realities—balanced between realism and abstraction. Such landscapes are hybrid images, essentially revealing—yet denying—easy identification, as they transform into specific yet universalized territories composed of earth, water, and plants. With these elemental forms, Fernandez indicates the reality of human experience and emotion through a synesthetic encounter wherein landscape becomes the emotion and experience of the artist's exile and bicultural life.

Architecture also appears as one of Fernandez's thematic subjects. His exploration of the Metropolitan Museum of Art's Trie Garden Cloister, located at the Cloisters in Fort Tryon Park, has occupied him for four decades, since he lived in New York City during the 1980s. As transplanted and reassembled architecture, the Cloisters are an especially suitable subject for Fernandez's meditations on his personal situation as an exile and an artist, and on the metamorphosis of time defined by lived experiences.[20] The Cloisters are a simile, a metaphor, and an allegory in stone of the exile experience, but also of the artistic process and the nature of the artist as observer, witness, and historian. The result of Fernandez's study is an ongoing series of paintings, drawings, and photography collages to which belongs *Trie Garden Cloisters 3* (ca. 2000, Plate 39). The series is formed from sets of four photographs, always taken from the same two places in the cloister, formed into composite collages that generate one image with overlapping edges that reveal that seemingly simple images are intensely complex.

The identity of the Cloisters as hybrid, transplanted, and reformed architecture provides Fernandez with a ready-made environment that he can interpret as a *hortus conclusus*, of hidden significance and meaning and past time lived by others, centuries ago. Yet, these lives and their history remain present in the Cloisters. Like the memories changed by departure, the Trie Cloister retains multiple identities of cloister, refuge, and transported museum. Reinterpreted across the years during which Fernandez has come to record it, Trie Cloister mirrors and reflects the times of his life as a transplanted exile, a naturalized citizen, an artist, a husband, a father, and an observer, removed from daily life by the cloister's walls. Trie Cloister is a synecdoche of exile reflected in the assembly of its four separate parts into one image. These juxtaposed parts "hold" the gaze by contrasting nature with architecture. Fernandez's iterations of Trie Garden Cloister's present articulate his interpretation of his existence and its meaning, which cannot be seamlessly joined—as Trie Cloister's architecture is kin to Fernandez's transnational life.

Humberto Calzada's paintings of architectural environments are unique to the Cuban Vanguardia and in Contemporary, Postmodernist art.[21] These invented, idealized interiors and exteriors are remarkable for their evocative ability to transport spectators to the artist's remembered, imagined, and carefully researched "Cuba" (*La tradición* [*Tradition*], 2017, Plate 40).[22] His paintings are also an important contribution to the history of Cuban architecture, wherein he incorporates consistent synecdoches of Cuba's landscape and architecture, such as palm trees and stained-glass windows. Calzada's paintings reconstruct a vanished world that defines his Cuban identity and evokes the actuality of Cuba through quotations that memorialize and preserve Cuba's architecture.

Calzada's thematic territory reflects the Exile Vanguardia's engagement with memory, identity, Barroquismo, and ostranenie, which surfaces in the tension between Calzada's idealized architecture and its total absence of inhabitants. The resulting emptiness of Calzada's world is disquieting.

Where have people gone? Thus, as idealization captures the gaze, the realization of absence disturbs the visual equilibrium. Absence is exile, its emotions and experiences. Hence, what on the surface appears to be an analytical and cool detachment is essentially a distillation of the complex emotions of exile presented within Calzada's memory-images of home.

In Calzada's paintings, Barroquismo surfaces in tiled floors, reminiscent of Dutch Baroque painting and of the Islamic-derived tiles often found in Cuban homes. The mathematical precision of Calzada's perspectives brings Jan Vermeer to mind, and the absence of inhabitants is reminiscent of Giorgio de Chirico's empty urban images. Classical architectural motifs, the foundation for Baroque architecture, recur transformed into a Postmodernist exploration of quotations. Calzada's interiors resonate with nineteenth- and twentieth-century Cuban academic paintings, such as Esteban Valderrama's *Dr. Carlos J. Finlay Discovers the Cause of Yellow Fever* (ca. 1940), which portrays stained-glass windows and arches like those found in Calzada's work, in turn evocative of Amelia Peláez's interpretation of vanguardia styles. Thus does Calzada's work blend Cuba's artistic heritage into his tropical Barroquismo.

Within the group of Exile Vanguardia artists, Demi's[23] work is outstanding for its focus on emotions expressed through color, line, and painterly technique and for her emphasis on representing children.[24] Adults are rare in her paintings. Born in Camagüey, Cuba in 1955, Demi has lived in Puerto Rico, Tarrytown (NY), Miami, and Madrid, the latter with her husband Arturo Rodríguez. Through her extensive travels in the United States, Europe, and Latin America, she has absorbed a global network of inspiration, reflective of Bourne's transnationalism. Therefore, her work is global, in Kraidy's definition of cultural incorporation of "traces of other cultures," and in her employment of U.S., Latin American, European, Asian, and Arabic influences on the literature and art found in her work.

Demi's complex painterly style can be described as fantastical, surreal, or as Magical Surreal, and akin to those of Frida Kahlo, Richard Dadd, Leonora Carrington, Remedios Varo, and the children found in the portraits of Diego Velázquez, which she studied at the Prado Museum in Madrid. As did the Cuban vanguardia painters, she uses Cuban landscape elements and costumes in her imagery. Renaissance artists, such as Filippo Lippi and Fra Angelico, also influence her work. *The Arabian Nights* and Günther Grass's *The Tin Drum* provide further inspiration for her work.

As an artist who draws from such a variety of global sources, Demi belongs within the stream of Barroquismo, delineated by Lezama Lima and Carpentier.

For Cuban-American artists who lived through Fidel Castro's takeover of Cuba, the experience left a permanent imprint that time has invariably mitigated. Demi's experiences were extreme, and included the aftermath of her father's execution (1960) by Cuba's Communist regime. This event is the subject of *The Execution* (2014, Plate 41). Two years later, Demi was separated from her mother and sisters and sent to live with relatives in Puerto Rico, until the family reunited in 1971. These traumatic events give energy and emotion to Demi's work, which situates her within the energetic territory described by Wilhelm von Humboldt's *energeia* (active doing) and *ergon* (the product of that doing).[25]

Demi's creative impulse, her *energeia*, produces *ergoni*, through which she expresses her anger and pain, in a re-creative manner akin to Classical rhetoric's *enargeia*, defined by Quintilian as mimetic recall through representation of memory and experience.[26] In re-presenting the narratives that retrace her father's execution, her separation from her mother and two sisters, her exile, her move to Miami, and her transformational life with her husband Arturo Rodríguez, Demi renders an *enargeic* recreation of her life in which she tells her stories.

The result is the creation of a space in which Demi and her audience share experiences of loss, trauma, anger, and renewal in the aftermath of devastation. These emotions are given form in the bodies, clothes, and environments of Demi's children—her chosen subjects. Through them, Demi conveys her message of changing fate, which can befall even the most privileged children, as they too can have their fates changed by abuse, as they transition from safety to the insecurities of an unknown future. In Demi's paintings, fate strikes children as an avenger, much as exile struck Demi's generation, whose homes disappeared and who became adults before their time. Demi's images resonate with anyone who has experienced events that divide their lives into times before and after or who mask emotional desolation with elaborate display.

As a Cuban-American artist of the Exile Vanguardia, Demi participates in a transnational artistic movement, marked by hybrid identities and grounded in memory and given form through her diverse knowledge of artistic culture. As a bicultural artist who has a significant place in the history of Cuban and American art, Demi's paintings are the most directly expressive of the emotions experienced by her peer group of children and adolescents. From her life, she has made art that has given her a unique place within her peer group through her individualistic, expressionistic territory.

Mario Bencomo (b. 1953) is unusual among Exile Vanguardia artists in his predominantly abstract style.[27] In paintings, drawings, and original, one-of-a-kind artist books, Bencomo expresses his group's core concerns with transnationalism and cultural hybridity, Bencomo's interest in them provoked by frequent trips throughout North America, Latin America, Europe, and Cuba, which he has visited frequently. Exile made Bencomo an observer and a historian of philosophy, literature, and poetry, whose oeuvre expresses a compelling desire to question and explore social justice in transformative political circumstances.[28]

Initially, Bencomo's totally abstract style emphasized spirituality through veils of color, kin to color-field painting. Without abandoning his early, metaphysical, and abstract meditations, Bencomo's later work evolved to accommodate his historical and political themes. This change transformed his style from pure abstraction to a style that has elements of realism—forms suggestive of foliage, earth movements, wind currents, and geography—even as text became incorporated into some of his ongoing work. Yet, Bencomo's liminal style continues, suspended between the ambiguity of pure abstraction and depicted realism.

Ecological concerns entered Bencomo's subjects decades ago, as manifested in his *Wind* series, initiated by the meltdown at the Chernobyl Nuclear Plant in Ukraine in 1986. In his *Stanley Park, Vancouver* series, Bencomo explored the spiritual mythologies of natural environments or preserved in national parks. In *Utopia: If Quebec Were in the Tropics* (2005), Bencomo explored geography as a metaphor for place and identity, while thinking about Montreal, the city he considers his muse.

For decades, Bencomo has been creating his *Elegy to Poetry*, a series of single works and one-of-a-kind artist books, in which he explores cultural hybridity, gained through travels in and extended visits to French Canada.[29] *Elegy* is Barroquista and includes a signature work entitled *A Mario Bencomo, on a Poem by Severo Sarduy* (2015), which features a poem Sarduy, the barroquista poet and writer, dedicated to Bencomo, about a work by Bencomo that Sarduy owned. Another work from this series is *Ode to Whitman, Homage to Lorca, Poet in New York* (2013, Plate 42), directly evocative of Bencomo's Spanish and Whitman's English, each representing Bencomo's bicultural life.

Bencomo's historical interests surface in his *Torquemada* series, begun early in his career, in which the Spanish Inquisitor Tomás de Torquemada becomes a metaphor for political oppression. Raised in a secular home, Bencomo is of maternal Jewish ancestry, but his interest in the Inquisition is more political than personal. From the *Torquemada* series emerge shapes evocative of the hoods worn by Inquisitors, or the pointed caps, or *corozas*, worn by their victims.

Bencomo's intellectual interest in global literature, philosophy, history, spirituality, and religions enables him to access diverse cultures for inspiration. His return to Cuba affirmed his Cuban identity, even as he remains a U.S. citizen who regularly visits Canada. He is transnational in life and eclectic in his Barroquismo, rooted in timely political, social, and environmental concerns.

In the work of the Exile Vanguardia artists discussed above, memories of their experiences as Cuban children and adolescents play a significant role, but others have no memories of their time in Cuba, such as Alberto Rey (b. 1960), who left Cuba at the age of three.[30] Rey lived briefly in Miami, but grew up in Barnesboro, Pennsylvania, becoming more American than Cuban. His paintings, installations, films, drawings, and photographs trace the trajectory of his transnational life.[31]

As Rey's work developed, issues of identity surfaced overtly in his *Icon Series*, inspired by Andy Warhol's canonical Campbell's *Soup Can*. In *Icon Series: Ancel Guava Paste* (1993–95, Plate 43), Rey memorialized the guava bar that is the Cuban equivalent of the American Campbell's soup, melding American aesthetics and Cuban identity into a transformed hybridity expressive of his hyphenated identity. This duality was the catalyst for additional exploration of his two cultures in landscape paintings of Cuba and of Western New York State, where he lives, a series that eventually took him to Cuba, after which he painted portraits of Cubans and Cuban Americans to memorialize his divided nation.

Rey has always been an angler, and his interest in fish (especially trout) and his immersion in their natural environment of rivers and streams led to Rey's social activism as a preservationist, which took him from Buffalo's Scajaquada River to Nepal's Bagmati River.[32] These transnationalist conservation efforts place Rey among today's most significant biological preservationists. From his interest in his identity to the leadership role he now plays in international environmental conservation, Rey is a link between the Exile Vanguardia and the fate of the world. Yet, for Rey, even with his ability to connect and expand his identity, home remains an elusive place. The displacement of exile, the life not lived, the absence of an integrated self, the life truncated by an imposed division, is a rupture that is never bridged. Pre-Castro Cuba, for Rey, is an absent presence that the older Exile Vanguardia artists were among the last to know, and yet it will always be Rey's lost "home."

For every member of the Exile Vanguardia, the prism of their memories of Cuba remains a filter through which they see the world. Belonging nowhere and anywhere, they adapt, assimilate, adjust, and acquire identities that enable them to communicate with others through their diverse identities and their ability to be as much at home in Nepal as in Miami. It was the Cuban Modernists (*La Vieja Guardia*) and the Exile Vanguardia who established Miami as a global artistic center. Artists who came to Miami later owe a great debt to the pioneers, who are equally important for the history of Cuban art, which extends into the twenty-first century.

Notes

1. See Jaime Suchlicki, *Cuba*.

2. See Ileana Fuentes-Pérez et al., *Outside Cuba/Fuera de Cuba*; Giulio V. Blanc, *Cuba/U.S.A*; Carol Damian, *Breaking Barriers*; and Lynette M. F. Bosch, *Cuban-American Art in Miami*.

3. For mature Cuban artists who came to the United States after 1980, see Andrea O'Reilly Herrera, *Cuban Artists across the Diaspora*; Holly Block, *Art Cuba*; and Luis Camnitzer, *New Art of Cuba*.

4. See Zeida Comesañas Sardiñas, *Great Masters of Cuban Art, 1800–1958*; Nathalie Bondil, ed., *Cuba*; and Gary R. Libby and Juan A. Martínez, *Cuba*, for Cuban Postcolonial to Modernist art. See also Bosch, "From the Vanguardia to the United States," 130; Martínez, *Cuban Art and National Identity*.

5. "Cuban Surrealist Wifredo Lam Fetches Record Price," *BBC News*, May 24, 2012. An unidentified collector paid $4.5 million for *Idol (Oya/Divinité de l'air et de la mort)* (1944).

6. On Cuban Modernists, see José Gómez Sicre, *Art of Cuba in Exile*.

7. See Gustavo Pérez Firmat, *Life on the Hyphen* and *Next Year in Cuba*.

8. On Wynwood, see "Wynwood Welcomes Return of Art Basel," *Miami Herald*, November 26, 2016, Letters to the Editor; "Wynwood Attracts Florida's First Design College," *Miami Herald*, November 28, 2016. The first Art Basel (2015) attracted about 77,000

visitors. Franz Schultheis et al., *When Art Meets Money*; Noelle Bodick, "A Brief History of Art Basel."

9. Arthur C. Danto, *After the End of Art*; Walt Whitman, *Song of Myself*. For a discussion of Fernando Ortiz Fernández's concept, see Sergio Valdés Bernal, "'Cuba es un ajiaco,' sentenció Fernando Ortiz." Ortiz was a cultural critic whose work is a touchstone for Cuban studies.

10. Marwan Kraidy, *Hybridity*.

11. Mieke Bal, *Quoting Caravaggio*. On Cuban neo-Barroquismo, see César Augusto Salgado, "Hybridity in New World Baroque Theory."

12. Salgado.

13. On neuroscience and memory, see Eric R. Kandel, *In Search of Memory*.

14. Selected collections: Metropolitan Museum of Art, New York; Jerusalem Museum, Israel; Vatican Museum of Contemporary Art, Rome; Smithsonian American Art Collection, Washington, DC; María Zambrano Museum, Málaga, Spain; Cintas Foundation, New York; Frost Art Museum, Florida International University, Miami. For examples of Rodríguez's paintings of exile, see Bosch, *Cuban-American Art in Miami*, Figs. 56–62. For his humorous paintings, see Bass Museum of Art, *Arturo Rodríguez*.

15. On ostranenie, see Viktor Shklovsky, "Art as Technique," and Alexandra Berlina, ed., *Viktor Shklovsky*.

16. *The School of Night* drawings were published in 2014. See Alejandro Anreus, ed., *The School of Night*. Interactive events at book launches included poets and musicians. In New York City: Barnard College, Columbia University (October 30, 2016), poets José Kozer, Bruce Weber, Laura Tartakoff, and Afro-Cuban jazz pianist David Virelles; McNally Jackson Bookstore, New York City, poets José Kozer, Bruce Weber, and Alejandro Anreus (October 31, 2016). At WDNA Gallery in Miami: showing video/drawings, and music with jazz pianist David Virelles (January 9, 2017).

17. Bosch, "Art Spirituality and Poetry."

18. Selected collections: Ringling Museum of Art, Sarasota, FL; Contemporary Art Museum, University of South Florida, Tampa, FL; Lawton Chiles Foundation, Tallahassee, FL; Center for the Arts, Tampa, FL; House of Representatives, State Capitol, Tallahassee, FL; Smite Museum, University of Notre Dame, Notre Dame, IN.

19. Jake Fernandez arrived in the United States in 1960, at the age of nine. See Martínez, *Jake Fernandez*; William Zimmer and Sheldon M. Lurie, *Abstraction*; Allys Palladino-Craig and Jorge H. Santis, *Jake Fernandez*; and Rebecca Sexton Larson, *Jake Fernandez*.

20. John D. Rockefeller purchased the Cloisters at Fort Tryon Park from George Grey Barnard (who bought them in France and Spain); Frederic Law Olmsted redesigned them from 1917 to 1934. See James Rorimer, *The Cloisters*.

21. Selected collections: Pérez Art Museum Miami; Blanton Museum of Art, University of Texas, Austin; Museum of Art, Fort Lauderdale, FL; Art Museum of the Americas, Organization of American States, Washington, DC; Centro de Arte Fundación Ortiz-Guardian, Granada, Nicaragua; Museo Nacional de Bellas Artes, Santiago, Chile.

22. Calzada was sixteen years old when he arrived in Miami in 1960. See Bosch,

Cuban-American Art in Miami, 110–14; Ricardo Pau-Llosa, *Humberto Calzada*; Lowe Art Museum, *Humberto Calzada*; William Navarrete and Jesús Rosado, eds., *Visión crítica de Humberto Calzada*.

23. Demi was sent abroad from Cuba at the age of seven (1962). At sixteen, she arrived in the United States. See Bosch, *Cuban-American Art in Miami*, 117–26; Pedro J. Martínez-Fraga, *Demi*; Bosch, *Demi*.

24. Selected collections: Smithsonian American Art Museum, Washington, DC; Fort Lauderdale Museum of Art, Fort Lauderdale, FL; Frost Art Museum, Florida International University, Miami; Lowe Art Museum, University of Miami; and Tampa Museum of Art, Tampa, FL.

25. Wilhelm von Humboldt, *On Language*.

26. Quintilian's *Institutes of Oratory*, Book 8.3.

27. Bencomo left Cuba as an unaccompanied minor, traveling to Madrid. In 1968, at the age of fourteen, he arrived in New York City, then went to Miami. See Veigas-Zamora et al., eds., *Memoria*; Bosch, *Cuban-American Art in Miami*, 126–31; Clearwater et al., *The Miami Generation*.

28. Selected collections: Metropolitan Museum of Art, New York; National Museum of Fine Arts, Havana; Art Museum of the Americas, Washington, DC; Pérez Art Museum Miami; Museo de Arte María Zambrano, Málaga, Spain; Museo de Arte Contemporáneo, Panama; El Museo del Barrio, New York; and Frost Art Museum, Florida International University, Miami.

29. Mario Bencomo, *Elegy to Poetry/Le cabinet de poésie*.

30. Rey was three when his family left Cuba for Mexico City (1963), then Miami (1964). In 1967, they moved to Barnesboro, Pennsylvania. Selected collections: Brooklyn Museum, New York; Bronx Museum of the Arts, New York; El Museo del Barrio, New York; Museo Extremeño e Iberoamericano de Arte Contemporáneo (MEIAC), Badajoz, Spain; Centro de Arte Contemporáneo de Caja de Burgos, Spain; Frost Art Museum, Florida International University, Miami; and Museum of Art, Fort Lauderdale, FL.

31. See Bosch, *Cuban-American Art in Miami*, 138–46; Bosch and Mark Denaci, *Life Streams*.

32. See Jason Dilworth and Alberto Rey, *Complexities of Water*; Smriti Basnet, "Sketching Bagmati: A Multimedia Project to Revive the Enthusiasm for Change and the Bagmati Itself," *Nepali Times*, November 18–24, 2016.

Bibliography

Anreus, Alejandro, ed. *The School of Night: Drawings by Arturo Rodríguez*. Miami: Island Project, 2014.

Bal, Mieke. *Quoting Caravaggio: Contemporary Art, Preposterous History*. Chicago: University of Chicago Press, 1999.

Bass Museum of Art. *Arturo Rodríguez: The Human Comedy*. Miami Beach: Bass Museum of Art, 2006.

Bencomo, Mario. *Elegy to Poetry/Le cabinet de poésie*. Miami: Miami International Airport, Mia Gallery, 2016.

Berlina, Alexandra, ed. *Viktor Shklovsky: A Reader*. London: Bloomsbury, 2017.

Blanc, Giulio V. *Cuba/U.S.A.: The First Generation*. Washington, DC: Fondo del Sol, 1991.

Block, Holly. *Art Cuba: The New Generation*. New York: Harry N. Abrams, 2001.

Bodick, Noelle. "A Brief History of Art Basel, the World's Premier Contemporary Fair." *Artspace*, June 17, 2014. https://www.artspace.com/magazine/art_101/art_market/a-brief-history-of-art-basel-52350.

Bondil, Nathalie, ed. *Cuba: Art and History from 1868 to Today*. Montreal: Montreal Museum of Fine Arts, 2009.

Bosch, Lynette M. F. "Art Spirituality and Poetry: A Preview to The School of Night." *Island Project* (blog), October 2, 2014. Accessed August 10, 2017. https://islandproject.info/blogs/news/16980991-art-spirituality-and-poetry-a-preview-to-the-school-of-night-by-lynette-m-f-bosch.

———. *Cuban-American Art in Miami: Exile, Identity, and the Neo-Baroque*. London: Ashgate, 2000.

———. *Demi*. Edited by Oksana Salamatina. Milan: Skira Editore, 2018.

———. "Regions of the Mind: The Paintings and Drawings of Jake Fernandez." In *Altered Realities*, edited by Jake Fernandez, unpaginated. Tequesta, FL: Lighthouse Art Center Museum, 2013.

———. "From the Vanguardia to the United States: Cuban and Cuban-American Identity in the Visual Arts." In *Cuban-American Literature and Art*, edited by Isabel Alvarez Borland and Lynette M. F. Bosch, 129–48. Albany, NY: SUNY Press, 2009.

Bosch, Lynette M. F., and Mark Denaci. *Life Streams: Alberto Rey's Cuban and American Art*. Albany, NY: SUNY Press, 2014.

Carpentier, Alejo. *The Baroque and the Marvelous Real*. Durham, NC: Duke University Press, 1995.

Clearwater, Bonnie, Jorge Hilker Santis, Helen L. Kohen, Giulio V. Blanc, Juan A. Martínez, César Trasobares, and Sue Henger. *The Miami Generation: Revisited*. Fort Lauderdale, FL: NSU Museum of Art, 2014.

Comesañas Sardiñas, Zeida. *Great Masters of Cuban Art, 1800–1958/Grandes maestros del arte cubano: Ramos Collection/Colección Ramos*. Daytona Beach, FL: Museum of Arts and Sciences, 2009.

Damian, Carol. *Breaking Barriers: Selections from the Museum of Art's Permanent Collection*. Fort Lauderdale, FL: Fort Lauderdale Museum of Art, 1996.

Danto, Arthur C. *After the End of Art: Contemporary Art and the Pale of History*. Boulder: University of Colorado Press, 1998.

Dilworth, Jason, and Alberto Rey. *Complexities of Water: Biological Regionalism—Bagmati River, Kathmandu Valley, Nepal*. Fredonia, NY: Canadawa, 2016.

Fuentes-Pérez, Ileana, Graciella Cruz-Taura, and Ricardo Pau-Llosa, eds. *Outside Cuba/Fuera de Cuba: Contemporary Cuban Visual Artists*. New Brunswick, NJ: Transaction, 1989.

Gómez Sicre, José. *Art of Cuba in Exile*. Miami: Universal, 1987.

Herrera, Andrea O'Reilly. *Cuban Artists across the Diaspora: Setting the Tent against the House*. Austin: University of Texas Press, 2011.

Humboldt, Wilhelm von. *On Language: On the Diversity of Human Language Construction and Its Influence on the Mental Development of the Human Species*. Edited by Michael Losonsky. Cambridge, UK: Cambridge University Press, 1999.

Kandel, Eric R. *In Search of Memory: The Emergence of a New Science of Mind*. New York: W. W. Norton, 2007.

Kraidy, Marwan. *Hybridity: The Cultural Logic of Globalization*. Philadelphia: Temple University Press, 2005.

Larson, Rebecca Sexton. *Jake Fernandez: Constructed Landscapes*. Maitland, FL: Maitland Museum, 2014.

Libby, Gary R., and Juan A. Martínez. *Cuba: A History in Art*. Gainesville: University Press of Florida, 2015.

Lowe Art Museum, University of Miami. *Humberto Calzada: In Dreams Awake—30-Year Retrospective*. Miami: Lowe Art Museum, 2003.

Martínez, Juan A. *Cuban Art and National Identity: The Vanguardia Painters (1927–1950)*. Gainesville: University Press of Florida, 1994.

———. *Jake Fernandez: Sites and Composites*. Miami: Miami Dade College, 1988.

Martínez-Fraga, Pedro J. *Demi: Searching for the Light*. San Francisco: Blurb, 2010.

Navarrete, William, and Jesús Rosado, eds. *Visión crítica de Humberto Calzada*. Valencia, Spain: Aduana Vieja, 2008.

Palladino-Craig, Allys, and Jorge H. Santis. *Jake Fernandez: Ethereal Journeyman*. Fort Lauderdale, FL: Museum of Art, Fort Lauderdale, 2001.

Pérez Firmat, Gustavo. *Life on the Hyphen: The Cuban-American Way*. Rev. ed. Austin: University of Texas Press, 2012.

———. *Next Year in Cuba: A Cubano's Coming-of-Age in America*. Houston: Arte Público Press, 2006.

Pau-Llosa, Ricardo. *Humberto Calzada: A Retrospective of Work, 1975–1990*. Miami Beach: Bass Museum of Art, 1991.

Rorimer, James. *The Cloisters: The Building and the Collections of Medieval Art in Fort Tryon Park*. New York: Metropolitan Museum of Art, 1944.

Santis, Jorge, and Luis Camnitzer. *New Art of Cuba*. Revised by Joe R. and Teresa Lozano. Austin: University of Texas Press, 2003.

Salgado, César Augusto. "Hybridity in New World Baroque Theory." *The Journal of American Folklore* 112, no. 445 (1999), 316–31.

Schultheis, Franz, Erwin Single, Stephan Egger, and Thomas Mazzurana. *When Art Meets Money: Encounters at the Art Basel*. Cologne: Verlag Walther König, 2015.

Shklovsky, Viktor. "Art as Technique." In *Literary Theory: An Anthology*, edited by Julie Rivkin and Michael Ryan, 15–21. 2nd ed. Malden, MA: Blackwell Publishers, 2004.

Suchlicki, Jaime. *Cuba: From Columbus to Castro and Beyond*. Lincoln, NE: Potomac Books, 2002.

Valdés Bernal, Sergio. "'Cuba es un ajiaco,' sentenció Fernando Ortiz." *Espacio Laical* 4 (2014): 69–75.

Veigas-Zamora, José, Cristina Vives Gutiérrez, Adolfo V. Nodal, Valia Garzón, and Dannys Montes de Oca, eds. *Memoria: Cuban Art of the 20th Century*. Los Angeles: California/International Arts Foundation, 2001.

Whitman, Walt. *Song of Myself*. Mineola, NY: Dover, 2012.

Zimmer, William, and Sheldon M. Lurie. *Abstraction: Four from Latin America*. Miami: Miami Dade College, 1998.

13

Cuban Art in the Diaspora

The "Chaos of Difference and Repetition"

Andrea O'Reilly Herrera

The quest to define national and cultural identity in the context of transformation and flux harkens back to the Cuban independence movement of the nineteenth century.[1] Following the establishment of the republic in 1902, Cuba underwent a period of intense nationalism.[2] As Alejandro de la Fuente observes, the avant-garde movement "emerged from the economic and political failure of the first Republic."[3] Shaped by this sociopolitical milieu, the first generation of Cuban *vanguardia* or modernist artists and writers collectively forged a set of fundamental motifs and elements that articulated a national identity apart from colonial Spain. Moreover, they established identifiable conceptual and thematic trends that reflected their physical *displacement from* and *reencounter with* a nation that had, on the one hand, officially suppressed its Indigenous and African roots and privileged European visual forms and traditions, yet was seeking to self-identify along the cultural lines of what Roberto Zurbano calls these "lost chapters" of Cuban culture.[4]

In addition to introducing modernism into Cuba, the avant-garde artists distinguished themselves according to their use of bright colors, patterns and baroque visual rhythms, which came to typify Cuban art. As Luz Merino observes, the vanguardia was "defined operationally by transformation and change . . . models were being reformulated . . . new spaces for representation were being created, and . . . an expressive inventory was being proposed in the service of [national] identity."[5] In his catalogue essay for *Outside Cuba/Fuera de Cuba*, Cuban poet and art critic Ricardo Pau-Llosa identifies four major trends or elements that originated with the vanguardia artists:

1. An exploration of Cuba's Indigenous and African roots, as well as the theme of *criollismo* (artistic and literary regionalism);
2. The presence of the landscape, including folkloric, pastoral subjects and symbols;
3. Colonial and regional architectural elements; and
4. Themes of rupture, violence, and oppression, linked to the subject of *criollismo*—especially regarding the role of the institution in relation to the individual (what some critics refer to as "themes of soil," vernacular art, and/or art of *social commitment*).[6]

While interviewing artists for my monograph *Cuban Artists Across the Diaspora: Setting the Tent Against the House*, these same fundamental themes—and the questions they inadvertently raise regarding what constitutes and defines a nation in the context of transformation and flux—emerged.[7] The artists participating in the itinerant art exhibition *CAFÉ*, the focus of *Cuban Artists Across the Diaspora*, all left Cuba under some form of political or economic duress. As established in the book's introduction, they clearly do not purport to represent Cuban diasporic expression in general; however, the structures of visual thinking first visible in the work of the vanguardia artists recur in various combinations in all their art and serve as the connective tissue that binds them together despite their differences. Although the *CAFÉ* artists individually forge a set of complex, compound cultural expressions out of disparate sources and integrate new elements into their work, certain *identifiable continuities* (to borrow Pau-Llosa's term) visibly link them directly to the vanguardia movement—a theme that provided the scaffolding upon which I organized *Cuban Artists Across the Diaspora*. This chapter, however, will focus exclusively on the presence of Indigenous and/or Cuban-African themes in the art of *CAFÉ* artists José Bedia, Angela Valella, Raúl Villarreal, and the chief curator of the exhibition, Leandro Soto.[8]

In *The Repeating Island*, Antonio Benítez-Rojo discusses the complex cultural expressions and forms that emerged in Cuba during the nineteenth century as a result of the *collision* among Europe, the Indigenous populations inhabiting the island, Africa, and Asia. Benítez-Rojo emphasizes the unique form of Creolization that burgeoned on the eastern side of the island—a confluence of multivarious influences springing "from the seeds that had . . . scattered from the richest stores of three continents."[9] In his seminal work, Benítez-Rojo acknowledges the "seam of continuous influence" from Africa (with emphasis on West Africa), unparalleled in any other Antillean nation except for Haiti. This influence combined with those of the various European presences that inhabited the island (including France), as well as the extant vestiges of Taíno culture.[10] These cultural forms took shape according to a process of stratification, striation, and sedimentation; and they remain *polyphonic* (to borrow Benítez-Rojo's term)—as opposed to having a single, fundamental tone—and, like the *ajiaco* or Cuban stew (as Fernando Ortiz described it), possess elements from their original sources that have maintained their integrity.[11]

In integrating Indigenous, Afro-Cuban, and *criollo* forms into their artwork, vanguardia artists such as Wifredo Lam (as well as scholars such as anthropologists Lydia Cabrera and Fernando Ortiz) cultivated a symbolic language that served to define certain fundamental aspects of what it meant to be Cuban.[12] Many of these artists idealized the *guajiro* or peasant and peasant life, and looked to the countryside for inspiration, as a repository of Taíno and African legends as well as *criollo* dance forms, music, and cuisine.[13] They also drew upon and romanticized icons such as the *guajira* or *guajiro* (female and male peasants) and the palm tree, which possessed sacred connotations and represented, for many, some sense of national cohesion.[14]

Although European, Asian, Mexican and North and/or South American aesthetics and forms have visibly influenced the artists featured in *Cuban Artists Across the Diaspora*, and many infuse their art with references to popular culture and traditional Western religious symbols, a metonymic *repetition*[15] of Indigenous and creole cultural elements and practices is evident in their work. Influenced by the work of avant-garde artists such as Lam, many integrate or fuse *criollismo* and Afro-Cubanism. Recalling the work of the artists in Grupo Origen (1974–78) and Grupo Antillano (1978–83),[16] others incorporate Taíno symbols, as well as elements drawn from Afro-Cuban religions such as *Palo Monte* and

Santería,[17] as fundamental sources of iconography as well as mediums of artistic expression in relation to the overarching theme of displacement.

As Benítez-Rojo comments, "When a people's culture conserves ancient dynamics that play 'in a certain kind of way,' they resist being displaced by external territorializing forms and they propose to co-exist with them through syncretic processes."[18] Perhaps one of the best examples of this impulse to conserve these *ancient dynamics* in the context of displacement yet also integrate new elements harmoniously is the work of José Bedia. Implementing an anthropological approach in his art, Bedia represents what Gerardo Mosquera terms *another form of decentering*, for he draws from the content of African-based worldviews of religious belief systems, "not by recreating forms, rites, or myths," but rather by "creating Western culture from non-Western bases, transforming it and thereby diversifying global contemporary culture."[19] Even as a child, Bedia recalled during our interview in 2005, he was interested in Indigenous art and exposed to images that frequently appeared in popular Cuban renderings of Native people and African Americans.[20]

Following his introduction to Palo Monte, Bedia began to weave both Indigenous and African elements into his work, as seen in works such as *Vive en la línea* (*He Lives on the Railroad Line*, 1989, Plate 44). According to the artist, the remnants of Indigenous culture in Cuba are *non-vital*, for Indigenous people had virtually disappeared and their culture has been reduced to something akin to *archaeological artifacts*. "What was definitely living and actualized," the artist ruminates, "were the Afro-Cuban traditions implicit in the Cuban population . . . I began connecting to these things through friends and my mother's people above all else."[21] "I have always been interested in the past," Bedia continues, "and the recurrence of elements in various cultures," as seen, for example, in Navajo sand painting or Yaqui masks. "The Yaqui included elements from nearly every group that crossed their path," Bedia observes. What has been for the artist an instinctive impulse to incorporate and transform signifies a way of comprehending and interpreting reality, and recognizing and acknowledging something *vital* and *functional*.[22]

Despite the idea that Bedia dismisses any essentialist notion of culture or human nature, his art strives to throw into relief what he terms certain fundamental *truths* or *realities* that continue to be *alive* and *useful*. Rather than focusing on difference, Bedia seeks what he characterizes as *verisimilitude*. His art emerges not exclusively from a single root or place of origin, but rather, it draws inspiration from the places he has traveled and the cultures and groups he has encountered. "I am searching for archetypal elements," Bedia muses, "which I want to explicate and make my own."

Indigenous elements and symbols are also centrally present in the art of Angela Valella (b. 1948). Having departed Cuba with her family in 1969 at the age of twenty, Valella seeks to reconnect with her Cuban past and heritage through her artwork. While studying art and pursuing dual minors in psychology and anthropology at Miami Dade Community College, she was introduced to the work of Mircea Eliade and Rudolf Otto, which contemplated totemic representations in nature; this in turn prompted Valella to research Taíno culture to learn more about pre-Columbian Cuba. This exploration enabled her to approach what she characterizes as an *essential aspect* of Cuban culture, which had been submerged or suppressed—though not entirely eradicated, as is widely believed. Valella's investigation consequently inspired her *Taíno* series, which she labored over for nearly a decade. Works such as *Deminan* (1999), for example, allude to the rich pantheon of Taíno mythography, as Deminan is the forbear of four male ancestors who oversee the elements, and the female spirit Caguama (Turtle Woman), the mother of humankind, who emerged from the swollen hump on his back and represents the fertility of the womb (Plate 45).

Valella's *Taíno* paintings gradually evolved into an exploration of the manner in which symbols and icons can be manipulated according to shifting ideological concerns; they became the foundation for a consequent series titled *Martí*.[23] In an impulse that runs parallel to the artwork produced in Cuba during the mid-to-late 1980s, Valella began to reconstitute national or patriotic symbols such as flags and heroes, and emblems drawn from mass culture and the popular media, to reference a range of nationalist discourses and ideologies. One painting, *The Idol* (1999), portrays the great poet and liberator José Martí as an organic, totemic figure (Plate 46). Valella visually links Martí's figure to Cuba's Indigenous cultures through a pattern of symbols. However, these symbols simultaneously point to the way Martí's image was reconstituted and employed alternatively as a nationalist symbol during the struggle for independence from Spain and, more recently, by the Castro regime.

Like Bedia and Valella, Raúl Villarreal (1964–2019) incorporates a combination of Taíno and Afro-Cuban elements into every aspect of his work, along with iconic images from the Cuban landscape. In his own words, the themes of "identity, hybridization, and transculturation" are a primary impetus for his art as he seeks to reconnect with his Cuban heritage.[24] Although, by Villarreal's own admission, European masters such as Jan Vermeer, Diego Velázquez, and René Magritte have profoundly influenced him, his integration of religious symbols, spiritual iconography, and autobiographical elements represents a personal exploration of his own ethnic and cultural roots. His exile, commencing in 1972 when he was only seven years old, and his eventual return visit to Cuba in 1992, prompted this artistic exploration.

According to Villarreal, his second trip to Cuba in 1996 represented a turning point in his art. Previously, his work had been largely "representational, figurative, and surreal."[25] Upon returning from this journey, Villarreal began depicting the Cuban countryside and incorporating more visibly or overtly Afro-Cuban and Taíno iconography into his paintings. The artist began to use what he characterizes as a form of *bricolage* to represent the *layering* of personal and historical memory. "My work," he writes,

> represents personal experiences, [the] assimilation of other cultures, and the appropriation of images from mass media. Through the use of assemblages and a process of layering, the work conveys unexpected connections between existence and identity within a postmodern and postcolonial context, thus fusing memories [from Cuba], experiences, and nostalgia.[26]

As an example, *El encuentro* (*The Encounter*, 2005) fuses folkloric references with personal and cultural elements drawn from both the past and the present (Plate 47). The painting portrays the island through a series of cloud formations. "The depiction of the shape of the island made of clouds," Villarreal comments, "alludes to the condition of exile, [for] it represents any sky under which we may find ourselves." In this series (titled *Roystonea Regia*), inverted palm trees—a leitmotif in Villarreal's work—reference Cuba's Indigenous population, which inhabited the island before Christopher Columbus's interventions on behalf of the Spanish Crown, as well as the African presence woven inextricably into the Cuban cultural fabric. Invoking the work of Cuban anthropologist Lydia Cabrera, Villarreal points out that the palm served as *an invaluable source of raw material* for Cuba's first inhabitants. Following the importation of slaves to the island, the tree became associated with one of the major

Afro-Cuban orishas (Yoruba deities), Changó, who resided on the crown of the royal palm tree, as well as with the *npungus* Siete Rayos (Palo Monte), the deity who commands thunder.[27] Functioning simultaneously as a phallic symbol, the palm suggests the erotic and sensuous nature of Cuban culture. Following a tradition established by Cuban poets José María de Heredia and Martí, both of whom resided outside the island in a state of exile, it is also a constant and sometimes painful reminder of the island's natural beauty, despite various interventions of colonial and neocolonial powers. The fact that it is inverted and solitary, Villarreal adds, bespeaks the ongoing political circumstances on the island and the lack of freedom because of the current totalitarian regime. "Contemporary Cuba," Villarreal tells me, "is a paradise turned upside down." Serving as a kind of visual palimpsest, the palm thus bridges both the past and the present in the same way as it links the various cultural presences that have inhabited the island over the centuries.

Inspired by his family's practice of Palo Monte, Villarreal also incorporates a coded pattern of religious symbols and colors into other works. A combination of Afro-Cuban, Spanish, and Taíno elements is distinctly visible, for example, in the richly textured border pattern and the overall color scheme of many of his paintings. In addition to including a range of Afro-Cuban religious symbols, as well as the iconic inverted palm and the crocodile shape of the island (subtly incorporated into the herringbone pattern that serves as a backdrop to the painting), a series of works features yellow, amber, and copper tones, which signify at once the orisha Ochún as well as her Catholic counterpart, the Virgin of Charity of Cobre. "[These] piece[s]," Villarreal observes, "[are] about experiencing different realities, cultures, and traditions, while maintaining your own culture. . . . The layering of images, the pulling back and forth [of] the two-dimensional surface suggests the complexity of migration." Ultimately, Villarreal's artwork portrays what he describes as *the postmodern condition* in that it bespeaks the complexities of transculturation and transmigration. In this sense, his art represents what he terms "'culture' on the brink of something unexpected."

Leandro Soto (b. 1956) also addresses fundamental issues regarding displacement, *cubanidad* ("Cubanness"), and transculturation through an exploration of Afro-Cuban and Indigenous cultural forms and practices. Soto, who left Cuba at the age of thirty-three—and has resided for significant periods in Mexico, various parts of India, Spain, Western New

York, Massachusetts, Phoenix, and more recently Barbados, Miami, and Mérida—freely aligns African and Afro-Cuban religious symbols with a score of newly acquired elements, which reflect the various cultures and artistic traditions to which he has been exposed in exile. Although he does not practice Santería (or belong to the Abakuá society), Soto's thematically unified series of installations titled *A Glance over the Garden* (1997), for example, was inspired by several conversations with a newly arrived Cuban couple whom he met "against the snowy [Buffalo, NY] winter background that covered every garden." Both husband and wife were initiated *santeros*. "For me as an artist," Soto explains,

> . . . it was extremely important to observe how their practices and beliefs were challenged, adapted and transformed by their new environment. . . . New places offer new opportunities, new places to rename, but at the same time they suppress a part of our cultural selves. . . . Elevating the presence of my African ancestors in this collection, as well as the experience of my friends in Buffalo, restores them within the Anglo context of this experience. In effect, I plant "a garden," a garden that functions as a metaphor of living together, of order, and of the appropriation and integration of this new land.[28]

Soto's exploration of the relationship between his own cultural roots and Indigenous culture began during his time in Tabasco, Mexico, and crystallized during his sojourn in Phoenix, Arizona. In 2005, he created a character based on the Abakuá deity Ireme with the assistance of fellow Cuban artist Nelson García Miranda (Plate 48).[29] During a performance at the New Contemporary Mesa Center for the Arts in Northern Arizona, Soto created an installation in collaboration with a second Cuban artist Dora Hernández, dedicated to his father and mother-in-law and Hernández's father, all of whom had recently passed away. A group of diasporic Cuban drummers, all of whom were living in Arizona at the time, danced and sang in the background as Soto/Ireme danced before a crowd, paying homage to the spirits of the dead. The dance took place in front of a palm tree located near the installation. Several members of the audience, who happened to be Mexican American and Native American, mistook Ireme for a kachina, or Hopi spirit. Following the performance, they questioned Soto's motives, thinking that he had confused or crossed what they believed were antithetical cultural elements. To their surprise, Soto revealed that Ireme was a Nigerian Abakuá spirit, not a kachina, and that this spirit was representative of his own personal heritage.

Prior to that point, Soto had been largely unfamiliar with Hopi culture. Despite the different cultural contexts from which they arose, the similarities between these two divinities were more than striking. As a result, Soto renamed his performance Kachíreme. Commenting on the experience, he observes, "Cuba is geographically opposite to what we have here in Arizona—it is surrounded by water and green. Being on the island is the opposite of being in the desert. Yet suddenly I was absolutely connected here in Arizona." This fortuitous discovery led Soto to an exploration of the links among U.S. Native, Afro-Cuban, Chontales, and Choles cultures (the last of which he encountered during his five-year tenure in Tabasco, Mexico).

Rather than focusing on difference, Soto—like Bedia—stresses the connective tissues among the Indigenous cultures he has encountered during his journey. Commenting upon this very subject, he insists that his work draws on the theory of *implosion*. In other words, things that are apparently separate are interconnected, or interwoven like a tapestry. Deeply influenced by his experience among various Indigenous communities in Southern Mexico, such as the Maya-Chol, Soto adopted a worldview that conceives of reality as an intricate tapestry of transpersonal or infinite energies woven together by some divine force or spirit.[30] He sees the trajectory of his travels—from Cuba to Mexico, Mexico to Spain, and subsequently to the United States, India, Barbados, Miami, and Mérida—as a *cumulative process* in which he is continually *editing* and *re-editing* his earlier experiences. "They are all connected," he assures me. Yet in the process of measuring his experience in the context of the new, Soto more clearly defines his own sense of cubanidad, as well as his cultural identity.

Commenting upon his own work, Soto explains:

> I work with the complexity of being Caribbean, a heritage composed of diverse cultural presences. To nourish these expressions, I have done a lot of anthropological research in the countries and cultures where I lived. I have used the term "cultural translation" to talk about this process. . . . I insist that I should become part of the communities in which I reside at any particular moment of my life. In order to become a "channel" (artist-shaman) for this community,

> I have to work with transpersonal thematics and transpersonal issues. . . . In my view, that which is apparently dispersed or diffuse is also linked to the magical, that is, I hold a vision of the world where reality is conceived as a tapestry of transpersonal energies. . . . [31]

Resonant with Bedia's practice, Soto emphasizes a concept he refers to as *religare.* Drawn from a Latinate tradition, this term signifies *reunion, re-connection, re-integration,* and *communion*—something that Soto and others characterize as a *non-Western approach to reality* and creative expression.[32] The works featured in Soto's installation project *A Glance Over the Garden* or paintings such as *Ireme Abacuá* (2005, see above) are visible manifestations of the heterogeneous and chameleonic aspects of Cuban culture given its long history of cultural intermixing and collision. In a discussion of these aspects of Cuban culture, with specific reference to *Eleguá* (one of his later installations, inspired by the Buffalo exhibition), Soto discussed the verisimilitude of visual elements:

> A good example of this cultural integration is the installation I devote to Eleguá—the god of new paths and avenues. I used maps of the routes I followed to go from Miami (my point of entrance in this country) to the Northeast of the United States (where I resided for a number of years). I displayed an image of Mickey Mouse—red and black, Eleguá's colors—as part of this installation because a mouse is Eleguá's favorite animal! Thus Mickey Mouse—who is black and red and a mouse to boot—is the perfect cultural object to explain and visually translate Eleguá Laroye. Also, I displaced a small version of the Statue of Liberty from its original location in New York City to the Miami area since, for many exiled Cubans, Miami is the most important city in the United States. I also used envelopes—black and red—from the United States mail overnight service in order to provide color and content for this installation.[33]

Soto's installations reconstitute and invoke a pantheon of orishas through familiar, iconic objects and images drawn primarily from U.S. popular culture. In liberally pairing the sacred with the profane, Soto suggests the integral and synergistic relationship between these two realms. In this sense, his installations blur the lines traditionally drawn between the supernatural and the natural. In Soto's view, art is *de palo pa' rumba*—a popular Cuban expression that refers to a sudden change in topic or theme during a conversation. Taken in more literal terms, it refers to a shift in conversation from the subject of Palo Monte (the sacred) to *rumba* (the secular or profane). Put another way, this expression suggests the coexistence of, and hidden links among, seemingly antithetical elements.[34]

Soto's thoughtful juxtaposing and counterbalancing of objects endow them, as Cuban art critic Tony Morales observes, with "the quality of expressing some universal principles emanating from a local perspective."[35] They suggest, moreover, the integrative and mediatory role the artist plays in bringing these elements together. Soto's creations—like Bedia's, Valella's, and Villarreal's—invoke the most fundamental tenets of these various religious traditions and allude to the all-embracing nature of Cuban culture itself. They simultaneously capture or make visible the *integral relationships* among seemingly antithetical objects, and recapture some essence that the vanguardia artists first recognized as fundamentally Cuban.

Notes

1. The subtitle of this chapter references Antonio Benítez-Rojo's seminal critical study *The Repeating Island*. Benítez-Rojo was indebted to Gilles Deleuze and inspired by the latter's groundbreaking work *Difference and Repetition*.

2. The first generation of Cuban vanguardia artists includes Víctor Manuel García, Eduardo Abela, Amelia Peláez del Casal, Antonio Gattorno, Carlos Enríquez, Fidelio Ponce de León, and Marcelo Pogolotti.

3. See Alejandro de la Fuente's edited collection and exhibition catalogue, *Grupo Antillano*, 57.

4. See José Veiga-Zamora et al.'s introductory essay in *Memoria*, as well as Zurbano in *Grupo Antillano*, 71.

5. Luz Merino, "The New Image in Everyday Life," 50.

6. Several essays in the exhibition catalogue for *Cuba*, edited by Nathalie Bondil, directly address this topic.

7. See Andrea O'Reilly Herrera, *Cuban Artists Across the Diaspora*. Excerpts from my monograph are reproduced in this chapter with the permission of the University of Texas Press.

8. Many of the participating artists in *CAFÉ* referred to themselves as *cafeteros*, loosely translated as someone who is fond of coffee.

9. See Benítez-Rojo's discussion in *The Repeating Island*, 52.

10. While the Taíno were virtually eliminated in the Caribbean, visible traces of their culture still exist and are manifest in language, folklore, cuisine, art, music, and religious emblems such as the Virgin of Charity of Cobre (Cuba's patron saint) who, as Benítez-Rojo argues, is "a fusion of the cults of Atabey (Taíno), Oshun (Yoruba), and Our Lady." See *The Repeating Island*, 46, 52. Although the Spaniards largely suppressed

the Indigenous presence in Cuba, it remained in evidence, as seen, for example, in the various manifestations and permutations of the Virgin of Charity of Cobre.

11. The Afro-Cuban folklorist Rogelio Martínez Furé articulated this concept in a personal conversation with Leandro Soto and Grisel Pujalá in 2002.

12. Wifredo Lam also integrated both Oceanic and Asian cultural elements into his work.

13. See Pau-Llosa, "Identity and Variations," 48.

14. Both José María de Heredia (1803–39), author of the famed poem "Niagara," and José Martí (1853–95) elevated the palm tree to the level of an emblem of Cuba and Cuban identity. That both poets employed this image while in a state of exile is noteworthy.

15. As mentioned early on, my use of the word *repetition* resonates with Benítez-Rojo's in that it suggests that memories repeat themselves over time and retain some of their essential qualities. However, rather than being mimetic in any Borgesian sense, they are also *as fugitive as the years,* as Marcel Proust suggested in the famous episode in *Swann's Way* with the crumb of *madeleine* and the cup of tea.

16. "The debate regarding the place and importance of Afro-Cuban cultural practices in the culture and identity of the nation," de la Fuente observes, "was revived after 1959" (58). Influenced and supported by Wifredo Lam, Grupo Antillano was a visual arts and cultural movement that emerged during what Ambrosio Fornet referred to as the *Quinquenio Gris* ("The Gray Five Years," 1971–76), a period of post-Stalinist censorship in Cuba. The movement emphasized and celebrated the leading role of Africa and Afro-Caribbean influences in the formation of the nation and consequently in national culture. Grupo Origen was Grupo Antillano's precursor.

17. In addition to Christianity, Cuba's two major religions are Palo Monte and Santería. The latter are religions of African origin that arose in the contexts of slavery and colonialism. Palo Monte (or Regla Congo or Palo) has three branches, the most prominent in Cuba being Palo Monte Mayombe. (Other branches include Briyumba and Kimbisa.) Palo Monte has traditionally been associated with slaves from central Africa, of Bantu origin primarily. Practitioners of Palo Monte emphasize ancestor worship as well as the relationship to the land and the spiritual forces that manifest themselves in the natural world. Santería is also known as Regla de Ocha in Cuba. To ensure their cultural survival, slaves (primarily of West African origin and specifically of the Yoruba culture of southwestern Nigeria) resisted acculturation by the Spaniards by integrating aspects of their folk religions with Christianity. According to the beliefs of Santería, at birth everyone is associated with a divine guardian or saint (orisha). Each orisha, in turn, has a Catholic counterpart. For example, the patron of Cuba, the Virgin of Charity of Cobre, is counterpart to Ochún, the orisha or goddess associated with love, sensuality, maternity, beauty, and art. Ochún's colors are yellow and orange, and she is associated with the number five.

18. *The Repeating Island*, 70.

19. See Gerardo Mosquera, "New Cuban Art Begins."

20. Personal interview, November 13, 2007, Miami.

21. Personal interview conducted and edited by Jorge J. E. Gracia, January 9, 2005, https://www.buffalo.edu/capenchair/exhibits/cuban-art/_jcr_content/par/download_1/file.res/iBedia.html.

22. Personal interview by Gracia.

23. Angela Valella's investigation into Taíno symbology and forms is akin to an impulse visible in the artwork produced in the context of the Mexican Revolution, as well as the ideological impulses that informed the Chicano Movement in the United States and manifest themselves in the work of Chicanx writers. In addition to seeking social justice and equity, the Chicano Movement sought to reclaim a lost or buried heritage that predated Spanish colonialism, as well as educate and encourage Chicanas/os to take pride in their ethnic and cultural heritage. A similar impetus was evident in the Mexican Muralist Movement, which included artists such as Diego Rivera, José Orozco, and David Alfaro Siqueiros. Aiming to create a new national cultural consciousness, their work contained nationalist themes that reflected their affinity with the school of Socialist Realist Art as well as Indigenous iconography. Related artists such as Frida Kahlo also incorporated Indigenous iconography into their work.

24. Personal interview, January 23, 2006, West New York, NJ.

25. Personal interview.

26. See Villarreal's unpublished master's thesis *(In)visible Traces*, 1.

27. Drawing upon the work of the Cuban anthropologist Lydia Cabrera, Villarreal points out that "because of its height, the royal palm is a natural lightening rod in Cuba; for this and other reasons it is associated with Siete Rayos." For more information on this subject, see Cabrera's *El Monte*, 221.

28. See Soto, "Cubans in the U.S.," 245–47.

29. Nelson García Miranda designed and painted Soto's *Ireme* costume.

30. Personal interview, May 20, 2005, Phoenix, AZ.

31. Isabel Alvarez Borland, "De Palo pa' Rumba," 168–69.

32. Personal interview, May 20, 2005. See also Alvarez Borland, 170.

33. Alvarez Borland, 173–74.

34. For more on this subject, see Alvarez Borland, 169.

35. For more information, see Tony Morales's "A Glance over the Garden," featured in the pamphlet distributed by Bit Orbit Gallery for the exhibition (September 20–October 25, 1997).

Bibliography

Alvarez Borland, Isabel. "De Palo pa' Rumba: An Interview with Leandro Soto." *Afro-Hispanic Review* 26, no. 1 (2007): 167–78.

Benítez-Rojo, Antonio. *The Repeating Island: The Caribbean and the Postmodern Perspective*. Durham, NC: Duke University Press, 1992.

Bondil, Nathalie, ed. *Cuba: Art and History from 1868 to Today*. Montreal: Montreal Museum of Fine Arts, 2009.

Cabrera, Lydia. *El monte*. Miami: Colección del Chicherekú [1954], 1986.

de la Fuente, Alejandro, ed. *Grupo Antillano: The Art of Afro-Cuba*. Pittsburgh: University of Pittsburgh Press, 2013.

Deleuze, Gilles. *Difference and Repetition*. Translated by Paul Patton. New York: Columbia University Press, 1993.

Herrera, Andrea O'Reilly. *Cuban Artists Across the Diaspora: Setting the Tent Against the House*. Austin: University of Texas Press, 2011.

Merino, Luz. "The New Image in Everyday Art." In *Memoria: Cuban Art of the Twentieth Century*, edited by José Veigas-Zamora, Cristina Vives Gutiérrez, Adolfo V. Nodal, Valia Garzón, and Dannys Montes de Oca, 50–52. Los Angeles: California/International Arts Foundation, 2002.

Mosquera, Gerardo. "New Cuban Art Begins." In *Cuba: Art and History from 1868 to Today*, edited by Nathalie Bondil, 314–29. Montreal: Montreal Museum of Fine Arts, 2009.

Pau-Llosa, Ricardo. "Identity and Variations: Cuban Visual Thinking in Exile since 1959." In *Outside Cuba/Fuera de Cuba: Contemporary Visual Artists*, edited by Ileana Fuentes-Pérez, Graciella Cruz-Taura, and Ricardo Pau-Llosa, 41–64. New Brunswick, NJ: Transaction, 1988.

Soto, Leandro. "Cubans in the U.S.: An Example of Ethnic Identity in the Making." In *ReMembering Cuba: Legacy of a Diaspora*, edited by Andrea O'Reilly Herrera, 245–47. Austin: University of Texas Press, 2001.

Villareal, Raúl. *(In)Visible Traces*. Master's thesis, New Jersey City University, 2005.

14

From Burning Paintings to Domestic Anxieties

Shifting Cultural Relations between the United States and Cuba and between Cubans on and off the Island

Jorge Duany

Journalists and scholars have told the story before, but its basic outlines are worth recalling.[1] On April 22, 1988, the Cuban Museum of Arts and Culture in Miami held a fundraising auction of 161 paintings, which included four artists who remained in Cuba and reportedly sympathized with Fidel Castro's regime: Mariano Rodríguez, Carmelo González, Raúl Martínez, and Manuel Mendive (b. 1944). A former paratrooper of the Brigade 2506, one of a group of exiled veterans of the 1961 Bay of Pigs Invasion in Cuba, bid $500 for one of Mendive's works, *Pavo real* (*The Peacock*). The brightly colored painting was a small, primitivist, oil-on-cardboard work portraying palm trees, birds, fish, a kneeling human figure, and, of course, a peacock. This last is a traditional visual representation of the orisha Ochún, the Yoruba goddess of love, beauty, and fertility revered in Afro-Cuban religion.

The man who purchased the painting, civil engineer José M. Juara, a resident of Key Biscayne in Miami, proceeded to burn it in the street outside the museum, before Cuban exiles protesting the auction. Juara later explained that he "burned that painting because [he] foresaw the ideological penetration from communist Cuba that was beginning to take place in the Cuban exile community." He also declared that the burning was "an act of repulsion against Marxist-Leninist propaganda" and "the Marxism associated with all Cuban Marxist painters."[2]

On May 3, 1988, after anonymous telephone threats, a pipe bomb exploded near the museum. The explosion damaged a car owned by one of the museum's directors, as well as the building's glass door and front wall. Seventeen of thirty-seven members resigned from the museum's board of directors a day later because they opposed dealing with art produced in contemporary Cuba. Founded in 1982, the museum eventually closed in 1999, following a prolonged battle to resist political pressures, avoid eviction from county-owned property, and respond to city audits of its financial records.[3]

Nearly thirty years after the Mendive incident, on January 18, 2018, the Pérez Art Museum Miami (PAMM) opened *Chapter 3: Domestic Anxieties*, the last installment in a ten-month-long exhibition of contemporary Cuban art from the Jorge M. Pérez Collection. Most of the works in the exhibition formed part of a gift of more than 170 pieces donated by Pérez, including those from artists living in Cuba, such as Mendive himself, Roberto Fabelo (b. 1951), Juan Carlos Alom (b. 1964), Alexis Leyva Machado (aka Kcho, b. 1970), Juan Roberto Diago (b. 1971), Yoan Capote (b. 1977), and Elizabet Cerviño (b. 1986). Curated by Tobias Ostrander, the exhibition included artists currently living in the United States and Puerto Rico, such as Zilia Sánchez (b. 1926), Luis Cruz Azaceta (b. 1942), José Bedia, Tomás Esson (b. 1963), and Teresita Fernández (b. 1968). The inauguration of *Chapter 3* featured a panel discussion with two Cuban artists: Glexis Novoa, who now divides his time between Miami and Havana; and Carlos Garaicoa, who moved from Havana to Madrid in 2007. The panel discussion attracted an audience of more than 100 persons, both Spanish and English speakers. No public protests—let alone burning of paintings or bomb threats—took place outside the museum, and the entire exhibition provoked surprisingly little controversy in Miami.[4]

How and why has the Cuban-American community changed in the last few decades? More specifically, to what extent have Cubans in Miami embraced the possibility of closer cultural exchanges between the United States and Cuba? How have diaspora cultural politics evolved to allow for the display and sale of artworks produced on the island, in the capital of Cuban exile? More broadly, how have cultural politics shifted because of demographic and generational transitions within Miami's Cuban community? Finally, how have recent changes in U.S. policies toward Cuba affected U.S.-Cuban cultural relations, especially after the announcement of the "normalization" of bilateral ties by then-President Barack Obama on December 17, 2014, and President Donald Trump's inauguration on January 20, 2017? These are some of the key issues addressed in this chapter.

U.S.-Cuban Cultural Relations since 1959

To contextualize the 1988 burning of Mendive's painting in Little Havana, let me provide some historical perspective on the long-standing geopolitical tensions between Cuba and the United States after Fidel Castro's revolution. The Eisenhower administration imposed a partial trade embargo on Cuba in October 1960, which the Kennedy administration extended to practically all imports and exports in February 1962, after the Cuban government expropriated U.S. companies on the island without compensation. The U.S. embargo, which remains in place today, made it very difficult to maintain contacts between Cuban and U.S. artists, musicians, writers, and scholars. For example, musical exchanges between the two countries—including recording and selling records; organizing performances, concerts, and tours; and playing songs on radio and television stations—practically ceased in the early 1960s.[5] Multinational music corporations all but abandoned the island until the late 1980s, when they could once again distribute Cuban records in the United States.

A similar isolation, due to ideological confrontations, marked the visual arts as well as literature and other cultural spheres. For decades, Cuban artists, writers, and other intellectuals residing on the island had little interaction with their counterparts in the United States and most countries of the Americas, except for those aligned with the international left, who had tended to support the Cuban Revolution since the 1960s. At the same time, major cultural institutions in Cuba such as Casa de las Américas, founded in Havana in 1959, largely turned away from the United States and toward Latin America and other regions of the so-called Third World. Cuba continued to export its culture—particularly its music, cinema, literature, and visual arts—on a large scale, but mostly to European and Latin American countries, not the United States.

In Cuba, the growing concentration of economic resources and cultural institutions in the hands of the revolutionary state paralleled the dismantling of prerevolutionary civil society, including independently owned magazines, journals, museums, galleries, theaters, publishing houses, and other venues for cultural debate and artistic expression. Most artists and other intellectuals were forced to depend on the state for their subsistence, join the newly founded National Union of Cuban Writers and Artists (UNEAC, in its Spanish acronym), and conform to revolutionary ideology; many chose exile or were marginalized in their own country. First uttered by Castro in a speech at Havana's National Library in June 1961, the ominous "Words to the Intellectuals" set the parameters for Cuba's cultural policies in the following decades: "Within the Revolution, everything; against the Revolution, nothing."[6]

The revolutionary government proceeded to provide unprecedented public access to cultural resources such as books, magazines, concerts, film screenings, theatrical performances, and museum exhibitions, as well as free art and music education, at the expense of increasing state control over creative expression. Debates about the "aesthetics of socialism" became more acute after Castro's proclamation of the socialist character of the Cuban Revolution in April 1961.[7] During the 1960s, Cuban authorities demonized rock music (including Elvis Presley, the Beatles, and the Rolling Stones) as a symbol of decadent bourgeois values and "the imperialist enemy" (one of Fidel Castro's favorite expressions). Revolutionary leaders even suspected that youngsters with long hair, tight jeans, and sandals were guilty of "ideological diversionism"—a term first used publicly by Raúl Castro in 1972 to refer to a lack of revolutionary commitment. The Revolution strove to create a noble "New Man," imbued with selfless collectivist values, but in the process persecuted homosexuals, Christians, and other "deviants" from the new socialist order.

The honeymoon between revolutionary Cuba and the international intelligentsia largely ended with the so-called Padilla Affair (1971), in which the prominent poet Heberto Padilla was censored, arrested, and forced to confess his "counterrevolutionary" sins, an episode reminiscent of Stalinist Russia. Also in 1971, the First National Congress of Education and Culture declared that homosexuals were incompatible with revolutionary goals and recommended expelling them from Cuba's Communist Party and removing them from their jobs as artists, actors, teachers, and diplomats. The first half of the 1970s, known as the *Quinquenio Gris* (the "Gray Five Years," 1971–76), is now remembered in Cuba as the worst period of ideological dogmatism, in which state bureaucrats unsuccessfully attempted to impose "socialist realism," largely imported from the Soviet

Union, on the island. Between 1970 and 1989, the Cuban government increasingly relied on the Soviet Union and its Eastern European allies as the island's main cultural referents, as well as its dominant political and economic models.[8]

During this period, U.S.-Cuban cultural relations were fraught with intractable obstacles, largely due to the legal and financial restrictions of the embargo. As a graduate student at the University of California, Berkeley, between 1979 and 1985, I can remember only a handful of cultural events in which artists and intellectuals from Cuba were represented in the San Francisco Bay Area: a screening of the classic film, *Memorias del subdesarrollo* (*Memories of Underdevelopment*, 1968), directed by Tomás Gutiérrez Alea; a dramatic performance by Teatro Escambray; a live concert with comedian and singer Virulo (Alejandro García Villalón); and a literary lecture by poet Nancy Morejón. Still, art historian Juan A. Martínez noticed a resurgence of U.S. interest in Cuban art during the 1980s, as expressed in several exhibitions at Miami's Cuban Museum of Arts and Culture, such as those devoted to avant-garde painters Víctor Manuel (1982), Eduardo Abela (1984), Carlos Enríquez (1986), and Amelia Peláez (1988).[9]

A basic impetus for increasing U.S.-Cuba exchanges in the visual arts was the lawsuit *Cernuda v. Heavey* (1989). In this federal case, heard before the Southern District Court of Florida, Cuban-American art collector Ramón Cernuda (the organizer of the 1988 auction at Miami's Cuban Museum of Arts and Culture) sued the U.S. Customs Service and the U.S. Department of the Treasury. The plaintiff requested the return of approximately 200 paintings produced in Cuba, seized by the U.S. Customs Service under the terms of the 1917 "Trading with the Enemy Act." The court ruled in Cernuda's favor, determining that paintings (and other cultural and artistic expressions) were exempt from the act, based on the First Amendment to the U.S. Constitution, protecting the right to free expression. This judicial decision led the federal government to revise its regulations to permit the importation, exhibition, and sale of Cuban art in the United States. Henceforth, the Office of Foreign Assets Control (OFAC) of the U.S. Department of the Treasury explicitly authorized the importation of "informational materials," including artworks, books, films, and musical recordings, from Cuba to the United States.[10]

Although federal courts proclaimed that the U.S. government could not censor Cuban art, local authorities in Miami attempted to limit artistic and other cultural activities with ties to the Cuban government. In 1996, the Miami-Dade County Commission approved the so-called Cuba Affidavit, an administrative ordinance that restricted Cuba-related musical performances, film festivals, and other cultural events. This policy prohibited any organization receiving county funds from doing business with the island's government. In July 2000, a Florida district judge issued a permanent injunction, barring Miami-Dade County from enforcing the "Cuba Affidavit" as unconstitutional political censorship against Cuban artistic and cultural expressions.[11]

The fall of the Berlin Wall in 1989, the demise of the Soviet Union in 1991, and the ensuing "Special Period in Times of Peace"—the profound economic recession on the island during the first half of the 1990s—created a relative opening for Cuban cultural production, particularly in popular music, creative literature, and the visual arts.[12] The 1990s saw the arrival of new commercial and foreign stakeholders in Cuban culture, including music producers, editors, filmmakers, art collectors, gallery owners, museum directors, and curators. The expansion of market transactions and the partial retreat of state institutions substantially transformed Cuba's cultural landscape.

An "alternative" public sphere slowly emerged in Cuba, one that did not depend entirely on the government for cultural production and circulation on the island and abroad. New opportunities to travel, perform, and record in the United States and other countries, such as Spain, especially affected Cuba's music industry, which had long been under state control. The Cuban Institute of Cinematographic Arts and Industries (ICAIC, in its Spanish acronym) could no longer monopolize filmmaking on the island. Cuban cinema began to show signs of ideological and financial independence, as directors entered into co-productions with European and Latin American companies or produced their own low-budget works of fiction and nonfiction. Some novelists (notably Pedro Juan Gutiérrez and Leonardo Padura) signed lucrative contracts with foreign publishing houses, which distributed their work outside the island and allowed them to prosper independent of state institutions. Similarly, the international art market increasingly engaged with Cuba through a network of museum and gallery exhibitions; artistic gatherings, such as the Havana Biennial; and specialized publications.[13]

Worldwide interest in Cuban culture—including popular music, dance, literature, film, and the visual arts—has exploded since the 1990s.

Several major exhibitions of contemporary Cuban art took place in the United States, including *Near the Edge of the World* (1990), organized by the Bronx Museum of the Arts, and *Cuban Artists of the Twentieth Century* (1993), organized by the Museum of Art of Fort Lauderdale. The well-regarded film, *Fresa y chocolate* (*Strawberry and Chocolate*, 1995), directed by Tomás Gutiérrez Alea and Juan Carlos Tabío, was nominated for an Academy Award for Best Foreign Film. The 1997 album *Buena Vista Social Club*, directed by Juan de Marcos González and Ry Cooder, as well as the 1999 documentary with the same title, directed by the German filmmaker Wim Wenders, became international bestsellers. Although critics have decried the film's nostalgic narrative and commercial exploitation of prerevolutionary Cuban music, it undoubtedly reflected a widespread fascination with Cuba's popular culture. In 1999, New York's Center for Cuban Studies created the Cuban Art Space to collect, exhibit, and sell the works of artists living in Cuba.[14]

The Montreal Museum of Fine Arts held the most comprehensive exhibition of Cuban art outside the island in 2008. Curated by Nathalie Bondil, *Cuba: Art and History from 1868 to Today* featured more than 400 reproductions of Cuban paintings, photographs, posters, drawings, and video art, mostly from the National Museum of Fine Arts in Havana. As U.S. art historian Gail Gelburd wrote in 2014, the Canadian museum did "what no American museum has been able to accomplish for almost fifty years—exhibit art held by the museums in Cuba."[15] The exhibition provided a panoramic view of the visual arts in Cuba over the last 150 years, interpreted by more than twenty curators and critics in Canada, Cuba, the United States, and France. However, the exhibition did not include any artworks produced by Cubans in exile after 1959. Perhaps this absence reflected the title of chapter 4 of the catalogue, quoting Castro's dictum, "Within the Revolution, Everything; against the Revolution, Nothing (1959–1979)."

Today, the embargo—which only Congress can lift or amend—remains the keystone of U.S. policy toward Cuba. Whereas some Democratic presidents have eased restrictions on trade with and travel to Cuba, Republican presidents have generally curtailed cultural and educational exchanges, family visits, and remittances to the island. The Carter administration (1977–81) started a rapprochement with the Cuban government, culminating with the opening of interests sections in Washington and Havana in September 1977. However, President Ronald Reagan (1981–89) attempted to tighten the embargo and isolate Cuba from international relations. In 1999, the Clinton administration (1993–2001) facilitated travel by Cuban artists and musicians to the United States under the legal figure of "people-to-people" exchanges. Once again, the George W. Bush administration (2001–9) strengthened the trade embargo and limited travel to and from the island.

During its second term, the Obama administration (2009–17) greatly relaxed U.S. regulations on travel, trade, and communication with Cuba, especially after December 17, 2014. Under the expanded rubric of "people-to-people" exchanges, Cuban artists and other intellectuals experienced growing opportunities to come to the United States and engage directly with U.S. cultural actors and institutions. The number and variety of cultural programs involving Cuban visitors from the island in the United States—including jazz and rap concerts, art exhibitions, film festivals, theatrical events, ballet and opera performances, and academic conferences—proliferated. To a lesser extent, U.S. musicians, artists, scholars, and other intellectuals have visited Cuba and become more familiar with its rich and diverse culture.

During the last two years of the Obama administration (2015–16), cultural exchanges between Cuba and the United States boomed through bilateral visits, formal agreements, and informal contacts. According to longtime Cuba analyst Sheryl Lutjens, the détente initiated by President Obama on December 17, 2014, represented "sea changes" in cultural and educational exchanges between Cuba and the United States. The restoration of diplomatic ties between the two countries during the summer of 2015 encouraged the flow of musicians, artists, writers, and scholars. For instance, a high-level delegation representing the President's Committee on the Arts and the Humanities visited Havana in April 2016. While in Cuba, the delegation announced new cultural initiatives ranging from art conservation programs to architectural fellowships to film festivals. In turn, the Smithsonian Institution planned to dedicate its 2017 Folklife Festival on the Washington Mall to Cuba, but failed negotiations with the Cuban government led to the plan's cancellation. Educational exchanges between U.S. and Cuban institutions also grew considerably during this period, including many involving universities and colleges throughout the United States, but declined in late 2017.[16]

In Miami, increased cultural contacts between Cuba and the United States have been scrutinized and disputed. Admittedly, recent U.S.-Cuban cultural relations have seemed lopsided—that is, more Cuban artists, musicians, writers, and scholars have traveled to the United States than their U.S. counterparts to Cuba. Moreover, the Cuban government has often denied entry visas to U.S. citizens—including Cuban Americans—who might openly criticize the Castro regime. Detractors of cultural exchange programs have therefore charged that they ultimately buttress the Castro regime more than they benefit U.S. interests. Prominent exiled artists and musicians—such as Miami singers Gloria Estefan and Willy Chirino—will not perform on the island under the status quo, even if the Cuban government authorizes them to do so.[17]

Since January 2017, U.S.-Cuban relations have chilled under the Trump administration. At the time of this writing (February 2019), cultural exchanges between the United States and Cuba are at a standstill, especially after the suspension of nonimmigrant visas by the U.S. Embassy in Havana and the U.S. expulsion of consular officials from the Cuban Embassy in Washington, DC.[18]

Cultural Politics in the Diaspora

Cuban refugees in South Florida have traditionally played a key role in U.S.-Cuban relations (or lack thereof). Numerous Cuban writers, artists, musicians, and scholars went into exile post-1959, particularly in Miami. At least 200 Cuban visual artists settled abroad during the first few years after the triumph of the Revolution. A partial list of renowned cultural personalities who fled the island during that period would include writers Jorge Mañach, Lydia Cabrera, and Lino Novás Calvo; painters Cundo Bermúdez and José Mijares; composer Ernesto Lecuona; and popular singers Olga Guillot, Celia Cruz, and La Lupe. During the 1960s and much of the 1970s, the politics of exile consumed the first generation of Cuban-American intellectuals, who tended to share a strong anti-Communist ideology, a belligerent stance against the Castro regime, and an unwillingness to negotiate with that government.[19] At the same time, supporters of the Cuban Revolution on the island and in other countries ostracized exiled writers and artists.

Between 1959 and 1979, members of the émigré community (including artists and other intellectuals) had very little personal contact with Cuba. Before the 1978 *Diálogo*,[20] most Cubans who left the island could not return home, even for short visits. The Cuban diaspora was largely cut off from its cultural roots in the homeland. For decades, Cuban exiles did not engage with Cuba's cultural production, except to oppose it on political grounds. In turn, Cuba's cultural institutions usually erased the names and contributions of writers and artists who had permanently "abandoned" the island.[21]

The South Florida population was mostly indifferent to Cuban art and culture during the first decades following the 1959 Revolution. At the time, local cultural institutions like museums, galleries, colleges, and universities paid scant attention to the exiles' artistic and cultural manifestations. Major stakeholders (including art collectors, curators, and critics) rarely recognized the work of Cuban-American artists, partly for aesthetic reasons, partly for ideological reasons.[22] Cuban exiles therefore founded their own cultural institutions in Miami and elsewhere, such as the publishing houses Universal and Playor, La Moderna Poesía and Universal bookstores, the Bacardí Art Gallery, the Cintas Foundation, Pro Arte Grateli, the Cuban Heritage Collection of the University of Miami Libraries, *Revista Mariel*, *Linden Lane Magazine*, and the now-defunct Cuban Museum of Arts and Culture. In addition, private schools, such as Belén Jesuit Preparatory School, and numerous voluntary organizations and periodicals sought to maintain a sense of *cubanidad* (Cubanness) in younger generations of Cuban Americans.[23] The transplanting of prerevolutionary cultural institutions, and the creation of others in exile, contributed to the flourishing of Cuban art, literature, music, and culture in Miami between the early 1960s and the late 1970s. Gradually, local museums and galleries collected the work of Cuban-American artists more widely, and affluent Cuban exiles were among the most avid collectors of Cuban and Cuban-American art.[24]

The Cuban exodus has undergone substantial transformations since the 1980s, as new migrant waves have reshaped the demographic, socioeconomic, and political profile of the Cuban population outside the island. The Mariel boatlift of 1980 brought to the United States a significant number of writers such as Reinaldo Arenas and Carlos Victoria, and visual artists such as Carlos Alfonzo (1950–91) and Roberto Valero (1955–94). Participants in the Mariel exodus and later waves of Cuban migrants seemed more open to maintaining ties to Cuba than earlier refugees did.[25] The Cuban diaspora increasingly diversified its locations, beyond the primary destinations in the United States and Puerto Rico. Cubans who resettled in Mexico and Spain were more likely than those who lived in Miami to remain connected to the island's culture and society. The expression "velvet exiles," sometimes used derisively by earlier refugees, alluded to a small core of Cuban intellectuals in Mexico who did not want to burn their bridges back home.[26]

Since the 1980s, younger generations of Cuban-American writers such as Cristina García, Achy Obejas, and Ana Menéndez, and visual artists such as Ana Mendieta (1948–85), Ernesto Pujol (b. 1957), and Alberto Rey have explored the theme of returning to Cuba, whether literally or symbolically.[27] An early attempt to forge and sustain contacts between Cubans on and off the island was Ruth Behar's edited volume *Bridges to Cuba* (1994), as well as its later reincarnation, *Bridges to/from Cuba*, the blog created by Behar and Richard Blanco. Through these multiple and sometimes overlapping initiatives, the borders between Cuban culture on the island and abroad seemed fuzzier than they were between 1959 and 1989.

Artists who left Cuba in the 1990s came from a very different socioeconomic and political context—the post-Soviet era—than earlier exile generations. Indeed, many did not consider themselves "exiles," and kept close ties to the island, even if they had ideological differences with the socialist regime. According to Eva Silot Bravo, "this new cohort included the most significant relocation of Cuban artists and musicians born and raised during the Cuban Revolution."[28] Some managed to maintain dual residences in Cuba as well as abroad, thus transgressing the binary geopolitical oppositions of the Cold War. A notable example is the installation and performance artist Tania Bruguera (b. 1968), who now lives and works between New York and Havana, even while becoming openly critical of the Cuban government. In the last decade, cultural exchanges between Cubans on and off the island have intensified, especially in the visual arts. *Dialogues in Cuban Art*, led by Cuban-American art historian and curator Elizabeth Cerejido, was one of the most significant projects to bridge the artistic gap between Miami and Havana. Supported by the Knight Foundation and PAMM, this initiative brought fifteen Cuban artists to Miami and took a similar number of Cuban-American artists to Havana in 2015–16.[29]

The Shifting Terrain of Cultural Politics

The recent evolution of U.S.-Cuban cultural relations has profoundly affected the Cuban diaspora in Miami. In 2010, Art Basel Miami Beach included for the first time the Cernuda Arte gallery, which exhibited Cuban artists such as Wifredo Lam, Amelia Peláez, Mariano Rodríguez, and others previously shunned by members of the exile community.[30] Furthermore, Art Basel has prominently displayed the work of Cuban artists such as Tania Bruguera and José Bedia (who first moved to Mexico in 1993 and then to Miami in 1994) without much opposition. In 2011, the Cuban Soul Foundation, affiliated with the Cuban-American National Foundation (CANF), began to sponsor cultural exchanges with young dissident artists such as Afro-Cuban rappers David Escalona (from Omni-Zona Franca) and Raudel Collazo (aka Escuadrón Patriota). The 2014 exhibition "One Race, the Human Race" at The Studios of Key West was touted as the "first U.S.-Cuba museum exchange in five decades." The exhibition featured works by the ubiquitous Mendive and other artists residing in Cuba, such as Fabelo and Sandra Ramos (b. 1969). The Key West exhibition did raise some polemics, mainly among Cuban exiles who still feel that U.S. museums and galleries should not display the work of artists living on the island.[31]

Nonetheless, Cuban-themed exhibitions have multiplied over the past decade in the United States, including South Florida. In 2009, the Lyman Allyn Art Museum in New London, Connecticut, organized a traveling exhibition with more than fifty pieces of Cuban art, *Ajiaco: Stirrings of the Cuban Soul*. The Frost Art Museum in Miami collaborated with the California African American Museum in Los Angeles on a retrospective of Mendive's fifty-year career in 2014. A year later, the Bronx Museum of the Arts inaugurated the exhibition *Wild Noise*, representing more than 100 artists from the collection of Havana's National Museum of Fine Arts. The Fowler Museum at the University of California, Los Angeles, inaugurated the first retrospective of printmaker Belkis Ayón (1967–99) in October 2016, which traveled to El Museo del Barrio in New York City the next summer. In November 2016, the American Museum of Natural History in New York City hosted its first-ever exhibition on the island's natural and cultural diversity. The Coral Gables Museum gathered one of the most extensive compendia of Cuban art in January 2017, previously shown at the Florida State University Museum of Fine Arts in Tallahassee, featuring Lam, Peláez, René Portocarrero, Mendive, Fabelo, and Tomás Sánchez (b. 1948).[32] In November 2017, the Walker Art Center in Minneapolis sponsored the largest U.S. exhibition of modern and contemporary Cuban art to date, *Adiós Utopia: Dreams and Deceptions of Cuban Art since 1950*. This traveling exhibition featured more than 100 works from the Cisneros Fontanals Art Foundation, headquartered in Miami. For its part, the John F. Kennedy Center for the Performing Arts in Washington, DC, organized *Artes de Cuba: From the Island to the World*, in May-June 2018, bringing together art, cinema, music, dance, theater, and fashion. This event gathered more than 250 artists living on the island, which was condemned by several Cuban-American lawmakers as "propaganda" for the Cuban regime.[33]

The polemics surrounding the collection, exhibition, and promotion of Cuban art have persisted in Miami. In June 2017, the Cintas Foundation announced that it would consider fellowship applications from Cuban artists, architects, writers, and musicians living anywhere, including Cuba. Although some exiled artists and critics opposed this decision, they did not resort to violent tactics as was common in Miami during the 1970s and 1980s. The decision to include Cubans on the island pitted the Cintas Foundation against other cultural institutions in Miami, such as the American Museum of the Cuban Diaspora, devoted exclusively to exile artists.[34]

During the summer of 2017, PAMM opened its three-chapter installation *On the Horizon*. Despite the pushback from some sectors of Miami's Cuban community, the exhibition attracted hundreds of visitors to the museum and was well-received by local critics. The last chapter of the exhibition, titled *Domestic Anxieties*, showcased the work of artists living in Cuba as well as in the diaspora, without any overt political overtones. Instead, the work focused on the visual representation of architectural spaces, public buildings, and intimate locations as emotionally charged sites for everyday life. This artistic turning away from epic narratives of politically charged events and icons related to the Cuban Revolution and exile may signal a growing trend for the future exhibition of Cuban art in the United States, particularly in Miami. Nonetheless, the PAMM exhibition rekindled the public debates of earlier decades, testing the limits of the exiles' tolerance of art produced in contemporary Cuba. Among other issues, local critics have insisted that exhibiting such work reaps economic benefits for the Cuban government, as well as restrains opportunities for Cuban-American artists.[35]

In some quarters, the old battle lines among artists, musicians, writers, and scholars residing on both shores of the Florida Straits are still drawn, but they now appear less politicized and clear-cut than in the past. Recent events suggest that paintings and other artworks, as well as music produced in Cuba, do not draw as much hostility from Cuban exiles as they did in the past. "Cultural exchanges" between Cuba and the United States still generate "domestic anxieties" among conservative sectors of Miami's Cuban community. At the same time, local museums, art galleries, and private collections have continued to assemble and exhibit art produced on the island after the Revolution. Some Cuban Americans once regarded displaying and buying art from post-1959 Cuba as traitorous to the traumatic experience of exile, which could lead to quick accusations of being a Communist sympathizer and spreading "Marxist-Leninist propaganda." Nowadays, owning a piece by Lam, Peláez, Portocarrero, or Mendive is usually a token of distinction, as reflected in the growing demand for such work in the local and international art market.

Conclusion

The Cold War severely curtailed cultural contacts between Cuba and the United States after the triumph of the Cuban Revolution. The breaking of diplomatic ties in 1961 and the consolidation of the U.S. embargo in 1962 obstructed trade, transportation, telecommunication, and even regular mail service between the two countries. Despite their geographic proximity and historical affinities, Cuba and the United States became ideological adversaries in a bipolar world, which undermined artistic and cultural contacts. Art became extremely politicized on the island, and the revolutionary government demonized those who left as *gusanos* (worms) and other epithets. In Miami's burgeoning Cuban enclave, the dominant exile ideology precluded any rapprochement with the Castro government and branded all artists, musicians, writers, and intellectuals remaining on the island as mouthpieces of the socialist regime.

The situation has changed noticeably in the past three decades. The collapse of the Soviet bloc between 1989 and 1991 deprived Cuba of its main trade partners and political allies, and forced the Castro government to reinsert the island into the global capitalist economy. Many of Cuba's cultural producers—among them musicians, filmmakers, actors, writers, and visual artists—suddenly entered into commercial relations with outsiders, who offered the possibility of profitable market transactions and perhaps the securing of independent sources of livelihood.[36] In Miami, the swift demographic transformation of the Cuban-American community, with the rise of a second generation born and raised in the United States and the arrival of a massive wave of immigrants since 1994, contributed to changing attitudes toward Cuba. Several public polls have confirmed the increasing support of the Cuban-American community for engagement with, rather than isolation from, the island.[37] This attitude—especially among younger and more recent émigrés—often extends to cultural activities originating in Cuba, such as live concerts, film screenings, theater performances, art exhibitions, and book presentations. Decades of mutual estrangement, animosity, and misunderstanding between Cuba and the United States have slowly given way to more direct encounters between the peoples of both countries, and the visual arts have been a building block of cultural bridges across the Florida Straits.

Notes

1. The Pérez Art Museum Miami (PAMM) commissioned the original version of this chapter for the catalogue of the exhibition *On the Horizon: Contemporary Cuban Art from the Jorge M. Pérez Collection*, ed. Tobias Ostrander (Miami: Pérez Art Museum Miami, 2018). I appreciate the kind invitation by PAMM's Chief Curator, Tobias Ostrander.

2. Lissette Corsa, "Art to Burn," *Miami New Times*, April 8, 1999, https://www.miaminewtimes.com/news/art-to-burn-6359117; José M. Juara, "Hay razones para quemar un cuadro," *El Nuevo Herald*, April 23, 1988, reproduced by the blog *Villa Granadillo*, September 23, 2012, https://villagranadillo.blogspot.com/2012/09/jose-juara-silverio-explica-por-que-le.html; Cammy Clark, "Cuban Cultural Exchange in Key West Draws Ire from Some Exiles," *Miami Herald*, March 8, 2014, https://www.miamiherald.com/news/local/in-depth/article1961040.html; my translations throughout.

3. For more details on the Cuban Museum of Arts and Culture in Miami, see Elizabeth Cerejido, "Museum as Battleground."

4. Nevertheless, Jorge M. Pérez denounced the Miami-Dade Board of County Commissioners for withdrawing $550,000 of its annual subsidies of $4 million to PAMM as "punishment" for including artists currently residing in Cuba. Instead, the commissioners assigned the funds to the fledgling American Museum of the Cuban Diaspora in Coral Gables. See Douglas Hanks, "Jorge Pérez Accuses Miami-Dade of Punishing Art Museum for Celebrating Cuban Artists," *Miami Herald*, December 6, 2017, https://www.miamiherald.com/news/local/community/miami-dade/article188316354.html.

5. See Leonardo Acosta, "Interinfluencias y confluencias en la música popular," 47.

6. Castro's complete speech appears in English translation in Lee Baxandall, ed., *Radical Perspectives in the Arts*, 267–98. The official censorship of the fourteen-minute film documentary *PM*, directed by Sabá Cabrera Infante and Orlando Jiménez Leal (1961), precipitated the meeting at the National Library. For more details on this episode and its repercussions, see Orlando Jiménez Leal and Manuel Zayas, eds., *El caso PM*.

7. See Rebecca J. Gordon-Nesbitt, "The Aesthetics of Socialism"; Abigail McEwen, *Revolutionary Horizons*.

8. Lourdes Casal, ed., *El caso Padilla*; Doreen Weppler-Grogan, "Cultural Policy, the Visual Arts, and the Advance of the Cuban Revolution"; Ambrosio Fornet, "El quinquenio gris." Still, Soviet models never entirely replaced the influence of U.S. popular culture on the island, and the Soviet Union left few traces in Cuba's cultural production after 1991. See Jacqueline Loss, *Dreaming in Russian*.

9. Martínez, *Cuban Art and National Identity*, 30.

10. Ramon CERNUDA and Editorial Cernuda, Inc., Petitioners, v. George D. HEAVEY, Regional Commission, United States Customs Service, and Department of Treasury, United States Customs Service, Respondents, case no. 89-1265-Civ. United States District Court, S.D. Florida, Miami Division, filed September 18, 1989. See also Gail Gelburd, "Cuba and the Art of 'Trading with the Enemy.'"

11. Joshua Bosin, "Miami's Mambo."

12. See Ariana Hernández-Reguant, "Multicubanidad"; Esther Whitfield, "Truth and Fictions"; Cerejido, "Replanteándonos la diáspora."

13. See Nora Gámez Torres, "'La Habana está en todas partes'"; Eva Silot Bravo, "Cubanidad '*In Between*'"; Cristina Venegas, "Filmmaking with Foreigners"; Santiago Juan-Navarro, "Cine-*collage* y autoconciencia en el nuevo documental cubano," 251; Cerejido, "Replanteándonos la diáspora."

14. Andrea O'Reilly Herrera, *Cuban Artists across the Diaspora*, 23; Tanya Katerí Hernández, "The *Buena Vista Social Club*."

15. Gelburd, 30.

16. Jordan Levin, "Forging a New Path to Cultural Exchanges with Cuba," *Miami Herald*, June 6, 2015, https://www.miamiherald.com/entertainment/ent-columns-blogs/jordan-levin/article23090049.html; Sheryl Lutjens, "The Subject(s) of Academic and Cultural Exchange," 260; National Endowment for the Arts, "Cultural Agreements Announced in Havana," April 22, 2016, https://www.arts.gov/news/2016/cultural-agreements-announced-havana-cuba; David Montgomery, "Smithsonian Cancels Plan to Feature Cuba at the 2017 Folklife Festival," *The Washington Post*, October 1, 2016, https://www.washingtonpost.com/news/arts-and-entertainment/wp/2016/10/01/folklife/?utm_term=.ffb710fdff58; Mary Beth Marklein, "US-Cuba Detente Paves the Way for Deeper Academic Ties," *Chronicle of Higher Education*, January 21, 2015, https://www.chronicle.com/article/US-Cuba-Detente-Paves-the/151333. However, twenty-four U.S. colleges and universities canceled their educational exchange programs in Cuba in the last months of 2017, in the wake of deteriorating relations between the United States and Cuba. *Diario de Cuba*, "Una veintena de universidades de EEUU ha cancelado

proyectos con instituciones cubanas," February 3, 2018, http://www.diariodecuba.com/cultura/1517667941_37128.html.

17. See, for example, Nora Gámez Torres, "¿A quién beneficia el intercambio cultural entre Cuba y EEUU?" *El Nuevo Herald*, July 21, 2014, https://www.elnuevoherald.com/ultimas-noticias/article2037369.html. An additional problem was that Cuban authorities mistrusted the cultural and educational exchange programs encouraged by the Obama administration, seeing them as subversive of the island's socialist regime. See also Nancy N. Balcziunas, *The Music and Politics of Willy Chirino*.

18. The U.S. government took these measures after the mysterious "sonic attacks" against twenty-four U.S. diplomats stationed at the U.S. Embassy in Havana between November 2016 and August 2017. In June 2018, two additional U.S. diplomats reported suffering various health symptoms in Havana, ranging from headaches and vertigo to hearing loss and mild concussions.

19. Ricardo Pau-Llosa, "Cuban Art in South Florida," 251. See also María Cristina García, *Havana USA*, 169–207; and Isabel Alvarez Borland, *Cuban-American Literature of Exile*. For analysis of the dominant political ideology among Cuban exiles in Miami, see Guillermo J. Grenier, "Engage or Isolate?"; Grenier and Lisandro Pérez, *The Legacy of Exile*, especially 85–99; and Grenier and Corinna J. Moebius, *A History of Little Havana*, especially 61–63, 80–81, 103, and 140.

20. In 1978, seventy-five Cuban exiles met with representatives of the Cuban government in Havana to negotiate the release of political prisoners, family reunification, and travel to the island. The so-called *Diálogo* set the stage for the visits of more than 100,000 Cuban exiles to the island in 1979.

21. Among those blacklisted on the island after moving abroad since 1959 were writers Lydia Cabrera, Gastón Baquero, Guillermo Cabrera Infante, Severo Sarduy, Reinaldo Arenas, Antonio Benítez Rojo, Zoé Valdés, and Daína Chaviano, as well as visual artists José Bedia and Carlos Estévez, and singers Celia Cruz, Gloria Estefan, and Willy Chirino. Nevertheless, Cuban cultural institutions have recently "rehabilitated" some exiled figures, who had been banned from the canonical narrative of Cuban culture on the island. For a discussion of the official exclusion of numerous exiled authors, see Rafael Rojas, *El estante vacío*. For an example of the attempt to reinstate some of them into the dominant discourse on the Cuban nation, see Instituto de Literatura y Lingüística "José Antonio Portuondo Valdor," "Apéndice."

22. Lynette M. F. Bosch has argued persuasively that much of the work of the first generation of Cuban-American artists was incompatible with the modernist and postmodernist agenda of the U.S. art establishment, especially in New York City. See Bosch, "From the Vanguardia to the United States," 138–39, and "The Cuban-American Exile *Vanguardia*."

23. See Lisandro Pérez, "Cuban Catholics in the United States."

24. In 1983, nine Cuban exile artists exhibited their work as part of "The Miami Generation" show at the Cuban Museum of Arts and Culture in Miami. For a case study of one of the leading members of this generation, see William Navarrete and Jesús Rosado, eds., *Visión crítica de Humberto Calzada*. The first comprehensive exhibition of

Cuban-American art took place between 1988 and 1989 in various locations throughout the United States and Puerto Rico. See Ileana Fuentes-Pérez et al., eds., *Outside Cuba/ Fuera de Cuba.*

25. See Jorge Duany, "Cuban Migration"; Susan Eva Eckstein, *The Immigrant Divide*; Silvia Pedraza, *Political Disaffection in Cuba's Revolution and Exodus.* For statistical evidence of the changing attitudes of Cuban Americans toward Cuba, see Grenier, "Engage or Isolate?" and Grenier and Hugh Gladwin, *2018 FIU Cuba Poll.*

26. See Rojas, "From Havana to Mexico City"; Tanya N. Weimar, *La diáspora cubana en México*; Mette Louise Berg, *Diasporic Generations.*

27. See Iraida H. López, *Impossible Returns.*

28. Silot Bravo, 30.

29. See *Dialogues in Cuban Art: An Artistic Exchange Program between Miami & Havana*, accessed March 8, 2018, http://dialoguesincubanart.org/. Another recent initiative is CubaOne, a nonprofit organization that sponsors travel to Cuba by young Cuban Americans. In July 2017, Ruth Behar and Richard Blanco accompanied ten Cuban-American writers to the island. See CubaOne, accessed March 8, 2018, http://cubaone.org.

30. The 2017 catalogue of *Important Cuban Artworks*, Vol. 15, published by Cernuda Arte, includes numerous paintings by artists still living in Cuba, such as Mendive and Fabelo, as well as others who remained on the island after the Revolution, such as Peláez and Portocarrero, and still others who moved abroad, such as Carreño and Bermúdez.

31. Christine Armario, "First US-Cuba Museum Exchange in 5 Decades," *Yahoo News*, February 21, 2014, https://www.yahoo.com/news/first-us-cuba-museum-exchange-5-decades-190748572.html; Clark, "Cuban Cultural Exchange," cites Cuban-American attorney Rafael Peñalver, president of the San Carlos Institute in Key West, as one of the most vocal critics of the exhibition.

32. See Frost Art Museum, *Things that Cannot Be Seen Any Other Way*; Florida State University Museum of Fine Arts, *Cuban Art in the 20th Century.*

33. Susan Crabtree, "Cuban-American Lawmakers: State Dept Facilitating 'Propaganda' Show," *The Washington Free Beacon*, April 30, 2018, https://freebeacon.com/issues/cuban-american-lawmakers-state-dept-facilitating-propaganda-show/.

34. In May 2016, the American Museum of the Cuban Diaspora in Miami canceled an exhibition with the Cintas Foundation after the announcement of the foundation's new policy. See Adriana Gómez Licón, "Miami Shows Embrace Cuba-Based Artists Even as Tensions Rise," *Orlando Sentinel*, July 24, 2017, http://www.orlandosentinel.com/news/politics/political-pulse/os-miami-cuba-art-20170724-story.html.

35. The Cuban exile attorney Marcell Felipe, president of the conservative Inspire America Foundation, accused Pérez of promoting the work of artists who "admire Castro and form part of the Castroite system of censorship, murder, and torture." See Miguel Fernández Díaz, "Polémica museológica en Miami," *Café Fuerte*, December 7, 2017, http://cafefuerte.com/miami/31456-polemica-museologica-miami/.

36. A new law, known as Decree No. 349, was supposed to come into effect in December 2018, strictly regulating artistic activities in Cuba. However, the Cuban government decided to implement it in a gradual and partial fashion, given widespread opposition

within Cuba. Once fully enforced, the decree will reduce the ability of independent artists and intellectuals to access state facilities on the island and to engage in economic transactions with foreign actors.

37. Between 1995 and 2016, the United States admitted 715,816 Cuban immigrants, the largest and longest wave of Cuban immigrants ever. U.S. Department of Homeland Security, *Immigration Data & Statistics*, accessed February 2, 2018, https://www.dhs.gov/immigration-statistics. For survey data on Cuban Americans, see Grenier and Gladwin, *2018 FIU Cuba Poll*; Bendixen and Amandi International, *Survey of Cuban-Americans*.

Bibliography

Acosta, Leonardo. "Interinfluencias y confluencias en la música popular de Cuba y de los Estados Unidos." In *Culturas encontradas: Cuba y los Estados Unidos*, edited by Rafael Hernández and John H. Coatsworth, 33–52. Havana and Cambridge, MA: Centro de Investigación y Desarrollo de la Cultura Cubana Juan Marinello/Centro de Estudios Latinoamericanos David Rockefeller, Universidad de Harvard, 2001.

Alvarez Borland, Isabel. *Cuban-American Literature of Exile: From Person to Persona*. Charlottesville: University of Virginia Press, 1998.

Balcziunas, Nancy N. *The Music and Politics of Willy Chirino*. B.A. thesis, Georgia Southern University, 2017. https://digitalcommons.georgiasouthern.edu/honors-theses/252/.

Baxandall, Lee, ed. *Radical Perspectives in the Arts*. Baltimore: Penguin Books, 1972.

Behar, Ruth, and Richard Blanco. *Bridges to/from Cuba: Lifting the Emotional Embargo*. Accessed February 5, 2018. https://bridgestocuba.com/.

Behar, Ruth, ed. *Bridges to Cuba/Puentes a Cuba*. Ann Arbor: University of Michigan Press, 1994.

Bendixen and Amandi International. *Survey of Cuban-Americans: One Year after the Normalization of United States-Cuba Relations. 17 December 2015*. https://bendixenandamandi.com/wp-content/uploads/2017/06/BA-Poll-of-Cuban-Americans-12.17.15-Web.pdf.

Berg, Mette Louise. *Diasporic Generations: Memory, Politics, and Nation among Cubans in Spain*. New York: Berghan, 2011.

Bondil, Nathalie, ed. *Cuba: Art and History from 1868 to Today*. Montreal: Montreal Museum of Fine Arts, 2009.

Bosch, Lynette M. F. "The Cuban-American Exile *Vanguardia*: Toward a Theory of Collecting Cuban-American Art." In *Picturing Cuba: Art, Culture, and Identity on the Island and in the Diaspora*, edited by Jorge Duany, 187–204. Gainesville: University of Florida Press, 2019.

———. "From the Vanguardia to the United States: Cuban and Cuban-American Identity in the Visual Arts." In *Cuban-American Literature and Art: Negotiating Identities*, edited by Isabel Alvarez Borland and Lynette M. F. Bosch, 129–48. Albany, NY: State University of New York Press, 2009.

Bosin, Joshua. "Miami's Mambo: The 'Cuba Affidavit' and Unconstitutional Cultural Censorship in an Embargo Regime." *University of Miami Inter-American Law Review* 36, no. 1 (2004): 75–113.

Casal, Lourdes, ed. *El caso Padilla: Literatura y revolución en Cuba. Documentos.* New York: Atlantis, 1971.

Cerejido, Elizabeth. "Museum as Battleground: Exile and Contested Cultural Representation in Miami's Cuban Museum." In *Art Museums of Latin America: Structuring Representation*, edited by Michele Greet and Gina McDaniel Tarver, 205–18. New York: Routledge, 2018.

———. "Replanteándonos la diáspora: ¿Arte cubano o arte cubanoamericano?" In *Un pueblo disperso: Dimensiones sociales y culturales de la diáspora cubana*, edited by Jorge Duany, 217–36. Valencia, Spain: Aduana Vieja, 2014.

Cernuda Arte. *Important Cuban Artworks*. Vol. 15. Miami: Cernuda Arte, 2017.

Duany, Jorge. "Cuban Migration: A Postrevolution Exodus Ebbs and Flows." *Migration Information Source*, July 6, 2017. https://www.migrationpolicy.org/article/cuban-migration-postrevolution-exodus-ebbs-and-flows.

Eckstein, Susan Eva. *The Immigrant Divide: How Cuban Americans Changed the US and Their Homeland*. New York: Routledge, 2009.

Florida State University Museum of Fine Arts. *Cuban Art in the 20th Century: Cultural Identity and the International Avant Garde*. Tallahassee: Museum of Fine Arts, College of Fine Arts, Florida State University, 2016.

Fornet, Ambrosio. "El quinquenio gris: Revisitando el término." *Revista Criterios* (2007). http://www.rebelion.org/noticia.php?id=45857.

Frost Art Museum. *Things that Cannot Be Seen Any Other Way: The Art of Manuel Mendive*. Miami: Frost Art Museum, Florida International University, 2013.

Fuentes-Pérez, Ileana, Graciella Cruz-Taura, and Ricardo Pau-Llosa, eds. *Outside Cuba/Fuera de Cuba: Contemporary Cuban Visual Artists/Artistas cubanos contemporáneos*. New Brunswick, NJ: Transaction, 1989.

Gámez Torres, Nora. "'La Habana está en todas partes': Young Musicians and the Symbolic Redefinition of the Cuban Nation." In *Un pueblo disperso: Dimensiones sociales y culturales de la diáspora cubana*, edited by Jorge Duany, 190–216. Valencia, Spain: Aduana Vieja, 2014.

García, María Cristina. *Havana USA: Cuban Exiles and Cuban Americans in South Florida, 1959–1994*. Berkeley: University of California Press, 1996.

Gelburd, Gail. "Cuba and the Art of 'Trading with the Enemy.'" *Art Journal* 68, no. 1 (2014): 24–39.

Gordon-Nesbitt, Rebecca J. "The Aesthetics of Socialism: Cultural Polemics in 1960s Cuba." *Oxford Art Journal* 37, no. 3 (2014): 265–83.

Grenier, Guillermo J. "Engage or Isolate? Twenty Years of Cuban Americans' Changing Attitudes Towards Cuba—Evidence from the FIU Cuba Poll." *IdeAs: Idées d'Amériques* 10 (2017–18). https://journals.openedition.org/ideas/2244.

Grenier, Guillermo J., and Hugh Gladwin. *2018 FIU Cuba Poll: How Cuban Americans in Miami View U.S. Policies toward Cuba*. Miami: Steven J. Green School of International and Public Affairs, Florida International University, 2019.

Grenier, Guillermo J., and Corinna J. Moebius. *A History of Little Havana*. Charleston, SC: History Press, 2015.
Grenier, Guillermo J., and Lisandro Pérez. *The Legacy of Exile: Cubans in the United States*. Boston: Allyn and Bacon, 2003.
Hernández, Tanya Katerí. "The *Buena Vista Social Club*: The Racial Politics of Nostalgia." In *Latino/a Popular Culture*, edited by Michelle Habell-Pallán and Mary Romero, 61–72. New York: New York University Press, 2002.
Hernández-Reguant, Ariana. "Multicubanidad." In *Cuba in the Special Period: Culture and Ideology in the 1990s*, edited by Ariana Hernández-Reguant, 69–88. New York: Palgrave Macmillan, 2009.
Herrera, Andrea O'Reilly. *Cuban Artists across the Diaspora: Setting the Tent against the House*. Austin: University of Texas Press, 2011.
Instituto de Literatura y Lingüística "José Antonio Portuondo Valdor." "Apéndice: La literatura cubana entre 1989 y 1999." In *Historia de la literatura cubana*, Vol. 3, 585–692. Havana: Letras Cubanas, 2008.
Jiménez Leal, Orlando, and Manuel Zayas, eds. *El caso PM: Cine, poder y censura*. Madrid: Colibrí, 2012.
Juan-Navarro, Santiago. "Cine-*collage* y autoconciencia en el nuevo documental cubano." In *Reading Cuba: Discurso literario y geografía transcultural*, edited by Alberto Sosa Cabanas, 251–66. Valencia, Spain: Aduana Vieja, 2018.
López, Iraida L. *Impossible Returns: Narratives of the Cuban Diaspora*. Gainesville: University Press of Florida, 2015.
Loss, Jacqueline. *Dreaming in Russian: The Cuban Soviet Imaginary*. Austin: University of Texas Press, 2013.
Lutjens, Sheryl. "The Subject(s) of Academic and Cultural Exchange: Paradigms, Powers, and Possibilities." In *Debating U.S.-Cuba Relations: How Should We Now Play Ball?* edited by Jorge Domínguez, Rafael M. Hernández, and Lorena G. Barberia, 242–65. 2nd ed. New York: Routledge, 2017.
Martínez, Juan A. *Cuban Art and National Identity: The Vanguardia Painters, 1927–1950*. Gainesville: University Press of Florida, 1994.
McEwen, Abigail. *Revolutionary Horizons: Art and Polemics in 1950s Cuba*. New Haven: Yale University Press, 2016.
Navarrete, William, and Jesús Rosado, eds. *Visión crítica de Humberto Calzada*. Valencia, Spain: Aduana Vieja, 2008.
Pau-Llosa, Ricardo. "Cuban Art in South Florida." In *Cuban Exiles in Florida: Their Presence and Contribution*, edited by Antonio Jorge, Jaime Suchlicki, and Adolfo Leyva de Varona, 251–66. Miami: University of Miami, North-South Center, 1991.
Pedraza, Silvia. *Political Disaffection in Cuba's Revolution and Exodus*. New York: Cambridge University Press, 2007.
Pérez, Lisandro. "Cuban Catholics in the United States." In *Puerto Rican and Cuban Catholics in the U.S., 1900–1965*, edited by Jay P. Dolan and Jaime R. Vidal, 147–247. Notre Dame, IN: University of Notre Dame Press, 1994.
Rojas, Rafael. *El estante vacío: Literatura y política en Cuba*. Barcelona: Anagrama, 2009.
———. "From Havana to Mexico City: Generation, Diaspora, and Borderland." In *The*

Portable Island: Cubans at Home in the World, edited by Ruth Behar and Lucía M. Suárez, 93–102. New York: Palgrave Macmillan, 2008.

Silot Bravo, Eva. "Cubanidad '*In Between*': The Transnational Cuban Alternative Music Scene." *Latin American Music Review* 38, no. 1 (2017): 28–56.

Venegas, Cristina. "Filmmaking with Foreigners." In *Cuba in the Special Period: Culture and Ideology in the 1990s*, edited by Ariana Hernández-Reguant, 37–50. New York: Palgrave Macmillan, 2009.

Weimar, Tanya S. *La diáspora cubana en México: Terceros espacios y miradas excéntricas*. New York: Peter Lang, 2008.

Weppler-Grogan, Doreen. "Cultural Policy, the Visual Arts, and the Advance of the Cuban Revolution in the Aftermath of the Gray Years." *Cuban Studies* 41 (2010): 143–65.

Whitfield, Esther. "Truths and Fictions: The Economics of Writing, 1994–1999." In *Cuba in the Special Period: Culture and Ideology in the 1990s*, edited by Ariana Hernández-Reguant, 21–36. New York: Palgrave Macmillan, 2009.

CONTRIBUTORS

Anelys Alvarez is an independent scholar and art historian, currently working as Assistant Curator for the Related Group in Miami. She previously taught art history at the University of Havana and at the Agrarian University of Havana. She has published articles and catalogues on Cuban and Caribbean art, and has lectured widely on Cuban and contemporary art in several galleries and other cultural institutions in Miami, Havana, and Mexico.

Lynnette M. F. Bosch is distinguished professor and chair of art history at the State of University of New York at Geneseo. She is the author of *Cuban-American Art in Miami: Exile, Identity, and the Neo-Baroque* and coeditor of *Cuban-American Literature and Art: Negotiating Identities* and *Identity, Memory, and Diaspora: Voices of Cuban-American Artists, Writers, and Philosophers.*

María A. Cabrera Arús is a postdoctoral fellow at the Andrew W. Mellon Foundation Sawyer Seminar at New York University. She holds a Ph.D. in sociology from the New School. She has written extensively on material culture in postrevolutionary Cuba, especially on fashion. She is the creator of the blog *Cuba Material*, dedicated to archiving and disseminating Cuban material culture from the Cold War era.

Iliana Cepero is a Cuban art historian, curator, and art critic. She has taught courses on Latin American art and photography at the New School, Hunter College, and New York University. She was also assistant curator of the Montreal Biennial in 2007, and co-curated the exhibition "Cuba: Art and History—From 1868 to Today" held at the Montreal Museum of

Fine Arts in 2008. She has written and lectured extensively on Cuban art and photography.

Ramón Cernuda is a publisher, editor, writer, and Cuban art collector. After thirty years pursuing a lifelong love of Cuban art as a private art collector and researcher, he established Cernuda Arte gallery in October 2000. The gallery specializes in the exhibition and sale of Colonial, Early Republic, Avant-garde, and Modern master Cuban paintings, as well as fine artworks by contemporary artists of unquestionable talent.

Emilio Cueto is a Cuban-American attorney and collector who specializes in Cuba's colonial graphic art and music. He is the author of several books and catalogues, including *Cuba en/in USA*; *Las litografías santiagueras del Departamento Oriental de la Isla de Cuba*; *La Virgen de la Caridad del Cobre en el alma del pueblo cubano*; *Cuba in Old Maps*; and *Mialhe's Colonial Cuba*. He has also published articles in journals such as *Cuban Studies*, *Espacio Laical*, *Herencia*, *Del Caribe*, and *Revista de la Biblioteca Nacional José Martí*.

Carol Damian is a retired professor of art history in the Department of Art and Art History and former director and chief curator of the Patricia and Phillip Frost Art Museum at Florida International University. A specialist in Latin American and Caribbean art, she has taught Pre-Columbian, Colonial, Spanish, and Contemporary Latin American Art, Modern Art surveys, and Women in Art. Her most recent work has focused on Latin American women and Cuban exile artists, on whom she has written numerous catalogues and articles.

Victor Deupi is professor of architecture at the University of Miami and former president of the Cintas Foundation. He was co-curator of the exhibit *Cuban Architects at Home and in Exile: The Modernist Generation* at the Coral Gables Museum. He is also the author of *Emilio Sánchez in Cuba, 1946–1959: Architectural Drawings from the Metropolitan Museum of Art*.

Jorge Duany is director of the Cuban Research Institute and professor of anthropology at Florida International University. He has published extensively on migration, ethnicity, race, nationalism, and transnationalism in

Cuba, the Caribbean, and the United States. He is the author, coauthor, editor, or coeditor of twenty books, including *Un pueblo disperso: Dimensiones sociales y culturales de la diáspora cubana* and *Blurred Borders: Transnational Migration between the Hispanic Caribbean and the United States*.

Alison Fraunhar is associate professor in the Department of Art and Design at Saint Xavier University in Chicago. She teaches courses in Modern and Contemporary, Latin American, and Women's Art and Film Studies. She has published numerous articles on Cuban visual culture and film, and is the author of the book *Mulata Nation: Visualizing Race and Gender in Cuba*.

Andrea O'Reilly Herrera is professor of literature and director of the Women's and Ethnic Studies Program at the University of Colorado at Colorado Springs. In addition to being a published poet and literary critic, she is the author of *Cuban Artists across the Diaspora: Setting the Tent against the House* and editor of *ReMembering Cuba: Legacy of a Diaspora*. She is also the author of the novel *The Pearl of the Antilles*.

Jean-François Lejeune is professor of architecture at the University of Miami, where he teaches architectural design, urban design, and history-theory. From June 2009 to December 2014 he was the director of graduate studies. In 2007, he was an affiliated fellow at the American Academy in Rome. His research field is the history of architecture and urbanism of the twentieth century, from Miami to Spain to Latin America.

Abigail McEwen is associate professor of Latin American Art History at the University of Maryland, College Park. Her areas of research and teaching interest span the modern Americas, with an emphasis on the art of twentieth-century Cuba and Puerto Rico, the transnational history of abstraction, and the postwar avant-garde. She is the author of *Revolutionary Horizons: Art and Polemics in 1950s Cuba* and is currently working on *Excentric Bodies: Exodus and Erotics in Post-Revolutionary Cuban Art*.

Ricardo Pau-Llosa is a Cuban-American poet, art critic, and curator specializing in Latin American art. He has curated exhibitions and written major studies of Cuban and Latin American artists. In 2010, the Snite Museum of Art at the University of Notre Dame put together the exhibition *Parallel Currents: Highlights of the Ricardo Pau-Llosa Collection of Latin American Art*, whose book-length catalogue explored the relationship among art, poetry, and philosophy in his life and work.

E. Carmen Ramos is curator for Latino art at the Smithsonian American Art Museum. In 2014, she organized *Our America: The Latino Presence in American Art*, a major traveling exhibition that presents selections from the Museum's pioneering collection of Latino art. She has written several exhibition catalogues and has also published in *American Art*, *African Arts*, and the *New West Indian Guide*.

INDEX

www.ingramcontent.com/pod-product-compliance
Lightning Source LLC
LaVergne TN
LVHW052350100826
845147LV00013B/802

* 9 7 8 1 6 8 3 4 0 2 0 9 1 *